Stephen King on the Big Screen

Mark Browning

Stephen King on the Big Screen

Mark Browning

intellect Bristol, UK / Chicago, USA

First published in the UK in 2009 by
Intellect Books, The Mill, Parnall Road, Fishponds, Bristol, BS16 3JG, UK

First published in the USA in 2009 by
Intellect Books, The University of Chicago Press, 1427 E. 60th Street, Chicago, IL 60637, USA

A catalogue record for this book is available from the British Library.

Cover designer: Holly Rose
Copy-editor: Heather Owen
Typesetting: Mac Style, Beverley, E. Yorkshire

ISBN 978-1-84150-245-8

Printed and bound by Gutenberg Press, Malta.

CONTENTS

INTRODUCTION

'I was surprised to find you as good as you are. As subtle as you are. I expected more hack and slash.'[1]

'Why do film-makers make life so hard for themselves by assuming that the original writer has got it all wrong?'[2]

The Autograph Man
In August 2007, a member of the public reported a man acting suspiciously in a Dymocks bookstore in Alice Springs, Australia, apparently defacing several Stephen King novels. He was later identified by the manager, Bev Ellis, as one Mr Stephen King. King has talked about his penchant for impromptu signings, especially on the cross-country road trip which he took in preparation for *Desperation* (1996) and putting his name to his work, marking it as his, seems to be important to him, reflecting the persisting cultural importance of the autograph – a tendency noted by Seán Burke.[3] The titles released under the pseudonym 'Richard Bachman' did sell but only became real bestsellers once King's talismanic name was attached. In 'The Breathing Method' story, in *Different Seasons* (1982), a private club meets with the toast, by way of D.H. Lawrence and Geoffrey Chaucer, that '[i]t is the tale, not he who tells it', and usually King is wary of biographical links between himself and his fiction, often paraphrasing John Irving's belief that writers appear to offer this, but only lie.

However an unquestioning auteurism in terms of King's own writing persists.[4] The stubborn endurance of auteur theory, represented most graphically by its ubiquitous presence on Film Studies degree courses, suggests that despite repeated attempts to kill it off by figures like Roland Barthes, it is a network of concepts which have not yet outlived their usefulness.[5] In terms of King's work, his first title to mention cinema directly, *Stephen King Goes to the Movies* (2009), repackages five previously-published texts (the literary bases for *The Shawshank*

Redemption, *1408*, *The Mangler*, *Children of the Corn* and *Hearts in Atlantis*). In effect, he is reclaiming, retroactively 're-authoring' films as works, which were not strongly linked to the King brand in their initial marketing. It is worth noting, however, that none of the scripts for these films were written by him.

Whatever debates there are about authorship, none of the films discussed in this book existed before King wrote the literary property, whether it be a novel, short story or screenplay. Therefore, although not applicable in a uniform fashion, adaptation theory is relevant to all the films in this book. I have discussed the historical background of adaptation theory elsewhere, including weaknesses in media-specific assumptions made by figures like Seymour Chapman, so I am not proposing to repeat that here.[6] Generally, however, approaches oscillate between George Bluestone's comparison of formal systems of media-specific features, which focuses on fidelity to the written text, or an auteurist approach, which emphasizes stylistic differences.

Historically, the Leavisite tendency has explicitly valued the written form over the visual; old media over the new; the single author over the industrial process (conveniently ignoring the fact that the single author is not alone, since he or she is part of a publishing industry). As Deborah Cartmell and Imelda Whelehan state, '[t]here is still the preconception that the novelist produces a work of quality, of "high" art as it emerges from the solitary efforts of the individual to express their distinct vision, untrammelled by concerns about the commercial value of the product'.[7] However, King has been struggling for critical acceptance for much of his career and, indeed, continues to do so. The decision to award him a National Book Award in 2003 was met with overt critical hostility from establishment figures like Harold Bloom. King's continued status as a bestselling author has been seen as fundamentally incompatible with notions of what constitutes 'art'; in other words, commercial success is seen by some critics as anathema to aesthetic value. Banned by public and school libraries at times, his work has often been vilified and seen as representative of a dilution of popular culture.[8] King's adaptations suffer twice over – in the eyes of judgemental, elitist critics, the films are associated with a cinematic sub-genre with historically low status (horror) and, secondly, the films are adapting an overtly popular, bestselling writer who is commonly associated with this particular genre in literature and, increasingly, on film. However, there is also a strange perpetuation in the notion of a high/low art divide in an inverted sense here. When his work has been adapted, especially by directors who have the popular reputation as auteurs, such as Stanley Kubrick, the resulting film is seen to have a higher cultural status than the written work from which it came, as in the case of Kubrick's *The Shining* (1980).

Despite what Brian McFarlane describes as, a tendency to be 'bedevilled by the fidelity issue',[9] there still seems an almost endless procession of critics falling into the trap of repetitive fidelity criticism, using a narrow, sexualized vocabulary (often based on notions of 'betrayal' and 'faithfulness'). The idea of 'fidelity', as in a romantic or sexual context, is very fluid and its meaning highly dependent upon contextual factors at any given moment. This becomes even more so when writers talk of being faithful 'to the spirit' or 'essence of a text, as if that was universally recognized. However, it is also true that the theorists have bemoaned this sufficiently and the time has come to suggest some more constructive ways out of the impasse.

Ultimately, arguments based around medium-specific issues, i.e. whether either film or literature is innately effective at particular kinds of expression, are just reductive. A more productive approach, according to theorists like James Naremore and Robert Stam, would be through the mechanisms of Bakhtinian dialogics and intertextuality. Stam's approach is influenced by Bakhtin's theory that any utterance is inherently linked to 'the entire matrix of communicative utterances within which the artistic text is situated' that was later developed into the conceptual area known as 'intertextuality' by figures linked to the *Tel Quel* journal, such as Julia Kristeva.[10] King has often said in interview that he writes with loud rock and roll playing and his own works are full of contemporary pop culture references (to the point where this has been routinely listed as a feature of his work). Other writers, such as Brett Easton Ellis, also uses the King trademark listing of brand-names, but more as a parody of consumerism than what has been termed King's 'stickerism masquerading as characterisation', a simplistic means of placing the narrative within a recognizable culture.[11] It is a contention of this book that adaptations are worthy of study in their own right and, more precisely, Stephen King adaptations represent a unique body of work in an intertextual context. There are authors who have been more frequently adapted, such as Shakespeare, or writers who have produced a smaller number of texts that have been repeatedly dramatized in many different versions, such as nineteenth century novelists like Charles Dickens, Jane Austen and Thomas Hardy. However, the films in this study are unique in that they are based on texts produced during the era of cinema and with a very keen awareness of popular culture linked to the moving image.

Thomas Leitch's 'grammar' of adaptation describes the choices available in any movement from text to screen. This includes adjustment (compressing or expanding the text), superimposition (introducing new material), colonization (changing the setting and chronology), metacommentary (using self-conscious commentary on the adaptation process), parody and pastiche, and secondary or tertiary adaptation. Leitch suggests that 'intertextuality takes myriad forms that resist reduction…there is no normative model for adaptation' and is therefore putting forward a flexible range of possible options, rather than a prescriptive list.[12] Leitch's proposal that we engage in a process of 'active literacy' has a more fluid notion of fidelity as an enabling concept; a flexible idea that provokes debate rather than closing it down.[13] This is an admirable intent and certainly, as Neil Sinyard reminds us, 'adapting a literary text for the screen is essentially an act of literary criticism,' which should serve to illuminate both source text and filmic version drawn from it.[14] With very few exceptions, it is difficult to see a Stephen King movie without being fully aware of this, due to King's status as the unrivalled producer of global bestsellers and since the marketing of his books foreground his authorship, from titles to high profile personal appearances. Since it is also quite likely that a notable percentage of the audience will have read at least some of King's work, if not the text used as a basis for any specific production, then to watch such a film becomes an act of adaptation and genre criticism.

However, in the case of the adaptations considered in this book, many of Leitch's categories (such as colonization) do not readily apply and those that do (such as adjustment or superimposition) tend to lead to the dead-end of fidelity-based observations. A more productive critical framework is provided by Gérard Genette's notions of narratology, which focus on what function an adaptation strategy fulfils. This offers a precise and positive way to consider the relationship between written text and film, particularly the term 'transtextuality', meaning 'all that which puts one text in relation, whether manifest or secret, with other texts.'[15] According to Genette, there are five types of transtextual situations: 'intertextuality', 'metatextuality', 'paratextuality', 'architextuality' and 'hypertextuality'.

Features in films, such as *Secret Window*, that problematize narrative structure force a viewer to reconsider the ways that meaning is produced, not just in that particular film, but also to look for similarities in other films, hence intratextual factors can also encourage intertextuality. Where intertextual references between the film text and any other work become knowing and self-aware, such as they clearly do in *Creepshow* (1982), with an animated 'ghoul', who addresses the viewer directly, one might speak of metatextuality. This is a feature of King adaptations from quite early on, where overtly literary references are playfully sited for King's cognoscenti to spot. In its opening five minutes, *Cat's Eye* (1985) features a number of visual references to *Cujo* and *Christine* (both 1983); *Sleepwalkers* (1992) has a number of visible contemporary horror directors in walk-on roles; and *Misery* (1990) even features a momentary glimpse of King himself as an idealized hero on the cover of a historical romance. Loyalty to the King brand can be measured by how many such references viewers pick up. A further level of metatextuality occurs in the plotline of *Misery*, where this process is overtly referred to in Annie Wilkes' desperation to be writer Paul Sheldon's 'Number 1 fan'.

Paratextuality is used to mean all those factors that affect the meaning of a film beyond the work itself, such as the author/director's own comments. King is a familiar presence on chat shows and in print and will happily discuss his latest works and books and films that he has recently consumed. As an arbiter of public taste, reflected in his regular column for *Entertainment Weekly*, the ubiquitous nature of his comments are hard to avoid, even if the critical precision of some of them in relation to film is highly debatable.

Architextuality refers to the significance suggested by the titles of a text. Nearly all of the major adaptations discussed in this study retain their original literary title, suggesting that a strong link to the author is important to film companies. Even in unusual and unwieldy titles, such as *Secret Window*, *Secret Garden* or *Rita Hayworth and the Shawshank Redemption*, there is an element of compression rather than outright alteration. A rare exception to this is *Stand by Me* (1986), originally *The Body*, reflecting the balance of power between writer and studio in the mid-part of King's career and also the overwhelming global marketing power of securing permission to use a recognizable song.

Hypertextuality describes the relationship between a core or 'hypertext' to a 'hypotext', which modifies the earlier text in some way. The running time of most commercial features means that many words must be cut in translating a novel into a film. Stam suggests that the process of adaptation can be seen as 'a source novel hypotext's being transformed by a complex series of operations: selection, amplification, concretization, actualization, critique, extrapolation, analogization, popularization, and reculturalization.'[16]

Several of Genette's notions can apply at the same time. In *Stand by Me*, elements in the plot premise (the discovery of a child's body) are loosely based on a series of real events in King's own childhood (the paratextual), the title change came after securing rights to B.B. King's eponymous song (the architextual) and, more substantially, the screenplay by Raynold Gideon and Bruce A. Evans, dramatizes King's short story *The Body*, collected in *Different Seasons* (the intertextual). Further paratextual meaning is derived from the music video (featuring not just clips from the film but cast members dancing alongside the singer) and an awareness of the, sometimes, tragic, later careers of the young actors involved (discussed in chapter 4).

Genre Theory
This book takes an original look at King adaptations through the prism of intertextuality and a closely-related concept – genre. In the words of Barry Keith Grant, the concept of 'genre' can be defined as 'those commercial feature films, which through repetition and variation, tell familiar stories, with familiar characters in familiar situations'.[17] Other theorists, such as James Naremore, offer a less rigid definition of 'a loose, evolving system of arguments and readings, helping to shape the commercial strategies and aesthetic ideologies',[18] while others like Robert Stam even question the validity of the notion of 'genre' and raise the possibility that it is merely an academic critical construct.[19] However, the notion of film genre is a term that is valuable to all the main parties in the film-making and consuming process, although, importantly, the meaning is slightly different in each case. For those making a film, genre provides apparent proof of a ready-made audience and a means to reach that audience by repeating certain situations, themes and collections of iconography. The closer the relation to existing film, the quicker and

easier it is for filmmakers to explain to potential financial partners what is being proposed. For audiences, genres seem to offer the promise of repeated pleasures, making a purchasing choice 'safer'. For Film Studies academics, genre offers a useful way to make connections between themes, stars, ideological concepts and stylistic choices, even in apparently disparate films. In a commercial sense, then, genre allocation is a process of simplification to make the finding of repeated pleasure and repeated sales more efficient. In an academic sense, it is also a simplification if it results in a stultifying, self-fulfilling taxonomy. The main point of considering genre critically in this book is to view the films in a way which has not happened before and to see how departures from generic expectations can lead to originality and added viewing pleasure, but also confusion and disappointment.

One weakness of theorists like William Wright or Thomas Schatz is that they tend to assume that development within a genre only occurs as a reaction to other work within that same genre, drawing on a fairly select number of those.[20] Rick Altman suggests the greater likelihood of cross-genre hybridization. His view of genre distinguishes between those elements that he describes as 'syntactic' (plots and themes) and 'semantic' (the presence of recurrent signs, locations and even stars).[21] Altman effectively posits a hierarchical scheme of generic evolution in which genres begin with some semantic elements but can only be regarded as complete genre pieces when they develop syntactic elements as well. To borrow a Darwinian notion for a moment, if genres only evolved from within their own species, so to speak, such an evolutionary process might take many years, but with borrowing between genres, larger developmental leaps become possible. Accordingly, this study is based on the assumption that generic development involves interwoven parasitical processes of borrowing, plagiarism, pastiche – in short, the business of intertextuality.

Critics like Barry Langford are right to point out that contemporary stars are not so tied by generic bonds as stars from classical Hollywood of the 1930s and 1940s, but even with greater financial clout and their own production companies, there remains a limiting factor in generic movement – the audience.[22] Notions of genre are intimately connected to concepts of positioning and constructing an audience. Although specialists in criminal justice rather than film, David Wilson and Sean O' Sullivan suggest a useful three-stage process of novelty, convention and exhaustion in how genres develop.[23] This leads to small changes in conventions to add an element of novelty, thus re-animating genres that were assumed to be exhausted but prove to be merely dormant. Jane Feuer also notes the pleasures of sharing a viewing experience with others who share our particular cultural experiences and tastes, thereby constituting an 'interpretive community'.[24] This may develop as far as the cultish sharing of ritualistic dress and behaviour to accompany films like *The Rocky Horror Show* (Jim Sharman, 1975) or even *The Sound of Music* (Robert Wise, 1965) but nonetheless, genre films function as a confirmation of cultural identity. According to Sonia Livingstone, '[d]ifferent genres specify different "contracts" to be negotiated between the text and the reader ... and the communicative frame (e.g. the participants, the power of the viewer, the openness of the text, and the role of the reader).'[25]

However, the balance is problematic. If films do not attempt some stretching of generic conventions, audiences may feel the narratives are too predictable and offer nothing original or worthy of viewing; if films move too far outside generic conventions, audiences may feel disappointed, confused and even angry. In the case of King's adaptations, the contract between producers and consumers rarely seems to work. What we tend to find is that despite apparently positioning the audience to expect a horror narrative, what is actually delivered rarely meets those generic expectations, either because they are extremely unambitious genre products operating entirely within predictable generic boundaries, or, more often, the deeper structure of these films is not overtly horror at all.

David Bordwell talks about the process by which viewers position a film generically as a series of 'framing' actions, metaphorically a little like Deckard in *Blade Runner* (Ridley Scott, 1982), searching a photographic image and by means of technology, zooming in on different sections of it.[26] However, for genre films to work, indeed for them to be perceived as such, audiences need to have sufficient knowledge of generic forms to understand and appreciate how a particular given text is exploiting, and perhaps challenging, conventions. This becomes more difficult when sub-genres are used that have become anachronistic, such as werewolf or mummy narratives (see chapters 2, 3 and 5). To use pseudo-Darwinian terms again, film genres need to include an element of novelty to expand the form and to keep it alive. This does not mean an ongoing process of refinement to ultimately produce a definitive example of a genre. The changes in generic patterns are closely related to audiences, for they are the factor that allows a genre to survive and, in a sense, are the 'environment' in which a film exists. Effectively, genres die out when they fail to mutate sufficiently to find the sustenance they need – a paying audience. Paradoxically, notions of genre help us to simplify and codify new and potentially complex viewing experiences but, at the same time, operate to generate mutations, sub-genres, that may in time evolve into their own fully-fledged genre, mutate further, lie dormant or die out altogether. Forces for change operate alongside forces for continuity. To use Thomas Schatz's metaphor of genre as a form of grammar, it may seem as if either there is little shared agreement or even understanding of what the grammar of a Stephen King adaptation is, or that there is a mismatch between the expectations of audiences and the films as they are packaged to fit the perception of the King brand.[27]

Criticism of genre films might suggest that there is insufficient content within an individual film to make it worthy of note. However, it could also be said that the process of making meaning from genre films is actually more complicated, as the act of interpretation and interrogation of a text begins before even seeing a film. Arguably, similarity in form allows greater focus to be made on distinctiveness of content. Genre becomes then a kind of shorthand, drawing on viewers' prior experiences, allowing meaning to be created more quickly and potentially more deeply, including the possibility of counter- or ironic meanings. This notion of genre means that meaning is primarily created in linkage with other films: i.e. it is inherently intertextual.

Also relevant here are what kinds of pleasures of are open to viewers of Stephen King adaptations. Part of the attraction is how a particular known written text is realized, so some consideration of changes and alterations is important. However, some films are either not closely associated with King or they may be titles that have not yet been read. In this case, a more significant question is generic: i.e. how successfully the films use known conventions to build on what is familiar and develop expectations in terms of style and content. Although referring to literature rather than film, René Wellek and Austin Warren's comment that 'the totally familiar and repetitive patter is boring; the totally novel form would be unintelligible – is indeed unthinkable' is relevant here.[28] The power of recognition cannot be underestimated. A film form that audiences recognize, and which appears to recognize them by providing references that only experienced viewers perceive, creates a powerful and cyclical synergy of viewing needs, desires and memories. These can extend beyond mere recognition to create a sense of empathy and escapism. Thomas and Vivian Sobchack's observation that contemporary directors and audiences are 'more keenly aware of the myth-making accomplished by film genres' is certainly true of the reception and uses to which *The Shawshank Redemption* (1994) has been put as an inspirational text since its release.[29] The dream-like, almost mythic closing scene provides a powerful element of wish-fulfilment – for the fictional characters but also for the viewer, who may wish to escape a life perceived as constrictive. More demanding narratives may create puzzles and problems to solve, constituting cognitive pleasure. Again, *Shawshank* provides one of the best examples of this as we, like the characters within the fiction, have to struggle with the information we are given to explain Andy's final escape. How will Dolores, in *Dolores Claiborne* (Taylor Hackford, 1995), escape prosecution? The presence, in both narratives, of some police involvement entails an investigation and a search for evidence and clues.

Genre Theory and Horror

It is easy to assume that there is general consensus as to what constitutes a horror film. However, horror is an incredibly diverse genre containing many sub-categories, such as the werewolf, vampire and zombie movie, the haunted house/ghost movie, slasher film, monster movies, demonic horror, apocalyptic horror, splatter film, survival horror and exploitation film. Indeed, it is so diverse, it is arguable that any single theory that attempts to accommodate all these sub-genres is unlikely to be wholly effective or convincing. Equally, what happens when some of the conventions apply for only parts of a film? This may seem idle speculation if it is assumed that most of King's work is based in the horror genre. However, on closer examination, this is not always the case: *The Shining* and *Cujo*, for example, whilst having a horrific climactic episode, for three-quarters of their length are closer to family dramas. Indeed, in both cases, a key part of the power of the final episode is the visualization of a family member (whether it be a father or a trusted pet) turning in on itself and attacking the institution from which it came.

Generic markers are usually based on a number of key criteria: plot; location; budget; iconography; the presence of key performers; genre-specific characteristics such as songs and special effects; or even production factors (such as Hammer horror). However, while even a fairly crude checklist of generic conventions – such as the presence of a villain; an isolated setting; scenes of graphic violence and death; the presence of the supernatural – would not suffice for many films that, generally, would be seen as horror, some of these characteristics might be apparent in genres other than horror, such as melodrama or western.

I have addressed the shortcomings of psychological approaches to horror elsewhere but here, in particular, Robin Wood's list of Others which he claims are repressed in the horror genre (women, the proletariat, other cultures, ethnic groups, alternative ideologies or political systems, children and deviations from sexual norms) could hardly be said to figure in the adaptations in this study as sources of monstrosity.[30] For example, of the films in this book, less than half have an entity that might be deemed a monster at all, and several of those are human characters who only develop or reveal monstrous aspects of their personality during the course of the film. At least nine films here are explicitly not horror. It would make little sense to apply horror theory to *The Shawshank Redemption*, *Stand by Me* or *The Lawnmower Man* (1992). Those films that appear to be closest to what most viewers might associate with horror are found in chapters two and three, and so horror theory will be used at that point where it helps illuminate the films.

If there is a scarcity of monsters in the adaptations here, a second archetype mentioned in the title of Andrew Tudor's *Monsters and Mad Scientists* (1989), is even more lacking.[31] There are few clear-cut examples here of a Frankenstein figure, whose scientific hubris allows uncontrollable forces to be unleashed which then go on to wreak vengeance on those responsible. We have Dr Lawrence Angelo (Pierce Brosnan) in *The Lawnmower Man* who is a scientist but not motivated by lust for power, and Captain Hollister (Martin Sheen) in *Firestarter* (1984), who is not a man of science but would like to exploit it for his own ends. Technology exceeds its bounds in these films, but there is no mad scientist (or even the absent doctor figure of David Cronenberg's work) and no visible act of creation (in Mary Lambert's 1989 *Pet Sematary*, where the reanimated corpses simply appear).

Horror allows, indeed expects, the expression of the unsayable; the socially-unacceptable. It explores transgressive states and taboo behaviour (often ultimately reaffirming social norms by the close). Horror visualizes fears of loss: of life, of self, of family, of the body, of sanity or of hope. It dramatizes how life might be if one or more of these factors was removed from our daily existence. However, unlike much contemporary horror, there is little graphic sexual or violent content in these adaptations. Crucially, viewing habits and tastes have changed over the last 30 years. Seen through the prism of contemporary horror, many King adaptations seem quite tame. Audiences who respond to the sadistic, brutal pleasures evoked by films like *Saw* (James Wan, 2004), are unlikely to have a similar visceral reaction to *Creepshow*. Whether this represents a growing desensitization in viewers of horror narratives, or is just part of shifting cultural tastes that will pass, remains uncertain, but what is clear is that King adaptations increasingly struggle to be heard in a horror marketplace with an emphasis on graphic violence, tie-ins with video games and where characters (major or minor) are readily sacrificed as the monster's next victim.

Goals of the Book

The theoretical approach of this book will be informed by Genette's terms in considering adaptation, but in the particular context of cinematic intertextuality and genre. It is not an aim of the book to produce or reiterate rigid taxonomies, which could become a mere exercise in generic book-keeping. This study will explore how the potential meanings of a text, cinematic or literary, can only be fully apprehended when considered by its interactions with other texts, and to what extent generic expectations are met, challenged or exceeded. This is a completely neglected area of King scholarship and is key to understanding why particular films are effective or not. It is the contention of this study that many audiences approach these films with inaccurate generic expectations and it is the mismatch between these expectations and the films themselves that goes some way to explaining the commercial and critical reception of the films considered in the book.

In the course of this study (especially films in chapters 2, 3 and 5), questions of value arise, in particular, why anyone would study films which appear to be of poor quality. Following the debate about 'badness' in film, often attributed to Jeffrey Sconce and the notion of 'paracinema' (but owing much to Pierre Bourdieu's notion, in *Distinction,* of valorizing the oppositional, the counterstatement and the rebellious), the last decade has seen a growth in writing about trash aesthetics, with degree courses rushing to offer modules on cult and marginal film. Sconce defines paracinema as 'an extremely elastic textual category [which comprises] less a distinct group of films than a particular reading protocol, a counter-aesthetic turned subcultural sensibility devoted to all manner of cultural detritus,' in which 'the explicit manifesto of paracinematic culture is to valorise all forms of cinematic "trash", whether such films have been explicitly rejected or simply ignored by legitimate film culture.'[32]

However, despite such a broad definition, and despite many of the films in this book being more innovative than they seem, associated, as they are, with poor quality, and displaying strong generic and intertextual elements, few King adaptations have been consumed in this way. They rarely inspire transgressive 'reading protocols' (they do not excite passionate fanaticism, group rituals or fan fiction), and aspects such as exploitation, explicit violence/sex, and non-conformist, even eccentric, narratives do not feature here. King's adaptations rarely favour open over closed endings and have neither the intention, form, exhibition environment nor the cultural status associated with 'paracinema'. To paraphrase a more recent Sconce book, these adaptations are not at the margins of taste, style or politics – precisely the opposite; they are, at heart, mainstream entertainment for a terrestrial TV audience.[33] Strangely, the two films that come closest would be the reception of *The Shawshank Redemption* on video through the 1990s and academic reaction to Kubrick's *The Shining*: seeking to place it in the oeuvre of an auteur. In both cases, one popular, one academic, the impulse has been to explain the enigmatic power of a piece of original filmmaking rather than celebrate low-grade tackiness.

Nonetheless, there are several reasons for including films like *Graveyard Shift* (1990) or *Creepshow*. Firstly, this completes the range of King adaptations. The point of this study is not to begin with *a priori* judgements and impose them on a limited selection of films – which is what has happened in the critical literature up to now. Secondly, it is important to question the residual high/low art division that persists, not just between literature and film but between different authors and genres of film. Like the tensions within the term 'paracinema', some of the adaptations in this book have been seen as worthy of study (especially those linked to auteurs like De Palma or Kubrick) but others as shoddy and low-grade trash. Like Joan Hawkins' refinement of Sconce's notion of paracinema, it is possible to collapse, or at least blur, distinctions, suggesting that 'high culture trades on the same images, tropes, and themes that characterize low culture.'[34] Some of the films here, such as the portmanteau films, have suffered pre-judgement several times over as a result of assumptions about the qualities of King's fiction, indeed any film adaptation, and particularly the horror genre. Thirdly, and most importantly, it is a contention of this book that some films are judged to be weaker because they fail on generic grounds to offer the kinds of pleasures that audiences expect.

Like Sconce's arguments about studying 'bad films' in order to understand so-called 'better' ones more fully, so generic elements are often only fully appreciated when we see examples where elements are absent or do not operate effectively. Although not deemed 'paracinema', the films here do strongly foreground matters of genre and intertextuality in the adaptation process: theoretical areas which all too often are approached separately but are inextricably bound up together. As Bourdieu notes, 'One can never escape from the hierarchy of legitimacies. Because the very meaning and value of a cultural object varies according to the system of objects in which it is placed' ('system of objects' here carrying the sense of 'genre').[35]

With a very large and loyal readership, Stephen King is the world's best-selling author and has been consistently successful for over 30 years. However, there remains a strange conundrum about films based on his work: why are so many Stephen King film adaptations deemed to be 'disappointing'? More particularly, why does the work of this best-selling author not translate into the world's most commercial and critically-acclaimed films? On closer consideration, it seemed to this writer that increasingly critical assumptions about the adaptations were often misplaced and even where they did apply, tended to be stated as a fact rather than actually drawn from analysis of the films themselves – something this book aims to address.

Any attempt to encompass either the writings of Stephen King or movies based upon his work has the obvious problem that, as he is so prolific and as there is such a buzz of activity around him that almost every day there is a fresh entry on an official or unofficial website announcing progress on a new novel or an update on various adaptations or some kind of new King-related product, any study on him has an almost built-in obsolescence.

Existing Critical Literature
Clearly, also, there are already books written about Stephen King, demonstrating the strength of reader interest. Stephen Jones' *Creepshow: The Illustrated Stephen King Movie Guide* (2002) is primarily a picture book with bite-sized summaries and cursory ratings of films. Stephen Spignesi's *The Essential Stephen King* (2001) and George Beahm's *Stephen King from A–Z: An Encyclopedia of His Life and Work* (1999) are both designed for reference use. *The Stephen King Universe* (2001) by Stan Wiater et al. is an attempt to unify King's works by theme, and Beahm's *Stephen King: America's Best-loved Bogeyman* (1998) largely reworks his *The Stephen King Story* (1994), constituting an on-going King biography. Mark Kermode's *The Shawshank Redemption* (2003) focuses on one specific film and Tim Underwood and Chuck Miller's *Bare Bones: Conversations on Terror with Stephen King* (1988) and Beahm's *Stephen King Companion* (1991) are collections of articles, interviews and various King-related material. Several titles that appear to cover the films: Jessie Horsting's *Stephen King at the Movies* (1986) Jeff Conner's *Stephen King Goes to Hollywood* (1987) and Michael Collings' *The Films of Stephen King* (1986), are now all over twenty years old and often out of print. With an average of nearly two King adaptations every year since 1976, there is a mass of material which remains unexplored.

Conner's study, covering thirteen films, is typical of the formula: plot summary, production history, general comment and initial critical reaction, usually capped by King's own verdict – as if that is the definitive judgement. There are also repetitive, bordered citations of its own text placed within each chapter and a tendency towards tabloid-style language, such as 'and all that other important script stuff that film instructors talk about'.[36] Collings' book covers only eleven films and tends to focus on changes to King's written text, assuming, as both titles suggest, a sense of ownership and influence from King, and both studies are underpinned by the belief that there is a perfect 'translation' from which all adaptations deviate to a greater or lesser degree. There is a constant shuffling and restating of a ranked position of quality without this deriving from analysis of the detail in the films themselves. Auteurism is accepted as a completely unproblematic concept, with certain films dogmatically described as 'King's' (such as *Creepshow*) with others dismissed as dilutions from 'King's original conception' as if this were transparent.[37] King himself is more aware that 'once you move from a single artisan working in his hut to the Hollywood film, the writer is no longer the one in control'.[38] He also explicitly sees that reading requires 'a certain degree of intellectualization', a demand which he claims is frequently subordinated in viewing a film.[39] He attempts to distil a certain 'Kingness' in the films, without ever really defining exactly what this might mean, and often presents judgements-as-facts and conclusions before analysis.[40] The study concludes with a look forward to *Maximum Overdrive*, which was to prove slightly optimistic.

Even more recent books on the subject, such as Ann Lloyd's *The Films of Stephen King* (1994) and Tony Magistrale's *The Hollywood Stephen King* (2003), assume that the meanings of the films are transparent and focus almost exclusively on whether a particular film is 'faithful' to what King intended, assuming that that is transparent too. Lloyd's text is largely a picture-book and, despite the title, Magistrale's work actually devotes less than 50 per cent of its text to discussion of the films. He himself admits in his preface that 'I am still very much a novice in the art of understanding film's nuanced language of technique' and that 'I leave the task of interpreting these films … to a scholar more adept at this specialised undertaking'.[41] The novels are portrayed as intrinsically superior to the films and there is very little consideration of the films as artistic expressions in themselves. Overall, apart from reviews written at the time of release, there is little detailed analysis of these films in journals or in books, even those with titles which suggest they provide this. Essentially, existing works are either fan-based and encyclopaedic, or products of US English professors seeking thematic unity for King's work and academic credibility for courses they run. As Stanley Wiater recognizes, 'the definitive book on this vital aspect of the author's career has yet to be published'.[42]

The titles of these works reflect the critical assumptions than underlie them. Lloyd and Collings both imply a sense of ownership on King's part, whilst Magistrale and Conner suggest both that King's works are taken on by the Hollywood film industry and that he is in some senses 'making it' in the home of movie glamour and success. Beahm personalizes King's work and views it as the product of a unique individual, and Wiater emphasizes the concept of King possessing a particular all-encompassing world-view. Lloyd follows the basic pattern of a plot synopsis, some quirky background facts and/or details of special effects and King's own 'verdict' on the film, which is explicitly given the weight of final approval or condemnation. The main characters are mentioned and it is stated how viewers respond to them, but not why, i.e. how such effects might be produced. Jones' book contains more detail than Lloyd's but still ultimately tends towards the formulaic. Each film entry has a plot synopsis; recounts how (sometimes at length) the film came to be made (such as how producers met); a brief verdict from a couple of film magazines (often *Fangoria*, *Shivers* and particularly *Cinefantastique*); and a fairly cursory critical view. With an interesting background fact per film and a focus on striking images, especially taken from film posters, the book fulfils its brief as an illustrated companion, intended to be read in fragments. It has an accent on background information, often detailing the most noticeable special effects, and a focus on magazines aimed squarely at fans of the horror genre; there is little attempt to analyse specifically what is actually on screen, beyond an implicit tendency to shift from opening each description positively and often ending the section ironically or even cynically. In terms of tone, each King adaptation is initially met with enthusiasm but, ultimately, the overall feeling is one of repeated disappointment.

Of any existing work, Magistrale's book advances scholarship around King adaptations the furthest and offers many valuable observations, laying out some important first steps. However, it is also important to look closely at the ways in which it falls short. Magistrale promises analysis of around 25 films and even then, only actually discusses a handful in depth. The book contains sustained commentary on only a small number of films, such as *Carrie* (Brian De Palma, 1976) and *The Shining*, some sections on others, such as *Apt Pupil* (Bryan Singer, 1998) and *Hearts in Atlantis* (Scott Hicks, 2001), but in general, the focus is almost unremittingly on the literary sources and on generalizations about the meanings of character actions. Interesting though this is, such pronouncements are often delivered *a priori* without any evidence, i.e. analysis of what is actually on screen and sometimes to the point where it is unclear whether Magistrale is talking about the books or the films (something King actually does more effectively in his interview at the beginning of the book, especially in relation to *Carrie*). With a writer like King, gaps are almost inevitable. However, despite claiming the need to 'abandon the threadbare and specious distinctions used to separate high and low definitions of art', films without literary antecedents, which play little part in English degree courses, such as *Creepshow* (I and II) drawn from comic book culture, original movie scripts such as *Sleepwalkers*, movies drawn from King's short stories like *Graveyard Shift* or portmanteau films such as *Cat's Eyes*, are barely mentioned, which undermines any conclusions drawn (although there actually is no concluding section).[43]

There is, in Magistrale's approach, an unremitting concern with fidelity to a source text and complaints about differences, or parts that are missed out, without accepting that any 90-page screenplay must inevitably reduce significantly the content of a novel of several hundred pages. The basic structure of each section includes a plot summary and nods to what previous critics have said, but the main focus is on analysis of relationships and themes that he perceives in King's work, with lengthy passages discussing the novels (and literary criticism of them) rather than the films, and characters are routinely treated as realistic psychological entities rather than fictional constructs. The book's organization around thematic categories highlights an approach which sees the meaning as a given and, time and again, character actions are described as if they were transparent, with very few comments based on film form, leading with assertions which are often interesting, but not wholly convincing. There are sections on technology and typical King heroes and, especially, family types (with separate chapters on children, mothers and fathers). Magistrale's basic approach is to extend his literary analysis to movies: finding the same points in the films and seeing it as a critical fault when such features are absent. He can see complexities in the books and discusses them but because he cannot see the same/related features in the adaptations, he assumes them to be inferior, as with De Palma's version of *Carrie*, which 'abandons the book's pseudo-documentary perspective' (a feature he is happy to analyse as it links nicely with Bram Stoker's 1897 *Dracula*).[44]

There are references to reviews of individual films but there is little sign that major figures like De Palma, Carpenter, Cronenberg and even Romero have a critical background; that positions have already been taken up; in short, that Film Studies as a discipline exists. Whilst there is no particular value in replaying the auteur question over and over about whose influence was greatest – the prime interest of this study is what is on screen rather than arguing about the relative merits of who put it there – by placing an interview with King right at the start, Magistrale strongly suggests that he (King) is the unquestioned 'author' of the works that he considers in the following chapters. Both Magistrale and Collings talk about films that are 'faithful' to King's novels, and can therefore be seen as 'his', and 'artists' who somehow 'deviate' from King's source, such as Kubrick, thereby commit the sin of unfaithfulness to a source text. Magistrale states from the outset that since all the texts share a common source, 'they must necessarily possess important elements of similarity', without arguing why this should necessarily be so.[45] Moreover, he is overtly and uncritically auteurist, without apparently being aware of this, openly expressing 'a desire to view these films according to shared similarities of themes, characters, motifs and narrative designs'.[46]

Magistrale struggles to accommodate films without a literary basis or to relate the films to the genre with which King is most closely associated – horror – and, at times, also struggles to articulate precise analysis of film sequences (see *The Shining*, where he spends several sentences struggling to express the breaking of the continuity line and high and low angles, or *Apt Pupil* where he describes the process of superimposition as 'the magic of film', or the misuse of the term 'pan' to describe the camera movement up to Coffey's face in *The Green Mile* from 1999).[47] Clearly, in order to grow and develop, Film Studies should be open to contributors from other disciplines. One only has to think, for example, of Slavoj Žižek, philosopher and social critic. However, imagine the howls of protest that would greet a Film Studies academic with the temerity to write about Shakespeare,

Charles Dickens or Herman Melville without knowing the difference between a metaphor and a simile. A little self-deprecation is one thing but to declare from the outset, as Magistrale does, that he has no 'formal training in cinema studies' and will only cover half the available material, does seem to undercut much of the validity of the exercise.[48] While Collings' earlier work may be more limited in scope, it is more precisely focused on the films. Magistrale notes the low critical status historically accorded King's written works, and the horror genre more broadly, but then goes on to perpetuate this by largely ignoring films like *Creepshow* or *Sleepwalkers*. There are assumptions about 'the average fan's curiosity' and 'audiences likely to go to a Stephen King film adaptation', as if there was a consensus about what such terms might mean.[49] The critical method used by Wiater, Beahm and Magistrale generally entails identifying thematic concerns in the novels and then spotting them in the films. Unfortunately, this becomes a self-fulfilling prophecy, producing descriptions, which are partial, repetitive and sometimes highly selective, rather than analysis of what is actually there.

This study, which will consider every single King film adaptation given a cinematic release, is the first such book written by a film-specialist. It is also the first to comment in detail on *Sleepwalkers*, *Dreamcatcher* (2003) and *1408* (2007) and the first to analyse the portmanteau films, such as *Creepshow I* and *II*, (1982, 1987), *Cat's Eye* and *Tales From the Darkside* (1990). It is not the aim of the book to salvage all of the films as great masterworks of cinema but, rather, to highlight how and why particular films are effective (or not) in meeting the genre expectations of their audiences. This book examines what things the films can tell us about King's novels, the process of adaptation and the a range of genres, with a clear focus on the films themselves and how they work on their own terms, rather than becoming hamstrung by questions of fidelity to a source text.

Authorship as a Branding Device
In terms of directors, almost all the big names of horror films have had at least one attempt at a King novel: John Carpenter (*Christine*), David Cronenberg (*The Dead Zone*), Brian De Palma (*Carrie*) and George Romero (*Creepshow* and *The Dark Half*). It is also clear that undeterred from having their name attached to a King project are stars such as Tom Hanks (*The Green Mile*), Morgan Freeman (*The Shawshank Redemption*) or Anthony Hopkins (*Hearts in Atlantis*). When *Carrie* was first published King was still relatively unknown: it was De Palma's movie that really brought his work to major national and international audiences. Since then, King has been very aware of how movies help bring his work to a wider audience, which has both artistic and clear financial benefits for him, and although he rejects the idea that he writes with an eye to being adapted, he works in the full knowledge that screen rights will be sold as a matter of course. He claims that 'I have never written with the movies in mind, but I have always written with them in my eye ... My books are the movies I see in my head, that's all'.[50]

However, this is a little disingenuous. King has an increasingly powerful role in the adaptation industry, both as an author and as a Producer. Furthermore, films completely permeate King's writing career. In *On Writing*, he admits to a 'quasi-professional life' in the film industry and describes himself as 'someone who has been in the film world but not of it ever since Paul Monash optioned my book *Carrie* in 1974'.[51] In 1961, at the age of fourteen, King made about 40 copies of a self-penned novelization of *The Pit and the Pendulum* after seeing the Roger Corman version; in effect producing his first bestseller. Indeed, King claims that '[w]hat I cared most about between 1958 and 1966 was movies', particularly 'horror movies, science fiction movies, movies about teenage gangs on the prowl, movies about losers on motorcycles'.[52] Productions have almost run alongside his writing – *Firestarter* was released while the novel was still on the bestseller lists. He has written original screenplays (*Sleepwalkers*), adaptations of his work (*Pet Sematary*), acted as Executive Producer (*Storm of the Century*, 1999) and Director (*Maximum Overdrive*, 1986). His interest in scriptwriting actually predates working from his own sources as his first attempt was a rejected adaptation of Ray Bradbury's 1962 novel, *Something Wicked This Way Comes* (filmed by Jack Clayton in 1983) – the carnival frame story finding its way later into the last part of King's script for *Quicksilver Highway* (Mick Garris, 1997). On the DVD extras for *Desperation*, he even mentions considering taking a Masters degree in screenwriting. He is a consciously analytical writer – he has theorized articulately in numerous interviews and in print about the writing process (*On Writing*, 2000) and on the horror genre (*Danse Macabre*, 1981), where his knowledge is seen as being broad and factually-detailed. In terms of formats, he has written TV mini-series scripts (*The Stand*, Mick Garris, 1994), full-length feature films and discrete episodes of long-running sci-fi serials (*The X-Files*, *The Twilight Zone* and *The Outer Limits*). His willingness to allow his shorter literary properties to be adapted by film students for a nominal fee – to produce his so-called 'dollar-babies' – also suggests an interest in fostering the next generation of filmmaking talent. Despite his clear association with the horror genre, much of his work extends beyond such boundaries: from 'domestic' films like *Dolores Claiborne* to pop videos (the story writer for Michael Jackson's *Ghosts*) and even musicals (co-writer of *Ghost Brothers of Darkland County*, in collaboration with John Mellencamp).

Although scriptwriting guru and sometime King collaborator William Goldman once famously observed that Hollywood 'knows nothing' about what will be successful or not (reflected in his own involvement as a King scriptwriter from the success of *Misery*, *Hearts in Atlantis*, and *Dolores Claiborne* to the mess of *Dreamcatcher* where he is uncredited), there is one fact that remains true: linking Stephen King's name to a project will ensure that (sometimes later rather than sooner) it will get made, and it will make money. Maybe not a lot but it will at least break even and, considering the number of films and TV mini-series based on his work, this alone makes him unique. He may not be a star director, producer or actor, although he has dabbled in all of those fields, but he is, in short, the most bankable name in

Hollywood and one of a small number of writers whose name appears in significantly larger font than the titles of his works. He is both a prolific and significant player in the world of publishing and movie-making. Remarkably, there has been at least one Stephen King-derived film in production every year, without a pause, for the last 30 years and, although their artistic quality and commercial success may vary, it does not seem to create funding difficulties for the next King adaptation. As Producer, Jeff Hayes notes on the DVD extras package for the *Nightmares and Dreamscapes* collection (2006), with King's name attached to a project, 'you don't have to sell too hard'.

His commercial status as a writer and an initiator of film projects is unparalleled. His standard deal with Castle Rock Entertainment is unique in terms of both its extent and longevity. Since the mid 1980s, he has been able to command script-, director- and cast-approval, with the option of ending the project at any point. Equally impressive is his 'gross participation' deal, which means he receives a percentage on every dollar spent on his adaptations at the box office, irrespective of profits. His direct day-to-day influence over the production process may vary from project to project but this basic deal means that he cannot completely wash his hands of responsibility for any of the films made from the novels which bear his name.

This bankability extends to that staple of the marketing of a new TV season, especially in the US – the TV mini-series. It is through internationally-syndicated TV versions that King's work is increasingly coming to a screen near you, most likely a screen in your own home. Linking King's name to an upcoming drama draws upon two central tenets of why the auteur theory persists. It draws attention (and hopefully viewers) from his millions of readers and it identifies a yet unseen product with the 'King brand'. The announcement of a Stephen King adaptation is increasingly used by American TV networks as a visible sign of their commitment to high quality prime-time drama. Since *Silver Bullet* (1985), film titles have included the key phrase 'Stephen King's...', denoting ownership and apparent approval. This is also why he is so keen to avoid association with films that damage the quality of that brand, reflected in the litigation over the use of his name in connection with *The Lawnmower Man*. Interestingly, in contrast, through the mid 1990s, film companies at times attempted to distance their products, like *The Shawshank Redemption* and *The Green Mile*, from direct linkage with King, anxious to avoid associating such films with the narrow horror label that still follows King from project to project.

His marketable name goes with an increasingly recognizable face: his picture adorns most of his book jackets; he makes himself available regularly to his readers via signings; he has made several appearances on US chat-shows; and is a sufficiently visible presence in contemporary culture to have taken part in an American Express adverts. The dramas of his own life, such as his near-fatal accident in 1999, are reported as national news, and his own literary status is finally being recognized, if not universally accepted. At the same time, film versions based on his work (if not overtly linked to him via marketing campaigns), have gained recognition: *The Green Mile*, secured four Oscar nominations and *The Shawshank Redemption*, seven – recently winning a poll of best films never to have won a Best Picture Oscar.

The bankability of King as a source author has even reached the point where remakes are now being made of his own films. The time loop between original and remake may seem to be shortening in contemporary cinema and this seems especially so in the horror genre, which appears inherently cannibalistic. Already there have been remakes of *The Shining* (1979 and 1997) and *Salem's Lot* (1979 and 2004) and sequels which feel more like remakes *Carrie* (1976 and 2002). These remakes are now clearly branded in their titles as 'Stephen King's...' as if previously they were not authored by him. In connection to the films discussed in this book, it is possible to see a sliding scale of King's authorship from no active involvement beyond the paratextual (legal wrangling over the use of the title *The Lawnmower Man*) to acting as director (*Maximum Overdrive*) or Executive Producer (Mick Garris' 1997 remake of *The Shining*). Even within the scriptwriting role there is a similar range of involvement from none, to an initial draft (which may or may not be taken further as with Kubrick's *The Shining*), to a series of drafts in collaboration with other writers, to complete and sole authorship (*Sleepwalkers*). There is the question of credited involvement and unaccredited involvement and the vexed question of rewrites appropriating material that King feels is his (in the case of *Cujo*). There is a growing tendency to underscore authorship with a director-possessive title in marketing other films, especially in the horror genre, such as *John Carpenter's Vampires* (1998) and *Wes Craven's New Nightmare* (1994). This has evolved into a franchise of more tangential endorsement, 'Wes Craven Presents...' preceding the *Dracula* trilogy – the latter two subtitled *Ascension* and *The Legacy* respectively (2000, 2003 and 2005). In some cases, like Stephen King's *The Shining*, where he wrote the screenplay, there could be a argument for slightly more authorial ownership, but in general it is part of a more visible branding of a product for global recognition.

This might be seen as indicative of a poverty of imagination in both producers and consumers but, looked at more positively by critics like Jim Collins, it reflects more keenly their creativity and ability and willingness to make connections between texts.[53] The standard possessory credit with a Stephen King adaptation may be one of the clearest signs that the films in this book are struggling for a corporate identity, which the texts alone at a surface level, do not always convey. Films increasingly refer to one another in dialogue, in situation, even in titles (such as *Alien vs. Predator*, Paul W.S. Anderson, 2004), blurring clear-cut generic boundaries and indicating that old-style generic categories are not yet redundant but are more of a useful starting point. As Jacques Derrida notes, [e]very text participates in one or several genres, there is no genreless text.'[54]

Structure/Content

What this book is

The book attempts to look at King's adaptations on their own terms and see how they succeed or fail in generic terms. Particular consideration will be given to the presentation of monstrosity, narrative momentum and credibility, the pressure to ameliorate endings, the presence of generic confusion, the presence or absence of generic ambition and a stubborn loyalty to anachronistic genres. The films are discussed generally in chronological, not alphabetical, order. They were produced in this order and to take them out of context would imply they have little relation to one another. That said, some of the films, for example *Apt Pupil*, have had a fairly lengthy, and even troubled, gestation period and some sequels, although produced years later (like *Carrie* or *The Shining*) are more meaningfully discussed juxtaposed with the original film, rather than placed hundreds of pages apart. The sections themselves are fairly porous – both *The Shining* and *Hearts in Atlantis* might equally have been placed in the chapter entitled 'Mind over matter'. Some consideration will be given to deleted scenes because, although their inclusion in a package of 'extras' is part of the justification for the relatively high price of DVDs, viewed more positively, the availability of previously-unseen material allows consideration of early intentions and, in some cases, forced decisions due to over-running of time or budget.

What this book is not

Please note, it is not an attempt to cover all visual adaptations of King's work – just those designed for a cinematic release. There are, however, a couple of exceptions to this basic structure. *The Shining* (1997) and *Carrie: The Rage* (2002) were made for television but are the sequel to feature films by Kubrick (1980) and Brian De Palma (1976), respectively, and so it makes sense for them to be discussed here alongside the originals. By contrast, *Return to Salem's Lot* is a film but was released straight-to-video in the US and is a sequel to the 1979 TV version, *Salem's Lot,* and the later 2004 remake was also made for TV. *Thinner* (Tom Holland, 1996) and *Riding the Bullet* (Mick Garris, 2004) both had extremely brief releases in certain territories only and although *Children of the Corn* (1984) and *The Mangler* (1994) were given cinematic releases, the franchise that the sequels became were all released (in most territories) straight-to-video. Rather than relegate King's work for the small screen to a final catch-all section, which tends to be how it is treated – explicitly portraying it as a visual 'poor relation' of his film adaptations, it is hoped to devote a complete companion study to this topic.

There will no attempt to distort the film material to fit one theoretical paradigm. With so many different directors, crews and writers, to attempt to throw a single critical blanket over the range of films would be inappropriate. In literary terms, there have been attempts by critics like Wiater to draw all of King's works together: to see the persistent cross-references of names, situations and themes as part of a coherent whole. This can be an interesting parlour game but the same does not work for the films. There will be references to horror theory where this illuminates texts, but nearly half of the films in this book do not fall into this category. Magistrale notes that it is striking 'how few of them (the films) fit the mould of the 'typical' horror movie'.[55] Anyone who has read and enjoyed King's books should be able to find the study accessible. It should make readers want to seek out films they have not yet seen and to look with fresh eyes at those they think they already know.

Notes

1. Gerald Olin describing the writing of Mike Enslin in Stephen King, '1408' in *Everything's Eventual* (London: New English Library, 2002), p. 432.
2. Sebastian Faulks, *Engleby*, (London: Vintage Books, 2008), p. 36.
3. See Seán Burke (ed.). *Authorship: From Plato to the Postmodern* (Edinburgh: University of Edinburgh Press, 1995).
4. Stephen King in Tim Underwood and Chuck Miller, *Bare Bones: Conversations on Terror with Stephen King* (New York: McGraw-Hill, 1988), p. 17.
5. See John Caughie, *Theories of Authorship* (London: Routledge, 1981); Virginia Wright Wexman (ed.), *Film and Authorship* (Piscataway, NJ: Rutgers University Press, Depth of Film Series, 2002); David A. Gerstner (ed.), *Authorship and Film* (London: Routledge, AFI Film Readers, 2002); and Barry Grant (ed.), *Auteurs and Authorship: A Film Reader* (Hoboken, NJ: Wiley-Blackwell, 2008).
6. See Mark Browning, *David Cronenberg: Author or Filmmaker?* (Bristol: Intellect Books, 2007), pp. 26–32.
7. Deborah Cartmell and Imelda Whelehan (eds.), 'Introduction', *Adaptations: From Text to Screen; Screen to Text* (New York; London: Routledge, 1999), p. 6.
8. See George Beahm (ed.), *The Stephen King Companion* (London; Sydney: Futura Publications, 1991), pp. 75–95.
9. Brian McFarlane, *Novel to Film: An Introduction to the Theory of Adaptation* (Oxford: Oxford University Press, 1996), p. 8.
10. Mikhail Bakhtin, cited in James Naremore, *Film Adaptation* (London: Athlone, 2000), p. 64.
11. See Thomas Tessier in Don Herron (ed.), *Reign of Fear: The Fiction and the Films of Stephen King* (Novato, California: Underwood-Miller, 1988), p. 74.
12. Thomas Leitch, *Film Adaptation and Its Discontents* (John Hopkins University Press, Bloomington and London, 2007), p. 126.
13. Ibid., p. 92.
14. Neil Sinyard, 'Introduction', *Filming Literature: The Art of Screen Adaptation* (Beckenham, Kent: Croom Helm, 1986), p. x.
15. Gérard Genette cited in Naremore, (London: Athlone, 2000), p. 65.
16. Robert Stam, cited in Naremore, *Film Adaptation*, p. 68.
17. Barry Keith Grant, (ed.), *Film Genre Reader* (Austin: University of Texas Press, 1986), p. ix.
18. James Naremore, 'American Film Noir: The History of an Idea', *Film Quarterly*, 49. 2 (1995–96), p. 14.

19. Robert Stam, *Film Theory: An Introduction*, (Malden, MA: Blackwell, 2000), p.14.

20. See William Wright, *Sixguns and Society*, (University of California Press, Berkeley, 1975) and Thomas Schatz *Hollywood Genres: Formulas, Filmmaking and the Hollywood Studios*, (Random House, New York, 1981).

21. See Rick Altman, *The American Film Musical* (Indiana: Indiana University Press, 1989).

22. See Barry Langford, *Film Genre: Hollywood and Beyond* (Edinburgh: Edinburgh University Press, 2005), p. 2.

23. See David Wilson and Sean O' Sullivan, *Images of Incarceration* (Bristol: Waterside Press, 2004).

24. Jane Feuer, 'Genre study and television' in Robert C. Allen (ed.), *Channels of Discourse, Reassembled: Television and Contemporary Criticism* (London: Routledge, 1992), p. 144.

25. Sonia M. Livingstone, 'The rise and fall of audience research: an old story with a new ending', in Mark R. Levy & Michael Gurevitch (eds.), *Defining Media Studies: Reflections on the Future of the Field* (New York: Oxford University Press, 1994), pp. 252–3.

26. David Bordwell, *Making Meaning: Inference and Rhetoric in the Interpretation of Cinema* (Cambridge, MA: Harvard University Press 1989), p. 146.

27. Thomas Schatz, 'Film Genre and Genre Film' in L. Braudy and M. Cohen (eds.), *Film Theory and Criticism* (New York: Oxford University Press, 2004), pp. 691–702.

28. René Wellek & Austin Warren, Chapter 17: 'Literary Genres' in *Theory of Literature* (Harmondsworth: Penguin, 1963), p. 235.

29. Thomas and Vivian Sobchack, *An Introduction to Film* (Boston, MA: Little, Brown & Co, 1980), p. 245.

30. See Browning, *Cronenberg: Author or Filmmaker?* op. cit., pp. 9–19 and Robin Wood, 'An Introduction to the American Horror Film', in Andrew Britton, Richard Lippe, Tony Williams and Robin Wood (eds.), *The American Nightmare: Essays on the Horror Film* (Toronto: Festival of Festivals, 1979), pp. 7–28.

31. See Andrew Tudor, *Monsters and Mad Scientists: A Cultural History of the Horror Film* (Cambridge Massachusetts: Basil Blackwell Inc., 1989).

32. Jeffrey Sconce, 'Trashing the Academy: Taste, Excess and the Emerging Politics of Cinematic Style' in *Screen*, vol. 36:4 (Winter, 1995), p. 372.

33. See Jeffrey Sconce, Sleaze Artists: Cinema at the Margins of Taste, Style and Politics (Durham, NC: Duke University Press, 2007).

34. Joan Hawkins, *Cutting Edge: Art-Horror and the Horrific Avant-garde* (Minnesota: University of Minnesota Press, 2000), p. 3.

35. Pierre Bourdieu, *Distinction: A Social Critique of the Judgement of Taste*, trans. Richard Nice, Harvard: Harvard University Press, (1997), p. 86.

36. Jeff Conner, *Stephen King Goes to Hollywood* (New York: New American Library, 1987), pp. 110–111.

37. Michael Collings, *The Films of Stephen King* (Washington: Starmont House, 1986), p.1.

38. Stephen King in Tony Magistrale, *The Hollywood Stephen King* (New York: Palgrave Macmillan, 2003), p. 11.

39. Conner, op. cit., p. 16.

40. Ibid., p. 32 and 52.

41. Magistrale, op. cit, p. xviii.

42. Stan Wiater in Stan Wiater, Christopher Golden and Hank Wagner, *The Stephen King Universe* (Los Angeles: Renaissance Books, 2001). p. 462.
43. Magistrale, op. cit., p xvii.
44. Ibid., p. 23.
45. Ibid., p. xvi.
46. Ibid., p. xviii.
47. Ibid. See pp. 91–94, p. 110, and p. 138.
48. Ibid., p. xviii.
49. Ibid. See p. xii and p. xvii.
50. Stephen King in Frank Darabont, *The Shawshank Redemption: The Shooting Script* (New York: Newmarket Press, 1996), p. ix.
51. See Stephen King, *On Writing* (London: New English Library, 2000), p. 260 and Stephen King, 'Rita Hayworth and the Darabont Redemption'– Introduction to Frank Darabont, *The Shawshank Redemption: The Shooting Script*, op. cit., p. xii.
52. Stephen King, *On Writing*, pp. 39–40.
53. See Jim Collins, 'Genericity in the Nineties: Eclectic Irony and the New Sincerity' in Jim Collins, Hilary Radner and Ava Preacher Collins (eds.), *Film Studies Goes to the Movies* (New York: Routledge, AFI Film Readers, 1993), pp. 242–263.
54. Jacques Derrida, 'The law of genre' in W J T Mitchell (ed.), *On Narrative* (Chicago: University of Chicago Press, 1981), p. 61.
55. Magistrale,, *The Hollywood Stephen King* op. cit., p. 147.

CHAPTER ONE

MIND OVER MATTER: TELEKINESIS

Public interest in psychic powers did not suddenly begin in the 1970s, but the decade produced a number of powerful cultural expressions of it from the emergence of entertainer/illusionist Uri Geller to the development of new cinematic subgenres. William Friedkin's *The Exorcist* (1973) reanimated religious horror and virtually single-handedly created the subgenre of the possessed child narrative. Along with *The Medusa Touch* (Jack Gold, 1978), *The Fury* (Brian De Palma, 1978) and *Scanners* (David Cronenberg, 1981), *Carrie* and *Firestarter* were amongst the first films to popularize the terrifying, possibly world-destroying, potential of telekinesis. In *The Medusa Touch*, John Morlar (Richard Burton) has the power to induce destruction on an increasing scale by power of mind alone, culminating in a political warning as, from a hospital bed, he scribbles 'Windscale' (the site of a nuclear power plant) on a pad. *The Fury* and *Scanners* also feature a shadowy government organization seeking to harness psychic gifts for malign ends. Perhaps because of its focus on the spectacular and the apparently impossible, the telekinesis subgenre had innate comedic potential, previously identified by such mainstream TV fare as *I Dream of Genie* (NBC, 1965–70). The protagonist in *Zapped* (1982), Barney Springboro (Scott Baio) gains telekinetic powers after a lab accident but then proceeds to use them for a range of puerile jokes, like undressing girls, echoing Carrie's shower scene but more precisely for prurient heterosexual viewers. Roald Dahl's novel *Matilda* (1988) and the film version in 1996 are benign versions of *Carrie*, where tables are turned on the bullying teacher Miss Trunchball by a number of telekinetic tricks (including tipping over a glass of water with a newt in it) but no real physical harm befalls anyone.

The key question considered in this chapter is how King adaptations attempt to dramatize the possession of psychic power. Cinematic representations of the subject tend to oscillate between the supposedly-scientific (and thereby undramatic) or the spectacular and performative, which rely on special effects to convey phenomena which viewers can find convincing. In *On Writing*, King describes writing as a form of telepathy and in his early works he explores telepathy as a form of art.[1] However, for King, a psychic gift seems to be only of limited value to the one who has it. Indeed, it seems more of a curse than a gift and cannot prevent an unjust and even sacrificial death (*The Dead Zone* and *The Green Mile*) or exclusion/exploitation (*Firestarter* and *Hearts in Atlantis*). Those King narratives focusing on psychic gifts seem to have at their centre a figure who is gentle, selfless but ultimately destined to meet a tragic end as the harsher realities around them exact a terrible price.

The approach in this chapter is predominantly an auteurist one as it is largely the input from directors Brian De Palma and David Cronenberg in their creative choices over camera placement and movement, and their ability to coax particularly powerful, even career-defining performances from their protagonists (Sissy Spacek and Christopher Walken respectively), that set *Carrie* and *The Dead Zone* apart from *Firestarter* and *Carrie II*. This is not an uncritical auteurism, but it is these areas of production upon which the chapter will focus and it is easier to attribute them to a director than constantly qualify any analytical comment made. It is ultimately what is on screen and how it works (or not), which is significant, rather than quibbling about who put it there.

Carrie (Brian De Palma, 1976)

'Blood, fresh blood. Blood was always at the root of it' (King 1974: 137).[2]

Robert Stam builds upon Steve Neale's model of an interdependent tripartite structure of needs and expectations between film and artist and audience model, and defines genre via four inter-related threads: blueprint ('a formula that precedes, programmes and patterns industry production'), structure ('the formal framework on which individual films are founded'), label ('a category central to the decisions and communications of distributors and exhibitors') and contract ('the viewing position required by each genre film of its audience').[3] However, it can be seen that, in terms of the films discussed in this book, there are often tensions between, in Stam's terminology, the 'blueprint' of a King adaptation based on assumptions about previous films, the generic 'label' which is often inaccurate or fails to deliver what audiences might expect and because of fault-lines in the 'blueprint' and 'label' terms, the 'contract' is subsequently also flawed.

Carrie, both in terms of the book and the film, was marketed squarely as a horror narrative – bloodied images of Sissy Spacek adorning video covers, movie posters and book reprints. The bloodshed at the prom; the infliction of a slow death on her mother from multiple stab wounds; the sudden shock ending with the hand rising into the frame; a screaming female character unable to sleep – there are certainly features of horror at the end. However, this overshadows the film up to that point.

For a good 80 per cent of its length, i.e. until the climactic prom scene, we have a greater generic emphasis on a high school narrative. It perhaps should not really surprise us that *Carrie* was a Broadway musical, albeit with a very short run. For most of its length, we have a darker, more mature version of *Porky's* (Bob Clark, 1982) or *Fast Times at Ridgemont High* (Amy Heckerling, 1982). We see Carrie as an ostracized victim of peer group bullying; a school leadership uninterested in her (reflected in the mistakes with her name); one sympathetic teacher trying to help; snapshots of lessons and preparations for annual rituals, like the prom.

The success of Brian De Palma's 1976 feature *Carrie*, the first movie based on a King novel, established King as a Hollywood player and effectively re-animated the horror genre. However, *Carrie* is very different in nature from the slasher narratives of the *Friday the 13th* and *Nightmare on Elm Street* cycles, foregrounding the anguish of US teen life, particularly around rituals like the high school prom. It would be another 26 years before there was a sequel to *Carrie* and the narrative in the first film, as scripted by Lawrence D. Cohen, is extremely linear and sequential, rather than the episodic nature of most slasher pictures. Cohen took King's original novel, constructed, like Bram Stoker's 1897 *Dracula*, in fragments of different communicational devices (such as interviews, letters, reports, and textbook entries) and recast it with a clear focus on one individual, trying to find a way to accommodate the religious demands of home, the physical/sexual demands of her own body and the social demands of school.

The standard criticisms of De Palma at this point of his career (of which Magistrale appears unaware – see discussion in the Introduction) is that his work is derivative (particularly of Hitchcock), and his representations of violent acts on and around women amount to a directorial (and possibly personal) attitude to women that can be seen as misogynistic. Both criticisms are not without some foundation but, often, such references constitute a critical cul-de-sac, ending debate rather than starting it. In particular, for the purposes of this book, more relevant is how De Palma creates scenes of effective horror. Despite a fairly modest budget ($1.8 million) and a demanding shooting schedule (50 days), De Palma's film was a critical and commercial success. Part of the reason for this was that *Carrie*, the novel, was fairly short (just over 200 pages), especially in the light of later King works (often 500–600 pages). Closer to a novella, the pared-down source text made Cohen's job that much easier. The novel has little suspense – we know who will die before the end. By contrast, the film displays a depth of artistry that makes other adaptations look extremely 'flat'. This is not just an emotional term – De Palma creates depth within his shots through a close understanding of film form. Take almost any sequence in the film and you can see painterly picture composition, elaborate camera positioning and movement and the creation of space across and through the frame, giving a greater sense of being involved in the action (and thereby more unsettled when unexpected things happen).

Allied to this is an extremely allusive style, self-consciously making intertextual references, which need to be teased out if we are trying to explain the impact of the film. Almost any discussion of De Palma in reviews mentions Hitchcock: the final split-screen ending, and the sudden dream ending. It is a further critical commonplace to say of De Palma's work that it is stylish (often with the implication of 'too-clever-by-half') without precise analysis, i.e. intertextuality is recognized as important but not specifically how. Whereas *Body Double* (1984) 'borrows' plot elements wholesale from *Vertigo* (1958) and *Rear Window* (1954), *Carrie* wears its Hitchcockian influences a little more lightly. Both *Carrie* and *Psycho* use mirrors as a symbol of a divided self and there is some obvious visual name-checking – for example Carrie attends Bates High School. The birds-eye shots of Carrie locked in her closet; of her mother walking around the kitchen table, contemplating the murder of her own daughter; and indeed the final blow itself – all evoke the shot above the stairwell in *Psycho* just before the murder of Arbogast. The opening camera positioning, perching bird-like on the rim of the basket above the volleyball court, has similarities with the cool, distanced, god-like point of view shot (POV) sometimes favoured by Hitchcock in films like *The Birds* (1963). As an image of indifferent fate, the shot is reprised at the end from high above the bucket apparatus set to drop over Carrie, suggesting that prowess or otherwise in ritual school events like the prom foreshadow the chances of success in later life.

Carrie's opening sequence and the bath after the prom trick that has covered her in blood mean that the film is 'book-ended' by parallels to the infamous shower scene in *Psycho* (1960). Both scenes have overtones of baptism, but whereas Hitchcock's heroine, Marion Crane, could be said to be trying to wash away a genuine sense of sin (in reference to the money she has stolen), Carrie seeks to wash away a sense of sin that is projected upon her: first by her mother and then by her so-called school friends. The murder weapon, the assailant and the method of attack (hiding behind a form of screen – here the bathroom door), are all similar, but whereas Crane meets her end by being stabbed by 'mother', Carrie completes her ablutions without interruption, only to be attacked afterwards by her real mother whom she destroys by telekinesis.

One of the more subtle links with Hitchcock here is De Palma's association with long-time Hitchcock collaborator Bernard Herrmann, who had already worked on *Sisters* (1972) and *Obsession* (1975). De Palma used Herrmann's music when he was putting a temporary music track on *Carrie,* and the final scene does still use a few bars from *Sisters*. De Palma openly uses a scaled-down version of Bernard Herrmann's speeded-up violins to signify an outburst of Carrie's murderous rage. One of the most unsettling moments in the film occurs when Carrie is in her closet peering into the mirror, which seems to distort and buckle, and is accompanied by a just a single violin note, making the viewer wonder if they heard it correctly. As De Palma admitted, 'the flexing sound is very *Psycho*'.[4] It is as if there is a hidden force pushing just beneath the surface, struggling to erupt into the everyday world, which by the end of the film, it has. Years before the kind of liquid, CGI-produced, special effects as seen in *Stargate* (Roland Emmerich, 1994) or *Donnie Darko* (Richard Kelly, 1991) to signal borderline states between different dimensions of reality, Carrie's low-budget alternative is arguably just as effective.

However the closest link with Hitchcock is not in superficial similarities of situation but in the meticulous composition of shots and sequences and their subsequent editing together. For example, early in the film, Carrie is waiting outside the Headteacher's office. She sits facing us and we can see through a window into the office as Miss Collins, the concerned PE teacher, discusses with the Head what happened in the lesson. In a following shot, Carrie, still waiting, is in the extreme foreground but now placed at right angles to a rather frosty-looking secretary. At the same time we still hear the conversation continuing in the office. In the first shot we see a figure in the extreme foreground being discussed in the extreme background and in the second we still see the character but only hear the character being talked about. In both cases, in a way, we are placed in a position to see and/or hear the relationship between the different planes of meaning, which the individual characters themselves are not, making them appear lost and helpless.[5] Later, by contrast, we are prevented from hearing phone dialogue when Mrs White takes a call from school. From her facial expression and subsequent violent striking of Carrie, we deduce that the school has just informed her about the incident in gym class.

A further example of how planes of meaning are constructed in conjunction with the soundtrack occurs later in Sue's mother's house. Mrs White has managed to talk her way into her neighbour's house when the phone rings and Mrs Snell goes to answer it. She walks away from the camera out of focal distance, becoming blurred. However, we still hear the conversation that she has with a friend, asking her to call her back; making it clear from her tone that she has a local nuisance to deal with. At the same time, a TV off-screen is showing a film featuring an argument between a couple in which the man cries 'I'd like to kill you'. Visual information and differing sound perspectives in the fore and rear-ground interact simultaneously with apparently random dialogue to coalesce around the central figure – here, Mrs White. Her presence as an unwanted, possibly threatening, figure is emphasized by the raised-hand gesture which she gives on leaving, praying that Mrs Snell find Jesus. A wish for spiritual health is accompanied by a gesture which seems closer to a threat and is echoed later when she raises the same hand to her daughter, this time carrying a large knife and with the clear intent to kill her, convinced that she is a witch.

The earlier secretary shot works a little like the Abba video 'Knowing Me, Knowing You' (Lasse Hallström, 1977), although that uses crash zooms to switch attention from foreground to background or vice versa, whereas De Palma sometimes keeps both in focus. In school, Tommy's grinning face in the extreme foreground is connected to

Carrie, who is shyly looking down at her desk in the background, embarrassed about her positive comment on the poem he wrote, suggesting there could be some kind of connection between them if peer pressure did not exert such a powerful hold on his weak character. De Palma also keeps both figures facing the camera so that we can see their full facial expressions even though they cannot see one another. Written text is also used in conjunction with purposeful framing for dramatic effect. When Carrie looks in the window of the gym, we can see a janitor inside cleaning away graffiti, including the prominent words 'Carrie White eats shit'. Looking through the literal frame with the quasi-subtitle emphasizes how little sense she has of the gut-hatred some girls feel for her. Similarly, in the coda, the line 'Carrie White burns in hell' daubed on her pseudo-gravestone continues the hostility beyond the grave.

This complexity of shot composition extends to even quite minor sequences. Walking home from school, Carrie is framed in extreme long shot on a footpath along a tree-lined avenue. She advances towards the camera whilst a boy on a bike approaches her, weaving in and out of the trees. There is movement towards and away from the camera and across the frame, creating a great depth to the shot and leading to the expectation that the vectors will intersect, i.e. that the bike will hit Carrie. However the bike misses her, denying us that expected contact. The boy decides to turn round and go for a second run. All of this is shot in one take – the first cut comes as the boy approaches again, now from behind her. De Palma shifts camera position, shooting from the other side of the trees, down the street in effect, in another long take so that the cyclist now appears and disappears from shot as he weaves back and forth around the trees. As the volume of his approach increases and he calls out 'Crazy Carrie', his taunt motivates a zoom in on her face and her eyes flash anger, causing him to fall from the bike. In a long shot, the boy (played by De Palma's nephew Cameron) looks up in pain, shock and fear as Carrie looks at him and then walks on. Long takes, careful shot composition, and movement through and across the frame: all create a sense of imminent conflict between different vectors, initially denied and then climactically delivered.

Suspense is created not only by what is shown but the rhythm of cutting. All through *Carrie*, working closely with editor Paul Hirsch, De Palma uses conventional shot-reverse-shot patterns of editing but extends the number of repetitions we might expect, so that we are left waiting for a cut to a different set-up, which almost feels as if it is never going to happen. It creates the sense that characters are about to voice concerns or fears that are beneath the surface but they just cannot bring themselves to do so. De Palma almost sadistically tests (and possibly at times exceeds) the patience of the viewer by drawing this process out. At the same time, he also speeds up the editing rhythm of cutting so that when a cut does come, it feels almost like a relief. This happens in the Head's office in the cutting between the extreme high angle POV shot of Carrie looking down at the ashtray and its reverse angle, which is repeated five times; in the seven shot-reverse-shot repetitions in the exchange between Carrie and her mother when she strikes her with the Bible; and the five repetitions that make up the final battle between the knife-wielding mother and the cowering Carrie, frantically scrabbling to escape.

The extended slow-motion of the initial shower scene does evoke the trope of soft porn as Magistrale notes but it also links to the finale with the bucket of blood. Slow motion clearly allows the viewer time to look at a shot more closely but as De Palma uses it in conjunction with fluid camera movement, it also creates the sense of a stalking camera. This is more obvious in scenes like the art gallery seduction in *Dressed to Kill* (1980) but even in *Carrie* the shower scene is prurient because it not only uses slow motion but tracks forward slowly like a voyeur's POV, first past lockers, then past girls in various states of undress before homing in on one shower cubicle and one naked girl in particular. The idea of invading the very personal space of the shower is one reason why *Psycho* still shocks but, here, De Palma manipulates our sympathies in a slightly different way. Hitchcock (with the help of Art Director Saul Bass) uses montage editing to make us feel we have seen more than the 83 shots actually contain – the sum is much greater than the parts. De Palma uses fluid camera movement, extended slow-motion and dissolves between shots, rather than harsher cuts, in conjunction with a score of lush strings and framed images of Carrie soaping and caressing her own body, her mouth thrown back in apparent ecstasy to create a sense of sensual liberation as well as evoking standard devices of soft porn. Although we might not feel wholly comfortable, it may only be with the change in score and the appearance of menstrual blood that we fully realize how we have been gently led into a highly personal space. This ambivalence extends to Carrie's panic when she sees blood on her hands. Looked at objectively, the behaviour of the other students in teasing her and pelting her with sanitary towels is reprehensible. However, in the context of the film, we see Carrie's point of view of the locker room as she looks for a source of help and then cut back to what the rest of the class see – a wide-eyed, screaming, naked girl running at them with blood on her hands. Just as Carrie cannot understand what is happening, so momentarily, through the ambivalence created by alternating POV shots, neither can they. It is only when Sue gives them ammunition and a tribal call ('Plug it up!'), that they can objectify what is a shocking scene for them, too. In the opening sequence, we do see a close-up of a screaming female face but she is horrified at the inexplicable things are happening to her body, and the humiliation of this happening in front of others. The reaction of the viewer is not horror but sympathy, which shifts into empathy as we experience fleeting POV shots from Carrie's view in the shower. To see a fictional character express fear does not necessarily mean we share that emotional reaction.

It is worth comparing this with an alternative opening scene that was shot but not used in the finished film. In this, the camera lingers over an unclothed woman (Stella Horan) who is rubbing herself (here with sun-lotion) and whose parted lips suggest an utter absorption in her own sexuality. However, a key difference, which might have gone some way to mitigating allegations of voyeuristic misogyny towards De Palma, is that this is *Carrie*'s gaze. A pre-pubescent Carrie stares through a hedge at her neighbour as she sunbathes. Motivated by sexual ignorance and shame about her own body, instilled in her by a puritanical mother who insists on calling breasts 'dirty pillows' that a 'good girl' would never develop, Carrie's insistent gaze and relative youth make the shot entirely appropriate. The scene is taken from the novel, where Carrie's curiosity is so great that she does not even hide behind the hedge for cover but stands right next to Stella, gawping in amazement.[6] Early drafts of the script thus followed one of King's favourite literary devices: the flashback.

The scene ends with Carrie, having been scolded by her mother for indulging in sinful talk, causing stones to rain down on their house. The novel describes the 'pebbles' clearly as hailstones but De Palma's script is a little more ambiguous, retaining the sense of them as small rocks.[7] The slight confusion (the novel opens with a news report: 'Rain of Stones Reported') is caused by the contradiction that it is hail that lands on the White house but what falls elsewhere is described as 'granite'.[8] The opening and closing of the deleted scene uses extreme close-ups of a globe-like pebble, raising the intriguing possibility that De Palma was attempting a homage to Welles' Boarding House sequence from *Citizen Kane* (1939), using a similar snowscape and white graphic matches to open and close the scene. The pebbles thereby function like the Rosebud symbol in the earlier film, providing a symbol for Carrie's core character motivation – a fundamental hardness, borne of religious/sexual suppression, producing a stunning and, ironically, beautiful rage. Both book and deleted scene describe Mrs White's treatment of her daughter as going beyond anger. When she spots Carrie talking to Stella, she emits an inhuman howling noise ('She just whooped. Rage. Complete, insane rage' and later 'bayed at the sky'), which quickly leads to violent action directed at Carrie, whom she slaps, and at herself (she claws at her own neck and cheeks).[9] Although the novel suggests that Carrie inherits her telekinetic ability from her father, the film suggests more strongly that it is Mrs White, a character whom we do see on screen, who is a more credible source.

Perhaps luck or fortuitous directorial decision-making plays a part in the film's success too. Another part of the original opening would have featured Sissy Spacek as a six-year-old Carrie, in children's clothes and an oversized set, which, whilst certainly ambitious, may also have tipped over into the absurd. Carrie's ability to rain stones is not mentioned in the finished film but would have helped motivate the final scene, which was also the very last sequence to be filmed. Originally it was planned that the White house would be destroyed in a rockfall caused by Carrie. However with money and time running out (it was already 4am), with the police on their way in response to complaints about noise, and the conveyor belt that was supposed to feed the rock-throwing machine getting jammed, the idea had to be shelved in favour of burning the set down. Unfortunately the interior shots with rocks falling through the roof had already been filmed, so the finished product has the rather odd sight of the house imploding and combusting with little obvious reason why, other than a Samson-type collapse induced by a guilt-ridden Carrie at having killed her mother.

De Palma's intertextual awareness, especially his knowledge of Hitchcock, is also reflected in his use of point-of-view shots. Magistrale takes issue with Clover's assertion that 'the majority position throughout … is Carrie's own' and declares the opposite that 'the camera's positioning always belongs to others rather than to Carrie herself'.[10] However, we are given many examples of shots from Carrie's own view, such as looking out of the shower cubicle in the opening scene; waiting outside the Headteacher's office, watching the corridor outside; inside the office staring down at the ashtray; peering in at the girls in the gym; spotting Tommy's car as it draws up outside her house; walking past the tables at the prom; approaching the stage after being announced as the prom queen; and even at the climax as she lies at the foot of the stairs, apparently helpless, watching as her mother approaches her, brandishing a knife. Magistrale even inadvertently admits the point in making much of the projected, subjective laughter Carrie hears and sees, imagining that her mother's warning ('They're all gonna laugh at you') has come true. The means by which we know this is a subjective shot from Carrie's POV via a prismatic lens, conveying her fractured relationship with everyone at the prom (including those like Miss Collins who have sought to help her) and also, since such lenses are also used in entertainment shows, particularly for youngsters, it acts as an ironic means to convey impressions which have consequences that are deadly serious. Magistrale attempts to question Laura Mulvey's theory of the male gaze and the objectification of women but does so by pointing out how weak the male characters are, which has little direct relevance for the Mulvey position at all.[11]

Like his use of depth cues to expand the spatial possibilities of a shot, De Palma carefully manipulates film form in chronological terms to extend what we might expect from a high school genre film. Slow-motion extends cinematic time, enriching a particular moment with greater significance. When Carrie is crowned queen of the prom, De Palma gathers the tropes of the climax of a beauty contest – a tearful winner in a tiara, beside herself with joy, and an audience keen to show their appreciation through applause and taking photographs to record the moment. In the epilogue, slow-motion allows us to be lulled into a false sense of security as we follow Sue into a cemetery-like building-plot to place flowers on the site where her house once stood; now a defaced grave. Although slow-motion is a trope used in dream sequences, the two previous uses of slow-motion were not dreams, and so we may be fooled sufficiently for the sudden emergence of the hand from the grave to make us jump. Furthermore, having cut back to Sue in bed, signalling the previous scene as a nightmare, De Palma includes one more frame of Carrie's bloody hand, conveying the sense of the nightmare bleeding into everyday life. To increase the unsettling sense that something is not quite right, De Palma shot the scene night-for-day and with the action running backwards, and then reversed the film (in the opening frames you can see a red car in the distance running backwards). Unlike the novel, which featured the destruction of the whole town of Chamberlain, De Palma's budget was too small to stage such a climax and the transference of a link between Carrie and Sue is established by this dream sequence.

The novel's ending is almost anti-climactic as Carrie dies from a heart attack caused by a mixture of shock, mental stress from over-using her telekinetic powers, and the stab wound from her mother. King gives one final, rather sentimental, exchange between Sue and Carrie, telepathically, underlining that Sue is Carrie's heir and providing a rather late attempt to underline Sue's motivation as blameless. Collings asserts that this shock ending 'startles; it does not terrify, horrify or touch any emotions deeper than neural response'.[12] Apart from the explicit devaluing of the visual and the visceral, Collings underestimates the effect of the scene. De Palma's ending is more ambiguous than King's: with the 'meeting' happening beyond the grave and in the place of a friendly resolution, he gives us a repeated nightmare. De Palma's use of subversive codas, also found in *Dressed to Kill* and *Body Double* (1984), is more a way to make audiences rethink what they have been watching up to this point than a way of motivating a financially-lucrative sequel. None of De Palma's films have yet to receive such treatment.

Slow-motion, especially through extended use, draws attention to itself as a cinematic device, and thereby to the person most closely associated with its use: the director. Even more so is the use of jump-cuts. These are used for moments of psychic force, mostly brought on by anger, as when the boy on the bike teases Carrie; in the destruction of the prom; and, finally, when Chris tries to run her down (changed from Billy in the novel, making her more of an overt villain). Sudden double jump-cuts on Carrie's eyes conveys the intensity and power of her anger. The five jump-cuts used when Carrie's mother cuts a carrot acts as a foreshadowing of her later attack on Carrie and the way in which Carrie will escape, using her telekinetic abilities to exact revenge on her attacker, also using sharp knives. More conventional use of jump-cutting, particularly the collapsing of time in showing a repeated process, appears in the comic interlude where Tommy and his friends try out different outfits for the prom. Stylistically, this sequence may seem out of sync with the film around it (there is even a few lines of speeded-up dialogue) but this brief segment of comic relief does provide contrast with the climax at the prom which follows.

Other bravura camera shots include the long take at the start of the prom scene as the camera slowly cranes across the whole room, before coming down and picking out Tommy and Carrie from the crowd, and the whirling shot around Tommy and Carrie as they dance, capturing the dizzy intoxication of the night for her. This later effect was achieved by placing Spacek and William Katt (Tommy) on a spinning platform while tracking the camera in the opposite direction. It is De Palma's meticulously-planned and carefully-executed compositional skills that make the final sequence effective. An extremely long take leads us, via tracks and pans, from the faking of the election results to the string that links the 'conspirators' to the unwitting Sue, to the bucket of blood. We are shown a literal chain of events, a visualization of cause and effect, from the guilty to those unwittingly caught up in their machinations. It may also remind us of the part that Sue played in the torture of Carrie in the opening scene, and that she still bears some part of the responsibility for what is about to happen. The shot only ends when there is a zoom past the bucket down to the figures of Carrie and Tommy, unaware of the plan, almost completing a full circle of action on set. The scene is De Palma's version of Hitchcock's definition of suspense, but instead of a ticking bomb beneath a table, we have a teen prank that will have explosive consequences. The suspense is established here by the absolute refusal to cut and the extended use of slow-motion, creating a sense of an inexorable fate that takes in the (relatively) innocent as well as the guilty, and by the dramatic irony of placing the viewer in a position where he/she can see what the central characters cannot.

As the camera reaches Sue standing backstage, the scenery effectively creates a split-screen effect, and Sue's shifting gaze directs the viewer's attention along the string as if it were a fuse-wire from one vector to another, from horizontal to vertical – following the string up. As Chris begins to pull on the rope, Sue literally makes the connection between different parts of the scene as the string runs through her hands. The extended slow-motion intercuts looks of realization and bemusement between Sue, coming round to see the conspirators under the stage, Tommy, looking down from the stage but not understanding what is going on and Miss Collins, looking off-frame at Sue's strange behaviour and ironically wrongly-interpreting it as some kind of prank. There is even a nod to gothic melodrama in the silhouette shots of Chris pulling on the rope like an enthusiastic executioner and the closing shot of Carrie standing at the main door, silhouetted by the blaze exploding behind her. This complements the method of humiliation itself; a literalization of one of Roger Corman's most famous horror-comedy pieces, *A Bucket of Blood* (1959); the Usher-like destruction of first the school gym and then later the White house; and the red light in which Carrie's face is bathed prior to being literally covered in blood – echoing another of Corman's Poe films, *The Masque of the Red Death* (1964). Spacek's stiff-body positioning both on stage and as she slowly steps down, almost like an iconic figurehead on a ship, marks her as a being who has undergone a complete transformation. After the bucket falls, the applause stops, allowing De Palma to focus our attention on tiny sound effects (the dripping of the blood and the creaking of the rope), and the break in the idyllic mood is signalled by the return to normal speed motion.

The split-screen effect at the climax is certainly not new in cinematic terms and was used in such seminal work as Abel Gance's *Napoleon* (1927) or even *Woodstock* (Michael Wadleigh, 1970). Its prime use is to convey simultaneous action. For example, in *Sisters*, police interview witnesses while the perpetrator cleans up the crime scene. Commonly used for showing telephone conversations, it allows two characters to act and react at the same time. Associated with the romantic comedy genre in particular, it was made famous by such stars as Rock Hudson and Doris Day in *Pillow Talk* (Michael Gordon, 1959) and later in *When Harry Met Sally* (Rob Reiner, 1989). Again, like slow-motion, it is a very self-conscious device; breaking the dramatic illusion as it is virtually impossible to concentrate on two parts of the screen simultaneously. It requires the viewer to be more active and to overtly search the frame for meaning. De Palma is famous for such meta-narrative devices, which draw the attention of the viewer to how the story is being told as much as what is being suggested. It reminds us that we are watching a dramatic construct and foregrounds the director. When asked whether this device alienated the viewer, De Palma replied 'No more than extreme angles or a top shot'.[13] However, *Carrie* is full of such devices, (like the picture composition of Billy, Chris and the other conspirators approaching the pigs whilst framed against a mural depicting a bucolic idyll, which momentarily disorientates us), suggesting that it is exactly such a self-conscious reaction that De Palma is looking for, or at least prepared to risk. We should remember this is the same director who went on to give us a demonstration of montage editing in John Cassavetes' explosion in repeated slow motion, from multiple angles, in *The Fury* (1978); a five-minute long take in the opening of *Bonfire of the Vanities* (1990); and an extremely elaborate staircase shoot-out in *The Untouchables* (1987) in his own slow-motion homage to Eisenstein's Odessa Steps sequence in *Battleship Potemkin* (1925), bouncing pram with baby and all. De Palma wears his film school credentials very much on his sleeve.

The split screen technique can convey a greater amount of information than a single image, and possibly from different points of view, but in action sequences it can also be confusing. It creates an appropriate sense of panic and disorder in this scene but De Palma remains ambivalent about its success here. Originally, the entire five-minute sequence was shot this way and De Palma spent weeks editing it before eventually adding some whole frames to make the viewing experience slightly (but only slightly) less intense. De Palma experiments with editing practices in ways which are both obvious and relatively subtle. He takes the conventional use of a split-screen a stage further by juxtaposing actions that are happening simultaneously and are also taking place in the same location. In this way, each shot condenses, one might even say doubles, the conventional amount of visual information in that it already contains its own reverse angle. We see Carrie looking and what she is looking at, at the same time. Cause and effect are visible simultaneously. The scene alternates between split-screen shots and whole frames so that we see Carrie's actions and their direct consequences but also the wider panic spreading through the room. In an action sequence later in his career – the boxing match assassination scene in *Snake Eyes* (1998) – De Palma uses a split screen again, but opted to show simultaneous action in the same place.

Mrs White's slow death, moaning in an apparent outpouring of religious and sexually suppressed ecstasy, and the slow tracking back from the dead woman, bathed in candlelight, give her facial features a peaceful almost beatific smile and parallels not so much a crucifixion of Jesus but the St Sebastian figure in Carrie's closet – she too has become a martyr to her faith by being stabbed to death. However there is also a less-widely noted cinematic parallel here. Dario Argento's *Suspiria* (1977), released around the same time as *Carrie*, also features surreal, nightmarish dream sequences, fluid camerawork, operatic violence, dark gothic houses and flying knives as a method of dispatching stalked and tortured heroines. Furthermore, Argento uses a school setting (a ballet centre rather than a high school), all-female changing room scenes, a focus on the paranormal (witchcraft rather than telekinesis); an ending in which a house is destroyed by fire due to unspecified supernatural means; and Argento's whole set, especially corridors, are bathed in blood-red light (from the outset, not just the climax as in De Palma's film).

In *Carrie*, De Palma blends Hitchcockian discipline in constructing his sequences with some of the darker, dream-like vision of Argento. By his composition in depth, bravura sequences with extended long takes and use of slow motion, experimental breaks with conventional editing practices, and a preparedness to openly reference other films, De Palma creates disturbing, effective and memorable scenes that, unlike many other Stephen King adaptations, retain much of their power over 30 years later.

The Rage: Carrie II (Katt Shea and Robert Mandel, 1999)

'She's one of us!' (Monica on Rachel)

A sequel is an overtly intertextual device, seeking (as with genre) to draw on a ready-made audience of knowledgeable and interested viewers. In many ways, *Carrie II* is more of a remake than a sequel, although it does provide a useful means to compare the stylistic lineage from De Palma's film. Paratextually, the title is something of a misnomer as no one named Carrie appears in the film. Some kind of bloodline with De Palma's film is attempted in setting the narrative twenty years after the first film, in the same high school, with a protagonist, Rachel Lang (Emily Bergl), who discovers that she shares Carrie's telekinetic gift. Partly to claim greater veracity to a source text, Amy Irving, one of Carrie's tormentors in the original film, now plays the part of counsellor, Sue Snell, redeeming her, and the final confrontation between Carrie and her mother follows the scenario of the book more closely (as a second draft of the original film had done), with Carrie slowing down her heartbeat to a stop – alluding perhaps to Edgar Allan Poe's short story, 'Tell-Tale Heart' (1843).

However, this film feels more like a standard high school TV series, suggestive of intertextual references to movies like *Clueless* (Amy Heckerling, 1995). Prefiguring her breakthrough role in Sam Mendes' *American Beauty,* released the same year, Mena Suvari (Lisa) appears as a sexually active, gossiping teen, and in Tracey (Charlotee Ayanna) we have the character she also plays in Mendes' film, particularly when she is outraged that Jesse (Jason London) should be seeing Rachel who is not 'someone, pretty, someone cool, someone who counts'. Tracey's friend Monica gets Rachel into the select party, declaring 'She's one of us!' echoing, probably unwittingly, the rallying cry from Tod Browning's *Freaks* (1932).

The notion of the film as an attempted revisionist remake is emphasized by an inversion of some gender roles from the first film. The ubiquitous and intrusive video camera catches examples of ritualistic 'Jock' behaviour, like the drive-by egg attacks from rival teams. Rather than Carrie's mother, it is Rachel's foster-father who is the oppressive presence at home – drunkenly slapping her for staying out and, earlier, wailing over the $300 income they will lose if she leaves: suggesting mercenary rather than philanthropic motives for taking her in. We see a male changing room with male buttocks on show (where characters argue about their feelings); it is predatory male sexuality which is denigrated by the narrative, and it is a male character who is humiliated (the sports coach insists he drop his pants to prove he does not have 'a tampon between his legs' in a clear allusion to *Carrie*'s shower scene). Along with the macho posturing, communal head-shaving and the coach addressing the teams as 'girls', this feels like an over-compensated impression of heterosexuality.[14] Provincial sexual politics is touched upon in passing, with under-age exploitation of girls being swept under the carpet due to family and political connections (a sexual parallel of the economic and industrial cover-ups in *The Mangler* and *Graveyard Shift*). Rachel rejects an offer of sex from Mark (Dylan Bruno) for the giving-up of the photos, adding that she is 'a dyke'. Although her later behaviour with Jesse would suggest this is not true, it does touch on an underlying element in *Carrie*.

Rachel's mother is a hollow echo of Carrie's mother. The credits and opening scene feature her acting oddly, painting a red line around the walls, across pictures and even her own daughter in an attempt to keep sin out: suggesting the kind of religious mania that marked the previous mother. However, in a lost dramatic opportunity, she is just taken away in a straight jacket and although she features slightly in the revelation about Rachel's father later (at the end of the film after a cut to a black and white POV shot of Rachel as a young girl) she just shuffles out of shot, screaming that Rachel is possessed.

Intertextuality is not just manifested by gender inversion or parallel characters; there are a number of direct references to the first film, many scenes closely echoing the original in location or style. In Sue's office, Rachel stares at a coffee cup and makes it fall; despite being shot by a flare-gun, her hand suddenly reaches up to grab Mark into the pool; and at the end, although not being covered in blood, her blood-red dress, stiff body posture with extended fingers and slow movement whilst all around her panic, are all reminiscent of Sissy Spacek (although her demise, crushed by a wall, is a very pale echo). The impaling of both a boy on the inside of the door and Sue on the outside with the same spear blends the demise of Carrie's mother with the staking of victims inside the house in *Halloween* (1978). The music of the love scene between Rachel and Jesse also feels like the lush strings before the dramatic climax in De Palma's film. There are some specific plot links, often quite improbable ones – particularly that Rachel has the same father as Carrie ,or that the ruins of the first school have been apparently left as a 'twisted memorial' to those who died. Metatextually, there are three explicit mini-montages from the first film, all as flashbacks from Sue (a rather lazy and illogical device). For example, when the Sheriff suggests that her zeal in pursuing Eric (Zachary Ty Bryan) is based on trying to redeem the events of years before, we cut to a snippet of the shower scene in a red colour wash. Later, her attempts at counselling are cut with extracts from the shock ending, linked to her own breakdown and time spent in the same institution as Rachel's mother, and the prom carnage is prompted by the obtuse psychological test, provoking Rachel to smash a glass globe. There is even a 'borrowing' from the second draft script of the earlier film: originally placed at the climax (and present in the novella) but here moved to the beginning, we see a 'For sale' sign on the White property and some graffiti – 'Carrie White is burning for her sins'. This gives the illusion of this film as a sequel, when it is really closer to a remake. The subtitle may also allude to King's early short story, 'Rage' (begun in 1966 but not published until 1977), another tale of high school humiliation and violent revenge which King has allowed to go out of print, anxious not to fuel the on-going phenomenon of high school shootings.

Most obviously, the film climaxes with a prank played on the heroine, whose outsider status is mocked, prompting an outburst of destructive rage. Instead of a bucket of blood, we have a secretly-shot tape of Rachel having sex with Jesse and the revelation of a book of scores for the girls. There is a similar use of a prismatic lens to show that Rachel feels laughed at; doors are slammed shut; death is caused by fire and flying objects; and the innocent as well as the victim die. However, there is scarcely anything of the artistry of De Palma's film (a few oblique frames cannot compare with the earlier split-frame sequence) but the final sequence does have a few interesting aspects. When provoked to draw on her telekinetic power, Rachel and her surroundings are shot in black and white, such as when, earlier, the Jocks attack her house to try and intimidate her, or, at the end, where she appears in monochrome which is then intercut with the colour around her. The extreme close-ups of her eye in black and white (linking back to her childhood), the distortion of images by crash zooms, wide angle lenses, and speeded up motion – all suggest the distortion of her reality (as well as using cinematic means to allude to *Firestarter*'s more mechanical effects). The method of despatch for her tormentors is appropriate: the vain Monica (Rachel Blanchard) is blinded when her glasses explode; sexual predator, Eric, is shot in the groin with a spear-gun, his genitals shown flying into the pool in slow-motion; Mark, who had tried to cover up Eric's rape of a minor, is suffocated by the pool cover. The film closes a year later with Jesse now at university, visited by Rachel. There is romantic music as they kiss but this is interrupted when Rachel screams and shatters into pieces – the scene being cast as a dream. The final shot shows Jesse mournfully gazing into the mirror, still haunted by her, and although we have a theoretically-clever shot using mirrors in front and behind him, the effect is not particularly profound.

There are a few effective shots, like the pulsating heart tattoo and the spread of the rose across her body as her powers grow, or the gradual reduction in sound as Sue speaks in counsellor-mode until it is cut completely for a few seconds, showing that, ironically, she has learned nothing about listening. However, overall, there is a strange mish-mash of music – scenes of the school are accompanied by hardcore rap and yet Billie Holiday is used for two scenes of Rachel at home, although she shows enthusiasm for more contemporary grungy fashion (her ears prick up at the mention of Garbage). The plot lacks credibility – that Rachel should be working in the precise place where the incriminating photos are developed is rather unlikely. The quality of the dialogue varies from the inappropriate but amusing ('Oh man … whose car is this?' on spotting Lisa splattered across a windscreen) to the ridiculous doctor talking about Rachel's injured dog, Walter, after the dog is shown being run over, and using, without a hint of irony, the language of a fallen war hero ('he's banged up pretty bad … but I think he's gonna make it'). As a hollow echo of *Carrie*, the film feels like a collection of plot and stylistic references to the earlier work without having anything more to say. Intertextuality can highlight lack of originality as well as increase the potential meanings of a given text.

The Dead Zone (David Cronenberg, 1983)

Sarah: They told me you were outside.
Johnny: I am.

David Cronenberg's *The Dead Zone* (1983) is of prime interest because of how the film extends generic expectations via Cronenberg's editing choices in the vision sequences; the melancholic aura that pervades much of the mise-en-scène; the career-defining performance that he gains from Christopher Walken; and the restructuring of the narrative. The film re-organizes King's 1979 novel, so that the character Stillson (with whom Johnny never has direct contact in the book) only appears in the final third of the film, providing a satisfying climax but with an inevitable loss of subtext for his character. King's own script was rejected (Cronenberg describes it as 'terrible' and the filmed version is credited to Jeffrey Boam but with input, in addition to Cronenberg himself, from Stanley Donen, Paul Monash, Andre Konchalavsky and even Producer Debra Hill.[15] It is an effective adaptation, crafting a clear three-act structure from the novel's interwoven plot elements (Johnny's romance, accident and coma; pursuit of the Castle Rock killer; and finally Stillson's rise and fall). The plot is moved 10 years on, making Johnny (and the narrative for the most part) more apolitical – removing anti-Vietnam elements and student protests. A skating accident acts as a catalyst for his visions in the book but this is cut in the film, where it is linked more closely and tragically with his love for Sarah, showing his first symptoms on a rollercoaster with her. Sarah's fate is contrived to entwine with Stillson's in a way that is not in the book but this is in keeping with the sense that Johnny has an inescapable, tragic destiny.

Given the extent of Cronenberg's creative control, and that those areas of production which make the biggest impact on the adaptation all come under his remit as director, it makes sense to view the film primarily in auteurist terms. Typical Cronenberg elements are present – a derelict hero whose psychic gifts suck the very life out of him; a tragic love story of a relationship fractured by a sense of almost biological destiny; and the death/suicide of his protagonist (rather than the enquiry in the book that follows the assassination attempt). However, *The Dead Zone* is not easy to place in Cronenberg's broader oeuvre. When Magistrale talks about *The Dead Zone* as 'Cronenberg's only really human movie,' it depends on a particular reading of *The Fly* (1986), which can be seen as highly personal.[16] Like *Firestarter* and *Carrie* (right up to the denouement at least), *The Dead Zone* is closer to science fiction than horror, and even lacks those few isolated horrific scenes which appear in later Cronenberg work, such as the trout farm in *eXistenZ* (1999) or the attack in the diner in *A History of Violence* (2005).

As with many King adaptations, the precise nature of the supernatural phenomenon is not clear. The "Dead Zone" of the novel is a small window of time during which the future can be affected (somehow caused by a brain tumour). However, in the film, the vision of the fire is more ambiguous. It occurs in the immediate present and allows for rather unlikely heroic pre-emptive action, but Johnny's view of Weizak's mother is post-cognitive and his vision of the boys falling into the pond is precognitive. All main tense forms are covered. Johnny's gift does articulate an underlying philosophical issue about free will. Weizak does not speak to his mother because he says 'it wasn't meant to be' and yet the vision of the fire allows an event to be prevented. The film closes with Johnny's heroic sacrifice to prevent a future nuclear catastrophe but by an attempted murder. The ethical question is explicitly raised when Johnny asks Weizak if it were possible, with the benefit of hindsight, whether it would have been right to kill Hitler, to which, after a pause, the scientist agrees wholeheartedly.

Our first view of Johnny is as a cheerful teacher, happily inspiring his class with a reading of Poe's 'The Raven', which shifts into a recital of a poem he clearly knows well. The intertextual allusions here add greater poignancy to the tragic character of Smith (Johnny), clearly portrayed through nomenclature as an Everyman figure. The inclusion of Poe (a typical Cronenberg addition, discussed by both Magistrale and Collings as Poe scholars), foreshadows Johnny's tragic loss of a beautiful woman and his immersion in (arguably) sentimental melancholia, and may have been prompted by a specific reference to 'The Raven' in the novel of *Carrie,* when Billy is setting up the bucket of blood (which De Palma chose not to put in his film). It talks of 'a bust of Pallas, used in some ancient dramatic version'.[17] The irony of Johnny's next recommendation, 'The Legend of Sleepy Hollow', a story about 'a schoolteacher who gets chased by a headless demon', is clear. He, too, is a teacher whose life will be irrevocably altered by his psychic ability, from which he tries to flee but ultimately cannot. Later he aligns himself with the reclusive anonymity of Ichabod Crane from

'The Legend of Sleepy Hollow' – 'as he was a bachelor and in nobody's debt, nobody troubled their head about him anymore'. Visually, Johnny is a bookish, slightly nerdy-looking teacher, whose jacket, tie, trousers and tank-top (as we Brits would say) do not match. He has a slightly nervous smile but flirts with fellow teacher Sarah in the corridor and seems happy and forward-looking. The future reading pleasures of the class anticipate his plans for a surprise date for Sarah – the narrative is looking to a future from which he is about to be excluded.

Later, he is invited over the threshold as a clear sexual offer, but he declines, claiming 'some things are worth waiting for'. In the novel, after a while together in the house, it is Sarah who declines because she feels sick and then Johnny goes home in a taxi rather than driving himself. Making both actions Johnny's responsibility gives the opening a more ironic pathos. However, the accident seems a little strange. Mid-shots through the windscreen and a side-on shot of the driver are conventional enough and the pathetic fallacy of the storm underlies the approaching tragedy as well as motivating poor visibility and grip on the road. Even with the nice touch of milk rather than blood splashing on the windscreen, the surreal shot of a tanker sliding crossways down the road is slightly undermined by the fact the road is straight, the car relatively slow and Johnny is hardly a reckless driver; suggesting the accident could have been avoided rather than a sense of crushing inevitability.

As with John Coffey in *The Green Mile* or Ted Brautigan in *Hearts in Atlantis*, the catalyst for Smith's visions is human touch (something they all crave but must deny themselves), and images are received in waves almost like electric shocks (in the hospital, Johnny's head crashes back on the bed in an over-the-shoulder shot). All three figures eventually seems tired of the suffering that their gift has brought them so that death or capture is seen as a welcome release, rather than something to be feared or shied away from. In Johnny's first vision, shot in close-up, he looks to the right of the camera and we cut to a doll's house on fire, accompanied by a single, high-pitched violin note. Key powerful images all jostle for our attention – a goldfish bowl in which the water is bubbling; the doll's house (like *The Shining*'s house-within-a-house microcosmic image and also ironically providing a more powerful effect than a big-budget fire scene); and a little girl cowering in a corner. We cut back to Johnny, who calls the girl's name and, on the third cut back to him, see he is still in bed in the same part of the frame, but now his bed is on fire, and the different bedding and wallpaper places him in the scene, possibly even in the girl's bed (a key Cronenberg addition, making the experience more subjective, personal and ultimately disturbing). Johnny turns back to look off-frame left to address the nurse, warning her that she still has time to save the girl. Conventional juxtaposition of locations (the windows in the girl's room blow in and, back in his hospital bed, he flinches) is taken a stage further in the shots in the middle of the vision: cross-cutting (different place – same time) is mixed with same place – same time editing.

Later, Johnny's vision at the gazebo uses the same technique but with the extra dramatic twist of concealing and slowly revealing the identity of a murderer. The high angle shot of the daytime gazebo, evoked sharply with the sound of fresh snow crunching underfoot, focuses on Johnny, who takes the hand of the victim – throwing him into a reverie. Night-time in the present, with a static camera, is intercut with bright snowy, daytime and a moving camera that allows Alma, the victim, to walk round the gazebo and then cranes up behind her to obscure the standing figure that she knows and calls up to. Johnny appears in the vision in the same kneeling position and we cut between his helpless witnessing of the crime and looking in the present towards Frank Dodd, who stands guard over the crime-scene. Johnny sees the scissors revealed as the murder weapon and we cut between the attack and Johnny, standing now, apparently present ('I was there') but unable to intervene ('but I did nothing'). The anguish of his gift is that it allows him to 'see' vividly into the past as if he was there, but he can only act in the present. Walken reprises a similar God-like visionary role in the 1993 David Fincher-directed video for Madonna's 'Bad Girl': unable to prevent a young girl from being violently murdered. Johnny no longer features in his own visions from this point on (visions of Chris drowning; Stillson initiating nuclear war and finally taking his own life), suggesting a steady diminution of his powers. We see visions perverted too – the accurately-named, emotionally-sterile Stillson claims that he has had a vision of himself as President, and in Johnny's own flashforwards, Stillson manically talks of the war as 'his destiny'.

Cronenberg has frequently mentioned his admiration for Bergmann, and it was one of Bergmann's protogés, Alf Sjöberg, director of *Miss Julie* (1951), who developed the use of protagonists appearing in their own visions; eschewing the-then conventional use of flashback 'markers' and problematizing past and present by putting characters from the heroine's past, such as her mother, within the same frame as the present.[18] This is effectively what Cronenberg does after Weizak is told about his mother, which creates the 'impossible' scene of Weizak hearing on the phone the voice of a person who he had assumed was dead. Originally, all the visions were to feature Johnny, including the hockey accident which still features a quick cut of Johnny's telltale beige-sweatered arm holding Chris underwater. Despite repeated attempts at withdrawal from interaction with society, Johnny's gift literally places him in his visions preventing this, meaning that he lives a fuller but briefer life.

The approach of scholar William Beard is similar to that of Magistrale in seeing characters as psychological entities rather than fictional constructs, identifying film texts by themes which are then 'found' within the narratives, and spending little time analysing specific film form. Beard sees Johnny's character as masochistic, and the pain that he experiences largely self-inflicted.[19] Whereas the novel attempts some explanation (through reference to a skating accident), the film does not, but Beard misreads the roller-coaster ride as a potential cause of the visions rather than just their first manifestation. Cronenberg often cuts childhood trauma scenes from source material, (which, in his view, make psychological interpretations too pat) such as in his adaptation of *A History of Violence*. Beard's reading of the hospital vision is rather strange, claiming that 'his (Johnny's) abrupt seizing of the nurse's arm cannot be plausibly motivated by anything other than the film's desire to create exactly this startling conventional effect.' However, as suggested in the analysis of the visions, the style in which they are shot is anything but conventional. Beard concludes that '[w]hat this tells us is that Johnny is the film's monster'.[20] This is quite a distortion of the material as all the visions are triggered by sudden touch and Stillson, who is corrupt, vicious and prepared to initiate pre-emptive Armageddon, is by far the stronger candidate for the title 'monster'. Even here Beard seems strangely contradictory. Beard reads Johnny as representing 'a kind of anti-monstrosity, consisting of a reified hypercompassion and a decorporealised abjection...[i]n this context, Johnny's passive and receptive "feminine" qualities are contrasted with the active "male" qualities of the sexual-sadistic Dodd and the outgoing manipulator, controller and actor Stillson, twin models of masculinity to avoid'.[21] However, Johnny does act to stymie Stillson's campaign in a way that leads to his own martyrdom.

Although the points Beard makes about Johnny's theatrical and, in some ways melodramatic, withdrawal are interesting, it is still ultimately reductive to ascribe emotional characteristics to particular genders: sensitivity, Johnny's key characteristic, is not restricted to the female half of humanity. The doppelgänger case that Beard seeks to make with Johnny and Dodd also lacks credible evidence – the bond the two share is that Johnny 'sees' what he has done, not that they are alter egos of one another. The glance they exchange through the window is of guilt and recognition, not complicity. There is no evidence that 'Dodd represents what Johnny fears he might be if he ever stopped repressing,' any more than Johnny might become like Stillson if he became politically engaged.[22] There are gaps missing in Beard's logic: to see the Dodd episode as 'a consequence of Sarah's fantasy-wife visit' ignores the fact that Johnny becomes engaged with the case through seeing a TV report he would have seen anyway – he was staying with his parents, not in order to see Sarah but, if anything, to avoid her.[23] Similarly, to suggest that the film 'advances a schema whereby houses represent life and nurture and the outdoors is lifeless and frozen' works in some ways but throws a critical blanket over material that does not always fit.[24] The Dodd's house is a dark repository of repressed sexuality; the nurse's home is a potential death-trap; and the gazebo scene is partly shot in bright sunshine. Ascribing symbolic values so generally is limiting and, as his phrase suggests, 'schematic': one thing Cronenberg takes great pains to avoid.

Several elements combine to produce a profound sense of melancholy, most particularly Walken's performance; the inadequacy of language at key moments; and sporadic melancholic moments. In a long and distinguished career, Christopher Walken here gives one of his greatest performances. Cronenberg describes the subject of the film as 'the loneliness and the melancholy and the impossibility of dealing with things. And yet the necessity to do it ... It's Chris Walken's face. That's the subject of the movie'.[25] As John Smith, we are drawn to what makes him ordinary as well as what makes him exceptional. Frequently shot in low angle, particularly as he prepares his rifle at the denouement, his status as an outsider is clear. His understated delivery gives lines a particular punch, so that, for example, the awkwardness between himself and Sarah is underlined by his half-hearted jokes. There is bemusement and some anger that Sarah has let someone else step into the life that should have been his. She notes that he has lost weight and his reply is tinged with bitterness and regret: 'Yeah, it's called the coma diet – lose weight while you sleep'. Weight is not all he has lost. His 'gift' makes him lose any human connection as soon as he tries to make it: his teaching job; a life with Sarah; with his mother who has a heart attack watching his press conference; then with Chris, a fellow outsider with whom he instantly bonds. Later, he responds angrily to Bannerman's moralizing with dialogue paraphrasing Johnny's interior thoughts in King's novel: 'God's been a real sport to me'.[26] His life plays out like his coma: he is unable to completely live or die – personifying an impossible and unbearable state of infinite deferral.

Johnny is aware from quite early on that he is undergoing some kind of bodily change, asking Weizak 'what's happening to me?' and there is pathos, as well as an allusion to Brundlefly's questioning in *The Fly* in the hero's awareness of his own bodily evolution, and his helplessness in preventing it. He knows that 'when the spells come, it feels like I'm dying inside'. His gift puts him in an unnatural state, reversing the patient-therapist role (he asks Weizak 'what's on your mind, Sam?'). In the eyes of the public, he is cast as some kind of spiritual guru onto whom a needy population project their problems, symbolized later by the bags of mail spilling unopened out of a cupboard. At several points in the film, he tries to disengage from life, but life will not disengage from him – Bannerman's public appeals for help; Roger Stuart's search for a tutor for his son; Sarah's campaigning for Stillson; all intrude upon his attempts at isolation and with each contact, he weakens. The restraint in the central character is reflected in Cronenberg's downplaying of the body-horror with which he was synonymous at the time. Although adding Dodd's horrific suicide, he still cut King's original opening scene featuring Stillson torturing a young boy, and a later scene where he kicks a dog to death.

Also at key moments, like in the final phone scene in *Dead Ringers* (1988), language, which might help to make sense of experience and make it bearable, is seen as deficient. On hearing from his parents that he has languished in a coma for five years and that his life with Sarah has gone, Johnny turns away and covers his face as the scene slowly fade to black, reflecting his grief. Weizak cannot speak to his mother, thereby denying us an overtly melodramatic scene and Johnny cannot speak to Stuart on the phone; he is just relieved that Chris is alive, symbolically holding the receiver to his chest. Later, Johnny's father confides 'I guess I'm not much good with tinsel' but the inexpressible grief at the loss of his wife is more powerfully conveyed by the tall Johnny hugging the older but smaller man. Reducing Chris from the eighteen-year-old Jock of the novel to a much younger, quiet, sensitive boy provides the plot with a suitable alter ego for Johnny, making their enforced separation much more poignant.

Cronenberg extends the notion of what is possible in a relatively narrow subgenre by a realizing this melancholic aesthetic through specific shot composition. Weizak visiting a reclusive Johnny is framed with a huge poster for Stillson, only half completed, suggesting his dual nature of respectable public figure and private psychotic. The tunnel where the first victim was killed is shot with backlighting (motivated by parked patrol cars), creating expressionistic long shadows and silhouettes of Johnny, Bannerman and Dodd. Within this cavernous setting, the camera cranes down as the figures walk forwards, creating a sense of space and depth through the frame. At Dodd's house, touched by his mother, Johnny realizes she knew about her son and failed to act. The mise-en-scène (partly taken from the novel) is wonderfully creepy.[27] In Dodd's dark bedroom, cowboy wallpaper, western comics and related toys create an unpleasant sexual undertone of arrested adolescence, like a backroom from David Lynch's *Blue Velvet* (1986) or *Lost Highway* (1997), and the rubber coat, which is more prominent in King's novel, (associated with the adjective associated with his self-image, 'slick'), is hung up here like the sexual prop that it is. The rather bizarre suicide, more theatrical than the novel's straightforward throat slash, appropriately uses the same murder weapon and is played out in front of a mirror: the main-stage for Dodd's deviant fantasy life. By contrast with the darker internal material, the more overt drama of the slow-motion shooting of the mother, and her hand reaching through the banisters for Johnny, seems less convincing and contrived.

Cronenberg's work is often permeated by a sense of loss, and here, even in the credit sequence, angular shapes appear on screen, gradually creating spaces which, in combination, define letters and finally words. It is the spaces which create the words, and presence is denoted by absence. Small but powerfully-melancholic moments punctuate the film: after visiting him as he recovers, Sarah pauses in the car to cry for a moment before driving off. In casting Brooke Adams as Sarah, Producer Debra Hill was clearly departing from King's description as tall and blond, but her performance is finely-nuanced, often framed in reaction shots.[28] Sarah's poignant visit to Johnny provides a glimpse of the life he could have had (symbolized by three generations eating together at the same table), especially since she knows exactly what she is doing and the visit is a single event, never to be repeated. She stands for a moment before approaching Johnny's house and later takes a deep breath before leaving her sleeping child, steeling herself for the emotional demands of loving and leaving Johnny. There is pathos in Johnny's desire to impress Sarah: hanging up his cane before walking stiffly out to greet her. Even reading with Chris, Johnny is strangely drawn to the section of Poe's 'Elinore' describing whether the hero will ever see his lover again, a thinly-veiled reference to Sarah, and the term 'sorrow' is repeated. On subsequently seeing Sarah again at his front door, he suddenly waves Chris away, crying and then putting his arm round him, motivating the vision of the hockey accident. Ultimately, it is the blending of such moments with the strongest driving force in his life, his love for Sarah, which gives the film its tragic power. Before he dies in her arms as she declares her love, the narrative closes with his letter to her – virtually a suicide letter, delivered via voiceover, explaining his assassination attempt, flawed in its execution by her cry which momentarily distracted him. However, right at the end, fate for once helps rather than thwarts his intentions and Stillson commits political suicide by grabbing her baby (the one she might have had with Johnny – an improvised suggestion from Walken) to use as a shield, and then actual suicide, seen by Johnny in his dying vision (additional to the novel).

Firestarter (Mark L. Lester, 1984)

Although in some senses a distant cousin of *Carrie*, the weaknesses of *Firestarter* are useful in counterpointing the relative strength of the earlier work, and underline what distinguishes a film that expands, and even defines a genre, and one that operates so fully within it yet is almost instantly forgettable. Although he is rarely thought of as a political writer, King's least principled organization is not an extraterrestrial one but the so-called Shop. The novels have the space to sketch this dimension out, albeit not always convincingly. Shorn of the necessary narrative space, such shadowy figures tend to appear in the movies as cardboard cut-outs and carry little dramatic weight. However, although in *Firestarter* we are not encouraged to sympathize with the position of the Shop operatives who seek to kill Charlie McGee, their attempts to neutralize the threat she poses are, to some degree, understandable. She has such potential destructive power (in Garris' *The Shining*, Halloran calls Danny 'an atomic bomb'), which can be unleashed at unpredictable times with unknown force that is not really fully understood even by those who wield it.

There is also an intertextual allusion here to H.G. Wells' *The Man Who Could Work Miracles* (1911), filmed by Lothar Mendes in 1936. This dramatizes a man who has sudden miraculous powers and stops the earth's rotation to demonstrate this. However Mendes has his hero, Fotheringay (Roland Young) intervene to prevent loss of life and reverse his action, like a spell in a fairy tale. A more ethically-challenging and overtly political work than King's adaptations, this film, with the looming threat of global fascism, suggests that absolute power can be resisted through self-control. However, a post-war generation, aware of the destructive potential of atomic devices may be less idealistic. This is the prime concern of Dr Joseph Wanless (Freddie Jones), a precursor of the mad scientist stereotype Todhunter in *Golden Years* (Kenneth Fink, Allen Coulter, Michael G. Gornick and Stephen Tolkin, 1991). Wanless repeats warnings about the girl, whom he wants to be killed, leading to his own death at the hands of Rainbird. However, the basic premise of *Firestarter*, shady government experiments leading to psychic powers which it then tries to exploit, is not original and better handled elsewhere in *The Fury* and *Scanners*. Tests upon a young girl with some psychic ability appears in *The Exorcist II* (John Boorman, 1977) and the opportunity for something terrifying here is lost as Charlie sets fire to some logs, later burns a hole through a wall and then transfers the heat-making capacity to a bath and huge blocks of ice. The childish whooping of Captain Hollister (Martin Sheen) is unlikely to be mirrored by the viewer.

From the outset, the narrative is focused on a pair on-the-run but director Mark Lester manages to achieve the apparently impossible in creating a whole new genre – the a tedious chase film. Apart from pace, effective chase narratives need a clear, coherent plot and a lack of sentimentality. We follow Andy and Charlie McGee as they run from airport to motel to homestead, but there is never any sense of real jeopardy created. The scenes of father and daughter together rarely go beyond the saccharine, and whilst Barrymore certainly has a very sweet look (a factor which Producer Dino de Laurentis felt would be a commercial winner), the plot plays out in a predictable fashion. Flashbacks, signalled via dissolves, punctuate the narrative, so that we see the Lot six experiment going wrong, Charlie setting her mother's oven mitts on fire and the abduction of Charlie. This latter example reflects the lifelessness of the film. King's novel slowly draws attention to a single bloody fingerprint on the glass porthole of the dryer but, here, Andy's discovery of his wife's body (showing signs of torture), flopping out of a cupboard, provokes no immediate or lasting reaction, and he just rushes off after Charlie. Even the final lines from Irv Manders (Art Carney) as he and Charlie enter the offices of *The New York Times*, 'You'll be safe now' and a skywards 'I love you daddy' from her, are the kind of sentimentality that also ruins the end of *The Shining* (1997).

The telekinetic subgenre suffers from one particular problem, which *Firestarter* brings into sharp focus. Stylistically, the conventional technique of a cut between a contorted close-up of a protagonist's face, twisted in concentration, and a special (or not so special) effect is hard to make dramatically convincing or, indeed, to avoid making it seem ridiculous. To draw on notions of explicit intertextuality, King has mentioned (without elaboration) *The Brain from Planet Arous* (Nathan H. Juran, 1957) as an inspiration for the novel of *Carrie*; but, in terms of the film, the main stylistic link is in a sudden close-up of the protagonist's face and a change to their eyes. In Juran's film, this shot is made stranger by deliberately invading the focal distance of the shot and having Steve March (John Agar) wear dark contact lenses. De Palma opts for a crash zoom and less gimmickry – we are lead to focus on the effects produced more than Carrie's twisted features as she produces them. In *Firestarter*, Andy's attempt to 'push' the taxi driver to see a $500 dollar bill, or Charlie's anger at an airport guard dumping his pregnant girlfriend, are both signalled in similar ways. Andy's pressing his palms to his temples and the zoom in to a close-up of Charlie with a wind-fan blowing her hair and a synthesized, echoing drum sound, in combination is reminiscent of *The Six Million Dollar Man*, where Steve Austin's 'bionic' capabilities are signalled by slow-motion and a similar stuttering sound effect. In combination with the ludicrous spectacle of The Shop operatives rendering Andy powerless by simply holding his arms at his sides, such allusions add to the sense of the film overall, not just in clothes and hairstyles, as closer to the 1970s than 80s. Tangerine Dream's ambient synthesizers produce an insipid echo of the unsettling score by The Third Ear Band from Argento's *Suspiria*. As with *Carrie II*, intertextual comparisons also point up weaknesses.

The character of John Rainbird (George C. Scott) provides a potentially-chilling figure, but his motivation is sketchy. He wants to have Charlie once the Shop has finished with her so that he can look directly 'into the face of God' before killing her, thereby assuming some of that power in an afterlife. There is something of the paedophile about his 'grooming' of a minor: inveigling himself with Charlie; posing as an orderly who is afraid of the dark during a power cut; sharing apparently-true nightmares about Vietnam; and taking her horse-riding. He could be an interesting example of a 'false father' (the horse he introduces her to is called 'Necromancer') but he kills Wanless, a postal worker, and Charlie's father without compunction or necessity; casting him more in the role of unmotivated psychopath. Magistrale's attempts to cast him as possessing 'all the unsavoury attributes of a Shakespearean villain,' just seem ridiculous.[29]

The climax, with Charlie destroying The Shop's installation in Virginia, is anticipated by a parallel scene earlier at the homestead, and shows what the ending of De Palma's *Carrie* might have been like. Charlie walks forward slowly, like a traumatized Carrie White, setting trails of fire up to Shop agents and sending fireballs into cars and buildings. This latter effect, pre-CGI technology, actually packs a visceral punch because of its immediacy and literal destruction. However, a few interesting shots (Hollister cycling to work rather incongruously or the X-File-like emergence from behind trees of suited agents to tackle the McGees once Rainbird has drugged them), do not make an interesting film. Conner notes the all-star cast as part of a 'disaster-film formula' but, unfortunately, *Firestarter* encompasses a very literal reading of that phrase.[30]

Conclusion

One feature which distinguishes cinematic forays into this subgenre is the lack of a coherent and rational explanation for the appearance of psychic powers. There is the small plot twist about the source of Carrie's gift, but nothing approaching a scientific explanation. Even comedies like *Modern Problems* (Ken Shapiro, 1981) usually attempt this, attributing Chevy Chase's telekinesis to his immersion in radioactive material after an accident with a waste disposal truck. The movie of the *Dead Zone* provides a dramatic incident in the form of an accident to explain Smith's powers by positing an accident (a brain tumour in the book) but the cause is really not dwelt upon in the concerted focus on the debilitating effect on Johnny. It is perhaps no coincidence that the one film in this section where psychic power is not used in a destructive capacity (indeed, its exact opposite: to help warn of current or near-future catastrophe), is the most complex and satisfying narrative. The simplicity of Carrie's or Charlie's blind rage allows for an intense reaction on-screen but not one we can easily share – Walken's character suffers pain, guilt and sadness over time: more nuanced feelings which we have time to understand and share. There is also a problematic fluidity to King's notion of psychic power in that it can, rather unfeasibly, encompass anything the protagonist wants at any point in the narrative; almost like the powers of a super-hero. Charlie's father in *Firestarter* is able to 'push' others into small-scale acts by suggestibility and Carrie's destructive rage can cause inanimate objects to move or prompt individuals to harm themselves, as seen in the killing of her mother or the prom massacre, respectively. This undercuts the seriousness of the narrative and makes the film's feel closer to entertainment for children. The problem with fantastic constructs is that if apparently anything is possible (from Charlie's ejecting coins from a pay-phone to sending fireballs to destroy her enemies), there is little sense of jeopardy.

In theory, the surface narratives of *Firestarter* and *Carrie* are similar. A young girl feels threatened and discovers irrational, destructive forces within herself, which she cannot completely control. However, it is largely the cinematic realizations that distinguish them. What sets them apart is the intelligence of De Palma's direction in extending existing generic boundaries, and even defining new ones. He achieves this by creating multi-layered depth within the image and of the performance he coaxes from Sissy Spacek, who is old enough to exude a maturity in her performance beyond that of a very young Drew Barrymore. The elaborate set-pieces in *Carrie* (such as the opening shower scene, the prom, and the shock ending), the counter-pointing of Carrie with the religious mania of her mother and the sense of pace in driving towards inevitable tragedy, find no counterpart in *Firestarter*. De Palma manages to linearize and elevate what is a fairly ordinary text, taking King's attempts at a modern-day *Dracula* with its juxtaposed, fragmented narrative form to a memorable and coherent whole.

De Palma's highly-allusive aesthetic and use of very ostentatious cinematic devices, such as split-screen and slow motion, inherently provoke the viewer to make connections with other film texts. It is such ambition in the film form and narrative structures that stretch and even define future generic boundaries (like the sudden shock ending of the slasher film) and helped increase the profile of Sissy Spacek. Possessing neither pace nor wit, *Firestarter* is a stillborn echo of *Carrie,* and *Carrie II* shows what a film looks like shorn of De Palma's direction and Spacek's charisma.

In *Phenomenon* (Jon Turtletaub, 1996), George Malley (John Travolta) suddenly develops telekinetic powers after seeing a sudden flash of light, but this is later 'explained' as a progressive brain tumour. With a press conference, at which George is overwhelmed, a sense of pursuit from an uncomprehending world, and the final death of the protagonist from his condition, there are superficial similarities with *The Dead Zone*. However, Cronenberg's thoughtful and challenging editing choices, particularly around the portrayal of visions, the persistent sense of melancholy in both script, and particularly Walken's haunting depth of performance, all serve to underline differences between a mainstream Hollywood project and one financed from sources beyond it (Dino De Laurentiis' Production Company).. At the end of

Andrei Tarkovsky's *Stalker* (1979), the protagonist's daughter, Monkey, is apparently able to move three glasses across a table, and the viewer is left to wonder whether this is an inexplicable psychic gift or the result of vibrations from a passing train. If telekinesis is to remain a subject outside the genre of comedy, perhaps it is best left unexplained; as part of an open ending rather than an only partially-convincing plot trigger.

Notes

1. Stephen King, *On Writing* (London: New English Library, 2000), p. 113.
2. Stephen King, *Carrie*, (London: New English Library, 1974), p. 137.
3. Robert Stam, in Robert Stam and Toby Miller (ed.), *Film and Theory: An Anthology* (Wiley-Blackwell, 2000), p. 14.
4. Brian De Palma, interviewed by Mike Childs and Alan Jones, *Cinefantastique* 6:1 (Summer 1977), p. 9.
5. Chuck Palahnuik uses the name that the Headteacher wrongly applies to Carrie, Cassie Wright, as the name for his abused, isolated heroine in *Snuff* (London: Jonathan Cape, 2008).
6. Stephen King, *Carrie.*, p. 32.
7. Ibid., pp. 36–38.
8. Ibid., p. 9 and p. 37.
9. Ibid., p. 33 and p. 34.
10. Magistrale, *The Hollywood Stephen King* (New York: Palgrave Macmillan, 2003) p. 30.
11. Magistrale, op. cit., pp. 28–29.
12. Collings, *The Films of Stephen King* (Washington: Starmont House, 1986) p. 40.
13. Brian De Palma, *Scene-By-Scene with Brian De Palma*, dir. Mark Cousins, first transmitted BBC2, 8/11/1998.
14. See Judith Butler, who talks of 'heterosexuality as an incessant and panicked imitation of its own naturalised idealisation', 'Imitation and Gender Insubordination', in Diana Fuss (ed.), *Inside/out: Lesbian Theories, Gay Theories* (New York; London: Routledge, 1991), p. 23.
15. David Cronenberg, in *Cronenberg on Cronenberg*, Chris Rodley (ed.), (London: Faber and Faber, 1992), p. 14.
16. See Magistrale, op. cit., p. 123.
17. Stephen King, *Carrie*, op. cit., p. 130.
18. David Cronenberg, in *Cronenberg on Cronenberg*, op. cit., pp. 11, 19, and 153.
19. William Beard, *The Artist as Monster* (Toronto: University of Toronto Press, 2001), p. 175.
20. Ibid., p. 178.
21. Ibid., p. 191.
22. Ibid., p. 186.
23. Ibid., p. 185.
24. Ibid., p. 194.
25. David Cronenberg, in *Cronenberg on Cronenberg*, op. cit., p. 111. See my discussion of the Deleuzian affection-image, in Mark Browning, *David Cronenberg: Author or Filmmaker?* (Bristol: Intellect Books, 2007), pp. 39–40.

26. See Stephen King, *The Dead Zone* (London; Sydney: Futura Publications, 1979), p. 254.
27. Ibid., pp. 295–6.
28. Ibid., p. 234.
29. Magistrale, op. cit., p. 35.
30. Jeff Conner, *Stephen King Goes to Hollywood* (New York: New American Library, 1987) p. 92.

CHAPTER TWO

TALES FROM THE DARKSIDE: THE PORTMANTEAU FILM

'Comic books are full of contraptions capable of performing multiple tasks.
Genre is usually seen as just such a device.'[1]

Robert Stam may not have been thinking of the films in this chapter when he made the connection above, but it is still a pertinent one. An advert for some of the 'contraptions' that he mentions is glimpsed briefly in the wraparound story at the end of both *Creepshow* films, and it is a useful way for thinking about the notion of 'portmanteau', also an umbrella term, which can hold different, possibly contradictory, meanings in a fruitful tension. It is also probably the most inherently intertextual film form discussed in this book – a key measure of how effective a portmanteau film is how effective links are between tales purely by juxtaposition or by overt comparison in some kind of narrative framing device.

These films are also amongst the most critically neglected (Magistrale mentions *Creepshow* once, the other films not at all), raising the question of whether these films are deserving of closer examination. However, it is tempting to see an element of cultural elitism in the treatment of these movies – they are already linked to a genre with low cultural status (horror), but these particular forms go one step further and associate themselves with a parallel print form: the comic, which may only serve to magnify connotations of low cultural value. The potential viewing pleasure of such low-budget efforts can be considered in generic terms – how well does the storytelling fit the limited time frame? What innovations are visible in the stories themselves? How do they relate to one another? Indeed, it could be said that, despite the critical rejection these films have received, they are actually amongst the most successful films of any King adaptation in that, at a basic level, they deliver generic expectations; in form at least. All of the films in this section are divided into three parts, apart from *Creepshow*, which uses five narratives; all have a wraparound story; and all have a cultural and visual link with EC comics – about which King has often spoken with both an informed knowledge and a nostalgic fondness.[2]

Short stories have seemed very appealing to adapt. As King notes, 'if you have a short story you can always expand it, whereas if you are working with a novel, you are always thinking of taking stuff out'.[3] However, that is the kind of simplistic approach which Studios have found to their cost. It is true that interest in King is such that recent adaptations include the *Nightmares and Dreamscapes* TV series of 45 minute dramas, *Secret Garden*, *1408* and *The Mist*, but it is too simple to assert that because the King source text is a short story or novella, that in itself produces a better film. True, *Carrie* and *The Shawshank Redemption* are based on novellas, but so is *The Mangler*. It is how the text is visualized that is important.

He has also shown an interest in comic-book culture in such as *Tales From the Crypt* (the adaptation of which he dubs a 'miserable failure') and the portmanteau film; both broken narrative forms, purposely episodic and often based around the motif of storytelling, where separate short tales are juxtaposed and/or given coherence by a loose frame story.[4] The production of a graphic novel based on *Creepshow*, with text written by King, reflects a strange circularity of production. The film was inspired by comics; involved the storyboarding of animated comic-book style sequences; was consumed primarily as a film in cinemas and latterly on video and television, and finally as a graphic novel, in a book format close to the original inspiration. The portmanteau form seems particularly suited to the horror genre in that, drawing on the literary basis of the genre, it can both accommodate short forms and benefit from the implied cultural prestige. Portmanteau horror films date back at least to *Dead of Night* (Alberto Cavalcanti, Charles Crichton, Basil Dearden and Robert Hamer, 1945) and the Amicus films of the 1960s and 1970s, including *Dr Terror's House of Horrors* (Freddie Francis, 1965), *Asylum* (Roy Ward Baker, 1972) and *From Beyond the Grave* (Kevin Conner, 1973). King claims that '[m]ost horror movies employing the frame-story device to tell three or four short tales work unevenly or not at all' but that does not seem to have dented his enthusiasm for the subgenre, also producing *Quicksilver Highway* (1997) for TV.[5]

For Altman,

[t]he repetitive nature of genre films tends to diminish the importance of each film's ending, along with the cause-and-effect sequence that leads to that conclusion. Instead, genre films depend upon the cumulative effect of the film's often repeated situations, themes and icons.[6]

However, of the three points being made here, the first is less pertinent in the horror genre, where the ending is often loaded with life and death significance, and particularly so in the portmanteau format, with its multiple endings within a single film; inviting comparison. More accurate for this chapter is Altman's observation that the repetitive and cumulative nature of genre films makes them also quite predictable ... The pleasure of genre film spectatorship thus derives more from reaffirmation than from novelty. People go to genre films to participate in events that somehow seem familiar.'[7]

Research would suggest that horror audiences behave differently than other audiences, and that a sizeable part of the viewing pleasure is in the shared nature of interactive rituals (not just for *The Rocky Horror Picture Show*).[8] The puns, the twists and the gore of these portmanteau films may well be welcomed by a knowledgeable horror-seeking audience, well-versed in the conventions of the genre. A key question to consider in this chapter is how the films attempt to achieve a stylistic or thematic coherence across separate narratives, and whether this represents an extension of generic conventions or whether they are content merely to operate within the narrow parameters defined by the expectations of a cine-literate audience.

Creepshow (George A. Romero, 1982)

George A. Romeo, director and co-editor of *Creepshow*, has had a long association with Stephen King and has dedications in *Christine* and *Cell*. King's first cameo was in Romeo's picture *Knightriders* (1981) as Hoagie Smith (a hick precursor of Jordy Verrill) and he was originally pencilled in to direct *Salem's Lot* but did not like the script's conception of Barlow and Straker, or the TV-mini-series format as opposed to a movie. He went on to direct *The Dark Half* and possibly will do so again for the heavily zombie-influenced *Cell*, for which he would seem a natural choice.

The critical treatment of *Creepshow* is typical of all the films in this section. It is often credited as King's first original screenplay but two of the five stories are actually based on existing stories, 'The Crate' and 'Weeds' (possibly missed as these are not as yet available in any published anthology). In contrast to King's TV mini-series work from the mid-nineties onwards, which often displays a lack of discipline – producing meandering plotlines and dissipating potential tension, *Creepshow*, with its five separate storylines, has a relentless focus on 'story'. However, given the structure and the fact that it had four different editors (with Michael Spolan credited with the first and last tale, including some of the more ambitious cutting, Paquala Buba for 'Jordy', Romero himself for 'Tide' and Paul Hirsch for 'Crate'), it is not surprising that the film has an uneven, episodic feel. This is the very nature (and some might say, appeal) of the portmanteau format in which juxtaposed stories overtly invite comparisons. The film is noteworthy for three main reasons – the use of unusual framing devices; King's extended cameo adopting an acting style more associated with silent film; and the integration of comic-book and filmic conventions – all of which challenge viewer's generic expectations.

The first segment, 'Father's Day', opens like a stagy, Victorian ghost story at the Grantham family residence, until mention of Aunt Bedelia motivates the first of many framing effects, as a tale of family scandal is told. The top two thirds of the screen is momentarily divided Battenberg-style into four squares, with the remaining third at the bottom. Hank Blaine (Ed Harris) and Sylvia (Carrie Nye) appear in the top two squares but our eye is taken by movement in the two squares below. The left one shows a car moving away in oblique framing and before this action is completed, we see, in the adjacent square, the reverse shot as the same car comes towards us. More than the standard continuity editing convention of an action begun in one frame being completed in the next, here we have some overlap of action (a stylistic feature of E.C. comics). We are encouraged to look for meaning from frame to frame, left to right and top to bottom, as comic book reading conventions dictate.[9] The bottom frame shows a closer shot of Bedelia driving, which is then expanded via a horizontal wipe to fill the whole frame.

The rich patriarch of the family, Nathan, is shown within a wobbly, animated border like a family portrait, railing against his money-grabbing relatives. His jealous reaction to his daughter's new love is dramatized via rapid cutting, in which a murder is passed off as a hunting accident. At first the image of a hunter in woods is enclosed by a narrow, horizontal border, which has the appearance of barbed wire, reflecting the trap the man is walking into. Then we cut to a Tower-of-Pisa-style frame, with the same border design, in which we see the man in a low, oblique angle, in non-naturalistic red light and walking not into the camera but just past it as if he is walking out of the frame. Returning to the first horizontal framing, we cut between a close-up of the man's feet and a rifle appearing from nearby bushes. As we occasionally cut back to the storyteller and listeners, so here we cut back to the sound of Hank striking a match as the rifle fires. Close-ups of the gun firing and the body falling into water are almost too fast to see and both are framed by a red, jagged border; the rapid cutting creating visual shock to complement the aural shock of the match/gun synchronization.

At this point we cut back to the family, who show Hank the heavy ashtray (which appears tucked away in all five stories) as the weapon used by Bedelia to gain revenge. He is only slowly becoming aware of the kind of family he is involved with; one who would condone a murder for mutual financial benefit. The burden of sharing this secret is also dawning on him as the hands of Cass, his wife, fall upon his shoulders in a gesture which could be affectionate or threatening. The occasion is now revealed as Father's Day, when the family meet up after Bedelia has laid flowers on her father's grave. It is both a commemoration and a sealing of a mutual pact of silence.

Framing choices signal not only flashbacks but ones containing lurid scenes with debatable moral choices being played out. The effect is expressionistic and acting styles theatrical, anticipating the imminent demise of a character, and simplistic motivation (suitable perhaps for a child's comic). At the graveyard we see Bedelia thinking, in flashback, to the act itself. A cake-shaped border outlines the cake for which her husband is constantly calling. A brooch-shaped border shows a busy kitchen and then a door containing the same shaped window literally swings into the frame, creating depth within the shot. We then cut to a larger brooch-shaped frame, as if the iris is gradually widening, containing a close-up of Nathan, repeating the previous family portrait effect. A series of shots using rectangular borders, his in portrait format, hers in landscape, alternating extreme high and low POV shots of Bedelia and her victim are intercut with a close-up of her hand reaching for the ashtray, create a primitive visual aesthetic akin to silent film. More expressionist framing follows with small fishbone-like borders intercut with bizarre cutaways of stuffed animals (a bear, a cat and a fox) who seem to be the only witnesses to the murder. At the precise moment that Bedelia brings her arm down, we have a landscape, rectangular border with a red, splinter-like design and a reverse angle showing the family portrait behind her arm, at first clear and then closer but strangely distorted, prefiguring the man's transition from burden to ghostly presence. Iris use, animalist symbols, occasional POV shots, dramatic backgrounds to a frame (acting like intertitles) – Romero is drawing upon a wide range of overtly-anachronistic Expressionist devices but whether his audience is sufficiently cine-literate to pick these up is unclear, beyond an overall effect of disorientation.

There are some more recognizable generic signposts – at the graveyard, at the mention of the word 'peace', a bloodied hand shoots up but the corpse does not attempt to grab Bedelia, *Carrie*-like; rather to dig itself out. An element of visceral gore appears in the corpse's maggot-ridden face, but more recognizable is his ironic mantra: 'I want my cake'; touching briefly on Paul Brophy's notion of 'horrality' but not in any sustained sense.[10] Humour is not used as a default position when we are faced by the apparently inexplicable. The fate that befalls Hank (he falls into the same grave, possibly punished for showing lack of respect by striking a match on a gravestone and taking a swig from the bottle he finds) or Sylvia's being decapitated to make a cake are not likely to elicit either response encompassed by the title of William Paul's study of comedy in modern horror, *Laughing Screaming* (1994), more than an appreciation of achieving narrative closure in a very time-limited genre.[11] Synthesizer chords mark the appearance of the corpse of the cook, framed through an oval window as Sylvia had been, moments before, but this is a fairly crude, higher-pitched allusion to Carpenter's use of lower notes in *Assault on Precinct 13* (1976) and *Halloween* (1978). Overall, 'Father's Day' feels very much like an experiment in the stylistic excesses of German expressionism of the 1920s. However, the fact that the narrative itself is not literally set in this period, nor are the audience used to such codes and conventions, makes it quite a self-indulgent experiment on the part of Romero.

Portmanteau films need to have some means of linking the narratives together. Here, the first story is introduced, as those that follow, by a graphic match from comic book to live action (ironically produced the other way round) and narrative information is conveyed by on-screen top-left captions, and in the character of a ghoulish MC, given to puns and rhetorical flourishes. The captions link the functions of comics and intertitles for silent films, whetting the viewer's appetite, underlining humour, giving information and providing a moral at the conclusion.

Of King's many roles to date, his cameo in 'The Lonesome Death of Jordy Verrill' is his longest on-screen presence, and a clearly meta-textual reference. The wraparound tale was also the screen debut of King's son, Joe, now a successful horror writer in his own right, reflecting a real-life shared appreciation of comic book horror and a passing-on of the muse.

Here King is virtually the only human character for one fifth of the film, apart from the man at the college to whom he takes the meteor or the doctor from whom he imagine seeking treatment (both, strangely, played by the same actor, reflecting Verrill's poverty of imagination). In contrast to the naturalism of other established actors in the film (such as Ed Harris, Leslie Nielsen, Ted Danson, Hal Holbrook), here we have King as hick Jordy Verrill scratching his head to express puzzlement, using excessive cross-eyed facial expression and an almost simian body posture and using an acting style more closely associated with silent film as if playing to the back-row of a theatre. Despite drawing some criticism, King was hardly attempting naturalism and is in keeping with Romero's anachronistic stylistic aesthetic from the first section of the film.

The wobbly-screen effect signalling his wish-fulfilment dream sequence at the college is conventional enough but the sequence itself is framed by a cloud-like border in its initial three shots, before assuming full-frame status; it uses low oblique angles and is shot in washed-out, sepia tones. A later dream sequence, motivated by his desire to phone for help, also uses black and white and extreme low angles but this is placed within a skull and crossbones border (reflecting an irrational fear of medicine) as a crazed doctor takes a cleaver out of a special steaming box in order to amputate Verrill's infected limbs.

The basic plot premise has intertextual echoes of John Wyndham's 1951 novel, *The Day of the Triffids*, to the BBC's *Quatermass Experiment* (Rudolph Cartier, 1953) or its later series, *Dr Who*, where the 1976 'The Seeds of Doom' story blends the arctic expedition of 'The Crate' with the infective vegetation of this tale. What is different here is the blend of comic book storytelling methods with live action and conventional editing practices with more expressionist framing, lighting and acting. The narrative does not have the tragic, existential quality of Brundlefly's interstitial identity in *The Fly* (1986) (particularly with King's horrified glance below his beltline) but it does ultimately end in a similar method of suicide via a rifle after a bathroom mirror scene (albeit here we have a father-son dialogue). Both here and in 'Father's Day', the minimal use of colour, melodramatic action, a single actor playing more than one part and exaggerated, theatrical acting styles, in combination, evoke a blend of silent cinema aesthetics with elements of Victorian stage melodrama.

In 'Something To Tide You Over', puddle-shaped borders frame shots of the house of Richard Vickers (Leslie Nielsen) after he has drowned his wife and her lover, Harry Wentworth (Ted Danson). Appropriately for Romero, the pair return as slow-moving zombie-like creatures, but even with oblique angles and close-ups of Vickers' face locked in a silent scream, the pale figures, covered in seaweed, surrounded by dry ice, look more like costume party gate-crashers than unsettling monsters. More effective are the distorted, 'liquefied' voices, the expressionist blue backlight when Vickers is scared and the intercutting of shots from his ubiquitous security cameras, which pick up no sign of the supernatural intruders (although this shows King's confusion in assuming some vampiric lore here). At the moment of their final attack, Romero uses a puddle-pattern border again but with concentric lines, as if Vickers is falling into a vertiginous whirlpool. The closing segment with Vickers buried in sand and claiming, as the water begins to strike his face, that he 'can hold his breath a long time', provides both a sense of closure in Wentworth's revenge and eternal return in that logically he might then haunt someone else as a similar zombie-like creature.

'The Crate' draws heavily on *The Thing from Another World* (Christian Nyby, 1951), featuring an entity brought back from an arctic expedition, here supposedly dating back to 1834 and blends this with a 'worm that turned' narrative as mild-mannered lecturer, Henry Northrup (Hal Holbrook), eventually stands up to his unprincipled, lecherous boss, Dexter and his own shrewish, indiscreet wife, Wilma, respectively saving him from – and feeding her to – the creature. Two unsignalled dream sequences show Henry call to Wilma at a social gathering, after which he shoots her and receives the applause of those present, and later attempt to strangle her, to which she does not react, casting both as subjective wish fulfilment only in retrospect.

The blend of roaring sound, devilish *Rosemary's Baby*-style eyes (also shown in motivated letter-box shot as Henry peers into the crate), hairy hands and ridiculous action, like the janitor putting his arm into the crate or the second victim deliberately crawling into his 'lair', make the 'monstrous' elements of the tale more like a Jekyll and Hyde parody. The monstrous features are mixed here too – the creature is clearly ape-like (hardly from an arctic region) but possesses huge sharp teeth, which he sinks into the necks of his victims, vampire-style. It feels like a hybrid of Pennywise from *It* and the killer ape from Poe's *Murders in the Rue Morgue* (1841) with questions like how it could have lived so long unfed left unanswered.

Obvious horror techniques appear, particularly the sudden movement into the frame, such as when Dexter drops a hand on the shoulder of the monster's next victim, Mike, or a sudden noise, like Henry tripping over a bucket. The attempt to drown the creature feels a bit like a trope from another age and as the ghoul MC reminds us:

'You can't drown your fears that easily'. The notion of horror as the eruption of that which is disavowed and suppressed feels closer to the obvious Freudian interpretations of films like *Creature from the Black Lagoon* (Jack Arnold, 1954). All of the tales feature a main character who seeks to repress an acknowledgement of a crime, for which they ultimately pay (or will do by implication in the future), with the slight exception of Verrill who is seeking to exploit something, which is perhaps less culpable.

Non-naturalistic, red backlighting is used at moments of supposed terror when the creature attacks (foreshadowing a similar use for Jack Torrance's in *The Shining* (1997), particularly in the case of Wilma who is surrounded by a red zig-zag design border too. As she approaches the 'trap' Henry has laid for her, the piano score makes the scene feel more like silent melodrama. A split screen is used for the call between the janitor and Henry and later this is followed by vertical and horizontal wipes, overtly dissecting the screen. As Henry wheels the crate out, Romero creates a further multi-screen effect like the opening of the Bedelia story in 'Father's Day'. Here the screen is split into thirds horizontally. In the top third, we see the hand poking out of the crate and in the bottom, a picture of the front of the university building – both of which are static. The middle third is divided by a vertical line, and as in the Bedelia example, we see simultaneous but also sequential movement juxtaposed as Henry brings out and loads up the crate. There is an automated vertical wipe bringing the bottom third up to full-screen size, almost like the sensation of projected film getting stuck between frames.

In 'They're Creeping Up On You', a scrupulously-clean apartment is gradually overrun by cockroaches in a *Bishop Hatto*-style morality tale. In the visual appearance of the protagonist, super-rich Upson Pratt (E.G. Marshall), with his bald head and spiky hair over his ears, his obsessive inability to distinguish between people and bugs, the running ticker tape of company profits and obliviousness to the suffering of workers beneath him, evokes Rotwang from Fritz Lang's *Metropolis* (1927), a further silent film reference. There is slight the feel of Burroughs' *Naked Lunch* (1959) and Cronenberg's 1991 attempt to 'linearize' that tale in the exchange at the door with the eye-hole distorting the face and voice of the underling sent to fetch a bug exterminator and the close-up eruptions of insect life from domestic orifices (sinks and grilles) and then physical ones from Pratt's body, as an image of misanthropy. This story is mostly shot in a naturalistic style but even here there is perpetual lightning and, right at the end, a red/black circular background and a border with hand-drawn roaches add a final expressionist touch. The frame story is completed by the garbage men (literalizing King's student column, 'King's Garbage Truck'), who pick up the comic only to find the ad for a Voodoo doll already missing. We cut to the father experiencing neck pain and the son gaining revenge by stabbing the doll he has bought. Red light and a zig-zag background blurs the comic book/reality border once more and we cut to the animated ghoul blowing out a candle in a rather abrupt denouement.

King, rather unconvincingly, attempts to explain the film's poor ratings by claiming that critics did not understand that it was 'not a send-up at all but a recreation.' of 1950s horror comics.[12] This is important, foregrounding genre over attempted parody. However, that distinction is hardly clear in the film, which has a campy, playful element throughout and even more overtly horror elements, such as found in 'The Crate', do not really deliver shocks or thrills an audience might reasonably expect. It is fascination with the medium itself, via Romero's direction, which is noteworthy. Overt comic-book conventions intrude upon the film with repeated use of page-as-a-wipe device to show the passage of time (to signal stages of Verrill's disease or Wentworth being buried on the beach), on-screen captions to show the passage of time or a change of location (when Vickers drives to a nearby beach), or both ('later that night in Henry's study' in 'The Crate') and letter-box style framing with a machine-driven pan (as we might scan a comic image), in the panoramic shot of Verrill's infected backyard.

King worked with legendary illustrator Berni Wrightson on the *Cycle of the Werewolf* novella and *Creepshow* comic book tie-in and, according to editor, Marv Wolfman, he 'understood comics and he understood how to write for them'.[13] *Creepshow* represents a defence of the pleasures of such 'trash culture' in the face of parental (and by extension, critical and academic) opposition. Billy's abusive and self-satisfied father condemns the comic (and by extension his son) as a 'worthless piece of shit'. He has no answer to the boy's argument that they are no worse than his father's 'sex books', which he assumed were a secret. Both represent guilty pleasures: the adolescent one openly acknowledged (and condemned); its adult equivalent violently disavowed. In throwing out the comic, the father assumes a literal and metaphorical smug pose of self-satisfaction, with his feet up, beer in hand and declaring 'That's why God made fathers'. Lacking fatherly affection, the boy is drawn into alternative imaginative worlds, in which what might looks macabre to adults seem accepting, even welcoming to the boy who shows no fear and indeed smiles at the skeletal figure outside his window. In the transition sequences we track swiftly across typical comic-book features (often only clear in freeze-frame), such as adverts for jobs (newspaper deliveries), fan letters and especially products for sale (X-ray specs, electro-buzzers and 'Muscle-Up' bodybuilding products), all familiar to the horror cognoscenti. Early-eighties effects technology was starting to allow live action and comic book sections to be integrated effectively in a mainstream, non-horror context (as seen in A-Ha's 1985 video 'Take On Me', directed by Steve Barron), partly under the supervision of long-time Romero-collaborator and zombie special effect expert Tom Savini (who also appears at the end as a garbage man). However, Romero's split screen experimentation challenges viewers to adopt reading procedures more commonly associated not just with comics but silent films – an increasingly obsolete combination.

Creepshow II (Michael Gornick, 1987)

Theoretically, there is a sense of continuity with *Creepshow*'s cinematographer, Michael Gornick, now elevated to director and George Romero as scriptwriter, but also a patchwork of residual matter – the three tales here were left over from the original film rather than written for this one. There is, perhaps consequently, generic confusion in the content of the tales themselves but also in the linking devices. The wraparound animation features Billy, a thirteen-year-old, so that, in a sense, the narratives constitute Billy's imaginative version of the stories he reads in the magazine: an early example of a cinematic version of a graphic novel. Hence, each story begins and ends with a graphic match from a frame of the magazine to a live action image. However, this struggles to mesh with the anachronistic Creep who delivers puns (Chief Moon has 'a high price toupee') in the mannered, theatrical voice of an MC from another age (especially when accompanied by a Rick Wakeman synthesizer score). The primitive animation style, poor sound quality and rudimentary make-up of the live-action Creep, even if linked to budgetary limitations, all seem fairly crude and hardly aimed at an adult audience. The relative, wide-eyed innocence of Billy seems inappropriate with the sexual content of Randy uncovering Rachel while she is asleep in 'The Raft' or Annie's flash of breasts in 'The Hitchhiker' and the discussion how much money she should pay for six orgasms. Indeed, the three tales seem to belong to different audiences: the first is almost a family, Disneyesque story until the violence at the end; the second is a teenage adventure; and the final one a moral tale of marital infidelity. Both first and last tales have a revenge theme, echoed in the ending of Billy exacting revenge on the bullies, who are eaten by his Venus fly-trap monsters, presumably bought through the magazine, which is advertising them.

The pace of the first tale, 'Chief Wood'nhead', is ponderous from the lengthy opening shot of the store to the exchanges between the couple, Martha and Ray, in which Dorothy Lamour's acting seems almost as wooden as the Indian figure outside. Ray's belief, in talking about the economically-dead town around them, that 'It'll come back to life someday' clearly anticipates the figure that revenges the attack on the store (although it does beg the question why he stands by and lets it happen in the first place). The three punks that rob the place are pure stereotypes, apart from the vain ringleader, Sam Whitemoon, who has delusional aspirations as a Hollywood star and is convinced he has better-looking hair than 'the guy with superhuman powers' (*Superman*'s Christopher Reeves, we assume). The deaths of the couple do not seem tragic or callous as we have hardly been dramatically drawn into their predicament. The revenge exacted on the three feels like a pale echo of *Christine*. 'Fatso' Gribbens is appropriately pinned to his chair by several arrows while eating a TV dinner; we see the shadow of Andy Cavanaugh stabbed with a tomahawk while, on the TV in the background, the Cisco Kid is ironically intoning 'You'll regret double-crossing me'; and the leader of the gang is cornered in backroom after a low-speed chase, pulled through a wall and scalped. The basic problem with plot momentum is genre-related (similar to problems with zombie-like elements in chapter 3). Unfortunately, as the chief can hardly move, there is no real ambiguity between when the statue is supposedly-animated and when it is not.

'The Raft', originally written by King as 'The Float' in 1968, has quite a powerful idea at its core but the problem comes in its visualization. On paper, the reader can imagine an amorphous, sentient entity with hostile intent but on screen all we get is some scummy-looking pondweed accompanied by a gloopy, sucking sound. King's slick emits hypnotic colours and seems to grow as it eats more victims. There is some effective picture composition. The overhead shot of Brandy swimming through the frame, followed a second later by the 'slick', is quite effective (used again in Andrew Niccol's 1997 *Gattaca*) but the boy's stroke-rate hardly looks like panic. When, he reaches the shore, turns and says 'I beat you', we almost applaud the 'thing' for rising up like a blanket and swallowing him. Both girls rise up from the slick in a slow-motion, balletic final pose like a synchro-swimming movement and the shot of the raft in the distance and the car, doors open, radio on, in the foreground, effectively telescopes the distance and encapsulates the tantalizing proximity of safety.

However, there is an inconsistent morality universe in operation in terms of victims, leading to a contradiction between EC conservatism and structural theories around the slasher film by figures like Vera Dika, who have mapped out quite rigid taxonomies in the sub-genre.[14] Those who are the most open in their drug-taking and sexual promiscuity, such as Deke, the stereotypical Jock, die, but so too does Rachel, who refuses a joint, and the shy Randy who has tried to protect the girls, hauling Rachel out from the water, and sees the risk of the slick most clearly. Sounding like a thinner version of Piggy from William Golding's *Lord of the Flies* (1954), he observes that 'no one knows we're here'. Possibly Deke is punished for the gratuitous lusting after Laverne and for allowing her to lie down (despite the fact that he has just seen his two friends die and knows that the slick can get suck them through the boards – which it duly does) but Rachel's curiosity (hardly a crime), in putting her finger in the slick, is punished as a hand-like tendril shoots up and pulls her in.

The portmanteau genre is fatally flawed in *Creepshow II* by a blend of clumsy narrative exposition with actions that carry more symbolic than dramatic weight. In 'The Hitch-hiker', Annie, the cheating wife, thinks aloud in unconvincing dialogue couched in full sentences, stops ridiculously quickly at least twice after escaping the figure and, predictably, the hitch-hiker reappears in her rear-view mirror, at her window and then through her sun-roof. The first tale articulates the economic depression underlying many Native American communities, the second touches upon possible environmental abuse as a cause for the slick and the third suggests the kind of economic apartheid, which like Tom Wolfe's *Bonfire of the Vanities* (1987), makes an affluent white character run down 'a black guy' (as the Stephen King cameo describes him), rather than pick up a hitchhiker. Ramming her Mercedes into his inert body five times as it leans against a tree, her deliberate reversing back over him and shooting him several times, suggests an underlying hatred as well as fear towards an economic (and racial) underclass. The unkillable figure grabs hold of the iconic Mercedes badge in hauling himself up and later breaches the fortress of her home to deliver his revenge on middle-class guilt.

Cat's Eye (Lewis Teague, 1985)

'Cats are weird'. (*Pet Semetary*)[15]

Where the *Creepshow* films draw upon conventions from graphic art, *Cat's Eye* attempts coherence in the portmanteau form through a literal common narrative thread (via the presence of one particular cat) and similarity of content (three cat-related stories). This is only partially successful, however, due to editing decisions which remove important content from the frame story and the actual content of the narratives themselves, which seem little more than a device to juxtapose feline tales rather than presenting any consistent and coherent thematic statement. Viewed as a whole, *Cat's Eye* is a slightly uneven package. In particular, the idea of tacking one story that is overt horror ('The General') onto two other tales which are clearly not, has only limited success. Both 'Quitters Inc.' and 'The Ledge' might be more accurately described as 'tales of the unexpected'. Cats (changed from rabbits in King's source story) are the unwitting means by which Jerry Morrison (James Woods) gives up smoking in 'Quitters Inc.' by their threatened torture and, by extension, torture of Morrison's wife and child. They are also the means by which Norris overcomes Cressner's henchman and turns the tables in 'The Ledge' and the saviour of the girl from the troll in 'The General'. King credits Producer Dino De Laurentis with the idea of using cats as a transition device but cats are mentioned in the original stories, where Cressner's wife warns Norris that her husband is 'like a cat...an old tom full of meanness'.[16] However, the weaknesses in the wraparound story mean that the attempt to distract the audience from the fundamental difference of the three tales only partially works.

What has been largely missed by critics is the intertextual and particularly the metatextual layers at work in the film, which go some way to make up for its surface inconsistencies. Despite being studiously ignored by Magistrale, *Cat's Eye* does have a literary basis. The basic structure of three tales linked by associations with a cat is not new. Richard Oswald's 1932 *Unheimlichen Gesichten* (Uncanny Stories) dramatizes two tales by Edgar Allen Poe, 'The Black Cat' (1843) and 'The System of Dr Tarr and Professor Fether' (1850), and one by R.L. Stevenson ('The Suicide Club', 1878). 'Quitters Inc.' and 'The Ledge' are both based on King short stories from his *Night Shift* collection, both have notable twists at the end and in the case of 'Quitters Inc.', there is a strong similarity with the 1954 tale 'Man From the South' by Roald Dahl, (both feature gambling, which leads to the wife of a minor character having the end of her little finger chopped off).

Transitions between segments in the portmanteau form need to be carefully managed so that viewers can understand potential shift in settings and groups of characters and quickly identify with them. Here, the cat seems lost amongst busy New York streets but then stops to look up at a mannequin in a clothing shop. At this point, some cuts of the film show a brief 'vision' which the cat has of a girl in danger and that motivates its interest and how it manages to let itself be captured by Junk, henchman to Mr Donatti at Quitter's Inc. However, in several versions of the film this sequence is missing and the precise narrative link between the three stories becomes confused. Junk's question ('What are you so excited about?') becomes a real one for us. The focus of our attention is switched twice here – first from the cat to the car that pulls up behind it (with a helpful 'Quitter's Inc.' sign on the door) and then, after Junk has bundled the cat into a box, we track him across the street and another car pulls up in mid shot, so that the dramatic focus now follows Morrison. The shifts here are quite smooth and effective and not overdone as Junk's action is complete in itself and we may already have tired of the antics of the cat. Woods is clearly the focus of the story and he is the figure we follow from now until the end of the first segment of the film.

He loses his nerve, but is intercepted on his way out by Donatti (Alan King). Casting choices, lighting and dialogue all have metatextual overtones here, which blur generic boundaries. Blinds are pulled and light falls directly in Morrison's face, making him recoil slightly, creating an air of interrogation (he had asked Jerry out in the car, 'Is this a quit smoking clinic or the CIA?'). At the moment we are not entirely sure. The impression is made more ambiguous by the casting of King. The short story describes him as 'vaguely familiar' and with more than a passing resemblance to the on-screen delivery of Humphrey Bogart and the deep, gravelly voice of a 40-a-day smoker, there is a contradiction between apparent absurdity and something more sinister.[17] 'Shall we get down to it?' Morrison nervously asks, to which Donatti replies 'Yes, of course. In fact, we've already started getting down to it' and automatically locks the door. Like the portrayal of the outer office, Romero creates a scene where characters act with unpredictable, emotional responses. After getting Morrison to meekly hand over those cigarettes he has with him, Donatti spreads them out slowly on the table, Morrison leans forward expectantly and the camera almost gives us his POV in a close-up of the cigarettes. Then Donatti's fists come smashing down into the frame and we cut to Morrison's sudden frightened and shocked reaction as he recoils. Donatti works himself up into a frenzy, scrunching, punching and pounding before calmly sweeping the mess into a desk draw and sitting down calmly. Through a mixture of generic references, all held in tension, we are unsure if we are in a Bogart-like thriller or a parody of such a genre. In this, we are being presented with a fantastical scenario and are unable to explain it instantly. Tzvetan Todorov's notion of the fantastic described such events as creating a moment of hesitation as we struggle to categorize experience.[18] What makes *Cat's Eye* interesting is how it manages to extend this moment into a significant period when we cannot, with certitude, ascribe a rational or even supernatural explanation to the events we experience.

The multigeneric references continue after Morrison humiliates himself with weak threats and an ineffective attempt to open the door. Donatti just ignores him and strolls over to the other side of the room, where he draws back a curtain with a remote control. There is the sense of a performance here, with Donatti as a showman with the patter ('Watch closely, Mr Morrison and you'll notice that at no time does my hand leave my wrist'), the light musical accompaniment, the gimmick (the glass-fronted room) and the sadistic spectacle (the cat on a wired-up floor). We keep cutting back to Morrison's horrified reaction at the sight of the cat jumping around to the sound of 'Twist and Shout'. In an arm lock, Donatti returns Morrison to his chair and gives him, and us, the back-story of how the 'family business' could be used to help people stop smoking. The low angle shots of Donatti, the Italian American accent and the ambiguous vocabulary blending business with organized crime, convey a blend of mafia boss and assertive supporter. His closing dialogue, much more dramatic and emphatic than the short story, captures that ambivalence in warning Morrison not to smoke because he will be spotted by Quitter's Inc operatives: 'You may see some of them all of the time. You may see all of them some of the time. But, believe me, you'll never see all of them all of the time.'

In keeping with the ambiguous generic features around Donatti, we cut from Morrison at home watching TV to a fantasy (signalled by a slightly blurred iris and a distorted soundtrack) in which Donatti is explaining the punishments for smoking, ranging from Morrison's wife and then daughter being tortured in the cat-room to sending a particularly 'disturbed individual' to rape his wife. King condenses and dramatizes the ten stages in the original short story down to just four and in answer to the question about a punishment for a fourth offence, Donatti just opens his jacket to reveal a gun. At this point we cut back to Morrison in his armchair, spilling his drink. It is not entirely clear if this was a flashback of an actual event or a fantasy, his own vision of the future which he can affect or 'dead zone', as it were. It is the first of several episodes (such as the creeping downstairs for a smoke, the party and the scene in the traffic jam), where the viewer is unsure of the exact status of an event, all effectively extending Todorov's period of hesitation still further.

Morrison's search for a crafty smoke uses straightforward horror clichés – creeping around a house at night with thunder and lightning, a momentary glimpse of his own reflection, a golf-bag that slumps out of a cupboard when he jerks the door open and he even spies some boots perhaps prefiguring a *Dressed To Kill*-style revelation, especially since we cut to a reverse angle from within the cupboard looking out – but the clichés still have some dramatic power due to the tonal blend of the absurd and the sinister, which prevents us from simply dismissing these devices as empty clichés. For example, he addresses the cupboard, declaring that he did not smoke the cigarette, and then withdraws. Morrison goes to pick up his disabled daughter (a son in the original story, possibly making her seem more vulnerable) and gives her a doll, which could be the act of a loving father or someone looking to salve his conscience, having put his family at risk.

The party, where almost everyone seems to be smoking, becomes surreal and hallucinations are introduced without any on-screen signals, expanding upon the two-line reference in the source story. Morrison sees a strange figure on the couch next to his wife who exhales smoke for an unnaturally-long period of time. At this stage we could be watching just a slightly heightened sense of reality but then he sees the sinister portrait from the Quitter's Inc. office whose eyes move and who blows smoke from his nostrils, a group of kids playing with cigarettes, and packets that walk around on their own legs. Some of these effects, like the boring acquaintance holding fistfuls of lighted cigarettes in each hand, are fairly conventional ways of conveying dream sequences but others, such as the waiter offering some egg-based snacks which are transformed into moving eyeballs, are more disturbing. Finally Donatti appears in a white suit, singing 'Every Breath You Take' (capturing the smoking and surveillance motifs), whilst blowing a huge cloud of smoke. Very like the party scene in *Jacob's Ladder* (Adrian Lyne, 1990), what begins naturalistically becomes a highly stylized sequence in which, to convey the protagonist's growing sense of paranoia, we are given no direct clue as to whether what we are seeing is 'real' or hallucination.

The original story lists a number of events from Morrison's life over the coming weeks, including sneaking a crafty cigarette in the darkness of a tunnel, generating no tension. However, in the film, Morrison risks a smoke whilst stuck in a jam over a bridge. Again the ludicrous mixes with the sinister (later he is so scared, he even picks up the phone with an oven glove). Here he checks there is no one on the roof of the car and puts on dark glasses, before hunkering down in the passenger seat. This reflects both his state of paranoia but also the social faux pas of holding up traffic and the litigious actions of the state in many western societies, progressively penalizing smoking as a socially-unwelcome activity.

The elision of self-help industries with organized crime is reflected in a generic blurring. Summoned to Donatti's office, Morrison is forced to watch his wife being tortured, as the cat was, in a trope from a gangster movie. The scene is unsettling as we are placed in the role of voyeur, alongside three men (two watching willingly, one under duress), which implies that cats and women are equally dispensable for male sadistic viewing pleasure. The twist that the arrangement changes from stopping smoking to losing weight reflects the corrosive integration of organized crime into everyday life (by now Morrison is quite chatty with Donatti) as well as the infectious nature of gambling. It is at first tempting for Morrison to dismiss the threats to cut off his wife's finger but the story closes with a dinner party with his friend Jerry and a toast to Quitter's Inc., which reveals in close-up the missing finger of Jerry's wife. It is only in this final scene that we have third-party corroboration of Morrison's experiences, casting the traffic jam and the party as 'real' and allowing the Todorovian moment of hesitation to pass.

From the outset, part of the coherence of the film is provided by a knowing, self-referentiality in the dialogue, even metatextuality – the man involved in betting with

Cressner tries to coax the cat to cross the road, by saying 'Don't worry about these big things – that's special effects.' The film is full of in-jokes for King enthusiasts. The dog that initially chases the cat is a Cujo-look-alike, sticking his foaming muzzle under an upturned boat, and is nearly run down by a 1958 Plymouth Fury, sporting a bumper sticker held in shot for several seconds – 'I am pure evil. I am CHRISTINE'. Later, Morrison is watching TV (Woods also reprising his role in Cronenberg's 1982 *Videodrome* here, along with subsequent ambiguous experiences which might be hallucinations) and declares 'I don't know who writes this crap', after viewing a scene from *The Dead Zone* (*Bullitt* in the original story), where Johnny is being interviewed by Dr Weizak. Finally, in 'The General', the book which the mother, Sally Ann, puts down, in order to talk about the problems of their little girl, is *Pet Sematary*. Intertextual references beyond the King canon also appear for the attentive viewer. Cressner alludes to *The Girl, The Gold Watch and Everything* (1962), a novel by John D. Macdonald, a King favourite (and Robert Hays, here playing Norris, starred in William Wiard's 1980 TV movie version). The pleasure of such allusions is in recognizing them – thereby becoming a more demanding generic feature and setting up hierarchies of genre recognition.

King's original short story, 'The Ledge', begins with Cressner's challenge to 'look in the bag', whose contents is only revealed at the end, as in the film. As with 'The Crate' section of *Creepshow*, and Ted's curiosity to open Straker's unusual crate in *Salem's Lot*, King exploits the reader's curiosity to find out what is hidden from view. The film adaptation increases the dramatic stakes to focus on the fulfilment of the bet and the cinematic possibilities of instant death in falling from a great height. The exact nature of Norris' crime (an on-going affair with Cressner's wife) is less clear in the film script than the original short story but this hardly matters as the focus is the wager – Norris' challenge to circumnavigate Cressner's building on a narrow ledge. The carrot is money, the removal of drugs planted in Norris' car and Cressner's wife; the stick is the revelation of the drugs to the authorities. Norris feels he has no choice and embarks on the challenge.

The body of the narrative, then, is the 'journey' around the building, with a series of obstacles, literal and dramatic, placed in Norris' way. Metaphorically, this sounds like a standard Hollywood film narrative but the problem is its literal manifestation – the hero in jeopardy on a narrow ledge is such a cinematic cliché that it is hard to engage with, and care about, Norris' fate. What follows is a series of extreme high angles to include shots of buildings opposite and sometimes down the side of the building to the street below, alternated with extreme low angles looking up at Norris edging slowly round, with the occasional close-up to show his fear as he flattens himself against the wall and a couple of shaky hand-held POV shots as he supposedly looks down; all of which ought to make us empathize with him.

However, despite the sterling attempts of effects expert Emilio Ruiz to make the miniatures look credible, there is not the same kind of creation of jeopardy that we feel on watching Harold Lloyd in *Safety Last* (Frank C. Newmeyer, 1923), a clear influence on this film. Norris even pulls a neon sign backwards in much the same fashion as Lloyd's iconic stunt with the clock face. Whatever viewers might feel about Ruiz's effects, they are ultimately studio-based and a key part of the effectiveness of Lloyd's stunts is the impression of people and traffic moving in the streets below. Predictably, a pigeon suddenly flies into shot and there are foot-level shots of Norris edging round and some arm-waving when he loses his balance. The obstacles put in the way of the protagonist are serial, not cumulative, and the series of dissolves used to convey the passing of time implicitly acknowledge the need to telescope time because nothing dramatic is happening. We see the power of the wind (with a wind machine and a sound effect, rather than the explicit wind gauge in the original story), Cressner with a flapping coat, a hose and then a horn and even a nasty, pecking pigeon. Also we do not know enough of the hero in 'The Ledge' to really care what happens to him. The casting of Robert Hays, whose 'drink problem' as hopeless pilot Ted Striker in *Airplane* (Jim Abrahams and David Zucker, 1980) involved smashing the glass into his forehead rather than raising it to his mouth, does not help.

However, other parts are more effective in reanimating this cliché. The horn (which turns out to be the object Cressner has been searching for) lurches into the frame unannounced and is blurred in the extreme foreground in a quick series of cuts. The slow-motion of the cat racing across the road earlier anticipates the slow-motion shot of first the horn and then Cressner himself falling from the apartment to the streets. The foreshadowing works well here, conveying the sense of Cressner's crumpled body, how he has been hoisted by his own sadistic petard, and of human life being innately ridiculous – Cressner ending with a squeak rather than a splat. The open ending of the short story, with ambiguity as to whether Cressner makes it back or not, is given closure here. The change to a horn from a New Year's Eve 'noisemaker' in the original story works well too, making Cressner more of an absurd and clownish figure rather than a credible mafia boss. We only hear this sound effect over a shot of the gaze of the cat, sheltering under a car before the screen fades to black. This echoes the demise of Brett in *Alien* (Ridley Scott, 1979), whose death is also motivated by a search for a cat, Jones, and conveyed partly by an extreme close-up of the cat's unblinking, and apparently indifferent, reaction to the xenomorph's attack. The film ends with a plot twist, not in the original story, with Cressner not just revealing the money but also the head of Norris' wife, which rolls across the floor and could be quite dramatic (as in Argento's *Trauma*, mentioned in discussing *Silver Bullet*) but it seems more funny than horrific and Norris' reaction is anger rather than shocked revulsion.

The transition to the third tale involves the animal acting as catalyst of plot coherence and resolution, hitching a train ride to Wilmington, N.C. where it will fulfil the mission to save the girl who had called for help at the beginning of the film. The cat plays a stronger central role in the narrative of the third tale than the peripheral role of the first two, where it was more of a linking device. In paratextual terms, all three films contain elements of what a cat sees (hence the title) but, here, this gains greater resonance as a form of protective early-warning system for the defenceless at night, echoing its namesake's function in traffic.

However, generically, it is an uneasy mix of the everyday and the completely fantastical. As a consideration of fears surrounding domestic pets, especially those that want to share our living space, and the folkloric superstition of a cat stealing a sleeper's breath, the final story is interesting. A troll-like creature living in her wall gives credence to the girl's fears and weakens the status of her parents' scepticism. Stylistically, we have elements of a horror film – a monster appears at night and seems to want to kill. We have both an 'objective' view of a hole appearing in the skirting-board to reveal a shape with two shining eyes and, in a reverse cut, we also have the troll's POV in silhouette from inside the hole, which might engender a measure of sympathy, possibly even empathy, for the creature. However, the manifestation of the 'monster' is innately ridiculous. It snuffles and giggles to itself like a blend of Chewbacca, Disney's Taz character and Beavis doing his Great Cornholio impression. There is something cartoonish about not only its 'voice' but also its actions, emerging like Jerry the mouse from a home-made hole in the skirting-board and climbing Sylvester-like up to the budgie cage. It scoots across the floor and, via a tilt-shot, we see it scaling the pole to the budgie cage. We have still only seen parts of the troll – its jester-like hat, its black body gripping the pole and its scaly, green hands parting the curtains at the top, and it is only after the despatching of the bird has been conveyed by a bit of shaking and a few feathers flying out, that the troll creeps up the bed until it shares a two-shot with the girl.

Much is made by Lloyd of the effects technology and record-breaking size of the oversized set used to create such sequences; an effect tried out by De Palma in *Carrie* but ultimately deleted and the results are not always convincing.[19] Lengthy close-ups of the creature show reptilian features and sharp little teeth but the effects tend to oscillate between stop-motion sequences which have some of the jerky unintentionally-comic effect of the *Puppetmaster* films, and the live action sequences basically look like a man in a ridiculous Halloween costume prancing in front of a blue screen. The long shots where the creature bounces off the bed and the gesture with the forearm to the cat just before he disappears back behind the skirting board, which miraculously reassembles (with the film run in reverse, a possible allusion to *Christine*), seem designed to be funny and make the creature look as if he is enjoying himself.

Our feelings towards the troll are ambivalent. It has some of the charm of an Ewok, being knocked off the bed into a drum from which it must heave itself out. It is a comically grotesque figure, with quick little steps like an old woman, but never really seems to convey a genuine sense of threat. The way in which it is supposed to take your breath involves pinching the nose, which looks more like a party game. The troll also just seems unlucky. When the cat finally works out a way to get into the girl's room, crashing down the chimney, Father Christmas-style, the troll's frustration is clear and we can sympathize with it, to a degree. The spectacular back flip it manages rather highlights the human acrobat inside the troll costume, and its subsequent climb up the doll's house echoes the plot of the previous story. It even gives out a laugh as it floats up, having grabbed a helium balloon, but then a comic 'uh-oh' as it starts to descend. The shot of the cat leaping up at the balloon is the weakest in the whole film but is redeemed by the troll landing on the record player, which is dextrously activated by the cat. The song played is the same heard in 'Quitters Inc', 'Every Breath You Take', adding coherence to the tales and, at the same time, being appropriate for the troll's avowed aim in relation to the girl, who is unable to scream having been partially asphyxiated. As the girl's parents burst in, the troll is despatched into a nearby fan.

What makes the tale generically unusual is that, within the fiction, the unbelievers (the parents) are shown direct proof of the supernatural (a little like the theatrical release of *1408*). Earlier, the mother had picked up one of the troll's bells from his hat but, at the end, they both see the mangled remains, small arm and sword included, and the hole in the wall. For the viewer, there is no moment of Todorovian hesitation. This particular monster does not challenge the viewer to reposition his views of the world – there is enough of the ridiculous about the look and actions of the creature for it to be dismissed as just 'silly'. However, these characters within the fiction are faced with a challenge to their understanding of the universe and, interestingly, their reaction is based purely on social standing and the concern that the girl will tell someone. She promises not to in return for being allowed to keep the cat. She has learned the value of emotional blackmail and they have learned about the 'reality' of monsters. What prevents the tale from being more powerful, however, is that the parents' world-view has to be realigned to accommodate the apparently-impossible whereas ours is not and, because of this, the dramatic status of the parents is diminished.

A deleted prologue would have begun with the girl's death and the mother's attempt at revenge, making the cat's vision a plea from beyond the grave. Concerns over the commercial effect of such a downbeat opening and reactions from animal rights groups, as the cat is pursued by a variety of weapons, prompted changes to the finished film. The cuts do erode narrative coherence but not to the extent that Lloyd suggests. Intertextuality and even metatextuality provide common threads and position the audience as particularly actively involved in the meaning-making process. The use of slow motion in 'The Ledge' foreshadowing Cressner's demise, and the ambivalent creature in 'The General', a mixture of the absurd and the sinister, work at times. The basic premise of 'Quitter's Inc.' seems to grow in prescience year by year as smoking becomes less and less socially-acceptable, foreshadowing more recent movies like *The Game* (David Fincher, 1997), where a shadowy institution offers life-changing intervention. If the tone is uneven overall, then this is largely due to the attempt to yoke together quite disparate narratives and unlike the *Creepshow* films and *Tales From the Darkside,* which stay firmly within the horror genre, *Cat's Eye* remains something of an anomaly in the King adaptation canon – a portmanteau film that is a truly mixed bag.

Tales from the Darkside: The Movie (John Harrison, 1990)

Preston: You're a monster.
Agent: I'm an agent. For an agent, being a monster's just credentials.

Like Joe Dante's 1983 portmanteau film *The Twilight Zone: The Movie*, the architextuality of *Tales from the Darkside: The Movie* reflects a generic ancestry not only from comics but filtered through the prism of a cult late-night TV series, fondly remembered by King from his youth. George Romero here acts as writer of the second segment (adapting an original King story), originally designed to be in *Creepshow II*, and the film (sometimes referred to as 'Creepshow III') also includes three short stories with a wraparound format – George Romero's 'Cat from Hell', 'Lot 249', based on a Conan Doyle tale, and 'Lover's Vow', both scripted by Michael McDowell. However, beyond occasional use of vertical and diagonal wipes in the first tale, there is little of the comic-book influence here. The dominant generic influence, particularly in the wraparound story, is from European fairy tale.

Despite a slightly anachronistic sense of dress (sporting a red long coat and hat), Betty (Deborah Harry) seems like a stereotypical suburban housewife arranging a dinner party. It is only when Betty opens a store-cupboard that we cut to a POV shot from inside the room, revealed as a cell. There is a bizarre shift from suburban kitchen to medieval dungeon with a wrought iron gate and crematorium-sized oven. At first, Harry's flat, emotionless intonation seems jarring but it suits the psychopathic lack of empathy that underlies the scene, dispassionately explaining the term 'evisceration' to Timmy (Matthew Lawrence). The boy has a slightly bigger role than Billy in the *Creepshow* films via a Scheherazade motif, helping calculate his own cooking time and delaying his demise by reading stories from the self-referential book, 'Tales of the Unexpected'. The generic ambiguity of the film is underlined by Timmy promise of a love story and Betty's avowed preference for romantic stories when she is calmly organizing kidnapping, murder and cannibalism.

'Lot 249' picks up the central motif of 'The Crate' in *Creepshow*, except here Ed Bellingham (Steve Buscemi) deals in antiquities to fund his studies. Paralleling Betty's plans for Timmy, Ed describes to Andy (Christian Slater), largely in the role of a passive observer on behalf of the audience, how the mummies were originally killed by having their brains pulled through their nose and torsos cut open to be filled with flowers – grisly details which are later taken up in the mummy's choice of killing method. However, the mummy horror sub-genre, despite brief popularity in the 1930s and 40s, is largely played out. Stephen Sommers' *The Mummy* (1999), *The Mummy Returns* (2001) and *The Scorpion King* (Chuck Russell (2002), are big-budget effects movies for family audiences. Here, director John Harrison is attempting to draw upon a pool of iconic references, such as Ed reciting a spell to raise the mummy, whose hand appears on the edge of the casket (minus one finger), that many viewers will more readily associate with parody than a source of fear. The bringing of such an anachronism into a suburban space, as it breaks into the house of Lee (Robert Sedgwick), seems more strange than frightening, although the tracking shot from Lee, searching for an intruder brandishing a tennis racket, to the mummy, fashioning a coat-hanger into a weapon, and back to Lee as an imminent victim, works well. The pounce is accompanied by *Psycho*-like falling fifths on the soundtrack and the despatching of Lee, albeit with a different weapon, recalls the domestic terror of Michael Myers in *Halloween*, pinning Bob Simms (John Michael Graham) to a door. The mummy appears piecemeal and in darkened rooms, when it initially cuts the power, to increase the fear of its victims but also so we do not see the whole monster at once.

The small element of slasher film here exemplifies an (arguably anachronistic) conservative morality as the mummy acts as an instrument of social justice, defending the poor-but-able student body against the exploitative, leisured classes, who are corrupting the academic system by plagiarism. There are small moments of suspense, such as the carefully-choreographed stairwell shot with the mummy lumbering up on the left side of the screen and Andy coming down unaware on the right. The sound of his phone makes him pause but he carries on, only to stop at the second ring, turn and bound back up, by the time the mummy has reached the point where they would have met. However, such shots can only temporarily conceal the same problem exhibited by Chief Wood'nhead – a lack of mobility in the source of monstrosity. Andy's lack of shock or fear on seeing the monster for the first time brings the fight, with him lopping off limbs, closer to slapstick than horror.

Unlike *Creepshow*'s consistency of form or *Cat's Eye*'s attempted coherence through the progress of one animal, 'The Cat from Hell' is just crudely juxtaposed without any overt thematic link, beyond the presence of a revenge motif. The revenge element (the money of wheelchair-bound Drogan (William Hickey) comes from drugs, developed by experiments on thousands of cats), the flashback structure and the use of expressionist space as Grogan wheels himself into the dining room, where the flashback of his sisters is played out in bluish, sepia tones, all seems like a less-effective version of similar devices in *Creepshow*. An expressionist aesthetic also permeates the dominant point of view – from the outset we share the cat's POV, using high angles, views obscured by railings and a bluish iris, but this fails to engender any sense of horror. After being tripped on the stairs by the cat, high and low angles show the first sister fall, leading to a tableau of her body at the foot of the stairs, which then forms a background 'screen' as Grogan leans into shot. His other sister, Carolyn, is killed by the cat creeping into her room at night and smothering her, drawing on motif referred to in 'The General' section of *Cat's Eye* but, unlike that film, the effect here is made ludicrous by the cat adopting an *Alien*-style face-hugging technique. Similarly, the attack on Halston (David Johansen), leaping onto his groin, alternates his POV with that of the cat's and just looks unintentionally funny. The climax comes, though, after Halston has inexplicably missed with a laser-guided pistol, only for the cat to literally force itself down his throat. As a Stan Winston effect, that might have worked but the sight of two automated wiggling legs looks as if Halston is trying to swallow a cheap toy. The effect in reverse for Grogan's return is like a perverse birth scene: the cat jumping onto his wheelchair and literally scaring him to death, although again there is a mixture of the horrific in the glistening nature of the cat as well as the unpleasantness of the idea itself, next to the poor quality animatronics (particularly the shot of the cat on the wheelchair in the bottom right of the frame). Less ambitious expressionist effects than *Creepshow* and poor quality effects (a rotating camera unbelievably representing a crashing car) erode the dramatic power of this segment, which operates well below generic expectations.

In 'Lover's Vow', unsuccessful artist Preston (James Remar) is accosted by a gargoyle-like monster who allows him to live if he agrees to a Faustian pact never to speak of what he has seen. The random nature of this makes a cohesive story difficult – Preston survives but Jer, the barman who was trying to help him get home, is killed. Preston quickly gains success after meeting Carola (Rae Dawn Chong) until the tenth anniversary of their meeting (information clumsily given via an on-screen caption) when he suddenly feels the need to confess. In terms of surface narrative, there are clear fairy-tale elements in the presence of a monster and a promise exacted and broken, linked to the passage of a very specific time-period. The supposed twist at the end, that she is the monster, is flagged up by her unlikely sudden appearance and the speed with which she agrees to go home with a complete stranger. Like 'Cat From Hell', this section is let down by poor quality effects – the transformation sequence is a low-budget version of *An American Werewolf in London* (John Landis, 1981) and *The Howling* (Joe Dante, 1981). However, the real twist is the appearance of their children as strangely-cute little creatures standing by the door. Carola-as-monster encircles him with her wings and bites his neck, vampire-style, before assuming the position of a real gargoyle, although, like the hedge creatures in *The Shining*, the chance of a really uncanny shot of a moving inanimate object is missed. The overall moral is hazy. Preston broke a promise but the world is full of people who do this and they are not eaten by giant gargoyles. The punishment hardly fits the crime. Moral accountability seems to be arbitrarily applied, which is not consistent with the brutal, punitive logic of how fairy-tale ideology usually deals with behaviour deemed sinful or socially-unacceptable.

Tim saves his life by telling his own story, blending intertextual tropes from different narrative forms – Hansel and Gretel and *Home Alone* (Chris Columbus, 1990). He throws marbles on the floor, making Betty slip, drop her keys and fall back on the skewers, allowing him to push her onto the trolley and into the oven. In a paratextual twist, knowledge of narrative helps Timmy turn the tables on an adult who means him harm (just as it does for the boys in the *Creepshow* films). The fairy-tale motif is complete with Timmy eating a cookie (the source of the trail in Hansel and Gretel) and declaring, with meta-textual awareness, straight down the camera lens, that 'I just love happy endings'.

Although some actors would later find success with bigger projects (Christian Slater, Steve Buscemi, and a particularly young Julianne Moore), perhaps the most striking aspect of the film is the wraparound story. If Betty is preparing a dinner party, there must be other cannibals whose domestic normality also conceals something a lot darker.

Conclusion

If publisher Marv Wolfman is right about King's knowledge of comic/graphic art, then the *Creepshow* films represents a knowing and ambitious attempt to transpose the grammar of comics into a different medium. Where their success is more mixed is in the avowed intention to evoke fear. King says that his intention with *Creepshow* film was to 'scare people so continuously that they'd have to crawl out of the theatre.'[20] It certainly manages low-budget shocks but this level of terror is conspicuously missing. One reason for that is the adoption of a fairly conservative moral code, typical of the E.C. comics but conventionally anathema to horror film, especially when this is emphasized at the end of each narrative. Morally-dubious behaviour is routinely punished. In *Creepshow 2*, murderous thieves are scalped in 'Old Chief Wood'nhead', drug-smoking, partying teenagers are picked off one-by-one in 'The Raft' and the murdered hitcher in 'The Hitchhiker' ultimately punishes the adulterous heroine, Anne.

In King's script and Romero's framing stylistic choices in framing there is an acute understanding of graphic art, especially the visual aesthetic underlying comic formats. However, there is a surprising, corresponding lack of understanding in terms of film. The pleasures on offer in the portmanteau films are generic. As Rick Altman states, '[g]enre film suspense is thus almost always false suspense.'[21] Within the conventions of this particular sub-genre, we do not expect fully-rounded, psychologically-plausible characters and are unlikely to feel the kind of terror to which King seems to aspire if we routinely expect immoral behaviour to receive its come-uppance. However even these pleasures are unavailable in narratives, such as 'The Raft' and 'Lover's Vow', where punishment seems arbitrary. The portmanteau films here offer a ritualistic view of genre, in which the audience can invest significance and meaning in a shared act of imaginative, transgressive play but also, arguably, they are being duped here into accepting overtly conforming forms of behaviour as a means to be happy in society (closer to an Althussian ideological/political model of discourse).

Perhaps there is here, as elsewhere in this book, an attachment on the part of King to culturally-obsolete forms and a slightly sentimental clinging to sub-genres and formulas from his own adolescence, which no longer resonate with contemporary audiences. David Buckingham suggests that, perhaps not surprisingly, viewers' generic understanding is related to age and their viewing experiences.[22] In relation to *Creepshow*, a viewer unused to conventions of reading graphic art, unfamiliar with the style and moralistic content of the E.C. products or the use of lurid colour and expressionist lighting and framing effects, may find it hard to engage with such a film. The animated ghoul that links the first films only serves to underline how painful punning is no longer seen as entertaining. There is also a slightly self-indulgent element in that the portmanteau form allows King to draw upon his back catalogue of short stories rather than purpose-written material that may be better suited to adaptation.

Cat's Eye's surface narrative is not particularly coherent but it contains elements of genuine unsettling subjectivity, when we are unsure of the status of what we are watching. Intertextuality, and more precisely metatextuality, adds resonance if we are acute enough to pick up references but, ultimately, King's confused notion of monstrosity casts the monster in 'The General' as comic rather than sinister. *Tales from the Darkside* is much less ambitious and achieves correspondingly less, failing to deliver even the limited pleasures of a purely genre film by predictable plotting, poor quality effects and an anachronistic narrative forms. This is the nub of the problem with the films in this section – the pleasures they offer are intertextual ones and the number of viewers well-versed in the disparate sub-genres that are alluded to is increasingly small.

That said, the portmanteau form itself invites comparison between tales and, inherently, the balance between variety and coherence is difficult. This is always going to provoke criticism, especially when the tales feature completely different casts, locations and are sometimes even produced by different scriptwriters, such as *Tales from the Darkside*. Certainly, they represent something of 'a mixed bag' in terms of quality but to reject the form outright misses the subtlety of Romero's editing and framing in *Creepshow* and the intertextual game-playing in *Cat's Eye*, and smacks of the kind of elitist high/low art division that prevents a more sober examination of the films themselves.

Notes

1. Robert Stam, *Film and Theory*, op. cit., p. 14.
2. Stephen King, *Danse Macabre* (New York: Berkeley Publishing, 1981), op. cit., pp. 36, 51 and 440.
3. Stephen King in Magistrale, *The Hollywood Stephen King*, op. cit., p. 9.
4. Stephen King, *Danse Macabre*, op. cit., p. 304n.
5. Ibid., p. 304.
6. Rick Altman, *The American Film Musical*, op. cit., p. 25.
7. Ibid.
8. See Matt Hills, *Fan Cultures* (London: Routledge, 2002) and *The Pleasures of Horror* (London: Continuum, 2004).
9. See Scott McCloud, *Understanding Comics: The Invisible* Art (New York: Harper Collins, 1993).
10. See Philip Brophy, 'Horrality: The Textuality of Contemporary Horror Films', *Screen*, 27:1, (January-February 1986), pp. 2–13.

11. See William Paul, *Laughing Screaming: Modern Hollywood Horror and Comedy* (New York; Chichester: Columbia University Press, 1994).
12. Stephen King, cited in Underwood and Miller (eds.), *Bare Bones: Conversations on Terror with Stephen King* op. cit., p. 42.
13. Marv Wolfman, 'King of the Comics' in Don Herron (ed.), *Reign of Fear: The Fiction and the Films of Stephen King* (Novato, California: Underwood-Miller, 1988), p. 14.
14. See Vera Dika, *Games of Terror: Halloween, Friday the 13th, and the Films of the Stalker Cycle* (Rutherford, N.J.: Fairleigh Dickinson Press; Cranbury, N.J.; London: Associated University Presses, 1990).
15. Stephen King, *Pet Semetary* (London: New English Library, 1984), p. 184.
16. Stephen King, 'The Ledge' in *Night Shift* (London: New English Library, 1979), p. 239.
17. Ibid., p. 275.
18. See Tzvetan Todorov, *The Fantastic: A Structural Approach to a Literary Genre*, trans. Richard Howard (Ithaca, New York: Cornell University Press, 1975), p. 25.
19. Ann Lloyd, *The Films of Stephen King* (New York: St Martin's Press, 1993), p. 43.
20. Paul Gagne, 'Creepshow', *Cinefantastique* (September/October, 1982), pp. 17–35, cited in Collings, op. cit., p. 20)
21. Altman, op. cit., p. 25.
22. David Buckingham, *Children Talking Television: The Making of Television Literacy* (London: Falmer Press, 1993), pp. 135–55.

CHAPTER THREE

SOMETIMES DEAD IS BETTER:
THE BODY UNDER THE SHEET

'We're afraid of the body under the sheet. It's our body.'[1]

'Death is when the monsters get you.' (Mark Petrie in *Salem's Lot*)

For King, '[t]he most obvious psychological pressure point is the fact of our own mortality'.[2] A key pleasure of the horror genre is the deferral of one's own death through the vicarious viewing of the demise of fictional surrogates. Death is the defining borderline state in classic horror fiction, film and novels. The return of the dead can produce ghosts (*The Shining* and *1408*), zombies (he has yet to write an explicitly zombie-based narrative, except perhaps the end of both *Pet Sematary* and 'Something to Tide You Over' for *Creepshow*), werewolves (*Silver Bullet*) or his own feline hybrid version of vampires (*Sleepwalkers*). The main jeopardy faced by the human characters is that the monstrous entity, having apparently cheated death, becomes the totemic 'unkillable thing', replacing one impossible situation (the surpassing of death) with another impossible dilemma – what can you do to something that is already dead? Luckily these cultural myths have developed their own lore, featuring solutions for despatching the monsters.

However, cinematic representations of death in this study often fall back on generic sub-genres which are largely obsolete, such as the werewolf movie. This particular example has a number of generic problems. The physical transformation of the werewolf, itself limited by linkage to lunar cycles, is cinematically demanding (and thereby linked to effects technology, by which it has become dominated to a degree). The relatively crude monster/human dichotomy of lycanthropia in *Dr Jekyll and Mr Hyde* (1886) appears simple by comparison with vampirism's literary inspiration, Bram Stoker's *Dracula* (1897), which is, in some ways, closer to nature (there are, after all, vampire bats) whereas lycanthropia has only ever been a delusional, psychological condition. There is also an emphasis on external changes in appearance, especially the acquisition of body hair, whereas the thrust of much modern horror is internal, to make insides visible. Vampire mythology is open to a greater range of interpretations of the blood/sex exchange as well as conveying a sense of *fin de siècle* bohemian decadence (reflected in the number of films that have and continue to be made featuring vampires), whereas werewolf plots seem limited in metaphorical application. To view the werewolf as symbolic of repressed adolescent sexual desire may make sense as a reflection of the constrictive culture of the 1950s and the emergence of the cultural and economic phenomenon of the teenager but, by the mid 1980s, this level of sexual repression simply did not exist in western visual culture.

In the specific case of *Silver Bullet*, a thinly-veiled mystery plot and empathy for the monster run counter to one another because, for much of the film, we do not know with absolute certainty who it is. Moreover, we do not see any scenes of transformation, internal struggle or ethical dilemma – the monster here just is. If the monster is a challenge to the dominant heterosexual, patriarchal values, the hero must defeat him to secure the affections of the female love interest. Here, however, this is denied because the female protagonist is the hero's sister – generically, this is a small-town, family drama, not a challenge of the incest taboo.

The acquisition of body hair might suggests a metaphorical link with adolescent fears about the onset of puberty but here we see very little of the monster itself.[3] Some werewolf conventions are referenced – it only strikes when the moon is full; it can only be despatched by a silver bullet (hence the title); and once killed it returns to human form. However, other conventions are missing – there is no sense that victims are then themselves transformed into werewolves; there is no excess of body hair, especially on hands; no pentagram figure on the body; and no extended index finger. Since horror is a genre where many sub-genres deal in myths, rather than directly referencing the everyday world in which we live, films often refer in their first instance to other, previous narratives of that genre. Five years after John Landis' *An American Werewolf in London* and Joe Dante's *The Howling* (1980), audiences of *Silver Bullet* would be accustomed to state-of-the-art transformation sequences, which we are completely denied here, giving *Silver Bullet* an inherently anachronistic feeling in purely generic terms. The lack of such scenes and references to birth and rebirth largely undercut approaches by theorists like Barbara Creed, denied those scenes that underline the monster's abject status. We do not see a feminized man, effectively giving birth to himself, and we do not see the man/Other as separated by a permeable membrane as they do not appear either in shot together or, in the case of the monster, hardly in shot at all.[4]

The werewolf myth exercises a strong attraction for Stephen King. *I Was a Teenage Werewolf* (Gene Fowler Jr., 1957) appears in *It* and as one of the manifestations of Pennywise (possibly also informing his make-up, sporting only a top row of razor-sharp teeth), and King talks warmly about the film in *Danse Macabre*. Unfortunately for King, in cinematic terms the werewolf sub-genre seems all but played out, as seen by the commercial flop of films like *Cursed* (Wes Craven, 2005) and possibly a contributory factor to why *The Talisman* (1984, co-authored with Peter Straub), which features a werewolf unimaginatively named Wolf, remains as yet unfilmed. True, there was a mini resurgence at the start of the eighties, but critical and commercial attention mainly focused on the special effects technology, largely inspired by Rick Baker and Rob Bottin respectively, used in the transformation sequences. It is a sub-genre associated with a bygone era (hence its use in *IT* to establish the teen culture of the late 1950s) and so often parodied, in such as *Teenwolf* (Rod Daniel, 1985), that it is hard to rehabilitate the sub-genre back into mainstream horror. In *Young Frankenstein* (Mel Brooks, 1974), when Gene Wilder, the eponymous hero, is being driven to his Transylvanian castle and asks Igor, played by Marty Feldman, 'Werewolf?' and gets the answer 'There wolf' as he points at a pack shadowing the coach, the nail really seems to have been driven into the coffin of the cinematic werewolf (a fact reflected in the failure of Anthony Waller's 1997 sequel to Landis' film – the imaginatively titled, *An American Werewolf in Paris*). There are occasional signs of life – Michael Wadleigh's 1981 political *Wolfen*, which tries to align the American urban underclass with an outbreak of apparent attacks but Romero's zombies fulfil this metaphorical role more convincingly. Mike Nichols' *Wolf* (1994) gives Jack Nicholson a chance to breathe new life into the myth but most of the screen time is devoted to his increasingly demonic face-pulling.

Silver Bullet (Daniel Attias, 1985)

So having selected an anachronistic and largely exhausted sub-genre, King produces a script, drawing on his 1983 novella *Cycle of the Werewolf*, which is largely bereft of anything either shocking or dramatically engaging. The title itself makes it fairly clear from the outset that the werewolf will be despatched and as soon as we see Marty Coslaw's new customized wheelchair with 'Silver Bullet' emblazoned across it, we know exactly who will be doing the despatching. As the titles roll, we have an opening shot of a full moon but although we are told by Jane, Marty's sister, via voiceover, that 'our nightmare began that night', there is a strange lack of any dramatic tension as we know the nature of the monster and that the main characters will survive.

The realization of the monster is important for any werewolf movie. However, the first attack sets the pattern for the rest. We have the monster's POV shots looking through bushes from where he is hiding, growling/heavy breathing on the soundtrack and deep synthesizer chords, referencing John Carpenter in *Halloween* (also used in the second and third attacks). Unfortunately, this in itself is not enough to generate tension. We do not know what these characters' inner lives are (indeed if they have them at all), including the monster – making any kind of empathetic connection all but impossible. There is a strange balletic beauty in the slow-motion flight of the head of rail worker, Arnie Weston, through the blackness, but Argento's later *Trauma* (1993) shows what macabre humour can achieve (the victim, played by Piper Laurie literally becomes a talking head, saying the name 'Nicholas' after being decapitated), rather than the hairy arm swiping through the frame here, which make the sequence more laughable than terrifying.

Generic clichés battle with clumsy editing. During the second attack, on a pregnant girl attempting to commit suicide with pills, a hairy hand enters the frame (here to climb a trellis) along with the ubiquitous thunder and lightning. The girl, oddly, starts to scream before the monster crashes through her window and then we have a montage of the girl's screaming face, the werewolf's jaws closing in, an apparent 'misedit' as we see the monster's hands gripping the girl's neck and an extreme close-up of its flashing red eyes, followed by a top shot with ridiculous head-waggling as he mauls her neck (like the attack on Mr Fallows in *Sleepwalkers*). The final shot of the sequence may not quite match the compositional depth of Susan's suicide attempt in *Citizen Kane* (Orson Welles, 1939) or the sex scene between Rutger Hauer and Theresa Russell in Nick Roeg's *Eureka* (1982), which also features door, bed and female body in similar positions, but it does at least show some generic ambition.

For the third attack there is still no real suspense or jeopardy. We have more monster POV, alternating with the victim's as he scans a garden shed with his flashlight. Pots shake inexplicably but the light that seems to filter through the slats of the shed does not herald a monster as original as Clive Barker's cenobites in *Hellraiser* (1987). In a single, unsettling moment, the camera follows the victim's feet as he climbs a short flight of steps and pauses momentarily half-way up to give us a glimpse of the werewolf's eyes, visible through the steps. The increased shaking of the shed creates an agricultural allusion to *Poltergeist* (Tobe Hooper, 1982) and when the man is impaled rather unconvincingly on an upturned plank, despite the blurred close-up of some kind of jaws, the snuffling noise of the creature, as in the third part of *Cat's Eye*, makes what could have been horrific merely silly.

More effective is the social dimension to the narrative, drawing on the crowd motif of German Expressionism. In the beginning we see Reverend Lowe address a communal event, where he praises the townsfolk of Tarker's Mill as representing 'the very definition of community'. Soon cracks appear in that community, as local trouble-maker Andy Fairton (seen later putting up an advert for shotguns, implying some profiteering) tries to rouse a local bar against Sheriff Haller. In this, he does have a point. Haller later imposes a curfew but seems powerless to do much to catch the monster and unwilling to call for outside help. He loses the battle to prevent mob rule, signified by the stream of cars, guns and dogs out into the woods. However, the generic markers are confused. Whereas the shooting parties in Romero's *Night of the Living Dead* (1968) do convey effectively the response of the wider community, including its underlying racism, reflected in the death of the final black survivor, here they just seem bizarrely out of place. They stumble around in the dark making huge amounts of noise, waving flashlights and, when one steps in a man-trap, he is initially released only for his rescuer to jump at a noise, letting the trap snap back on his ankle. This portrayal that makes them figures of slapstick comedy rather than horror continues in the shot where the bartender's hand, using his baseball bat on the monster, with the bat raised above the mist, is shown to change from human to that of the monster.

Generically, there is an awkward mix of the surface features of a horror film and a deeper structure that is closer to children's drama, which is reflected in Jane's voiceover that had virtually disappeared after the opening but now returns when Marty tries to convince Red about the incident on the bridge, and which seems intrusive and unnecessary. The assumption of a mystery identity for the werewolf and the extremely limited range of possible candidates (it can only really be Red or the Reverend) also plunges the film firmly into a narrative closely associated with a cartoon like *Scooby-Doo*, i.e. for a children's audience. Despite the R-rating for violence, scenes such as where Marty rides his new customized chair up and down a virtually empty road, or Jane's embarking on a search for the mystery man with one eye by trailing around town with a trolley, supposedly collecting bottles and tins for charity, seem to belong more in a Disney children's film than a horror narrative (closer to the original audience demographic of *I Was a Teen Werewolf*, perhaps). Similarly, the attempt to rid the town of the Reverend by posting anonymous letters, pasted together from newspaper lettering seems closer to Enid Blyton than Stephen King, emphasized in the closing lines of the film in which brother and sister exchange 'I love yous' and Jane underscores the lesson she has learned – 'I wasn't always able to say that but now I can'. Although, as mentioned in Chapter 2, an underlying conservative morality has been linked to slasher narratives, the pattern of the nature of the victims here also reinforces the sense of anti-establishment behaviour as the target, i.e. a sententious moral for a teen audience. We have a drunk; a girl, pregnant out of wedlock, attempting suicide; and an abusive, drunk father, showing a lack of respect to the disabled ('Damn cripples always end up on welfare,' he mumbles to himself'). Emblematically, in an action that is pure Disney, victim number four, Marty's friend Brady, had pushed a practical joke too far and, in waving a snake at Jane, made her fall back into a puddle.

The final attack appears to offer some generic variation as director Daniel Attias uses a slow zoom in on a door, the expected means of entrance, but then the werewolf crashes through the wall. However, predictably, Marty shoots the creature, who then regresses – the stages of transformation now in reverse, (in a clear reference to Landis' climax) – until he is human again. Even here, there is a strangely unwittingly ridiculous element as the Reverend suddenly lurches up before falling back, clearly dead. The horror trope of the unkillable thing, and the *Carrie*-style shock ending, just seem childish without the intention of parody.

The generic confusion works on occasion but that is more by default than design. In the church, the Reverend tries to counsel patience but cannot counter the mantra of 'private justice'. We then have a mass transformation scene as several characters begin to change into werewolves, at which point the Reverend wakes up and we realize that this was a dream. Without devices like a wobbly screen or a blurred iris, this evokes a similar sequence in *The Company of Wolves* (Neil Jordan, 1984), effectively disorientating us and arguably making the revelation of the Reverend as monster a little less predictable, although it is also yet another direct 'steal' from Landis' film, with its 'double-dream' sequence in hospital.

A more typical example of generic confusion occurs when the Reverend attempts to run down Marty. Despite the plot situation having potential for action, suspense and empathy, the sequence delivers none of those pleasures. The 'action' seems quite cartoonish (even passing a sign for an unsafe bridge ahead, *Road Runner*-style) and short-lived – Marty's vehicle runs out of petrol, he is forced to coast into the covered bridge and run to a stop. For a few seconds, there is some effective tension created as the boy tries to make the engine start, and the pace slows as he looks back through the hole he made in the boarded up entrance and sees the Reverend's car slowly approaching. Unmotivated sound (the sound of the door slamming) and obscured vision (the sight from Marty's view of the lower half of the Reverend's legs), all create a sense of dread. However, this is dissipated as soon as the Reverend comes close enough to speak. Although he is framed in low angle, he is sporting an eye patch and with terrible dialogue, calling Marty 'a meddling little shit', we are right back in the generic clichés of cartoons once more. There is one final chance to salvage the sequence when Marty spots a man passing on a tractor and calls for help but he initially appears not to hear. There could be an agonizing near-miss here but then the man does hear, comes to investigate and the Reverend just walks away.

Attias and King, who wrote the script, seem unable to deliver the generic features of a werewolf narrative without recourse to literal references to other werewolf films, unhelpful generic confusion drifting into cartoonish, family adventure film and, when the two collide, as in this last scene, the horror elements just 'retreat'. Ironically, the film is perhaps most convincing in its tangential generic portrayal of small-town tensions (complete with a *To Kill a Mocking Bird*-like female narrator), but it does show the problems of using scenes of graphic violence to conceal a sub-genre that is no longer culturally or cinematically credible.

Pet Sematary (Mary Lambert, 1989)

'A kiddie story with gruesome undertones – Winnie the Poe.'[5]

In *Danse Macabre*, King discusses one attraction of the horror as a preparation for one's own death and in *Pet Sematary* this issue is foregrounded explicitly, with intertextual allusions to Poe's *Premature Burial* (1844) and WW Jacobs' notion in *The*

Monkey's Paw (1902) (mentioned explicitly in King's novel) that you should be careful what you wish for – especially if, according to baleful neighbour Jud Crandall (Fred Gwynne), it is the reanimation of your dead son.[6] The film opens with some effective low-budget, theatrical tropes in the visualization of the cemetery, stylized like an Expressionist nightmare with crooked crucifixes, a stone-lined path and rising mist. It is a backlit gothic wasteland, bathed in blue and white light, becoming more of a mental landscape than a physical one, reflected in the momentary vision of a face in the rocks.

However, despite superficial differences with *Silver Bullet*, *Pet Sematary*, scripted by King (his first from a full-length novel, discounting *Cujo*), is also basically a small-scale family drama with a supernatural element superimposed upon it. The narrative draws upon a *Frankenstein* motif of male characters punished when they try to (re)create life, usurping the biological role of women, and resist intractable realities about the nature of mortality. The flashback to Zelda, the sister of Rachel (Denise Crosby), represents one physical reality of death – monstrous, needy, close, familial, suppressed (she is placed in a back bedroom) and left to the daughter to tend, traumatizing her and making her hate her sister for what she had become. Picture composition underlines the familial nature of the drama – Louis Creed (Dale Midkiff) and his daughter, Ellie, in the background, asking what happens when people die, are overheard by a tearful and unseen Rachel, in the foreground. Like *Cujo*, there are tensions in this marriage, but here they remain at the level of a minor tiff, centred around how to tell a child a difficult truth, which is quickly resolved by a kiss at the gate, producing an iconic image idealized family – mother and child waving goodbye to the husband on his first day at work. The real horror is man-made – not just the trucks which pound past the Creed's new home day and night, *Maximum Overdrive*-style, but the inability to accept death and the attempt to pervert older religions in order to prolong life. However, rather than an overt horror narrative, this is mediated through the family, and the management of death in its social aspects (graveyards and funerals) is seen at Gage's funeral, where family hostilities boil over, leading to an undignified fight and the knocking over of a tiny coffin.

The status of Victor Pascow (Brad Greenquist) is a good example of the film's generic ambiguity. Lambert presents audiences with some of the gore they might expect from a horror narrative in the close-up of a boy, later identified as Victor, placed in the extreme foreground, deathly pale, badly injured with part of his skull missing and some brain matter visible. For all his qualifications, Louis can do no more than close the boy's eyes and a sense of underlying panic, verging on hysteria, is suggested by a the handheld camera and distorted, overlapping dialogue used during the boy's admission. However, there is ambiguity between mainstream and more transgressive manifestations of the supernatural. Victor's graphic first appearance is subsequently contradicted by a Casper-like role as Louis' good angel through the course of the narrative (he says in the cellar that he wants to help). Bearing in mind how Louis uses the knowledge given to him and Victor's sense that all will not be well,

Victor's character might be read as a malign tempter (King's novel gives him the key command of Hamlet's ghost, 'Remember'), drawing Louis on to an evil act (why else show him the cemetery and then warn him not to go there?). Later, Victor warns him that 'the barrier was not meant to be crossed' but he was the one who showed Louis that it could be.

The difference here with *Silver Bullet* is that different generic elements sometimes complement one another, and that intertextual allusion is more than just simple referencing. Like *Silver Bullet*, there is a further appropriation of the 'double dream' device, with Creed waking from a nightmare still to find Victor at his bedside. However, here the technique effectively problematizes the boundary between borderline states of sleep and waking (Louis says 'I don't like this dream' to which Victor replies: 'Who said you were dreaming?') and when Louis tries to distance himself from his 'dream', throwing back the sheets, he reveals his muddy feet.

Victor, King's second foray into using ghost figures in a comic-horror sense after *Creepshow*, is given a range of powers – he can levitate, appear and disappear at will and, later,Louis is able to walk right through him. He appears to know what will happen but also issues warnings to Louis. The difference between Louis' perception of Victor and that of Rachel, who cannot see him but can hear something, makes for dramatic (and comic) irony but is strangely inconsistent. Victor comes to be like Hopkirk in the TV drama series *Randall and Hopkirk (Deceased)* (Roy Ward Baker, 1969–71), popping up to deliver a comment and then disappearing just as quickly. Rachel, waking on the plane to Chicago, casts the previous scene with her sister as a nightmare but the dream sequence is unsignalled and exactly where it starts is unclear, suggesting the borderline between sleep/walking and life/death has become porous, especially since we then cut to a shot of Victor sitting a few rows back from her, unseen and smiling. He then holds the boarding door open and prompts the car-rental receptionist to find a car for her, however beaten-up. He can affect objects and other characters in the real world but it appears to be an effort for him and, here, it is not clear why he is helping Rachel to get home as he states later that it will not end well – giving his actions the appearance of a trap. He declares to us more than to her (she cannot hear) that this is the 'end of the line' and that 'I'm not allowed any further' but there is no explanation as to why. Rachel rallies and says 'I'm sure everything will be fine' to which Victor adds 'I'm not' before disappearing. That said, the generic impressions surrounding his character are inconsistent rather than being contradictory, as in *Silver Bullet*.

There are some effective moments of horror, such as the foley effect of peeling the dead cat from a frost-covered lawn. Similarly, there is an element of restraint in the images of gore – the cross-cutting of the family picnic with the racing truck and the toddler following the kite focuses on a single frame of a bloodied shoe (like Ray Bowers in *Stand by Me* and Loman in *Maximum Overdrive*, both drawing on Billy the Kid shooting a man out of his boots in Arthur Penn's 1957 *The Left-Handed Gun*). The slow motion and father's kneeling scream are a little clichéd but the 'mini-montage' of snapshots of mother and baby, father and baby and family together leads well enough into Louis poring over photos in the kitchen. At the end, Cage stalks Rachel off camera and we only hear Rachel scream and see a flash-cut of the moment the truck struck Cage, his last moment of life.

Unfortunately, some fruitful generic tension gives way in the final section of the film to a clumsy realization of the supposed demonic boy as a Chucky-like figure. Since *The Exorcist*, the possessed child has become so much parodied that a snarling sound effect is not enough to create an unsettling scene. The quick shot of the wound that Jud, kneeling by the bed, receives to his Achilles tendon takes our eye from the obvious small puppet arm that makes it. The discordant music, the screwed up face of Cage, the virtual standing on the chest of an adult victim, all feels like the dominant stylistic motifs of the low-budget *Puppetmaster* films (David Schmoeller, 1989). More snarling sounds and the inexplicable vampiric gesture of biting Jud's neck suggest both a crudity and confusion in the film's conception and realization of monstrosity.

Generic confusion is reflected in weaknesses in the script (Zelda reappears although no one has moved her corpse to the reanimating burial ground) and technical flaws (in their final confrontation, the eyelines of Cage and Rachel do not match). However, up until the final ten minutes, the generic balance between family drama, aided by a restrained use of gore and ambiguity around the figure of Victor, and a darker, philosophical horror film is mostly maintained. Even in the denouement, the film almost redeems itself. Louis turns stalker himself and, as he looks through Jud's house, a transformation in the mise-en-scène takes place, with an ordinary house transformed into expressionist space for the living dead – misty, muddy and the family pictures all lopsided. with even a creaking sound like a ship at sea, slightly reminiscent of Barker's reanimated house in *Hellraiser* (1987) and foreshadowing *1408* (2007). Cage's final actions evoke the clumsy sweetness of JF Sebastian's toys in *Blade Runner*, declaring that it is 'not fair' and wandering round the corner in an attempt at a tantrum, but he collapses drunkenly, pulling a final face at Louis, and we have a flash cut of the beautiful child he was, holding his kite.

However, derivative generic horror elements predominate. Sudden movement into the frame cannot disguise the lack of dramatic tension. Rachel's hanging body suddenly falls on Louis from an attic door and Cage, a virtual double for Chucky at this stage, flies down (clearly a dummy on a wire) and there are several ridiculous close shots of Louis fighting with a doll (which, like similar shots at the end of 'Cat From Hell', undermine the horror of the scene). The final attempt at a poignant scene does not work as overt horror motifs overwhelm family drama (the motivation for which has been left behind). The romantic piano score does not overcome the inconsistency of Louis embracing Rachel, knowing that she is not really his wife (she is missing an eye and oozing blood). We cut to black after she reaches for a knife, we hear a 'No', a bloody strike and then The Ramones' rock and roll title track comes up abruptly on the closing credits. This final scene could work as a delusional love being greater than any sense of physical repulsion but we have not really seen that in Louis' character up to this point. Man's heart may be 'stonier', according to Crandall, but here it also seems weaker. Whereas Rachel has to cope with the circumstances around the loss of her sister, Louis seeks an 'easier' path, avoiding the reality of death, ultimately leading to his own.

Pet Sematary II (Mary Lambert, 1992)

The sequel, also directed by Mary Lambert, feels more like an unambitious remake and is a good example of how intertextual cleverness cannot overcome generic shortcomings. The film opens with knowing self-referentiality. Jeff Matthews (Edward Furlong) sees his mother, Renee (Darlanne Flueghel), a horror movie 'scream queen', electrocuted when a special effect goes wrong. Later, in a nice metatextual touch, Lambert shows him watching a clip of Flueghel in Sergio Leone's *Once Upon a Time in America* (1984). It is hard not to see Furlong's performance through the prism of *Terminator II* (released two years later), also concerned with feckless parenting. The demonic Sheriff Gus Gilbert (Clancy Brown) is a stereotypically abusive step-father to Drew (Jason McGuire) – he is drawn to drink, violence (shooting Zowie), ribbing Drew about his weight and grubbily pawing Drew's mother, Amanda. When Gus is murdered, and then miraculously reanimated as a more docile individual, Drew feels for the first time as if they are 'a real family' at breakfast. Although Gus eats like a pig, Drew pushes a flap of skin to hide his neck wound in a symbolic action that acts as a precursor of Sarah Conner's discussion of fatherhood at the gas station in *Terminator II*.[7] Drew would rather have a member of the undead as a parent, provided he is more socially responsible towards his family, suggesting in both films the rarity of such virtues.

However, the soundtrack, including The Jesus and Mary Chain's 'Reverence' and The Ramones' 'Poison Heart', like the inappropriate rock used for *Carrie II*, undermines the visual generic references. Unlike his character John Conner in *Terminator II*, where at least he is involved in a cash-point card scam, Jeff and the school environment hardly suggests teen rebellion. Whilst Furlong himself is a slight figure, the 'bully' who picks on him, Clyde Parker (Jared Rushton) barely conveys a sense of credible threat. Drew and Jeff's chatting on their bikes on the way to school makes this feel more like the world of Marty in *Silver Bullet* or Todd on his way to school in *Apt Pupil*; like the two previous films in this chapter, the inclusion of flashes of nudity in the dream sequences and the use of ex-porn star Traci Lords singing 'Love Never Dies' only serves to underline that the narrative's deep structure is that of wholesome family film with a veneer of generic horror superimposed on top and aspiring to a higher age rating than its narrative can really deliver.

The 'horror' is derived from a list of predictable stylistic features such as sudden movement and noise (a cat leaping into shot in the animal hospital). Jeff's father, Chase (Anthony Edwards), has a dream of his wife, which might suggest the working of evil through dreams (like his son's earlier) but it seems more like a gratuitous sex scene in a low quality blue colour wash. The idea of the re-animated corpse wanting to shower and worrying about making a mess on the carpet is a nice touch but the shift into a zombie narrative, like the first film, does not really work. On several occasions, King has chosen to work closely with George A. Romero, who is closely identified with the zombie sub-genre. Several of King's monsters exhibit zombie-like tendencies as if he is drawn to the type but without necessarily appreciating the conventions and constrictions associated with it. Romero's narratives work because they are set in very confined locations (a farmhouse, shopping mall, or military facility) and carry a metaphorical weight. In King's work there is no sense of the zombie as a metaphor for the mass, for consumerism or for twentieth century modernism. To bring zombies out of their generic element makes them look ridiculous. Chase sequences become redundant as the undead cannot move very fast (the stiff, lurching walking movements of Arnie in *Terminator* films are smoothed over by giving him a motorbike as a means of transport). Here, Amanda does not realize her lover is a lumbering corpse until he is already in bed with her, and the same lack of pace occurs as Gus and the dog supposedly 'chase' Jeff through his house. In contrast to chase sequences in films like *Alien 3* (David Fincher), Steadicam here underscores this problem rather than solving it.

Overall, this is a pale echo of the original. The problems are generic and cannot be papered over with intertextuality. A slow motion, *Cujo*-style leap through the window by the possessed Zowie does not provide a moment of dramatically-engaging shock, and when the gang sit around telling ghost stories, the comparison with *Stand by Me* makes this seem flat and humourless, in both writing and performance. There are intertextual references to the thematic undertone of *Terminator II* (using a central cast member, similar familial relationships and even using a close-up shot of a squashed object, here a potato, as Gus drives off in pursuit of Jeff and Amanda) but it does not have the complexity of characterization, structure or, it must be said, budget (less than a tenth of James Cameron's epic), to carry it off. It is perhaps not surprising that Mr King did not give permission for his name to be used in the title.

Sleepwalkers (Mick Garris, 1992)

Sleep'walkers. N. Nomadic shape-shifting creatures with human and feline origins. Vulnerable to the deadly scratch of the cat, the sleepwalker feeds upon the life force of virginal human females. Probable source of the vampire legend.

Chillicoathe Encyclopaedia of Arcane Knowledge, 1884.

Central to audience reaction to this film is its conception of monstrosity. The definition above appears on screen in the opening frames of *Sleepwalkers*, possibly displaced from an early concept of *Salem's Lot*, which, originally, was to feature a similar introduction to the novel.[8] King introduces us to a new monster: a strange hybrid of vampire and Egyptian cat-god and one that appears to contain the seeds of its own destruction. It is incestuous, raising questions from the outset about its likely longevity. The final shot of the opening titles shows the screen apparently slashed by a set of claws accompanied by a cat-like hiss, foreshadowing the demise of the central pairing. However, questions remain about where these creatures have come from, how they developed, how they procreate and why there are only two left. They appear to display vampire-like teeth in their half-way state but become more feline after full metamorphosis. The extent to which the pair can make themselves invisible at will is inconsistent and shifts the film into cartoon territory again as, like super heroes, they reveal their special powers as the need arises. On the DVD for *The Shining* (1997), King recalls how the Studio's first choice director (whom he does not name) came up with lots of 'crazy' ideas such as a history for the creatures (and even their own planet). In retrospect, a back-story might have been helpful. Mary's final combustion on being scratched by a cat is rather dramatic and although it has been suggested as a possibility from the opening titles, it still begs the question of why she goes outside if she knows such a threat is possible.

The film opens with allusions to a contemporary erotic thriller, the beginning of *Basic Instinct* (Paul Verhoeven, 1991), with a long-take, panning past a windswept beach, waving palms and busy cops on to a crime scene. It is only when we reach the house previously occupied by the Bradys that we see what marks this scene as unusual – the presence of many cats, left hanging. However, these are not markers of crime drama but rather a crude attempt at horror. *Star Wars'* Mark Hamill, in an uncredited role as Lieutenant Jennings, initiates the clumsily-expository dialogue from his side-kick cop, who provides us with facts about the last known occupants, and the cop's question: 'What d'you think happened here?', answered by his superior's 'I dunno but somebody sure doesn't like cats', seems more funny than horrific.

As soon as the cops enter the house, we are immediately presented with a series of horror clichés. Despite the fact that it is daylight outside, no one opens the curtains, relying instead on flashlights. We alternate between a reverse tracking shot as the pair pass further into the house and POV shots of what they see (blood on the wall and a cat's corpse). Although this is a modern dwelling, the oblique camera angle, the darkness and the hushed dialogue ('looks like the place has been empty for a hundred years'), convey a greater impression of entering a haunted house. The echoing effect on the soundtrack is motivated as we share the POV of the cops as they slowly approach a closed door; a hand enters the frame to open the door and a cat predictably jumps out, with a squeal. Director Mick Garris, in the first of several outings at the helm of Stephen King adaptations, attempts to reanimate genre clichés with fluid camerawork and does provide a nice second jump by allowing us a moment to recover before an emaciated corpse falls out of the cupboard. However, as critic Nigel Floyd points out, Garris 'deploys every kinetic camera movement and unusual angle at his disposal to weave some clever but redundant visual patterns around an essentially pointless plot'.[9] Scenes such as when Mary slaps Charles tread a very fine line between the effective and the ludicrous. Here, Garris cuts between a reverse tracking shot of the mother advancing and a forward tracking shot as Charles backs away. Like the tracking shots up the stairwells in both their house and Tanya's, and the running into the cemetery for the picnic (not the most romantic setting, it must be said), the fluidity of Garris' camerawork, could be said to show a director exploring generic possibilities, although the camera tracking over underwear to signal a sex scene is such a cliché that it renders any romantic or erotic potential redundant.

The tight shot of Mary's sudden appearance in front of Tanya (Mädchen Amick) brandishing some scissors, only to cut her a rose, seems more of a parody of an unstable psychotic than genuinely unsettling. King's first full-length original script must bear some responsibility for this ineffective attempt to play with generic elements. The mock ironic quips ('It finishes you somehow') increase in number in the second half of the film, and Mary's character becomes more and more outlandish as she commits one act of violence after another (smashing Tanya's father in the head with a vase, breaking Mrs Roberts' arm and throwing her through a window, before biting off the fingers of a cop and also snapping his arm). This reaches the level of slapstick when she smashes the heads of two cops together as they stand bewildered before her house.

A key part of contemporary horror is the delivery of spectacular, visceral abuse of the body by special effects. Disbelief is hard to suspend when 'effects' are sometimes not that 'special' – the cop who is picked up and impaled on the picket fence is obviously a dummy; Charles' and later Mary's wrestling with a rather unconvincing cuddly toy masquerading as a murderous cat seems ridiculous; Mary manages to make two patrol cars explode with a single gunshot each, and the foley department gives us a sound like a gunshot with a silencer when Charles' eye is removed with a corkscrew, making that action at first unclear. Most ridiculous of all, perhaps, is that the cop in Tanya's house manages to fire numerous shots that miss Mary, standing only about ten feet away, and then is stabbed in the back by Mary with a cob of corn.

There is also a rather strange generic mismatching in some elements of the visual style of the film. Although the pair, the boy especially, seems to be quite at ease in 1980s America, much of the iconography around them seems, for no apparent reason, stuck in the 1950s. In the first shot we have of Charles, he is about to carve a T in his arm whilst fawning over a yearbook photo of Tanya. As Charles and Mary make love, the pair listen to a 45 single (Santo and Johnny Farina's 1959 instrumental 'Sleepwalk') played on a fairly ancient-looking record player. The car that Charles drives, and Tanya's painfully virtuous character, seem a throwback to an earlier age (certainly she feels at some distance from her fellow pupils, who do not share her prudishness about sex). There is an almost anachronistic coyness about the chaste and cheesy, lengthy, grins exchanged between the two; the father picking the girl up, acting almost as a chaperone; and Charles sweeping Mary up in his arms and carrying her up the stairs, with the camera stopping firmly on this side of the bedroom door as it is closed in front of us. The fact that Charles changes at the moment he kisses Tanya in the cemetery suggests that sexual desire is equated with the revelation of monstrosity and that boys are just monsters beneath the surface, looking for virgins to deflower and steal their life-force. Perhaps such cultural anachronisms convey a sense of the oppressive conservatism of small-town America or that the pair have outlived their time, but neither is really convincing. When we see Tanya working in the foyer of the local cinema, she is wearing a personal stereo but the sound she is listening to, and that we hear on the soundtrack, is Berry Gordy's 1962 song 'Do You Love Me?'

There are other strangely anachronistic generic elements elsewhere. The cop disturbed by Charles speeding past, the ensuing car chase, the call to base, the sudden wheel-spins to change direction, the upbeat rock music, the wheel-level camera positioning, the ground level shot blowing up leaves and Charles' means of entering and exiting via the windows – all evoke the iconic CBS TV show *Dukes of Hazard* (1979–85) and ABC's *Starsky and Hutch* (1975–79). While the car used in the film, a Pontiac Firebird Tans Am (also used in *Creepshow 2*), does not appear regularly in either show, the weight of visual references in this sequence makes it feel like it belongs in a 1970s prime-time TV show.

Midway through the film, however, there is quite an abrupt change of generic style. The Sleepwalkers' first victim is Mr Fallows, Charles' English teacher, given to outbursts of sadistic violence: slamming his ruler down on the knuckles of unlucky students (another throwback). The generic shift is signalled by the rock music played in Charles' car (Extreme's 'Monster') as he is pulled over by Fallows, who has been following him. Confronting him over his falsified records, the teacher is shown in extreme low angle, looming into the car (as he had been shown in close-up with a wide-angle lens, putting his face right up to the boy passing a lewd sketch in class earlier). Whereas, up to this point, Charles had seemed the model of politeness with everyone, now he suddenly shifts into the wise-cracking, self-aware killer of a slasher film. The teacher makes a sexual pass, to which Charles replies: 'People should really keep their hands to themselves,' and proceeds to sever Fallows', giving it back with the quip 'Here's yours'. Once such lines are used, it is impossible to generate real fear in an audience – the gore and any potential horror are undermined by a parodying aesthetic. The pursuit of the teacher through the bushes in POV Steadicam makes him look ridiculous, especially since he runs straight into a tree and the rotating shot from above of the ferocious feeding on the man's neck looks more like a vampire parody. Once Garris starts to openly play with horror conventions, it is impossible to take them seriously, moments later. Having despatched the cop with a pencil, Charles declares him to be 'Cop kebab' and declares: 'I don't think you fired a warning shot officer' before shooting him with his own gun. Similarly, Charles' calm reaction to Tanya's resistance to being raped: 'I don't think you're entering into the spirit of this', places the film firmly in the parody genre inhabited by films like *Scary Movie* (Keenan Ivory Wayans, 2000).

However, despite all the preceding points, the film does have some effective sections. There is a moment during the first car chase when Charles, having allowed the police car to pull alongside unaware that there is a cat in the car, suddenly undergoes a facial change. Admittedly, it is very clearly shot against a blue screen but, as an early example of 'morphing', it does provide the cop and us, with a momentary, uncanny shock. The subsequent ability to make both himself and the car invisible may associate itself with the kind of cartoonish effect one might expect in a programme like NBC's *Knight Rider* (1982–86), primarily designed for an adolescent audience, but in combination with distorted POV of the cat, who can still see the car, it seems unsettling (more so in fact than the whole of *Christine*).

There are direct intertextual allusions as Tanya relaxes in a bath and lies back with a flannel over her face. Garris' tight shot on her face pulls back to give us a split-second shot of Charles, mortally wounded, and without fictive markers, we do not know if this was just a dream. It is not a bathroom scene that relies on a slow build up like David Cronenberg's parasite attack in *Shivers* (1975), or overtly misogynistic threats of violence via a phallic glove of knives as in *Nightmare on Elm Street* (Wes Craven, 1984), although Tanya bears a strong physical similarity to Nancy (Heather Langenkamp) here, but as a basic intrusion into the most personal of spaces (surely one of the key points about *Psycho*'s shower scene), it is oddly effective, the more so for its brevity. The iconic shot, craning up from ground level, of the lawn and roof absolutely covered in cats, is certainly eerie but, without a clear causal connection between Sleepwalkers and why they fear cats, it is difficult to generate a real sense of threat. Hence when Tanya is shown the dying Charles, there is little sense of pathos or tragedy and, equally, not really the kind of horror that might be intended when Mary suggests they dance. Indeed, the miraculously animated corpse, stumbling around in a parody of a dance to the same song used in the opening dance/love scenes, is more ridiculous than unsettling.

Generically, perhaps the most potentially-interesting aspect of the film is in the nature of the relationship between the Sleepwalkers. Examples of incest do not abound in films shown on terrestrial TV. It may say more about the 'ghettoization' of horror – a genre into which the powers-that-be do not delve too deeply and therefore miss plotlines which would be deemed unacceptable in other genres. In some ways, the pair has a parent-child relationship – she asks if he is going out, fishing for some juicy gossip and expresses a wish that the girl is 'nice'. It is a very odd *ménage-à-trois*, in effect based on self-interest, which means that the mother actively wants her son to seduce and murder a series of virgins. He asks her if she is jealous, to which she replies: 'Shall I be jealous? Would you like that?' In order to live, he has to 'cheat' on her and she has to share him sexually. Later, when he comes home, she quizzes him but now not as an anxious parent, rather as a Queen needing to be fed by a drone. She asks him how far he went with the girl, but not in the sense of a censorious parent – more to determine the likely virginal state of the girl. Their source of nourishment sets up a basic problem. As he says: 'What kind of a girl would go out with a guy she just met?', to which she answers: 'Not a very nice one, I suppose'. There is a co-dependency that bonds them together, but also makes them vulnerable – if one is caught, the other will die. Later she pleads: 'Did you get me anything?', casting her more in the light of a needy drug addict with him as her dealer. The old depend on the young to hunt for them, he reminds her: 'What if something happened to me? You'll starve'. He is dependent on her emotionally and cannot bring himself to consummate a relationship with Tanya, in part because he feels like he would be cheating on his lover.

In a film with an overtly incestuous plotline, the in-joke of the murder scene, where a number of King's favourite horror directors all share a few seconds of screen-time, is strangely suitable. With narrative momentum sacrificed to ironic gags to accompany a series of kills, decontextualized intertextuality is foregrounded. King himself as the Cemetery Caretaker witters on that 'I'm not taking the rap for this,' followed by Clive Barker, Tobe Hooper (Forensic Technicians), Joe Dante and John Landis (Lab Technician and Assistant respectively), minus George A. Romero who was originally supposed to appear in their place. The planting of references for King fans to spot includes Tanya, in school, responding to Charles' story with exactly the same simple phrase, 'I liked it', as used in a parallel situation by Carrie White, suggesting a bond with a girl who feels herself to be an outsider, and the film playing when Charles goes to see Tanya at the cinema is *They Bite* – Garris' next project.

Sleepwalkers has some promising features, especially in its genre-challenging incestuous plotline. The narrative does have a tragic inevitability about it in the way the cats gradually gather around the Bradys' new house, copiously avoiding the traps laid for them but, unlike the gathering flocks in Hitchcock's *The Birds* (1963), also alluded to in the opening setting of Bodega Bay, the lack of generic coherence in conceptions of monstrosity, linked to anachronistic cultural iconography, undermines the film's ability to unsettle viewers.

Conclusion
King recognizes three hierarchical levels of emotional reaction involved in writing horror – terror, which he terms 'the finest emotion' but if he cannot achieve this, he will 'try to horrify' and if he cannot do this, 'I'll go for the gross-out'.[10] The last category is relatively straightforward – the gag reflex often associated with low quality horror (in print and on-screen). Here we might place the digression about Lard Ass Hogan in *Stand by Me*, the 'Father's Day' section of *Creepshow* or the emotionally-uninvolved despatching of victims in *Pet Sematary II*. More difficult is the distinction between 'terror' and 'horror', although a useful parallel might be the

difference between empathy and sympathy. 'Sympathy' implies a fellow-feeling for someone outside the self – a feeling of pity but also of a residual distance; a sense of thankfulness that the individual in distress is not us. 'Empathy' is a step further, where we might put ourselves literally in the place of someone in pain, distress or misfortune. It is this, more refined, notion of identification that is correspondingly the more difficult to evoke in art. In *On Writing*, King shows an interest in the mechanics of how his writing works, but that same curiosity does not extend to film. In this chapter, we see several examples of films that initially aspire to 'horror-terror' but which rapidly descend to the 'gross-out', often due to a lack of apparent understanding of the genre in which they purport to operate and a slippage into the style of anachronistic parody or children's film.

Notes
1. Stephen King, *Night Shift*, op. cit., p. 12.
2. Stephen King, *Danse Macabre*, op. cit., p. 86.
3. See Walter Evans: 'stirred by innocence and purity … by the full moon, which for millennia has variously symbolized chastity, change, and romance, the Wolfman guiltily wakes to the mystery of the horrible alterations in his body, mind and his physical desires – alterations which are completely at odds with the formal strictures of his society.' Cited in Jonathan Lake Crane, *Terror and Everyday Life: Singular Moments in the History of the Horror Film* (London and New Delhi: Sage Publications, 1994), pp. 26–27.
4. See Barbara Creed, 'Dark Desires' in Steven Cohan and Ina Rae Hark, (eds.), *Screening the Male: Exploring Masculinities in the Hollywood Cinema*, (London; New York: Routledge, 1993), pp. 124–125.
5. Stephen King, *Pet Sematary*, op. cit., p. 290.
6. Ibid., p. 257.
7. Sarah Conner (Linda Hamilton) in *Terminator II*: 'Watching John with the machine, it was suddenly so clear … It would never hurt him or shout at him or get drunk and hit him or say it was too busy to spend time with him. And it would die to protect him. Of all the would-be fathers that came over the years, this thing, this machine, was the only thing that measured up. In an insane world, it was the sanest choice.'
8. Stephen King, 'Interview with Michael Kilgore', in Underwood and Miller (eds.), op. cit., p. 102
9. Nigel Floyd, *Sleepwalkers* – a review, *Sight and Sound* 2:4 (August, 1992), p. 63.
10. Stephen King, *Danse Macabre* (London: Warner Books, 1993), p. 40; See also p. 39: 'terror on top, horror below it, and lowest of all, the gag reflex of revulsion.'

CHAPTER FOUR

BOYS TO MEN: RITES-OF-PASSAGE

'Rites-of-passage' is an often-used, rarely-defined term in discussions of both literature and film. For our purposes here, it is taken to mean a ritual associated with a key phase of maturation in a young person's life, often including an increased awareness of mortality and the possibility of loss. As such, it has both universal applicability and cultural-specific manifestations. A potential source of greater precision for the term could be in anthropology and studies of cultural rituals. Ethnographer Arnold Van Gennep identified three phases in rites-of-passage: separation, and re-incorporation.[1] In the first phase, individuals withdraw from their existing community and move towards an unknown place or status. There is often a detachment from the former self in this phase, signified by symbolic actions and rituals. In the third phase, they re-enter society, having completed the rite and assumed a new identity. Victor Turner refined Van Gennep's ideas, noting that in the transitional state, the liminal phase, individuals remained in a limbo, an ambiguous period characterized by humility, seclusion, tests, sexual ambiguity, and communitas (defined as an unstructured community where all members are equal).[2]

As a narrative form, rites-of-passage is difficult to make dramatically effective as it is overtly concerned with a character's personal development, which needs to be empathetic and convincing without becoming cloyingly sentimental. An obvious pitfall is lack of pace, linked to an overly-sententious narrative producing a purely 'genre film', which viewers feel to be too bland and forgettable. The means of character development is important, particularly how conflict with engaging characters is generated and the pace sustained. Usually, such films cannot fall back on crowd-pleasing elements like graphic violence, explicit sexual content or socially unacceptable language to 'spice up' predictable situations and dialogue.

For the generic label to have resonance, the learning experience must be pro and life-changing. This might occur even at the level of religious faith (the itself certainly carries such overtones). Children or adolescents are often i characters, providing opportunities for breakthrough performances by unknown actors but also notoriously difficult for directors to get right, and just as learners are key, so are those who have wisdom to pass on (often pseudo father-figures) and their relationship with the learner, which may sit at the heart of the narrative. If the learning process becomes too prominent, the dialogue becomes overly sententious and then, as Michael Ryan and Douglas Kellner note, 'once the generic conventions are foregrounded, the genre can no longer operate successfully as a purveyor of ideology.'[3]

Since rites-of-passage narratives are often personal in nature, they lend themselves to projections of authorial biographical relevance. Some of the most powerful King adaptations seem to focus on relationships across generations, particularly (surrogate) father-son relationships, with limited casts, theatrical limitation of location, and feature a strong sense of loss as inherent in the transition from innocence to experience (as in *Hearts in Atlantis* and *Apt Pupil* and less successfully in *Dreamcatcher*), allowing King to tap into powerful semi-biographical feelings of childhood and its passing. However, whilst in King's case that may be partially so – the discovery of the body in *Stand by Me,* for example, may be more a reflection of the desire by audiences to elide first person narrators with an identifiable author figure. The notion of events 'on the cusp' creates a strongly elegiac tone in work like *Stand by Me*, especially since the boy-protagonists seem to intuitively feel the transitory nature of that moment in their lives. Like the genre itself, the acquisition of adult status is an ephemeral concept – age plays a part, certainly, but the gaining of sober perspectives on life, a realization of the darkness and the deceptive nature of life are also important. What perhaps marks the films in this section is a willingness to recognize human duplicity at the same time as not denying other more life-affirming possibilities.

Stand by Me (Rob Reiner, 1986)

'The boy's just being honest. It's a privilege of boys. A privilege that men must sometimes give up.' (Dussander in *Apt Pupil*)

Initial reaction to *Stand by Me*, based on the novella 'The Body' collected in *Different Seasons*, was mixed. It was the first film adaptation to avoid overt linkage with King's name and preview audiences expecting horrific content were a little disappointed. The last minute name-change, dictated by the availability of the B.B. King title-track, allowed an unexpected focus on a sense of brotherhood and solidarity at a key moment in the lives of the characters. Reiner certainly deserves credit for eliciting impressive performances from his child stars. His touch was less sure in *North* (1994), a child-centred narrative that was a critical and commercial flop, but it seems that with a background as a successful and Emmy-award-winning actor in the 1970s in the CBS sitcom *All in the Family* (1971–79), it is as a director of character-centred dramas that he has gained most success. Both *When Harry Met Sally* (1989) and *Misery* (1990) have been produced as stage-plays and both display the same intelligently-scripted, human-based drama. Reiner should share credit for the depth of characterization and poignant humour, not just with his young cast but with writers Raynold Gideon and Bruce Evans, who (in collaboration with Reiner) manage to craft an articulate script that is intelligible but also sounds true to the characters.

A three-stage rites-of-passage structure, as outlined by both Van Gennep and Turner, certainly appears in the film of *Stand by Me*. A pre-liminal phase establishes the boys in their home environment, a liminal phase covers the journey itself (which only lasts two days and a single night but seems longer as it occupies such a central part of the film) and a brief post-liminal section that shows the boys' return, their reintegration into society and how they have been changed by their experience. In terms of thematic content, the narrative is centrally concerned with processes of maturation, a growing awareness of mortality and an increased sense of disillusionment as to what adult life will be like. This is represented in the surface narrative by a series of tests, rituals and punishments, both real and imagined.

Of the four stories in *Different Seasons*, three have been adapted into effective films (*Apt Pupil*, *The Shawshank Redemption* and *Stand by Me*). It could be simply that they are better stories than the vast majority of King's output elsewhere, in particular that in the novella format he finds the need for the precision of a short story but slightly more freedom to expand or digress where he wishes. What makes *Different Seasons* particularly powerful is the construct of time – all four stories are about characters on the cusp of changes in their lives. *Four Past Midnight* deals with time too, but more so in perceptual terms – the possibility of cracks in reality and the potential existence of alternative universes running parallel to our own. *Different Seasons* is rooted very much in the human domain – there are no paranormal happenings here (unlike *It* and *Dreamcatcher*, which also feature all-male groups bonding for a common cause). Also the particular age that King focuses on in 'The Body' and 'Apt Pupil' is male adolescence (one an ensemble piece, one a loner). The ensemble male 'bonding' narrative also appears in *It* and *Dreamcatcher* but neither quite manages to capture the sense of a moment in time, glimpsed even as it vanishes, as well as this first example. All the boys sense the special quality of their being together on this shared adventure – even before they get very far, they describe the experience as 'really a good time' (Vern), 'the best' (Chris), 'a blast' (Teddy). The voiceover cuts in to underline the point, albeit a little heavy-handedly – 'There was more and we all knew it. Everything was there and around us. We knew exactly who we were and exactly where we were going. It was good.' Like Wordsworth's 'emotion recollected in tranquility', such statements are open to the charge of nostalgia, particularly when trying to recreate the sense of childhood from the position of an adult, can seem like an imposition.[4] However the story entitled 'The Body' is placed beneath a subheading 'The Fall of Innocence' and it is this quality which creates the poignancy in both story and film, which follows the written narrative fairly closely. It dramatizes a moment when all four of the protagonists sense there is the potential still to change their lives (fast disappearing perhaps, especially for Teddy and Chris) and that after this adventure, things will never be the same again. It represents a defining moment of their lives up to this time, but also where their lives will lead from here.

According to Van Gennep, death underlines the rites-of-passage process and despite the fact that it is not a horror tale, something horrific does lie at the heart of the novella and the movie – literally, this is the body of the title; the mortal remains of Ray Brower, a twelve–year-old boy who, just like any of the protagonists might have done, went picking berries and was struck and killed by a train. As King has frequently noted, a key attraction of the horror genre is the possibility of playing out one's own death vicariously at one remove and the narrative opens with an adult Gordie Lachance trying to understand the nonsensical death of his childhood friend, Chris, in attempting to break up an argument in a fast-food queue. Random, senseless, shockingly sudden – these seem to be the features of death here. The boys are energized by the possibility of seeing a dead body and claiming it as theirs: a kind of perverse treasure, which will guarantee them notoriety and possibly the height of their dreams of fame – their pictures in the papers. More broadly, the case of Ray Brower is carefully followed by both gangs of boys (the younger gang know instantly who is being referred to; the older boys we see listening to a radio bulletin later) – this one individual representing the potential fate of any one of them.

However, more precisely it is the working out of Gordie's feelings about his dead brother, Denny, that really lie at the heart of the narrative, in book and film. The ability of bad parents to keep on damaging their children, nicely represented by the close-up on a mailbox decorated with 'Home Sweet Home' just before being smashed by a baseball bat, is something Magistrale considers at length. Gordie's parents are still in a state of shock and we see him, (in flashback) at first ignored at the dinner table as the couple heap questions and praise on the older boy and then ignored around the house in their stupified grief. In a symbolic tableau, we see Mrs Lachance hanging a sheet in the foreground, Mr Lachance in the mid-ground gardening and Gordie, small and ignored, up at the window in the background. At one point Gordie needs his canteen and searches the Miss-Haversham-style shrine of Denny's room, a time capsule to his youthful potential now never to be realized, the plethora of trophies and photos of sporting triumphs standing as a visual indictment of Gordie's own lack of sporting prowess. King presents us with parents who think they have a monopoly on grief and cannot look beyond their own feeling to see how much they are underestimating the emotional turmoil that young people can feel. Gordie even has a nightmare later in the woods about Denny's funeral and his father turning to him and saying: 'It should have been you'. This may be more a sense of projected guilt as we do not see Mr Lachance saying that elsewhere but it is a clear departure from the novella where it is Denny, converted into a monster, returning from the grave still sporting the injuries that killed him, who utters those words. What makes this portrayal of grief unusual is that King has Gordie unsure of his own feelings. The age gap between the brothers means that he does not really feel he knows him and, despite the few glimpses we get of the two together (giving Gordie a special cap, play-fighting and Denny trying to act as his advocate to his parents, praising a story that Gordie has written), Gordie feels a sense of loss, but not as deeply as he feels he should, and it is guilt at this lack of passion as well as being ignored by his parents which gives his character real depth. In the film, Gordie admits to Chris that he did not cry at the funeral but unlike King's novella, which suggests that Gordie does not really know his brother, in the film, Reiner stresses that it is more a matter that Gordie does not know how to express his grief and can only say to Chris, 'I miss him. I really miss him'. In the novella, Gordie reads Ralph Ellison's *The Invisible Man* at school and finds himself identifying with the hero's lack of visibility. This briefly-mentioned, but nonetheless powerful, symbol does not make it to the film but is converted into Gordie's voiceover – 'that summer at home, I had become the invisible boy'. The stolen cap, symbolic of Gordie's bond with his dead brother, becomes elided with the body, which he will not let Ace steal from them at the climax.

In the apparent digression in the shop where Gordie goes to buy provisions, we see how close Denny is to the surface of his thinking. The shopkeeper's wittering about having lost a brother in Korea and the supposedly-comforting religious platitude that 'in the midst of life, we are in death,' triggers a flashback to a family meal where Denny's advocacy of one of Gordie's stories, Gordie's requests for potatoes, and indeed his whole presence, are all being ignored whilst Denny is being urged not to think about girls, who might distract him from future greatness. The shopkeeper's false sentiment, apparently recognizing Gordie from a physical similarity to Denny (not immediately apparent in the casting of John Cusack in that role), his lack of interest in listening to Gordie and the blunt question: 'What do you do?' mark him as yet another unsympathetic adult who judges youngsters by superficial achievements only. The spurious nature of his views and his manipulative nature are a little clearer in the book, where he also overcharges Gordie and tries to cheat him by putting a thumb on the scale whilst weighing goods. Gordie's worldly savviness, his willingness to speak up against injustice, against a more selfish, superficial and exploitative minor character in the shopkeeper – such nuances are lost in the film, where the adult roles are somewhat diminished, focusing more precisely on grief than on adult hypocrisy.

Lengthy digressions are largely eschewed in favour of forward narrative momentum. Reiner cuts the novella's coverage of Gordie's first published story, a derivative piece of tough-talking crime drama, 'Stud City', with a thinly-veiled Gordie-surrogate character involved in a rather grubby sexual encounter and dreaming of escaping his small town. Such a sexual episode would fit the 'Fall of Innocence' subtitle, perhaps, but it would strike a definite post-puberty note and distract from the all-male ensemble interaction that lies at the heart of the film. The story-within-a-story also features the violent death of a brother in a car accident (an attempt by Gordie to imagine the circumstances of Denny's death) but the film deals with this in sporadic flashback as the past affects the fictional present. This is actually a meta-textual reference as both 'Stud City' and 'The Revenge of Lard Ass Hogan' were actual early King short stories, published in 1969 and 1975 respectively, so that Gordie's development very much dramatizes King's own development as a writer.

The pre-liminal phase, accompanied by examples of habitual behaviour, is seen in the scene in the tree-house, where we have a microcosm of male adolescent rituals: playing cards, smoking and sharing jokes (not all of them politically-correct). Adult postures are literally mimicked (Chris putting his cigarette packet up the arm of his T-shirt) and adult language frequently parodied in the expected practice of exchanging curses and insults. It is a group bound by closed rituals (secret knocks), established practices (wiping palms to signify being quits) and clearly demarcated taboo areas (insulting mothers is accepted and even expected, not so fathers). More particularly, they are bound together by an acceptance of difference – Teddy's poor vision and his burned ears; Vern's tubbiness and inability to remember the secret knock; Chris' drunken, abusive father. When Gordie asks Chris, 'Am I weird?', Chris replies 'Definitely... So what? Everyone's weird'. They show, too, a great propensity for laughter – bursting into fits of giggles every few minutes, especially at Teddy's non-sequiturs like 'a pile of shit has 1000 eyes,' which still makes Chris laugh several lines later.

Shared rituals extend to the joke routines themselves – when a breathless Vern tries to explain his exciting news, he is interrupted not once but twice by the others breaking into song at Vern's use of 'I ran all the way home'. His need for attention and recognition is clear in his looking down disconsolately as he cannot find the words (and later how he quickly perks up at the idea of getting a medal) and when he manages the simple question 'You guys wanna go see a dead body?' he has their full and immediate attention. The fact that there is no need to explain references and back-story between each other, the familiar ease with which language and jokes are all understood, is symptomatic of long-term relationships, meaning that, here, 'We all knew what Vern meant right away' cues Reiner's dissolve to the scene beneath Vern's house where he is still searching for a jar of pennies he buried and has forgotten. The excitement of any overheard secret, but especially one about a body to boys still excited by treasure maps, is conveyed by the crosscutting from Vern's POV shot of Eyeball and his friend talking about Brower, and Vern, so frantic to hear that he crawls manically along and looks up, getting a faceful of dirt in his eye. The random nature of good and bad fortune is clear here – if you are in the right place, you hear some juicy gossip; if you are in the wrong one, you are hit and killed instantly by a train. Ironically, and perhaps sadly, the camaraderie in the early tree-house scene suggests that Turner's notion of 'communitas' already exists between the boys when they can escape their everyday lives – especially pressure from their families.

The novella uses the image of railway tracks as a symbol of their destiny and, as the boys set out, Reiner tilts up from ground level as the boys walk towards the camera to give us an iconic image of American youth. The railroad, the dominant means of westward expansion in pioneering times, here represents a journey – if not quite into a heart of darkness, then at least a wilderness against which the boys can test themselves. Turner suggests sexual ambiguity as a key factor in ritual behaviour and certainly the boys' dialogue is highly sexualized, both in terms of jokes and insults. As the distance ahead slowly dawns on them, Vern suggests hitch-hiking but Teddy dismisses this as 'pussy' and then articulates the whole point of the experience: 'Vern, did your mother ever have any kids that lived?' Dangers can be sudden and largely unpredictable, such as the appearance of the train whilst the boys are on the bridge, which only Gordie foresees having felt the vibrations in the rail. Reiner gives us a huge wide shot of the landscape with the boys slowly entering the frame bottom left, singing. However the pioneering spirit does not last long as the small matter of food appears to have been completely forgotten.

As Van Gennep suggests, the narrative is very episodic and divides neatly into a series of tests which the boys must overcome. Teddy's self-imposed challenge to the train (which bizarrely shows no sign of slowing down at all) is cross-cut by Reiner like *The Lonedale Operator* (D.W. Griffith, 1911), between the oncoming train, Teddy's resolve to stand his ground and the increasing panic of the other boys. Chris proves his qualities as leader of the gang by manhandling Teddy clear and enduring the wrath of the other boy for his greater good. Teddy is trying to live up to the bravery of his father, who supposedly stormed the beaches at Normandy, but whom we later hear from Milo is actually institutionalized. Teddy's awareness of his family situation, especially his violent and unstable father, his eccentric appearance and character and an oddly-perceptive nature, create an illogical rage, which boils up in him from time to time, that he cannot articulate but which the other boys know and accept.

Amongst the group, adult knowledge is paraded – Chris' warning to Vern, 'If they'd known you were there, they'd have killed you' and Chris' later assertion about the gun, 'It's a 45' to which Gordie replies contemptuously, 'I can see that'. Round the campfire, later, Chris states gnomically that 'a cigar tastes best after supper'. The group repeatedly fall out and make up, the rituals concerning the latter requiring a knowledge of oaths and hand gestures. Even Ace Merrill's bullying observes strict codes, giving Chris the opportunity, after calling him an asshole, to 'take it back', and the mindless vandalism of the baseball game has rules which Ace insists his gang adhere to. The boys' whole existence, and the progress of the narrative, is based around ritualized transgressions: going into forbidden areas (the junkyard, the rail track and the site of the body); touching forbidden things (Chris' procurement of a gun); and perhaps most obviously, using forbidden language (frequent cursing and insults). The insults to each other's mother has a particular status, such as Chris' 'Hey Vern, I think your mum's been out driving again' on seeing the wrecks in the junkyard. As the adult Gordie explains on the voiceover, '[f]inding new and preferably disgusting ways to degrade your friend's mother was always held in high regard.'

As Turner notes, in a rites-of-passage process, role-playing and dares abound. Gordie and Chris race each other but only after Gordie has shouted 'Go' and started. Chris plays with him, adding a mock commentary and applause from a fictional crowd when he wins. It is one of many roles which the boys play with, dramatizing other lives they aspire to or recognize they will never have. When Gordie tells them to shut up, the other three instantly drop into a mixture of parental parody and playground rhyme: 'I don't shut up, I grow up and when I see you I throw up'. Like the song they dip into instinctively to delay Vern's initial story and the little dance number that Teddy and Vern do later to 'My Girl Lollipop', these are shared routines, polished through practice and used to give structure to lives lived out largely in a parental void.

Van Gennep and Turner do not focus on the creation of narratives but for King, as an author, this an important way to come to terms with new experiences. Although, as previously noted, some source references to Gordie's writing are cut, stories from a more oral tradition play a big part in the boys' lives. Vern's initial account of overhearing the location of the body kick-starts the plot but we also get little anecdotes that add local colour, like Milo's fabled instruction to Chopper his dog to attack specific body parts, Chris' account of the theft of the milk money and, most obviously, Gordie's campfire tale. In each case, the myth is seen as more important than reality. Like Vern's disavowal in the novel that his brother has already stolen his buried money, there is a shared willingness to believe the interesting fiction over fact, even in the face of overwhelming evidence to the contrary, such as Teddy's repeating of slogans that refer to his father as a war hero.

Gordie's story about Lard Ass Hogan, strangely unmentioned by Magistrale, marks out the teller as a future writer but is an important episode more widely. Like *Carrie*, it is a tale of an outsider gaining revenge against high school bullies, pupils and teachers alike and ends with a tour de force of visceral excess. King often uses the tale-within-a-tale device (see 'The Revenge of Becky Paulson' in *The Tommyknockers*) but it becomes particularly appropriate amongst teenage boys given to swapping enhanced truths about family, sexual conquests, bravery in the face of adversity – indeed, almost any potential experience is crafted into some kind of myth. The campfire is the ritual place of storytelling and the most obvious example of Turner's notion of 'communitas' with the timing of Gordie's story constituting their version of an after-dinner speech, complete with a smoke. The boys are on a quest to find a body and Gordie uses corporal means to interest his listeners, describing the otherworldly growl and gurgle of Lard Ass' stomach. Interestingly, while King might manage to gross his readers out here, Gordie's narrative, blending extreme disgust with carefully-worded detail ('he sat back and enjoyed what he had created – a complete and total barthorama'), only pleases his peer audience.

The reader's desire for complete closure to their satisfaction is satirized in Teddy's disbelief at the tale's ending, demanding 'then what happened?' In the novella, Gordie states the reason for so-called open endings: 'When you don't know what happens next, that's the end'.[5] What should be the mark of a successful tale (that you care enough about a character to wonder what might happen beyond the end of the narrative) is taken literally as a sign of betrayal by Teddy, who fills in the end with a more satisfying one (Lard Ass goes home, shoots his father and joins the Texas Rangers). It is a thinly-veiled attempt by King to answer literal-minded critics whose expectations have somehow not been met, prompting disappointment and even anger. Vern, as representative of a different kind of literal-minded reader, cannot see past pedantic, irrelevant details: 'did Lard Ass have to pay?' Gordie tries to give his listeners what they want by suggesting that maybe Lard Ass went home and celebrated with a couple of cheeseburgers, but King is underlining how the tale is clearly weaker when the author merely reflects what his audience want rather than what his characters might do, given the internal logic and artistic integrity of the story.

The campfire 'debates' show Reiner's craftsmanship at its best in a cinematic version of 'communitas'. In a slow tracking shot (or it could almost be a pan from the fire's POV) we see a series of question-and-answer topics that engage the boys' attention – the shot holding Gordie's question 'What's Goofy?' dissolves into Vern's 'If you could only have one food for the rest of your life, what would it be?' so that, momentarily, we almost have a two-shot. Topics jockey for our attention and the dissolves convey both the passing of time and the circularity of debate, so that we come back to Chris' 'It can't be a dog – he wears a hat and drives a car' in a credible way through the logic of apparent non sequiturs. Hypothetical questions around food (a prime concern for tubby Vern) alternate with understanding how the fictional world of Disney matches up with reality and how TV reflects but also distorts the world around them, such as the belief that TV shows are fixed and that *Wagon Train* never seems to get anywhere. They question the meanings of some fictions in their life but not the pleasure, and maybe even the necessity, of believing in them.

As we move closer to the climax, there is an element of looking forward to the return: Van Gennep's reincorporation phase. The potential pomposity of Chris and Gordie's discussion about the profound changes about to happen when Gordie starts college courses, and Chris will be making birdcages and ashtrays, is undercut by Teddy and Vern's debate about who would win a fight between Mighty Mouse and Superman. Teddy is dismissive of the issue as one is only a cartoon, whereas 'Superman is a real guy'. Vern nods in agreement, concluding: 'Be a good fight though.' The exchange between Chris and Gordie, possibly reflecting King's own feelings towards his long-absent father who walked out on their family when King was just two, does seem a little contrived. Chris may be a mature figure, perhaps, but it stretches credibility to almost breaking point when he replies to Gordie's sarcastic 'Thanks Dad' with 'I wish I was your dad'. The sententious 'Kids lose everything unless there's someone to look out for them ... If your parents won't do it, maybe I should', certainly fits with the underlying theme of the group having to be their own parents (and also with the later argument about Vern wanting to turning back, when Teddy rounds on Chris and says

'What are you, his mother?') but, in linguistic terms, it feels out of joint with what the characters say elsewhere. It also casts the frame-story, and thereby the whole film, in a slightly different light. If Chris has acted as a responsible parent and looked out for Gordie (and the implication is that he has since Gordie has realized his ambition to become a writer), then Gordie as an adult is mourning the loss of a parent, a true parent.

Van Gennep identifies danger as a key part of the tests and challenges in a real rite-of-passage experience and the lives of the boys here are precarious – a fact they perceive, in part: Chris retells a time when he caught Teddy by his hair when he once fell from the tree-house. In reality he saved him but replayed in a dream, he drops him. As is often the case, King's narratives use a series of similar or repeated events so that we realize what potential consequences might be and tension can be raised without always having to deliver an expected outcome. In a narrative based around a journey, we see a series of races: for fun between Gordie and Chris; out of fear, between Gordie and Chopper; and for survival between Vern, Chris and the train. In a rare example of a self-conscious, intertextual reference, the slow-motion race between Gordie and Chris, with Gordie running, head-back like Eric Liddel (Ian Charleson) in *Chariots of Fire* (Hugh Hudson, 1981), is reprised in Gordie's race to the fence pursued by Chopper.

Both the film and King's original story constitute an almost anthropological study of small-town adolescent boys in the 1950s and a sociological study of male 'courtship'. Cinematic versions of rites-of-passage processes often find forward narrative momentum difficult as pauses for introspection stifle dramatic interaction but Reiner, for the most part, keeps his characters physically moving, which in a very literal sense suggests that the characters are not emotionally self-indulgent. As Teddy walks away from the junkyard, having escaped the ferocious Chopper, he cries at the insults that the owner has thrown at him and his father. After Chris has tried some consoling words, they all fall silent – they know when not to speak (except Vern who starts to sing and gets a stare from Chris before stopping). They pursue mechanical actions while they talk, such as lobbing stones or, later, spitting water into a tin can (shown in close-up), which frees them from any social pressure to maintain eye contact or take what they are doing too seriously.

Whilst the group are in their liminal state, they do also think about what place they might take in society on their return. More broadly, we see a group of characters who feel the weight of expectation upon them, mainly from their family (Gordie's father calls his friends 'a thief and two feebs') but also from the wider community. Chris is a thief because that is how he is generally perceived, despite the fact that he tried to give the stolen milk money back and the real thief (the teacher, 'old lady Simons') is of a social class that places her above suspicion. The pressure of their social destiny presses down upon them and they all feel it keenly. As Gordie say about Chris, 'he came from a bad family and everyone just knew he'd turn out bad'. However, later in the film, we see Chris challenge this way of thinking, especially in Gordie's attempt to put friendship before potential in offering to stay with Chris as they enter High School and thereby 'dumbing down' his writing ability. However, in retelling the milk money story, Chris wails that he wants to go to 'a place where nobody knows me'. Part of the film's poignancy is this battle to escape what seems like an implacable destiny when faced by the living example of elder brothers who have become small-time criminals and big-time losers.

Interestingly, in the film we do see two gangs – the older clearly paralleling the younger one, even featuring some members of the same family. This is, in part, to show the threat to the younger group but, also, many of the same behaviours are paralleled, creating the effect of a flash-forward in the present, literalizing what will happen to them if their lives do not change. As leader of the younger group, the implication is that if nothing significant happens, Chris will turn into Ace Merrill. He already has a gun, paralleling Ace's production of a blade, and Chris is the one Ace challenges on the sidewalk when he steals Gordie's cap, as if he senses a future pretender. The tree-house card game will become the mailbox baseball and the petty crime that already touches them (Chris' theft of the milk-money) will grow into 'boosting' cars. Both groups share a common goal (the claiming of the body) find secrets hard to keep, they are not shown around girls and they dream that discovery of the body will mean they may get their names in the paper or even appear on TV. Their imaginative life is highly-influenced by TV. When Chris shows Gordie the gun, which he claims he has in case they see a bear, he asks: 'Wanna be the Lone Ranger or the Cisco Kid?' When Charlie suggests anonymously calling the police, Billy ridicules this because the calls can be traced – 'I've seen it on *Highway Patrol* and *Dragnet*'. It is all just a game at the moment but just as the gun accidentally fires, the time is fast approaching when playing at lawbreaking will become the real thing. The ubiquitous abusive sexual references suggests a pose of heterosexuality which is protesting just a bit too much – Ace calls Chris and Gordie 'girls' when accosting them on the sidewalk (something Chris also does to calm the argument about who will fetch food) and refers to quitters in the baseball game as 'homos'. With 'Great Balls of Fire' on the radio, there is a sense with the older group of the build-up of small-town frustration of a sexual nature. Phallic baseball bats reflect their social impotency as a group of mostly unemployed, or at best low-paid, low-lives (Ace mentions that he wants to finish the game, 'before I collect my social security').

Gordie is the most imaginative of the group – he it is who quickly comes up with the elaborate interlocking alibi stories to fool their parents. Humour is an important part of the film's success and largely absent from anthropological work. We see the verbal wit of pre-teen boys in Gordie's answer to Vern's complaint about what he bought with their money ('I guess a more experienced shopper could have got more from your seven cents'), or his more pointed question to Teddy, 'Does the word retarded mean anything to you?' and Teddy's equally rhetorical and equally memorable question later to Vern, 'Is it just me, or are you the world's biggest pussy?' It is Teddy's slightly left-field take on life, as well as his suppressed vulnerability, which makes his character so appealing. When Gordie tells him to stop ducking Vern and 'act his age,' he replies with perfect logic, 'This is my age. I'm in the prime of my youth and I'll only be young once', to which Gordie replies, 'Yeah but you're gonna be stupid for the rest of your life'. When Vern is worried about crossing the bridge in case a train comes, Teddy derides his fear and says that he will be waiting for them on the other side and 'relaxing with my thoughts'. Having narrowly avoided both the train and the fate of Ray Brower, Chris's sardonic observation, 'now we know when the next train's due', lightens the atmosphere but acknowledges how cheap the life of a child seems to be in this community.

The return phase of the journey and the reintegration into society are both given minimal screen time. It is the journey rather than the destination, that is of prime importance to the narrative. The return journey is a subdued anti-climax and almost dismissed in passing – the important features of the narrative have happened; all that remains is for their consequences to work themselves out. The farewell as the four go their separate ways takes on an added significance as Gordie's voiceover tells us: 'As time went on we saw less and less of Teddy and Vern until eventually they became just two more faces in the halls'. The boys may not come back as fully-fledged adults but they are changed by their experience. In the novella, Gordie is the only one left alive by the end of the narrative – Chris' tragic death follows the same pattern but the original story also has Vern and Teddy dying senseless deaths in a house-fire and a car crash respectively. Perhaps Castle Rock Studios felt audiences would only accept so much snuffing out of youthful potential and Gordie-as-adult describes Teddy becoming an odd-job man and Vern a fork-lift operator, eking out modest but bearable lives.

Similarly, the film retains the 'victory' of the younger gang over the older one, whereas the book makes the Pyrrhic nature of their victory clear by having Ace catch up with each of them and inflict physical damage, some of it lasting. The novella has Chris firing the warning shot with the pistol whereas the film transfers the action to Gordie, making him emerge as the real spokesperson of the group, signifying his coming to terms with death and strengthening the Gordie-as-adult character (Richard Dreyfuss) who, after preview audiences had suggested they wanted a greater sense of resolution, bookends the story and to whom the last word is given, via the computer screen on which he writes: the last word of his book becomes the last word of the film.

There is also a blurring of film and real life concerning the four protagonists of an elegiac and tragic nature. For, while Jerry O'Connell managed to outgrow the tubby frame of Vern Tessio to become a notable TV success as a romantic lead in prime-time shows such as Fox's sci-fi series *Sliders* (1995–2000) and NBC's crime drama *Crossing Jordan* (2002–2007), Wil Wheaton was later to feature as Wesley Crusher in *Star Trek: The Next Generation* (1987–94) and Corey Feldman, overcoming personal problems with drink and drugs, went on to appear in a number of teen-movies such as *The Lost Boys* (Joel Schumacher, 1987) and *The 'Burbs* (Joe Dante, 1989), River Phoenix was not so lucky. Although showing great promise in films like *Running on Empty* (Sidney Lumet, 1988), for which he gained an Academy Award nomination, like his character in *Stand by Me*, Chris Chambers, he died tragically young, victim of a drug overdose. The fact, that by the mid-nineties audiences knew what had become of these boys, adds poignancy to their narrative of youthful potential and casts a long shadow over the film.

Apt Pupil (Bryan Singer, 1998)

'What was it that made certain people do what they did and other people do nothing at all?' (Todd Bowden's History Teacher)

You're a monster. (Dussander to Todd Bowden)[6]

We do not have a literal journey and an ensemble cast, as we had in *Stand by Me*, but an educational one for an individual, as Todd Bowden (Brad Renfro) comes to realize what evil Dussander (Ian McKellen), and humanity more generally, including himself, is capable of. There are a series of tests for both main characters but rather than in a purely linear form, such tests use an alternating structure as the balance of power shifts back and forth between them. At their first meeting, Todd is, by turns, solicitous and threatening. There is the appearance of power in Dussander's threat to call the police but Todd calls his bluff and watches as Dussander hangs up impotently, the old man legs almost giving way, forcing him to sit down by the phone. At this stage, it looks as if Todd is in control, smiling smugly as he completes part of Dussander's jigsaw, suggesting a sadistic pleasure in spoiling the old man's fun, and overestimating his power over the situation. At this stage, the Holocaust is just a collection of 'stories', which he almost seems to find hard to believe. However, after only a month of such stories, Dussander is invited for dinner where he plays the perfect charming raconteur, allowing him to show his abilities to fictionalize his own life and at which Todd can only look on in disgusted horror.

Possibly inspired by the 1963 'He's Alive' episode of CBS's *The Twilight Zone*, featuring Peter Vollmer (Dennis Hopper) as a young American neo-Nazi inspired to murder by the ghost of Hitler, *Apt Pupil* delivers a powerful parable about the ubiquity of evil. It may be flawed (for some viewers possibly fatally) by a couple of implausible coincidences – the fact that schoolboy Todd should recognize Nazi war criminal Dussander on the bus and that later, in hospital, Dussander is placed right next to a survivor from the very concentration camp where he led a murderous regime. However, the fact that the film can survive this is due to its structure and the strength of the two central performances. Parallels help to hold the plot together: Dussander claims to have a dossier of his own on Todd, which would incriminate the boy; we cut between the two dreaming as they start to share nightmares (possibly also implying responsibility) about the gas chambers; and Todd threatens to phone and inform on Dussander, but, like the old man earlier, he cannot. We see Dussander's powerful storytelling (it is after all the reason for Todd's visits) and he is quite open about his ability to lie to judges and reporters, challenging Todd: 'Can you do that?...I know I can'. It should be no surprise then really that he can craft a tale about his own dossier on Todd: a fairy tale that keeps him safe, a story about 'an old man who was afraid' and a boy, bound together because 'each knew something the other wanted to keep secret'. Ironically, it is Todd, not Dussander, who frenetically tries to burn all evidence of the presence of a war criminal in an attempt to exorcise the 'stories' and the complicit guilt which they bring in their wake. What makes the film distinct is the unconventional character arcs in Brandon Boyce's script. As soon as we feel that we have a sense of the dynamic of the two protagonists, it shifts. Todd thinks he can control the forces that he unleashes (in himself as well as Dussander) but he cannot.

An example of the shifting balance of power between the two occurs when Todd buys Dussander a present. Like the later post-exam celebration, there is the initial appearance of a common ground, a 'communitas' in Turner's phrase, but this is only illusory. There are also hierarchies of ritualistic behaviour here – established and newly-revealed manifestations. Todd comes into Dussander's house without knocking and approaches the man, slumped at the table, who suddenly revives. Both are shocked – Todd because he thought the man was dead and Dussander because he did not expect to see the boy at the weekend. The nature of the present is held back as Dussander spends several seconds opening the box and reacting verbally and facially before lifting out the contents – a new Nazi uniform. The scene is full of subtle reactions which play against expectations – Dussander is appalled at the tastelessness of the gift and Todd seems genuinely surprised ('I thought you'd like it'). Commanding him to put the uniform on (against Dussander's wishes), including the hat, and rapping out military orders, Todd appears in complete control, with Dussander, weak and servile, moving stiffly and somewhat ridiculously. However as Dussander begins to march with greater gusto, he is shown in a more powerful low-angle and moves more fluidly under his own command, causing Todd's composure to break, and the drill ends on a climactic Nazi salute (shot in a slightly high angle with McKellen looking directly at the camera as if making eye contact with an unseen deity). It is Dussander who is aware of the forces Todd has released, having seen them first-hand, not the boy, whom he warns against 'playing with fire'. Decontextualized close-ups of the leather gloves and belt, (foreshadowed in his first appearance on the bus, carefully rolling up a black umbrella) capture a sense of the sensual (possibly even sexual) apparatus of Nazism, and a loss of self in ritual action, reflected in films like Leni Riefenstahl's *Triumph of the Will* (1935).

Both characters are made more likeable than in the novella, Todd especially, which allows the protagonists to learn more about themselves. Singer cuts a description of Dussander wearing his new uniform to sleep in out of choice, the actual baking of the cat, and Todd's unmotivated murder of four derelicts. Todd becomes isolated from his friends, unable to relate sexually to Betty Trusk (but not as aggressive as King's Todd, even when taunted about his sexuality) and given to daytime hallucinations. In a single shot, problematizing the division between dream and waking reality, Singer tracks in to a close-up on Todd in the school showers, with his hands over his face, before draining the colour from the image and then panning left and then right, showing his companions now as old Jewish men. It is only then that we cut back to a longer shot showing Todd alone with a red mark on his neck, suggesting he has been there several minutes.

His only sign of overt aggression, prior to the tramp episode, is the basketball practice where he flings the ball against the backboard, provoking a response from his friend, who calls him an idiot, to which Todd reacts with the prickly response: 'What did you call me?' However, when playing alone, Todd shows that he can shoot perfectly well (Magistrale erroneously states that 'all through the film Todd has been unable to make a basket').[7] As with his gratuitous killing of the wounded pigeon, he is discovering, and revelling in, his ability to dissemble and exercise power over those weaker than himself. In the first half of the film, Todd's apparent control, and his (and by extension our) ability to distance himself from Dussander, is eroded by a growing inability to concentrate, caused by lack of dream-free sleep. This is made more stressful by Dussander's skilful posing as his grandfather at an interview with Mr French. Van Gennep's role-playing and dares appear in Singer's use of Todd's POV as he enters the counsellor's office, panning right to reveal Dussander. In contrast to his first scene, when he had been cringing beneath the phone, here Dussander is sitting back, looking relaxed and in charge of the situation, which is driven by his acting ability and his force of will (as French notes, 'he's a very persuasive man'). In this, the film avoids one of the conventions of a rites-of-passage narrative – characters being honest with one another. Both protagonists keep secrets from each other and from the viewer (right until the end, there is no sense that Todd will necessarily get away with his deception). Furthermore, the morality of the film is not just transgressive but celebratory in tone as well: as Todd ultimately gets away with murder, developing the ability to deceive is seen as an important element in leading a successful life.

Another deceptively pivotal moment happens as Dussander seeks a bottle to toast Todd's achievement in school. The Scheherazade game of the stories is over; the hold that Dussander has over the boy seems to have gone, of which he is overtly aware (and indeed describes as he is moving) and we share Todd's POV as he approaches the prone, older figure, reaching for a bottle just out of reach at the top of the stairs. A close-up of Dussander's stance on tip-toes visualizes the temptation to Todd to give fate a little push. However, Dussander's tale shifts onto the dossier that he has written (or so he claims) and his new narrative closes with 'he felt safe'; the power shifts again and he turns with perfect balance, a knife in his hand, and starts singing 'Que Sera Sera'. Dussander has a far greater understanding of the complicity of evil and can articulate the bond they share more precisely in pseudo-sexual terms: 'We are fucking each other'. The lesson that Todd learns – the intoxicating, corrupting and sometimes parasitic nature of evil – is far more brutal than anything Gordie learns in *Stand by Me*.

What Dussander might learn from this process is given less screen time and is correspondingly less persuasive. Despite a very powerful performance, McKellen's Dussander gives us few specific clues as to his motivation. This causes occasional scenes which seem out of place, such as Dussander trying to force his cat into a gas oven, even if discussion of the past has supposedly re-animated his bloodlust. He describes what he did, the experiences of those in the gas chambers, but the film does not attempt a coherent explanation of Nazi philosophy. He talks about wiping a village off the face of the earth because 'a door had been opened', suggesting responsibility lay elsewhere and that he was just finishing off a necessary job. The levels of personal evasion is reflected in McKellen's accent, carefully layering English actor, American citizen and Nazi criminal, and he ultimately dies an enigma (in an amazing close-up as if smiling), eluding the viewer as well as his frustrated investigators. It is hard to imagine Nicol Williamson, the original choice for the part in the aborted 1987 version, matching McKellen's dramatic range or subtlety of performance (although the first choice at the time, James Mason, who unfortunately died before production could begin, would certainly have been interesting).

Rites-of-passage narratives focus on an educational process and we should consider what Todd learns. In the novella, he does not really wonder why people do the things they do and, at the end of King's narrative, he is a lone shooter, going off to snipe randomly at traffic before he is 'taken down'. Like Brett Easton Ellis' protagonist Patrick Bateman in *American Psycho*, King gives us his hero's (mostly unspoken) violent and misogynistic impulses through italics. The film softens the character of Todd, making him more of an ordinary teenager (riding his bike, playing basketball and finding school dull), albeit an outsider with sadistic impulses, who is drawn to Dussander's experiences and, crucially, not made into a homicidal maniac. He outsmarts Mr French rather than brutally murdering him. The novella conveys the making of one psychopath whereas the film manages to make a more general comment about the seductive and corrosive nature of evil. Cycling down a tunnel, lit by the setting sun, there is something almost Disneyesque and innocent about some parts of his portrayal, a scene which is later paralleled in blue light, rapid cutting and the sense of a hallucination as he is thrown from his bike by the sight of Nazi graffiti. He is an 'apt pupil', integrating what he has learned – to manipulate circumstances and the wills of others to his benefit. Perhaps bizarrely, he also learns the value of hard work. It is only through the bullying of Dussander's deal with Mr French that Todd knuckles down. There is something of the 'tough-love' of a concerned parent in Dussander's visible pleasure at Todd's successful report card and his suggesting a celebratory drink and even doing a trumpet impression on the way to fetching it.

Brad Renfro (with a look of a young Ethan Hawke) conveys right from the start an ability to be manipulative via his rather unlikely dossier of fingerprints, photos and other evidence, which he has single-handedly amassed. What he learns is how to apply this, creating a darker version of the grade manipulation of *Ferris Bueller's Day Off* (John Hughes, 1986) and the pre-college criminality of *Risky Business* (Paul Brickman, 1983) in order to manipulate the system, suggesting that, ultimately, Machiavellian corruption is the logical apex of amoral entrepreneurialism (Todd is specifically framed at school in front of Mount Rushmore poster with the slogan 'Dare to be a Leader'). David Schwimmer's naïve counsellor, Mr French, sounds a little like Beavis and Butthead's hippy teacher, Van Driessen, which weakens Todd's victory over him. His 'you can't do that' is met with the strictly factual 'you have no idea what I'm capable of doing', blending a more chilling version of Tom Cruise's mantra delivered behind shades whilst sweeping leaves as he prepares for Princeton, in Brickman's film, with a strong echo of the ruthless directness of Charlie Decker in 'Rage', refusing to be talked down to by school authorities.

What the treatment of war criminals should be and the nature of complicity involved in Todd's project are both interesting side issues but the question from the teacher at the opening seems to suggest a central exploration of human evil, casting Todd as a Jack-style character in a *Lord of the Flies*-type scenario, who is seduced by having life-and-death power over others, which he momentarily experiences with the tramp. However, perhaps a more unsettling element of the film is an American education system in which arguably the most evil period of human history is dismissed within just a week and students are left to their own curiosity to pursue further details. It dramatizes the inability of education to convey the real horror of the Holocaust (the novella repeats the number of dead, six million, as an 'unprocessable' fact), shying away from graphic elements which adults may feel are pandering to prurient bloodlust. However, this does a disservice to boys like Todd who are looking for an honest approach to the seductive and pleasurable nature of ultimate power ('what they are too afraid to tell us in school'). In a way, Todd does exactly what the system expects – he wants more knowledge and having exhausted the library, he seeks out first-hand testimony to know what it was really like to have performed such deeds.

Clearly the film juxtaposes an alienated and impressionable teen who has the potential for evil and the real thing (Dussander's more accomplished evil is reflected in his better skills at imposture and forgery). An initial reading might see Todd as a fascist-in-waiting but (up until the pigeon episode) he shows no cruelty in other areas of his life, only curiosity, suffers nightmares about the gas chambers and there is no evidence that he wishes Dussander ill-will – he is not collecting material for a blackmail scam. According to Mr French, Todd is all set to be top of his class and is only scrawling swastikas on his schoolwork because he is obsessed with knowing more, not because he glorifies the regime. However, it is arguable to what extent a full insight into this horror is corrupting in itself or whether only someone sick would really want to know so much. The film opens and closes with a slow close-up on Dussander's eyes and could be seen as Singer's attempt to make us see through them. However, the film also closes with a superimposition of Dussander's face over an icon of American suburban normality – a basketball hoop. In this, the film is an indictment of western education but also of the limits of human understanding to grasp a meaning in the Holocaust, an event which perhaps defies and even destroys meaning.

Hearts in Atlantis (Scott Hicks, 2001)

Hearts in Atlantis is an elegiac, slow-moving, character-driven narrative focusing on the relationship between eleven-year-old Bobby Garfield (Anton Yelchin) and the mysterious Ted Brautigan (Anthony Hopkins), temporary lodger and surrogate father. Like *It* and *Stand by Me*, the narrative is placed at a key moment of adolescence: childhood friendships are more intense than anything experienced as an adult and the hero undergoes a rite of passage in connection with his closest friends, during the 1950s, in a way which shapes his adult life. The frame story, the death of a childhood friend, both motivates the flashback that constitutes the body of the film and provides closure at the end, as Bobby rather miraculously bumps into the grown-up daughter of his childhood sweetheart (credibly played by the same actress, Mika Boorem). Romance, continuity and coherence allow the film to close on a graphic match between the adult Bobby driving away through sunlit woods and his younger self cycling on the same road towards a future, some of which we already know.

Like *Apt Pupil*, the focus is on one individual boy and what he learns from a key period in his life. However, stylistically, there are also intertextual cinematic references to previous King adaptations, making this a slightly more self-aware and manipulatively-sentimental work. There are visual references to *Stand by Me* in the shot of Ted, Carol and Sully playing on a railway track and *Christine* in the persistent use of 50s tracks to complement the action. The latter feature appears in Chubby Checker's 'The Twist' (1959), used to convey the kids' youthful energy and The Platters' 'Only You' (1955) for Bobby's adoration of the bike in the window, swiftly transferred to Carol who persuades a buyer to purchase a different one. Even *Sleepwalkers* is evoked in the use of the twanging guitar of Santo and Johnny Farina's 1959 instrumental 'Sleepwalk' as Bobby and Carol play by the river. Paratextually, the title refers to a sentimentalized, nostalgic view of pre-teen innocence as if lived in a different realm of experience, before children 'grow up and our hearts break in two'. This is conveyed by montages of the kids at play, especially running in open spaces (down roads, across baseball diamonds, and around woods and rivers), always without the encumbrance of adult supervision. The sequences showing Carol on the steps, running up the road and later, in her rescue, are the only ones filmed using handheld camerawork, giving those shots a particular spontaneity and vivacity.

However, at the same time as including sentimental imagery, the film also has a darker edge, missing from the other two films in this chapter, in particular in what Carol and Bobby's mother learn. A kinder, gentler age is juxtaposed with the violence performed upon women by men, such as the attack on Carol by Richie O'Rourke (Joe T. Blankenship), the bully, and the 'rape' of Bobby's mother (Hope Davis) by her boss. Both these are conveyed with restraint: the attack on the girl represented by a book falling in the stream and Mrs Garfield's situation recognizable to a female passer-by, who can sense pain beneath her attempt at a dignified walk. Beyond family and friends lurk the FBI-style 'Low Men' and the world of exploitation, only read about in the newspaper and spoken of rather mythically by Ted. The dark suits, flashy cars and coded messages on telephone poles seem to Bobby like the stuff of fantasy but they prove all too real in the thinly-veiled H-men who haunt the ending of the narrative. The repeated shot of one of these men signalling to a passing car, shot in silhouette with rising, hellish steam, *Exorcist*-style, casts them as anonymous, almost demonic figures who abduct individuals to do their bidding. The town is closer than it appears to *The Village of the Damned*, which Bobby later goes to see, where children are taken over by malign outside forces.

Problematically, the rites-of-passage genre is very much grounded in discovering a 'reality' or 'truth' of life, which runs diametrically opposed to notions of the fantastic. Perhaps sensibly, William Goldman's script makes the 'Low Men' credible, shadowy threats from this world, severing all links to the alien intelligences in King's *Dark Tower* novels. Instead, the film is partly about vision, opening with the adult Bobby (David Morse) now a successful photographer, shooting through a rotating glass globe. The body of the film dramatizes how Ted acts as a prism, making Bobby re-evaluate what he thinks about love, books and his father, and shows the importance of the photo of Carol that Bobby has carried all his life – the image that Bobby focuses on to block out the predatory passing car. The concern with metaphorical vision also extends to the cinematic apparatus of filmic representation. The set used for the living space of both the Garfields and Ted is unusually theatrical in that both are often shot in long takes, with internal doors left open so that we see both Ted and Mrs Garfield pass into the bedroom or kitchen whilst talking to Bobby in the foreground. Indeed, the only closed door in the whole film is towards the end when Bobby goes into his bedroom, after his mother has betrayed Ted, and by extension, her own child. Angles within this set are often at table height, i.e. closer to the eye-line of a child. Such a setting suggests that there are elements of Bobby's life with his mother which co-exist but are compartmentalized (such as what he knows and feels about his father) and which Bobby must bring together and connect.

Hopkins plays Brautigan with some intertextual allusions to the same measured mannerisms of Hannibal Lector, effusing the same soft-spoken delivery that can be avuncular and charming (to Bobby) or threatening (in his confrontation with the bullies). His stance, with his head tilted back slightly as if listening to faint music that only he can hear, is slightly reminiscent of the distracted air of James Mason in

Salem's Lot but here there are lighter, human sections too, mixing citations of Samuel Jonson with jokes about flatulence. Ted seems a comparative innocent in a manipulative world, and certainly his brand of gentle knowledge seems out of place in a cynical world as Mrs Garfield shows mistrust in his dealings with Bobby and his help, later, with Carol's dislocated shoulder – leading in part to her informing upon him. The contradictory forces working on Bobby are symbolized in the attempt by his mother to recruit him as a 'spy' too and tell her if 'anything unusual happens' around Ted. There is, if not an overt spirituality, a transcendent quality to his character – he recreates the circumstances of a football game where a 'miracle' happened, in which the hopes and dreams of the crowd were lived out by the heroic actions of one older player. Later, Bobby acts out that role in slow motion, with the roaring crowd coming back on the soundtrack, as he carries the injured Carol to get help. Repeat edits convey the confusion, fear and almost out-of-body awareness in the physical and emotional stress involved. Bobby starts to develop some psychic abilities himself, most clearly in the fairground card game (an unfilmed incident from the novel of *The Dead Zone*) but, perhaps sensibly, Goldman's script ultimately plays this down. The lasting legacy from Ted is an educational lesson in self-improvement through books. He persuades the boy that an adult library card is a present worth having and the final dialogue we hear from Bobby is his reciting the anecdote about Jonson.

Paradoxically, Bobby learns to question his parents more closely and yet also retain a willingness to believe in them. Ted is the catalyst through which Bobby comes to know more about his father, unwittingly tracing his footsteps to his favourite bar, discovering from a barmaid that he was a talented gambler, a generous man and not the loser his mother has repeatedly insisted he was (although the signal between Ted and the barmaid remains ambiguous, problematizing the veracity of what she says). The photo given to him is juxtaposed in the following scene with him sporting a hat for the first time, suggesting he has a new role model against which to measure himself. Flickering black and white images of fictional heroes such as The Lone Ranger and a tellingly-brief glimpse of rough play between his friend Sully (Will Rothhaar) and his father as they load the car, which Bobby enviously watches, are both unattainable models of masculinity for him. Although Ted has mysterious power, he uses it for good (helping Bobby save for the bike he knows he wants, sending the bullies away and anticipating Carol's injury) and is not the monster that Bobby jokingly suggests with his crucifix when Ted talks of kissing. Bobby may be the son Ted never had but it is hard to say as we know little more of him at the end than at the beginning. Before they part, he allows himself to be hugged (which we see in a lengthy, chest-level shot) and, as he is driven away, shouts that he would not have missed it for the world, putting his hand to the window to 'touch' Bobby's in a gesture which is extremely sentimental but also quite moving.

He is often framed in doorways and windows, frequently in reflection (as Bobby's first image is, suggesting a link between them) and does, literally, seem a 'shadowy' figure, shown first by his feet only and later on, meeting Bobby properly, as a figure seen through frosted glass or with his head cropped from the frame. At times, he is left blurred in the background whilst Bobby is sharp in the foreground, and is often lit by a single light source within a dark scene. He also smokes, which can denote a pleasurable habit in a 1950s context or, more recently, a sinister vice à la Cigarette-Smoking man from *The X-Files*. He may not be malevolent but he does not speak of home or family, jobs or his past – he just is a man with a psychic talent, which he, like many King characters, finds more of a 'burden' than a gift. His deceptiveness proves to be different from that of Mrs Garfield's boss, who is hidden in the frame by her form as she phones her son with an excuse why she has to work late, suggesting he is using her. Ted's face is also obscured in the following scene (here by a pillar) as he sits on the veranda but his evasiveness is for self-preservation rather than self-fulfilment.

At the same time as containing clearly sentimental scenes, Goldman's script resists easily-won emotions. Bobby's emotional farewell to Carol is cut short by her directness, jumping to 'I love you too', and feeling is under- rather than overstated as they look at each other amongst the sheets – she has to 'go and fix the salad' rather than spend all day swapping clichés. *Hearts in Atlantis* is the film *Firestarter* could have been. At its core lies a father-son relationship which only gains its full significance with an awareness of its transience – a level of sensitivity and sophistication entirely absent from the earlier film. By choosing to use only the dove-tailed opening and closing sections of King's text, the film focuses on the possibility of youthful hope and leaves out the darker loss of innocence and idealism in Vietnam – the central part of the book. By the end of the film, the roles of father and child almost reverse (Bobby promises 'I won't let the boogeyman get you') but with the nightmarish, powerlessness of the slow-motion passing of the car, he has to learn one of the hardest lessons of all about growing up – that, try as you might, you cannot completely protect those you love from harm.

Conclusion

Although *Stand by Me* follows notions of a rites-of-passage narrative most closely in its quest format, all three films have as their protagonist a young boy at a formative age, questioning certainties about his parents and needing to look outside his immediate family for potential answers to troubling questions around death, loss and adult expectations. It might be said that the looser the generic bonds on a narrative, such as in the case of *Apt Pupil*, the more difficult it becomes to predict accurately how that narrative will be resolved, making it perhaps harder to market but arguably more pleasurable to experience as a text.

There are a number of similarities in all three films with William Golding's 1954 novel *Lord of the Flies,* another rites-of-passage narrative where an adventure teaches the main character about evil but also the value of friendship. The book is frequently mentioned by King as one of his favourites and the source of the name of his favourite fictional town and the production company, Castle Rock, who deal with most of his film work. In *Stand by Me*, Chris' paternal concern for Gordie is a little like Piggy's for Ralph, in particular as 'a true, wise friend.'[8] For his part, Gordie, as a natural leader, mature beyond his years, can be seen as Ralph; in Vern's tubbiness and cowardice, we have close parallels for Piggy; and Teddy, misunderstood, ready to sacrifice himself, becomes a version of the enigmatic Simon. Overall, we have a virtually all-male cast undergoing a series of tests in uncivilized surroundings and without parental influence, forcing a process of bonding between siblings. *Apt Pupil* is also centrally concerned with the human potential for evil and there is lack of parental contact in all three films, caused by death of a brother (*Stand by Me*), a mysteriously-absent absent father (*Hearts in Atlantis*) and parents who are simply uninterested (*Apt Pupil*).

Notes

1. Arnold Van Gennep, *Rites-of-Passage* (New York: Routledge, 2004; first published 1909).
2. Victor Turner, *The Ritual Process: Structure and Anti-Structure* (Aldine Transaction, 1995; first published 1969).
3. Michael Ryan and Douglas Kellner, *Camera Politica: The Politics and Ideology of Contemporary Hollywood Film* (Bloomington: Indiana University Press, 1988), p. 78.
4. William Wordsworth, Revised Preface to the *Lyrical Ballads* (Oxford: Oxford University Press, 1969; originally published 1800), p. 173.
5. Stephen King, 'The Body' in *Different Seasons* (London: Warner Books, 1992; originally published 1982), p. 414.
6. Stephen King, 'Apt Pupil' in *Different Seasons*, op. cit., p. 137.
7. Magistrale, *Hollywood's Stephen King*, op. cit., p. 114.
8. William Golding, *Lord of the Flies* (London: Faber and Faber, 1954), p. 223.

CHAPTER FIVE

THE RISE OF THE MACHINES: 1950S SCIENCE-FICTION B-MOVIE

'I'm scared by machines. Machines frighten me because I don't know how they work in a lot of cases.'[1]

King's rather irrational fear of machines (by his logic, most of us would share it) is one reason why the films in this section struggle to be effective. Often shorn of the political subtext in the original text, we are left with the spectacle of a special effect which may be limited by budgetary factors. All the films here, except *Christine* (originally conceived as a short story) and *Dreamcatcher* from 2001, were originally short stories from the 1970s and, typically, these narratives have a relatively short running time, which may suggest a slight over-reaching in producing a feature-length film: an idea stretched too far. These films explore the dependency of modern life on technology and dramatize, not terribly originally, the consequences of machines that no longer follow orders. Several of the films in this section might also fall within the broader heading of 'terror of the everyday' – it is mostly ordinary, domestic machines which appear to be conspiring against their users.

Superficially, this group of films might seem to reflect one of the central concerns of the 1950s B-movie as discussed by scholars like Peter Biskind.[2] King himself recognizes that '[g]reat horror fiction is almost always allegorical'.[3] However, there is little deeper resonance to many of the tales here – they are all denotation, little connotation. There is little fear of political or social subtext of those movies – the films here show no fear of radiation, no so-called Red Menace and, apart from *Graveyard Shift*, there is little of the 'nature run amok' subgenre. Even the machines that run out of control do so without any sense of this as a punishment for human hubris: an over-reaching into areas best left alone. Science as such does not figure here; there are no credible Quatermass-like, scientist figures, mad or otherwise (Jobe in *The Lawnmower Man* comes closest and he is the subject of experiments rather than their guiding hand).

The very titles of Kendall R. Phillips' *Projected Fears: Horror Films and American Culture* (2005) or David Skal's *The Monster Show: A Cultural History of Horror* (2001) reflects a theoretical approach stretching from figures like Leo Baudry, who see fictional genres very much as reflections of the dominant cultural values of the times, to Stephen Greenblatt's New Historicism and notions of 'resonance' (albeit in a literary context).[4] With the films in this chapter, a very obvious problem exists in trying to transpose a 1950s B-movie to the 1980s and beyond – it is no longer the 1950s and B-movies as a cinematic form no longer exist; the spectre of the Second World War is not a powerful cultural undercurrent; and the political metaphors of the Red Menace, or mutation resulting from nuclear testing, no longer resonate. Low-budget monster movies, lacking the invention of an exploitation director like Roger Corman and a metaphorical deeper structure, exist primarily as a collection of surface features. Even though an anachronistic literary source need not necessarily produce an anachronistic visual adaptation and although many of King's shorter, machine-based narratives were written when the oil crisis might have created resonance at fear of dependency on petrol-driven vehicles, there is nonetheless a strange, Luddite tendency in these works.

The machines that King uses are not human in form but based around industrial-model combustion engines – no other sentient powers are on display, even to the point of the trucks in *Maximum Overdrive* being rendered powerless simply by running out of petrol. These are not the unkillable, self-aware cyborgs of the *Terminator* films. The trucks are threats from the industrial age in the real world, not of anything supernatural. However, there really is not enough in the films to formulate a case that they constitute some grand anti-capitalist statement. It is the attribution of sentience to these machines, which is literally rather than metaphorically realized, that causes them to start to attack workers. In *Danse Macabre*, King suggests that nearly all monster movies can be reduced to three basic types: 'the Vampire, the Werewolf and the Thing without a name.'[5] Chapter 3 included one werewolf and one slightly vampiric narrative (*Silver Bullet* and *Sleepwalkers*) but it is the final category which is dominant here, perhaps suggesting that that is where King's real interests lie and also how difficult it is to get right.

A central weakness of the films in this section is the lack of a threatening monster. None of the most memorable monsters of the last 30 years – Ridley Scott's xenomorph, the *Terminator* series, even the human monstrosity of Anthony Hopkins' visualization of Thomas Harris' character, Hannibal Lector – are derived from King adaptations. The monsters in King adaptations struggle to work as metaphors when they have such literal life: when the monster is a machine, whose only sentience consists of acts of violence. This prevents any sense of fellow feeling and inhibits the development of a creature like Frankenstein's monster, an outsider, with whom we may feel some spark of empathy. These films do not have outsized creatures, often under the influence of radiation, such as *Them!* (Gordon Douglas, 1954), *It Came from Beneath the Sea* (Robert Gordon, 1955), *The Incredible Shrinking Man*, (Jack

Arnold, 1957) or Godzilla, one of the few creatures to have a cinematic life beyond the 1950s. Atomic waste plays no part in the King adaptations in this chapter.

Also, Harry Benshoff's notion of monstrosity as a challenge to heterosexual norms rarely has any relevance in this section as there is little sense of a gendered monster, except in *Christine*.[6] Here, there are suggestions of the car as sexual substitute, but it is of a jealous, feminine variety. In book and film, it serves to split up the potential relationship between Leigh and Arnie, who, in his transformation, exaggerates his heterosexual credentials. Carpenter removes King's ghostly back-story so that the car is evil as an unmotivated given and makes the machine an instrument of surrogate libidinous revenge, but there is no darker, political sense of the film – it is not a cautionary tale of car ownership; indeed, its wider context is closer to the *Grease*-style celebration of cars as liberating youthful sexuality. Intertextuality and generic hybridity are more profitable approaches in looking at *Christine*, particularly due to John Carpenter's willingness to reference other film works, the use of a soundtrack that acts as an ironic commentary upon the visual imagery and the combination of these two elements, which is a prime means by which Arnie Cunningham's transformation is conveyed.

Christine (John Carpenter, 1983)

'Cars are girls. Didn't you know that?' (Leigh Cabot to Arnie Cunningham)[7]

At one point, Alfred Hitchcock was going to feature a body being discovered on an assembly line in *North by Northwest* (1959) but he could not find a workable plotline. In *Christine*, director John Carpenter takes up the idea but makes the fatally-flawed decision not to use the rotting corpse of Roland LeBay from King's novel as the cause of the car's malevolence, instead designating the car itself as evil from the very outset. Christine is not really given any 'character' as such, except through the ironically placed 1950s tracks that periodically burst from her radio. The evil of the car can only really be suggested rather than felt, underscored by George Thorogood's 'Bad to the Bone'. The car takes revenge by killing a worker, who messily stubs out a cigar but also maims another, dropping her bonnet on his hand, like the bite of a shark, for no apparent reason. On the suggestion of cinematographer Donald Morgan, the opening scene is the only one shot on Fuji film, the different stock giving a slightly softer, brownish colour and setting it apart from the remainder of the film. The assembly line creates a motivated tracking shot, like a mechanical version of Jean-Luc Godard's jam in *Weekend* (1968). The intersecting vectors of Carpenter's camera positioning here and the initial lack of film music to guide our sympathies, work in a similar way to the car wash scene in Cronenberg's *Crash* (1996). Tension is created as we see the clock showing five, the supervisor walking across the line and looking puzzled but without Carpenter giving us an easy reverse angle to show what he can see – just faint sound as if from a car radio. The camera follows the man as he slowly walks up to Christine, still with her lights on, and cranes up and over the car to give a bird's eye view as he opens the door and a body flops out.

In terms of visible characterization, nerd-as-hero Arnie Cunningham (Keith Gordon) undergoes a transformation under the influence of Christine, casting the film as a love story. He is first seen, wearing thick spectacles taped together and carrying rubbish bags that split everywhere, being handed his lunch by his mother. He is a stereotypical, self-conscious virgin and Christine (given a female name) clearly acts as a sexual surrogate for Arnie, so that he spends more time with her than Leigh (a jealous Christine tries to choke her at the drive-in) and the changes in Arnie's manner and appearance reflect a growth in sexual maturity. On visiting Dennis at the hospital, Arnie has dispensed with the glasses, is sporting more fashionable clothes (his collars almost visibly grow during the course of the scene) and he speaks with a calm confidence not seen before, particularly to Detective Junkins (Harry Dean Stanton). The decrepit seller, George LeBay, states that a new car is 'the finest smell in the world...except for pussy', making the sexual substitution clear. When Arnie first puts the radio on in Darnell's, the camera repeats the movement from the opening scene, up and over the windscreen, but here we have Arnie framed in almost orgasmic ecstasy. He addresses the car with affection ('they can't hurt us now we're together') and, in a turning point in their 'relationship', we see, in long shot, Arnie walk away from the car, turn and command Christine to 'show me', at which she miraculously makes herself whole again via Roy Arbogast's hydraulics, which suck the panels in and then the film is run in reverse. With a slinky saxophone track, a tracking shot up to and over Arnie's shoulder and the sexual tone of the command, the sequence feels like a supernatural strip-tease, a private show of her capabilities. However, neither the film nor the book ever reaches the disturbingly-uncompromising psychopathology of JG Ballard's 1973 novel of *Crash* or Cronenberg's film.

Like *Carrie*, *Christine* is a high school drama but here with greater sexual and romantic frustration. We see Arnie lusting after new girl Leigh (Alexandra Paul) as she walks down the corridor and then being bullied in the Auto shop class (including Buddy Repperton taunting him sexually, calling him 'Cuntingham'), represented by the slow crushing of his glasses in close-up and alternate extreme high and low angles as Arnie looks up helplessly at Buddy waving a knife in front of him. Arnie's ecstasy on first spotting the car feels like love at first sight, an illogical infatuation. Dennis opines 'it's a piece of shit' and many viewers may agree. When he asks Arnie 'What is it about that car?' he answers, 'I dunno. Maybe for the first time in my life, I've found something that's uglier than me.' When Dennis protests that he is not ugly, Arnie replies 'I know what I am.' Possession of Christine has been the catalyst in the development from self deprecation to self-knowledge. The source of the protagonist's name from *Happy Days* (Ron Howard, ABC, 1974–84), blending a central character, the hapless Richie Cunningham with the teen hang-out 'Arnie's', underlines that this is teen entertainment, shorn of a darker subtext. Arnie's name and later fashion sense, Christine's car design, and the constrictive morality of Arnie's parents, all evoke overtones of Nicholas Ray's *Rebel Without a Cause* (1955) but in a more explicit context. Car ownership carries with it the heavy symbolic weight of potential sexual freedom and, in Arnie's case, is a clear break with the wishes of his parents, in front of whom he swears twice during rows about it. Particularly powerful, later, is his action at the foot of the stairs when he grabs and holds his father by the throat for a second or two in an iconic moment as he breaks with his family for good, in an updating of the family strife from the 1950s. The slow, lengthy shot of Arnie driving Christine into Darnell's, and carefully parking it, emphasizes the care taken with the car and the depth of the shot. After a false start, Arnie gives some encouraging words and it fires up, the radio playing Dion and the Belmonts' 'I Wonder Why', expressing Arnie's newfound love, which he cannot fully explain.

The way Carpenter realizes his source of monstrosity is interesting, since paratextually the car is the star of the film. Under $10 million, it is a very modestly budgeted film and much of this is designated for the numerous cars needed to portray Christine. There are no A-list stars in the film but Keith Gordon (seen in De Palma's 1980 *Dressed to Kill*) does an effective job in conveying the transformation of Arnie from nerd to tacit killer. Elsewhere, Carpenter draws upon the intertextual background of character actors playing minor roles. Robert Prosky, whose superficial unpleasantness as Darnell conceals a slightly less unpleasant interior (he offers Arnie the junkyard to salvage parts), suggested adding the superfluous dialogue about 'putting the toilet rolls on the little spools'. Harry Dean Stanton's Detective Junkins does not have much to do but his questioning of Arnie uses a similar picture composition to the first scene with Christine outside George LeBay's shack. In both cases, Christine occupies a dominant half of the frame and comes right up to the camera in a way which is quite disconcerting and is as if she is 'alert' to being talked about. Roberts Blossom (LeBay) with only two scenes conveys a strangeness, represented by his wearing of a tattered back brace in the first scene and a formal jacket over it in the second scene, as if to designate upward mobility now he has sold the car. He also reminds us of his absent brother Roland from the novel who also wore such a brace.

The car as sexualized space places the film once more generically as teen-pic. The attack on the car is a darker moment; the gang slash the seats with knives and, especially Buddy with his phallic sledgehammer, penetrate and violate not just Darnell's but Christine's interior, making it a form of rape. However, the soundtrack is again used as ironic, intertextual commentary with a bar or two from Little Richard's 'Keep A-Knocking'. At the drive-in, the camera slowly comes up to and then circles the car like a stalking voyeur. Leigh struggles free, however, and appears to feel an instinctive repulsion for the car, ('I can't … not in that car') and if we had not got the jealousy idea, she openly states 'You care more about that car than about me', mainly because of the time he lavishes on Christine at Darnell's. Some slightly odd camera placement shows him from Leigh's passenger POV looking right at the camera but the reverse shot feels more as if it comes from the dashboard, making her appear more direct and possibly trustworthy – he has become evasive in and around Christine. She hits the seat in frustration and when he tells her not to, she responds with 'Don't you like me slapping your girl?' Later in the scene with Junkins, Arnie gives the bonnet a proprietorial wipe where the detective had momentarily leaned against the car. Teen-pic shifts towards horror with a top shot over the car and Leigh's head thrown back, not in ecstasy but choked by some invisible force. A strange blue light illuminates the interior, contrasting with the dark outside and, shot mostly in close-ups, the scene creates some tension as a warning that she will not tolerate Arnie's attention drifting elsewhere.

There is a further generic shift, a 'refinement' of the horror idea towards an attempted slasher narrative, as Christine, the killer, starts with Moochie, the fat bully (although the school revenge motif links it back to *Carrie*). Moochie's dialogue ('Hey, Cunningham, you ain't mad, are ya?') is ironic by this stage and also, with the blacked-out windows, we do not know who is driving or whether Christine is acting alone. Moochie is chased in clichéd terms, turning round periodically and unlike the car as threat in *Assault on Precinct 13*, Carpenter holds the car in shot, which reduces the sense of dread, and the metronomic percussion beat and screaming wheels (to match Moochie's own scream) are less powerful than the rising and falling volume drum-track and strong synthesizer chords of the earlier film. Moochie's demise, seen via a top shot, conveys the will of Christine, as she squeezes into a parking bay apparently too narrow for her, and ends with a 'gore-free' fade to black as the camera runs right into Moochie's substantial midrift. The detective says later that they had to 'scrape him up with a shovel' but this is only stated, not shown. However, even accounting for subtle little touches like the 'Danger' sign by the parking bay or the chase down the alleyway, shown in alternate POV shots, with a slightly wide-angle lens to distort the image of the car and seem to bring it closer, the sequence does not really disturb. *Blue Thunder* (John Badham, 1983) also has a sequence of a pedestrian being chased and run down by a car, but there we feel engagement with the victim because he is a more rounded character, because we see a driver, the man chased is handcuffed and gagged and the sequence uses dramatic low angles, bonnet shots and close-ups, which are largely denied us here. Moochie's death feels more like an execution; a contest he is always going to lose.

After careering into a gas station in pursuit of the other two bullies, Carpenter uses the same POV shots as the Moochie attack. On the open road, the fireball that the car becomes creates a superbly demonic image against the night. As with the ruthless pursuit of the protagonist's wife and child in *Mad Max* (George Miller, 1979), the sequence is shot in low-angle but despite a similar sense of inevitability, there is much less empathy with Buddy who, as a bully without family ties, seems to deserve his fate.

The theorizing scenes between Leigh and Dennis about Christine are amongst the weakest in the film. Deleted material shows how a longer cut might have made their growing closeness clearer but you can see why Carpenter wanted less of this. Implausible leaps of logic, more akin to the clumsy narrative exposition and theorizing of children's films, anticipate similar (and equally painful) scenes in *Silver Bullet*. In both films, there does not really seem enough evidence for the theories advanced, especially here – Arnie may be acting possessively but there is no more proof than that.

The climactic attempt to trap the car at Darnell's contains some unexplained bulldozer skills from Dennis, (unlike Ripley's prowess with the lifting equipment in James Cameron's *Aliens* (1986)) but accounted for in the novel. Arnie, underlit to heighten his Caligari-like make-up, dies a sexualized, automotive death like Vaughan in *Crash*, as he is lacerated by shards of windscreen glass in the office but finds time to stroke the grille one last time. The novel's narrative conclusion seems a little cursory by comparison as it is Arnie's father Michael whose body comes through the windscreen, while Arnie's death (and that of his mother) due to a mysterious car accident, are described briefly. The final battle does not feature a bulldozer but a tank truck called Petunia, so Carpenter ditches King's girl-on-girl action in favour of a straight battle of the sexes.

Like Stanley Kubrick's problem in *The Shining*, King would have us believe that an inanimate object can be inherently evil. He describes Christine as 'a hellish haunted house that rolled on Goodyear rubber' but, on film (apart from the one shot of the car on fire), we do not really believe this.[8] Christine looks like an ordinary American car – a 1958 Plymouth Fury was deliberately chosen by King as a car without cultural baggage. However, a central problem with *Christine* is that it could share a tag-line with *Knight Rider* or more likely the *Herbie* films – each are about 'a car with a mind of its own'. The same basic premise is supposed to lead to comic hilarity or spine-tingling fear. Even with different music, in truth neither hoped-for response is likely. Even the eponymous mechanical hero of low-budget TV-movie *Killdozer* (Jerry London, 1974) has a visible, motivated reason for its evil via an extra-terrestrial meteorite. To the untutored European eye, Christine looks like a stereotypical American car, designed to reflect the owner's economic and social status. Large cars, being driven aggressively, often with tinted windows, are now so ubiquitous in urban areas of the developed world that it is hard to see Christine as unsettling. For that to happen, we would need some kind of displacement effect like Nic Roeg's placing of a modern car in an anachronistic setting in *The Man Who Fell to Earth* (1976), where a couple of brief glimpses of David Bowie's character driving through a pre-industrial landscape creates a sense of otherworldliness, making eye witnesses doubt their own senses. The 'unkillable' machines of *Westworld* and *Terminator* (with which the regenerating Christine bears a strong resemblance in the climactic battle) are simply more threatening than a car which can drive and regenerate itself but can otherwise do little more than a 'normal' car. The sudden appearance or disappearance of something in one's rear-view mirror or the relentless approach of an unknown vehicle is more unsettling in Steven Spielberg's directorial debut in *Duel* (1971), a film of which King is very aware, discussing its merits in *Danse Macabre,* or even in the more recent *Jeepers Creepers* (Victor Salva, 2001).[9] At the end, the slow track up to the rectangle of compacted metal that Christine has become is more funny than scary as we hear some music, motivated, as it turns out, by a passing junkyard worker carrying a ghetto-blaster. The slight movement represents how evil has not been wholly vanquished but, more likely, leaves the way open for a sequel, which has yet to be made, largely because the idea is played out to exhaustion in the film.

If the film does have an enduring appeal for some viewers, it may not be due to the articulation of timeless themes as much as the strongly nostalgic 1950s aesthetic; knife fights, drive-ins, rock and roll all make it feel like some kind of demonic alter ego to Randall Kleiser's *Grease* (1978), a film mentioned in passing in the book.[10] On the DVD, Producer Richard Lobritz might like to cite *Time* magazine's description of the film as 'Carpenter's best since *Halloween*', but ignores the fact that that was only five years before and bizarrely overlooks *The Thing* (1982). Ultimately, *Christine* must largely be viewed as a missed opportunity. The speed with which the film flew into production (the book was still on the bestseller list at the time) may have played a part. He admits on the DVD that 'for a long time in the film, nothing really happens to anybody'. Seeking to avoid comparisons with John Landis' *An American Werewolf in London*, Carpenter tones down obvious gore, but does not replace it with any compensatory sense of dread or strangeness (as in the first half of *Alien*). It is telling that the musical theme Carpenter used for his opening scene was chosen by Cameron in the tongue-in-cheek bar-room scene in *Terminator II*, when Schwarzenegger appropriates some biker clothing without killing anyone. It works as parody, not as a literal signature of evil. At the end of the novel, Dennis recounts two dreams he had: one about Christine driven by a rotting Roland Le Bay and the other, which he says is worse, features a driverless Christine, regenerated and with a radio blaring rock and roll. After watching the film, it may seem that Dennis, King and even Carpenter chose the wrong dream.

Maximum Overdrive (Stephen King, 1986)

'Where's your sense of loyalty?' (Wanda June to the trucks)

The basic premise of a group under siege, who are picked off one-by-one has been used before but whereas films like John Carpenter's *Assault on Precinct 13* are full of tension, here there is virtually none. King may have taken his inspiration from Hitchcock's *The Birds* but machines acting on their own, in itself, is not necessarily dramatic or interesting. There is something strangely anachronistic, almost nineteenth century, about a fear of machines, whose presence in everyday modern life is so completely normalized, running amok. Like the problem with *Christine*, the machines on display act without human agency (we see lots of trucks driving around without drivers) but they display little further signs of sentient life. We are not faced by an army of machines with powers beyond imagination – this is the terror of everyday life. The trucks driving aimlessly round the garage is redolent, not of supernatural entities but of stereotypical Indians in old-style westerns.

The opening sequence of the Wilmington Bridge has some effective elements. It may not be Eisenstein's *Strike* (1925) but the tipping bridge does produce some interesting juxtapositions and collisions between vehicles, both gradual (not just due to slow-motion) and sudden. The visceral power of the violence is enhanced by using real vehicles rather than computer animation – a similar basic concept on a much vaster scale and budget in James Cameron's *Titanic* (1997) does not necessarily yield a proportionately more powerful outcome. However, apart from abusive ATMs, calling their customers 'assholes' or bank signs that shift between temperature readings and less polite messages like 'Fuck you', revealing what institutions really think about their customers, there are few further examples of wit in the remainder of the film.

There is an element of 'the building of the team' as Brett, the hitcher, and Loman, the Bible salesman, the newlyweds, and eventually the boy on the bike, all find sanctuary at the garage. However, unlike *It* or even *Red Rose*, there is no attempt at characterization or generation of much in the way of empathy for these figures. Connie, the wife from the newly-wed couple, has such a nauseating character and voice that it is not surprising that actress, Yeardley Smith, went on to find fame as the voice of Lisa Simpson. There is some faint social comment in Hendershot's exploitation of Billy (and by implication the others in his employ), making him work overtime for no more pay because of his parole status, but this is not pursued, although one might see some poetic justice in his demise as an illegal arms trader, being shot by an automatic weapon.

There are a few interesting ideas, such as the truck tilting its side mirrors to see Billy and Brett flirt or, later, 'nudging' Billy back towards the fuel reserve, encapsulating the conflict in the wider film, or the crane shot up to see a line of trucks stretching away into the distance. The jump to the floor-level, POV tracking shot of the electric knife is evocative of a low-budget exploitation picture and here, as in later attacks, King uses a synthesized version of the *Psycho* violins at the moment of the attack. The idea of the kid, Deke, being stalked by an ice-cream van playing 'King of the Road' could be unsettling (as it is in *Assault on Precinct 13*). And the first time we see it, it appears in the background and comes through the shot, passing through the spot where the boy had been, seconds earlier. However, the idea is quickly dropped and the van is blasted with a rocket quite easily at the end. The appearance of Handy's truck symbolizes the evil threat of the trucks, with the ironic slogan 'Here comes another load of joy' down the side, the Pennywise-style clown on the back which delivers death with a smiling face and, most of all, the green monster attached to the front. From the opening scene at the garage, we see the first of many shots inhabiting the truck's POV, through the cab window, signalled by a darkening tint to the image. This is closer to King's own view as he is the first character we see in detail in the film, putting up darker lenses on his sunglasses. Unlike the POV sequence at the opening of *Halloween,* however, this lacks coherence as the implication of sentience is neither consistent nor explained.

The concept of a horror film with a moral aesthetic only operates sporadically. A waitress, late with orders, is cut on the arm and foot by an electric knife, and an unnamed coloured character, stereotypically given to criminality, pays the price for too many video games (and for stealing from the change machine) as he becomes mesmerized by the patterns on the screen, only to be electrocuted. However, the kid flattened by the roller after the baseball match, and Duncan, the guy who gets diesel in his eyes, are hardly culpable (except possibly the latter for not seeing the clownish gag coming).

In a narrative with pace and imagination, plot holes would not necessarily matter but with characters grouped in a siege situation, and with little to do but contemplate the basic scenario, it legitimizes (and indeed invites) the audiences to do the same. If all electrical appliances are affected, why does the narrative focus so narrowly on trucks? The key question to the supernatural opposition, ('What do you want?') appears late in the narrative and to which there appears no unequivocal answer. There are also credibility issues – would a garage owner really have a private stock of rocket launchers? Why would a superior intelligence communicate in Morse code, relying on Deke to be able to translate? Loman is not struck hard enough to push him over, let alone knock him out of his shoes into a ditch. The fact that he later regains consciousness almost salvages this inconsistency but then he dies from his 'injuries'. The timing of the survivors using the drainage tunnel to escape at the precise moment the trucks attack the garage is as unbelievable as the fact that neither group pursued these actions earlier. The concept of Wilmington as a microcosm for global catastrophe is supposedly conveyed by radio bulletins and Deke cycling around his neighbourhood strewn with dead bodies but Armageddon feels like a strictly local affair. Haven Island, to which the survivors escape at the end, is conveniently close and the on-screen 'explanation' that a UFO was destroyed by a Russian 'weather satellite' two days later leaves the cause of the whole situation unclear as to whether it was a rogue comet (as suggested by the opening text-on-screen, a fairly overt borrowing from the plot ambiguity in John Wyndham's 1951 *The Day of the Triffids*) or something more calculating, which Billy, earlier, unbelievably articulates as 'the broom' to sweep away humanity prior to an alien invasion.

The weaknesses in the film can be laid very much at King's door, as the opening credits clearly tell us that this was 'written for the screen and directed by' him. Most of his decisions are fairly predictable – a self-indulgent soundtrack plays wall-to-wall AC/DC, whether the images and context merit it or not. Crashes are shown in slow-motion, both in the opening and, later, as the newly-weds are chased along the freeway. For King, this was his first and last experience of directing. It underlines very clearly the difference between literature and film in that a knowledge and proficiency in one does not automatically give you the same ability in the other and, more precisely, that an appreciation for a particular genre in one's youth does not make you an expert in recreating it 30 years later.

Graveyard Shift (Ralph S. Singleton, 1990)

Graveyard Shift is a rare example of a King film adaptation that, like the most enduring 1950s B-movies, retains an underlying political subtext. Usually, such elements are stripped out (*Hearts in Atlantis*) but here there is the clear sense of the machine having a representational quality. Like the Moloch machine in Fritz Lang's *Metropolis* (1926), the maw of the machine and the rats who feed upon it reflect the parasitical nature of the capitalist process and the absent/detached owner, who benefits from it. The film features large, industrial-sized machinery that exploits its workforce, conspiratorial managers who are happy for workers to be devoured by the machines they serve and who bribe local officials to turn a blind eye to dangerous machinery, and ends with a battle in the 'secret place' at the lowest part of the works. The machine, which drowns out all but a few fragments of the dialogue between the foreman Warwick (Stephen Macht) and Kelly (Jane Wisconsky), is crucial to the mill, which in turn is vital to the economic life of the town. The machine, here, is dominated by spinning wheels, sharp teeth, unbearable heat and few guard rails – gloves and a small first aid box provide little protection for workers. The working conditions are noisy, dirty, dark and dangerous, in short almost as Dickensian as the mill flashback in *Kingdom Hospital*.

The hierarchies of exploitation exist between the workers themselves as Carmichael, the sole black character, is made to jump, like in a western, by Brogan (Viv Polizos), drunk with the power of his pressure-hose. Earlier we see the groundless antagonism that leads Brogan to put a rat in a burger for Hall (David Andrews), a macho, workplace equivalent of the high school bullying of *Carrie*. When Warwick unexpectedly appears, Hall explains his brandishing of a catapult with 'I thought you were a rat', which is true in Warwick's promiscuous infidelity (a photo in his desk, suggests he has a wife somewhere) but also in the way he treats the workers. He knowingly allows the workers to be devoured by the monster beneath the machine and Kelly describes a sexual harassment charge that she was advised to drop by her union as she could not prove it in court. After being put on cleaning duty too, she takes revenge by smashing up Warwick's car in a very public act of rebellion and it is only Hall holding back his arm that prevents Warwick from punching her in revenge. He offers Hall minimum pay, unsociable hours and no union protection for the first month, knowing that, as a drifter with a murky past that is never explored in the film, he will not be able to refuse. Warwick flatters Hall that he 'likes his style' and is 'hand-picked' to be in the clean-up squad (lines he has used with previous workers). Ippeston (Robert Alan Beuth) tries to organize some protest against their exploitation in working as exterminators rather than cleaners but in a direct confrontation, Warwick isolates and sacks him. Cleveland, the Exterminator (Brad Dourif), is not immune either. Hall notes he is working late, to which he replies that there is a lot of competition for his line of work, suggesting times must be quite desperate economically.

Although *Graveyard Shift* is usually marketed as a horror film, there is a science-fiction narrative here as its monstrosity is motivated by a specific scientific cause. Warwick blackmails the Exterminator to get rid of the rats as, in theory, he was responsible for the dumping of toxins into the river. Without any proof that he was only following the orders of the mill-owner, Bachman (whom we never see and possibly, like King's pseudonym, used as a cover for illicit activity), Cleveland has no choice. The political aspect is underlined by Hall demanding that Warwick be his partner as 'the management should be represented in this little adventure'. Ever the cowardly general, Warwick sends Hall down first and later, underground, demands that Carmichael take the lead.

However, as soon as they break through underground, there is a corresponding generic shift and realism is largely suspended. Warwick undergoes a sudden conversion to mad psychopath, blacking his face and pursuing a personal vendetta with Hall. The landscape becomes a strange mix of man-made and natural environments: part dry mineshaft and factory workings, part wet graveyard and cave. As the literal setting breaks down, so do the generic bearings of the film, falling back increasingly on intertextual shorthand. Brogan panics and runs, only to fall through some stairs into a darker version of the garbage disposal scene of George Lucas' *Star Wars* (1977). A whole new underground realm is visible, including a giant cavern filled with bones. In a bizarre echo of the flooded mine in Émile Zola's *Germinal* (1885), Hall and Kelly use a coffin to help swim out of a flooded cave.

However, as we found with *The Dark Half*, it is difficult to literalize a metaphor and accept it as a realistic entity, reflected in the extremely inconsistent (and derivative) appearance and nature of the monster. The first kill seems a justifiable act of revenge for sadism towards the rats, which are deliberately dropped into the picking machine. The second kill is a direct reference to the scene with Brett (Harry Dean Stanton) in *Alien* (lightly hinted at in the first scene, with rats all lined up watching impassively rather than Jones, the cat) – in a dark, dripping setting, a monster, which had been part of the background, gradually reveals itself. Later, we pan from a petrified Carmichael, flicking his lighter, onto the monster right by his side, like the death of Dallas in *Alien*. Here, rather than Ridley Scott's chains, hanging sheets blend with bat-like wings, to camouflage the creature's attack. Earlier, it has a dog-like snarl, a long-fingered claw and, in the pool where Brogan falls, we see a long tentacle. Here, the creature, only shown for a split second, looks like some kind of giant fish. However, later, it is eventually seen more fully, where it blends features of the

Xenomorph from the early *Alien* films, (it glistens, can hang off the ceiling and has claws) with the later evolution of the slow-moving Queen in *Alien Resurrection* (Jean-Pierre Jeunet, 1997), showing a bat-like head and vampiric teeth. There is the slight sense that this could be exploited and polluted Nature fighting back à la John Frankenheimer's *Prophecy* (1979) but it does kill several members of the workers forced to do the work rather than those running the machine. The creature is enticed forward, trapping its tail in the workings of the machine and, with a Goliath-style sling shot, Hall's catapult starts the machine going – chewing up the creature, whose remains are feasted upon by the rats.

Cleveland's lurid stories of rats used as instruments of torture in Vietnam draws intertextual resonance from Winston Smith's greatest fear in George Orwell's *1984* (1949) and the sadistic fascination of Quint's mythic shark tale in Stephen Spielberg's *Jaws* (1975), casting his job in the light of a personal vendetta, as well as foreshadowing the end of Nordello (Ilona Margolis) on the stairs as the rats attack her stomach. There is also some effective meta-textual self-awareness in the script, with Cleveland declaring that he is not one of those 'fuck-ups you see Bruce Dern playing', only shortly after demonstrating his ankle holster, his ludicrous claim that his little terrier is a good rat hunter and later offering a handshake to Hall whilst holding a bloodied, dead rat and waving the offer of a cigarette away as if it would be bad for his health.

The confused notion of monstrosity, the blatant borrowing of generic elements, which feels more like wholesale theft than creative allusion, (particularly from *Alien* where Ridley Scott integrates an economic caste system within his character dynamics) and the consequent confusion over a political subtext all weaken the film. A quick shot of a sign heralding 'new management' closes the film, leaving the way open for a sequel, but the jokey dialogue montage under the end credits reflects an excessively derivative aesthetic which is likely to render such a film redundant.

The Lawnmower Man (Brett Leonard, 1992)

'This technology will free the mind of man or enslave it'. (Dr Lawrence Angelo)

The Lawnmower Man is the only example of a film where King has gone to court to remove his name from association with a product. The significance of this is less in the quality of the film, more that it reflects the change through the nineties in terms of King's level of control over his material, particularly the use of his name as a brand.

The film follows the standard genre trajectory of 1950s science fiction, featuring technology which could help further human development but somehow runs out of control, and does so in a very derivative way. The basic premise is not original – Ben Bova's 1969 novel *The Duelling Machine* is set in a VR game, and Cronenberg's

Videodrome explores the porous nature of reality around a high-tech game. Brett Leonard took an existing script, *Cybergod*, which he had co-written with Gemil Everett and fairly blatantly sought to tack King's name onto this project. Leonard's *Virtuosity* (1995) shows what he could do with a more rounded villain in SID 6.7 (Russell Crowe) and Cronenberg again problematizes VR game-worlds with greater subtlety in *eXistenZ* (1999). Experimenting on apes, which become violent, the subject of the opening sequence, is also the focus of George A. Romero's *Monkey Shines* (1988) but here the ridiculous over-the-shoulder monkey POV shots down the corridor undercut the potential interest of its thought processes in looking at the torturous Catherine Wheel-style gyroscopes. On-screen information has been used before in *Terminator II* and hand-held camerawork and paws entering the frame (both in picking the lock of the cage and within the VR game-world), seem dated and predictable, making the opening sequence, cast as a nightmare when Angelo wakes, ineffective.

In the hands of an actor like Johnny Depp, the man-child character of Jobe Smith, with echoes of Peter Sellers' Chance the Gardener in *Being There* (Hal Ashby, 1979), has the potential to achieve some wit and intelligence. First seen with dishevelled hair, Jeff Fahey's portrayal of Jobe has him bandy-legged like an old man and with his tongue sticking out in concentration, but quickly evolving physically so that, after a few short weeks, he becomes more erect, smoothes his hair down, takes an interest in his appearance, reveals apparently-new musculature and can verbally out-reason his abusive church 'master' who had been offering him shelter at a spiritual and physical price. He shifts from sharing an enthusiasm for comics with the kid next door to speed-reading textbooks, and from showing no interest in his flirty neighbour to a full-on sexual (and adulterous) relationship – the ethics of which remain unquestioned, apparently justified by the husband's open abuse.

Angelo's use of Jobe seems like only a slightly different form of abuse, blending animal testing with something akin to paedophile 'grooming', eliciting a promise from Jobe to keep their arrangement a secret and offering to make him smarter. Jobe's actions in burning up the priest, attacking his lover's husband with the mower, implanting an image of a mower chewing up his brain in the mind of the bully at the garage,who earlier punched him, and 'pixillating' Angelo's manipulative line manager, Timms (Mark Bringleson), all seem acts of revenge. However, Jobe's subsequent slide into evil and plan to project himself into the mainframe as an entity of 'pure energy' has no clear motivation, any more than his act of generosity in freeing the kid who has wandered unbelievably onto the site, now primed with explosives by a disillusioned Angelo.

There are a few effective shots, such as a close-up of the lawnmower pulling back to reveal that it is now running on its own, directed only by Jobe's will. The closing of the film as phones start to ring signals the birth cry of Jobe as a virtual being, but overall the film is unconvincing. The secret institution, 'Virtual Space Industries' (renamed with a William Gibson allusion as 'Virtual Light Industries' in the sequel), looks like a precursor to Falco Plains in *Golden Years*, with no greater scientific credibility. The ease with which Jobe finds a perfectly-fitting VR suit for his lover is typical of how plotting is not thought through. Typically, the scenes featuring Timms, reporting via a large video screen to his superior, shown only in close-up, seem closer to *Thunderbirds* (Gerry Anderson, 1965–66, ATV) or even *The Wizard of Oz* (Victor Fleming, 1939) than an image of the future, undermining any sense of The Shop as threatening. The problem with such intertextual overtones, as with the hedge creatures in Garris' remake of *The Shining* and the cropped shot of Coffey in *The Shawshank Redemption*, is that the texts they most closely resemble are often entertainment for children or comedies, i.e. they undermine the generic integrity of the text in question.

Dreamcatcher (Lawrence Kasdan, 2003)

'I don't think I want to see this' (Beaver to Jonesy)

Dreamcatcher does have elements typical of King narratives elsewhere in this study – small-town America, the quintessential male bonding of the hunting trip, *It*-like links between childhood and adulthood. However, overriding all this is the basic science-fiction plotline of a crashed alien spacecraft. It is not a large part of King's *oeuvre* but resurfaces in TV movie *The Tommyknockers*. Of the films in this chapter, it is the closest to the 1950s B-movie with its crash-landed aliens (like *The Thing from Another World*, 1951, Christian Nyby; produced by Howard Hawks, who also helped direct, uncredited), with which it also bears similarities in choice of location, saucer-shaped spacecraft containing an apparently-hostile alien force, political infighting, and infiltration of the human population without obvious physical mutation (as in Jack Arnold's 1953 *It Came from Outer Space* and Don Siegel's 1956 *Invasion of the Body Snatchers*, although without the birthing-pod mechanism). However, the largest threat to the individual comes not from invasion from outside (the standard 1950s symbolic threat of communism) but rogue forces from within their own government. Therefore the narrative needs to repel both the invader and the forces of order, towards which one might reasonably expect to turn in a time of crisis.

Hawks' work often explores variations of masculinity under pressure, and this finds a parallel here in the cabin scenes, but this more thoughtful element is soon lost amidst the battle with the 'shit weasels'. According to Chris Steinbrunner and Burt Goldblatt, 'Hawks believed that the essence of drama was the pitting of strong, individualistic men against odds within a stark setting,' and 'where tough men faced (with few weapons except their own courage, loyalty and camaraderie) a nearly overwhelmingly hostile nature.'[11] *Dreamcatcher* boasts a virtually all-male cast, even if not all the main characters are tough and, despite being on a hunting trip, quick wittedness does seem to be the only effective weapon they have. There are small stylistic allusions too. Kenneth von Gunden and Stuart H. Stock identify 'humorous overlapping dialogue' as a feature of Hawks' work and that also appears in the scene around the dinner table in the cabin.[12] However, whereas Hawks' movie dramatizes conflict between scientists who want to keep the alien to study it and the military who want to destroy it, if it presents a danger, *Dreamcatcher* elides these functions – science is used as justification for the military to exert control over a dispensable civilian population.

There is a clear 'flying saucer era' feel to King's original novel, which opens with a selection of newspaper headlines about alien sightings, beginning in 1947, and incidents at Roswell. However, there is a specific intertextual *X-Files* link here, not just in the location and visual style of the film but that Curtis' position is similar to that of 'the smoking man' in that the human population is kept in ignorance of repeated alien threats and the violence that is directed towards them, supposedly for their own greater good. In this, *Dreamcatcher* reflects an element in invasion movies, explored by Melvin E. Matthews Jnr., in how the fear of an alien other is used to erode civil liberties, both in the 1950s and post-9/11, and how fictional extra-terrestrial infiltration parallels the current media portrayal of Islamic extremism.[13] More specifically, the film touches upon a situation in which public faith is placed in technologically-based authority and in which public health is the mechanism and justification used to exercise mass control and brutality beyond the rule of law. Mark Jancovich notes, in discussing Fordist policies during the 1950s, that they exposed 'a growing anxiety about technocratic regulation of American social life'.[14] This is not a dominant part of *Dreamcatcher* but the holding of American citizens in enclosures secured by barbed-wire, open to freezing temperatures, and the tiny action of a minor character identifying himself by means of a Blockbuster video card, are superficial manifestations of much deeper tensions (as well as underlining the ubiquitous nature of multinational companies in forming our cultural identity and, at an extreme, even our sense of self).

'You can't do this to people in America' a minor character declares to Owen, Curtis' second-in-command, touring a hospital unit. The rapid loss of civil liberties is a given in *The Stand* (1994) and, here, victims are held in concentration camp-style compounds prior to their extermination by Curtis and his self-chosen 'Project Blue Boy' personnel. Colonel Curtis (Morgan Freeman), originally Kurtz in King's novel, would seem a conscious echo of Joseph Conrad's Kurtz from *Heart of Darkness* (1899) and may seem purely psychopathic at first (he calls himself 'a monster'). However he has been dealing with a resilient enemy over 25 years that shows no sign of wishing to negotiate with humanity but only colonize or destroy it. The obsessive zeal with which he enforces quarantine may be the only way to save humanity. As far as he is concerned, his job is 'not to get all gooey about the little picture' but 'to take care of the big one'.

The film is noteworthy primarily for its manifestation of monstrosity in its literal and metaphorical forms. King is at pains in interviews to stress how *Dreamcatcher* is an attempt to break the taboo of what lies beyond the door of the toilet: the room where the first signs of cancer may well be found. However, it is highly debatable to what extent audiences are drawn by the hope of experiencing such a discordant blend of high-flown ideals and extremely base expression. The body is certainly in a state of revolt, with the protagonists confronted with chronic flatulence and diarrhoea. The first client of therapist Henry (Thomas Jane), lying on the couch, his fingers locked across his fat stomach, later eats himself to death but it is hard to ascribe metaphysical significance to such literal images. This surfaces elsewhere; for example in 'ringing' Jonesy (Damian Lewis), using Owen's (Tom Sizemore) revolver, it is not clear why Henry needs a similar-shaped physical object to achieve a metaphysical idea. The film works better as an examination of what Beaver (Jason Lee) terms, 'the scuzzy facts of life'. Beaver and Jonesy say nothing about Rick (the first victim) and his overpowering stench, only rushing to the windows after they have laid him in bed. Social propriety and the denial of bodily functions govern actions, even when at a distance from 'civilized society'.

However, the literalism of a monster in the toilet bowl is more reminiscent of urban legends about alligators in sewers, and more interesting is Beaver's need for a toothpick. He strains to reach the only one that has fallen on an unbloodied tile. Like Toomey's paper ripping in *The Langoliers*, Beaver's compulsive behaviour does not save him and, here, actually leads to his death. The suggestive quality of a ripped shower curtain (a nod to *Psycho*) or Beaver's glasses falling (a lack of vision in moving from the seat), is undercut by the thing which lands on his back and grabs him between the legs with a two-pronged claw. Henry's discovery of the eggs and the recently-hatched worms could be full of tension (his matches could fail or he could catch fire himself) but nothing happens and he burns everything without incident.

The 'weasels' themselves combine features of snakes, in their slithering movement and egg-laying, and slugs, in the slime-trail they leave, but they can also apparently jump, as they do at Jonesy, who slams the toilet door on one, and at Henry in the final confrontation. The weakness, as elsewhere in King's work, is less in the realization than in basic conceptions. There is an effective blend of stalking with sudden movement, as when Beaver looks down to see his fingers mostly gone after a sudden blurred lunge. However, the hand-to-hand combat shots just look ridiculous as Beaver keeps a weasel at bay with a toilet brush and wrestles with it as if it were a draught excluder. Unlike the *Alien* franchise, where the creatures coherently develop and evolve, here the conception of the aliens seems confused. The exact relationship between Mr Grays 'A', standing behind Jonesy in the cabin – tall, slightly luminous, almost jelly-like with an interior glow – and Mr Grays 'B', involved in the ground attack, which scurry around in panic like human-sized tadpoles, remains unclear.

Like the weasels themselves, it is very much a hybrid film. The opening credit sequence dissolves between black and white aerial photos with a rotating camera, partial shots of dreamcatchers and snowflakes, distorted into swirls in a similar way to the credits for *Alien Resurrection* (Jean-Pierre Jeunet, 1997). The combined effect is to establish an icy setting, shifting identities and the linkage of past and present.

As the pursuit of Jonesy intensifies, the cross-cutting between pursuer and pursued is often achieved with a slightly blurred vertical wipe, a device closely associated, in modern cinema at least, with *Star Wars*. Captions of time passing in an isolated, snowy landscape evoke *The Shining*'s intertitles. In a film featuring advanced CGI effects, the choice of a very simple and theatrical method of showing Jonesy's possession seems incongruous. On the snow-scooter, he is shot from alternate sides of the 180 degree line, disorientating the viewer slightly perhaps but the juxtaposition of his 'normal' speaking voice (although with a fake American accent) with a plummy English accent, smiling gestures and rapid head movements, does seem an odd choice and in taking a patrol car, and with his ability to impersonate the policeman he killed, he seems more like a low-budget of *Terminator II*'s T-1000.

A number of plot-holes remain. Whereas, elsewhere in this book, such weaknesses serve to underline a lack of pace, here it is narrative structure and characterization (along with blurry notions of monstrosity) that undermine identification with dramatic action. For example, we are unclear about the reason for Henry's suicidal impulses, why Beaver's enhanced sense of danger does not warn him about the shit weasels and Jonesy's accident, after which he is described as 'changed' but does not seem much different (apart from the limp). The exact reason why Duddits beckons him across the road only to be run-down, how Curtis' single helicopter could evade the whole US military and why the aliens need to travel to a particular water-plant if one worm can kill the world – all remain ambiguous. The idea of making a human chain to reach someone trapped in a pipe is unrealistic and strangely cut (when only one person is being held) before we see how obvious this is. Like the hand-to-hand fighting of the aliens in *The Tommyknockers*, the need for direct body-to-body contact for infection to take place hardly seems symptomatic of vastly more intelligent beings. The mystery of who Duddits is and his relation to the boys (explained half an hour into the film via a flashback sequence) does not easily dovetail with the alien crash-landing plot. Duddits message, revealed later as 'Ask for/hello Mr Gray' and the idea that a retarded boy with a speech defect is really an alien whose job it is to save mankind, takes more narrative time to make convincing than we have here. It is important to emphasize here that such examples are not part of a pedantic approach to credibility – plenty of fiction contains many aspects which are not 'realistic' or 'believable' in a literal sense but the point is that there are so many, often linked to central characters, that this fatally weakens the dramatic impact of the film. Extra-terrestrials are a good example of where lack of experience in the real world means we are obviously more likely to draw upon our generic knowledge to make sense of them. Key questions over their motivation and powers and the reaction of the human protagonists need to be answered for us to engage with such a narrative.

The notion of the 'Memory Warehouse' is an interesting one, although, like the weasels, part of a strong sense of literalism in the film. While Henry is driving with Duddits to the water plant, as soon as he thinks of something, we cut to a shot of it. The warehouse's notion of psychic space as physical office space has been seen before from Kafka's *The Trial* (Orson Welles, 1962), *Brazil* (Terry Gilliam, 1985) to

Being John Malkovich (Spike Jonze, 1999). Here, there is a strangely anachronistic element, deliberately predating electronic data, as we see Jonesy moving box files and wheeling trolleys of crates around a circular building, which has the feel of a nineteenth-century library. After his own serious accident in 1999, King himself had to rethink how he learns things. We see Jonesy organize boxes of 'Rock and Roll lyrics', computer instructions ('How the damn thing works') and other categories, 'Jerk-off fantasies' and 'Sports humiliations', which humorously merit sub-categories of their own. Material to be forgotten is burned in a *Citizen Kane*-style furnace to the accompaniment of 'Blue Bayou' (the song that calms Duddits after they rescue him).

After explaining the 'warehouse' idea, we cut to a blue-screen shot of the cabin scene with Jonesy outside looking in at his own life. It also occurs when Jonesy is on the motor-scooter and could herald a more thoughtful film – along the lines of David Cronenberg's *Spider*, released the same year. However, nothing is made of this beyond suggesting that the whole film could be projected subjective fantasy or the memory of Jonesy from his innermost and most precious office in his warehouse. This too is literalized, as a different-looking monster pursues him through the warehouse, although why it can only peer into his inner sanctum (via a wide angle lens shot) and seem unable to penetrate an ordinary wooden door is unclear. These sections descend into conventional monster-movie mode as we cut between obscured shots of the monster, tail thrashing and its red-washed POV shots of Jonesy furiously trying to hide all the files on Duddits. The logic of why Jonesy should see Pete (Timothy Olyphant) being killed on the scooter as if on a giant omniscient cinema screen of his own, or why he still limps here in his own projected fantasy, is also not clear.

Possibly the strongest elements of the film that enrich the generic mix are seen when King draws metatextually on his own rite-of-passage works. There are clear echoes of *Stand by Me* and *It* in the plot and in its visualization. Like *It*, there is the same image of a group of five friends holding hands in an act of solidarity to help solve the disappearance of young people (a girl is found in a sewer pipe) and, like *Stand by Me*, there is the iconic shot of a group of young boys wandering along a railway line. The back-story of *Dreamcatcher*, like *Stand by Me* and *It*, is set in small-town America, includes the facing down of bullies and features a group of lifelong friends on the cusp of adulthood who bond together to battle forces greater than themselves, thereby sharing a traumatic experience (with the supernatural in two of the three narratives), which casts a long shadow over their adult lives. The quick interchange of Jock-style chat about movie trivia (pure William Goldman) around the table in the cabin, especially with the *Roseanne*-style rotating camera and the quick exchanges between Pete and Beaver in the cabin, feel like an adult version of the tree-house dialogue in *Stand by Me*. It is quick, colloquial and full of sexual euphemisms (distinguishing between a 'fuckaree' and a 'fuckaroo' in their life of casual and meaningless relationships).

The ending can only really be described as a mess. It is true that the agents of extra-terrestrial evil are vanquished but the plotting problems with the aliens are brought into sharp focus. The conventional ending on the DVD has Duddits inexplicably transforming into a different kind of alien, battling Mr Grays and saving the world but being reduced to a cloud of red dust, momentarily in the shape of a dreamcatcher. Jonesy stamps on the baby worm just before it can poison Boston's water supply and the film closes weakly on a freeze-frame after an exchange of names between Henry and Jonesy. Originally, there was no baby worm at the end and Duddits kills Grays by blasting him with a finger 'wormhole' effect. Here, the film closes with a cemetery scene, paying tribute to Duddits' sacrifice as Jonesy and Henry sing 'Blue Bayou'. Before this, having vanquished Mr Grays, Duddits throws up his arms in a two-armed victory salute and shouts 'Duddits' ('Done it') – the significance of the name being completely lost in the revised ending.

There are some thoughtful shots which do attempt to add to the genre, particularly in terms of establishing an otherworldly setting, such as the snowflake that falls in slow-motion onto Beaver's glasses as he looks up whilst hunting. There is also not just the night-time, birds-eye shot over a car winding through woodland, but an interesting variation, looking forward, shooting across the tops of the trees as snow falls, which in retrospect could be the POV of the alien craft crash-landing. The music of James Newton Howard, reminiscent of some of David Sylvian's early instrumental work, uses chimes with a limited range of high notes to convey a dripping effect. The shot of Jonesy and Beaver watching various creatures fleeing an unseen danger, *Bambi*-like, establishes that some disaster has befallen the area which animals perceive before people. A subsequent reflected window shot shows both subject and object of the gaze simultaneously, followed by the actors stepping outside so that actors and CGI images intermingle in the same screen space, creating a greater sense of credibility.[15] Pete and Henry's later approach to the kneeling, hooded woman cuts between their POV and shots in the same direction but behind them, so we do not see the woman's face until they reach her – a little reminiscent of the nightmarish female dwarf at the end of Nick Roeg's *Don't Look Now*, although the cutting is too slow and the music insufficiently threatening to create a similar sense of dread. There is some witty dialogue: Pete elicits a promise from Henry before he goes for help that, if Pete dies, he will not tell anyone that the infected woman was his date and, later, talking mostly to himself, he nominally addresses the woman, intertextually drawing on the language of commercials – 'I find you very attractive also ... the truck that handles like a luxury car.'

Overall, the film feels like *The Thing from Another World* (Christian Nyby, 1951 and the John Carpenter 1982 remake – an isolated, snowbound setting; aliens crash-landing and subsuming humans; an infected individual, seeking help, crashes into a group of male characters) blended with *The X-Files* (pursuits in dark forests; shadowy government agencies vying for supremacy). There is some ambition in small examples of form but the derivative and confused plot fails to bind different elements together. The film feels like a big-budget mess and is likely to be remembered, if at all, *Friends*-style, as 'the one with the shit weasels.'

Conclusion

Dreamcatcher is symptomatic of a notion of monstrosity in several King adaptations that can, at best, be described as fluid and more often, fuzzy. It is one thing to be faced by a fictional adversity that can change its shape but the manner and relationship between the two types of alien in the film is confused and confusing. Unlike Robert Wise's *The Day the Earth Stood Still* (1951), there is no element of communication between alien and human, preventing any level of understanding of motive and development of empathy. We are even denied the option of parody, as in Tim Burton's *Mars Attacks* (1996).

Fear of technology exceeding human control is a mainstay of science fiction films, stretching back at least as far as the robot Maria in Fritz Lang's German Expressionist classic *Metropolis*. What makes King's personal phobia more out of step with its time is that his fear is directed not at machines that look or act like humans: his objects of supposed dread are not the robots of Asimov or even James Cameron but the humble automobile. If there was political criticism here, like Aldous Huxley's parody of Fordism in *Brave New World* (1932), environmental protest as in Heathcote Williams' long poem *Autogeddon* or an Amish-style religious objection to technology per se, that might make sense but none of the films in this section mention the dehumanizing, ubiquitous or sinful nature of the car as the source of its danger – its malign nature just simply is. There is none of Philip K. Dick's problematizing of borders between man and machine. None show possession by some satanic entity, like Elliot Silverstein's *The Car* (1977), which, with speeded up motion, blackened windows and extended long shots building an element of dread at the steady approach of the car, at least tries to create a sense of threat. This is all the more surprising since King knows about such films, showing appreciation of *The Car* in *Danse Macabre*.[16] A car that runs out of control is not difficult to imagine – when we drive, we need only let our concentration drift for a second or two and the consequences are clear. The cars and lorries we see in this section do not drive faster than they would with human agency, just differently, as if imbued with the spirit of the meanest drivers we can imagine. The problem is, with the advent of 'road rage' as a recognized cultural phenomenon, we already see around us examples of driver behaviour not far from what King would have us believe is apparently apocalyptic. Broader, sociologically-engaged themes seem of little interest – we do not have atomic testing, paranoia about Communist invasion or wider questions about mankind's place in the universe. The cod-scientific 'explanation' for the events of *Maximum Overdrive* seems a clumsy plot contrivance rather than an attempt at a political point. King's focus, and that of the films in this section, is unremittingly small-scale – it is the technology of personal transportation and the industrialized workplace. He dramatizes machines that we might see and use ourselves, placing these films closer to the final chapter – which really is terror of the everyday.

There seems an irresistible, nostalgic pull on King to recreate the cinematic monsters of his formative years but they no longer resonate with contemporary audiences (reflected in weak sales of *Cycle of the Werewolf*). It is telling that his coverage of horror in *Danse Macabre* dwells on those films of his youth in the 1950s especially, rather than those closer to his time of writing (1981). Many of the films in this section may look, at first sight, like monster movies from the 1950s but, surface features aside, they do not deliver those particular pleasures associated with this subgenre effectively. Looked at more closely, they often lack even the surface features that might have made them more convincing genre pieces. Undercut by confused notions of monstrosity, King's idiosyncratic view of technology, hamstrung by low budgets which cannot deliver special effects to an audience who may well expect spectacle, and detached from a political context that might have lent a metaphorical coherence to the manifestation of the Other, they disappoint because they do not deliver the pleasures that generic predictions might reasonably expect.

Notes

1. Stephen King, 'An Evening with Stephen King at the Billerica, Massachusetts Public Library', in Underwood and Miller (eds.), *Bare Bones: Conversations on Terror with Stephen King*, op. cit., p. 20.
2. See Peter Biskind, *Seeing is Believing: How Hollywood Taught Us to Stop Worrying and Love the Fifties* (New York: Pantheon Books, 1983).
3. Stephen King, *Night Shift*, op. cit., p. 14.
4. See Kendall R. Phillips, *Projected Fears: Horror Films and American Culture* (Westport: Praeger Publishers, 2005), David Skal, *The Monster Show: A Cultural History of Horror* (London: Faber & Faber, 2001) and Stephen Greenblatt, *Learning to Curse: Essays in Early Modern Culture*, (London: Routledge, 2007).
5. Stephen King, *Danse Macabre*, op. cit., p. 66.
6. See Harry M. Benshoff, *Monsters in the Closet: Homosexuality and the Horror Film* (Manchester: Manchester University Press, 1997).
7. Stephen King, *Christine* (London: New English Library, 1984), p. 233.
8. Ibid., p. 493.
9. Stephen King, *Danse Macabre*, op. cit., p. 191.
10. Stephen King, *Christine*, op. cit., p. 95.
11. Chris Steinbrunner and Burt Goldblatt, *Cinema of the Fantastic* (New York: Galahad Books, 1972), p. 221.
12. Kenneth von Gunden and Stuart H. Stock, *Twenty All-Time Great Science Fiction Films* (New York: Arlington, 1982), p. 32.
13. See Melvin E. Matthews Jnr., *Hostile Aliens, Hollywood and Today's News: 1950s Science Fiction Films and 9/11* (New York: Algora Publishing, 2007).
14. Mark Jancovich (ed.), *The Horror Reader*, (New York: Routledge, 2002), p. 51.
15. See Slavoj Žižek's notion of 'the metasuturing of the interface' in *The Fright of Real Tears* (London: BFI Publishing, 2001), p. 53.
16. Stephen King, *Danse Macabre*, op. cit., p. 190.

CHAPTER SIX

THE GREAT ESCAPE: PRISON DRAMA

The term, 'prison movie' is a little problematic. Intertextuality as a viewing strategy comes more strongly into play when the situation described in a text is alien to the audience's experience. A little like schema theory in Psychology, it could be said that in relation to fictional genres where we have no direct personal experience, such as science fiction, the prime way in which viewers make sense of narratives is by comparisons with other texts. John Fiske talks about the example of car chases but we might also apply this notion to the prison movie.[1] Even given the increase in the western prison population, relatively few viewers will have firsthand experience of life in a high-security jail, meaning that our view of prison is more influenced by fictional representations, which, in Fiske's terms, act as a 'prospectus' for filmmakers and audiences who 'encode' and 'decode' these conventions. This is all the more so in genres which are rarely made, providing a more limited source of coding material and making the relatively few examples proportionately more influential. *The Shawshank Redemption* and *The Green Mile*, even given the opening and ending of the former and the flashback elements and organized 'outing' in the latter, are both firmly set within the confines of a correctional facility. Indeed, their very titles refer to the name of a specific prison and one of its established rituals.

The pleasures of watching prison films are harder to explain. Most do not feature explicit sex, chase sequences and, by their very nature, are somewhat limited in terms of locations. All the films in this chapter have recognizable stars, with whom we might identify, but it is the roles they perform rather than their sheer presence that makes the difference. Crucially, *Shawshank* and, to a lesser extent, *The Green Mile* not only both deliver the generic expectations of a prison movie but exceed them. In a genre whose setting is inherently bleak and repetitive, both manage to create inspirational and aspirational narratives. Many prison movies focus on stoicism as a coping strategy, sporadic escape attempts and the brutality of those in charge (the last two features providing action sequences in fairly static plots) but what sets the films in this chapter apart is how these elements are realized.

Initial, and sometimes surprising, brutality is the norm, such as Captain Kennauer beating Paul Crewe in *The Longest Yard*, (UK title, *The Mean Machine*, Robert Aldrich, 1974). In *Shawshank*, violence is portrayed as unexceptional but its open manifestation in sexual violation is particularly rare. Unusual, too, is the reaction to violence. In contrast with Alan Parker's *Midnight Express* (1978), which shows a brutal and brutalizing system, from which the hero only finally escapes by indulging in equally violent acts: killing a guard, albeit accidentally, or *Scum* (Alan Clarke, 1979), where a male rape is ultimately revenged by vicious attacks on an informer, including the animalistic biting off of his tongue, director Frank Darabont rejects such scenarios. Brutality here is conveyed in a throwaway aside at the table the following morning; the victim unnamed. By contrast, the hi-tech exploding collars of *The Running Man* are only a technological and ironically less imaginative version of the chain gang system and *The Green Mile* casts all its brutality in personal terms on one deficient individual, Percy.

Stoicism is often shown as one possible strategy to get through one's prison term but in *Shawshank*, through the characterization of Tim Robbins, greater depth is added by a saintly selflessness and enigmatic quality missing even from Paul Newman's eponymous hero in *Cool Hand Luke* (Stuart Rosenberg, 1962), or Alec Guinness' Nicholson in *The Bridge on the River Kwai* (David Lean, 1957). In these examples, the hero suffers repeated punishments, including beatings or other physical deprivation designed to break his spirit. Steve McQueen's Captain Hilts in *The Great Escape* (John Sturges, 1963) and Henri Charrière in *Papillon* (Franklin J. Schaffner, 1973) endure through a tight-lipped, tenacity of spirit. This stoicism can include small, often Pyrrhic, victories against the system, sometimes providing a film's most memorable moment. Hilts and Nicholson endure the apparently 'unendurable' in solitary, Crewe engineers sadistic acts of revenge against the guards in the context of a football game and Colin Smith (Tom Courtenay) in *The Loneliness of the Long Distance Runner* (Tony Richardson, 1962) shows the reverse situation by deliberately losing a race.

Nicole Rafter suggests that prison movies tend to exist beyond alignment to a particular era, recognizable by stock characters, themes and plots.[2] These include 'the prison innocent', 'the Rat' or 'Snitch', the experienced buddy who befriends the new inmate, and a head guard who may be initially fair-minded films but become progressively more brutal and egocentric. Not all of these generic features appear in the films discussed here, such as the informer – often the most reviled figure in prison narratives. There is an element of this function in Percy's 'connections' in *The Green Mile* but this is more to protect his own incompetence than to act as a parasite within the jail.

The motif of the arrival of a new prisoner differs in *Shawshank*, where Dufresne is part of a large-scale system in which the individual is reduced step-by-step with the removal of clothes (and thereby dignity), the addition of powder (almost like a baby) and the compulsory wearing of uniform, signalling a process of juvenilization. In *The Green Mile*, inmates arrive singly to some fanfare and are in some ways treated as minor celebrities. For a short time, before the state kills them, they occupy a literal and metaphorical place reserved for the privileged few: 'the green mile' of the title. Ironically, in this place where all hope (legal and emotional) appears to have gone, it is Edgecomb's avowed intention to maintain a level of breezy efficiency and thereby endure the apparently intolerable. This might be seen to have the inmates' spiritual needs at heart but it can also be read as a more Machiavellian wish to keep order, to keep the wheels of a discredited system turning (he shortly leaves after Coffey's execution, unable to sanction a system in which he no longer believes).

Generic features may not disappear from one era to the next but they do evolve and mutate, reflecting shifting public perceptions about prison as a successful punitive or reformative tool.[3] In particular, Deral Cheatwood identifies a shift from a reform-minded Warden to a megalomaniac, and the innocent inmate to a greater alignment with an action hero, certainly reflected in *Shawshank*'s Warden and Schwarzenegger's Ben Richards in *The Running Man*. Cheatwood suggests a four-stage model: the Depression Era (1930s); the post-war rehabilitation era (1942–60); the containment era (1963–80); and the administrative era (1981–the present). Shawshank has Cheatwood's elements of scale in its mass incarceration (think of the helicopter shot across the yard) filled with lifers without hope of parole, yet Red's apparent contrition and ultimate rehabilitation would place it later than the Depression era. Rafter and Cheatwood's theories are persuasive for the films they interrogate but narratives are most memorable where they expand and even question generic boundaries.

The Shawshank Redemption (Frank Darabont, 1994)

Andy: I'm a convicted murderer who provides sound financial planning.

Director and screenwriter Frank Darabont had already some experience with King on his 'dollar-baby', *The Woman in the Room* (1983), and would go on to work with him again on *The Green Mile*. The film, based on King's novella 'Rita Hayworth and Shawshank Redemption', was nominated for seven Academy Awards but failed to win any, losing out particularly to *Forrest Gump* (Robert Zemekis). However, since then year-by-year, the critical stock of the film has steadily risen to current top ten status in public polls of all-time favourites.

The film is more radical than it appears in its basic narrative form. It is a critical commonplace in reviewing King's fiction that its power lies in its page-turning quality. *Shawshank* also explicitly foregrounds storytelling features – particularly apt in a film about the creation of a myth. Usually, overt voiceover narration would be seen as too obvious but the key difference here is Morgan Freeman's acting persona and the sheer charismatic power of his oratory. A white, ginger-haired Irishman in

King's text, the casting decision seems perverse until we hear the power of Freeman's voice. With the exception of acting against type in *Hard Rain* (Mikael Solomon, 1998), he has specialized in roles requiring gravitas and integrity. He manages to combine obedience and respect for authority with a slightly ironic undertone as Hoke Colburn in *Driving Miss Daisy* (Bruce Beresford, 1989) and Azeem in *Robin Hood: Prince of Thieves* (Kevin Reynolds, 1991), loyalty as Detective Lt. William Somerset in *Seven* (David Fincher, 1995) and even a credible President in *Deep Impact* (Mimi Leder, 1998). Steven Spielberg chose him to narrate events of global import in *War of the Worlds* (2005) and there are few actors who convey unquestionable character integrity through voice alone, making him the natural choice as God in Tom Shadyac's *Bruce Almighty* (2003) and *Evan Almighty* (2007). Freeman's Oscar nomination for Best Actor in a Leading Role is actually a strange choice, in a way, as he does relatively little on screen but his presence, through the voiceover, is what binds the film together. Darabont also chose to prerecord all of Freeman's voiceover and use it on playback during filming, i.e. it is not added in post-production, giving the words a real sense of running commentary rather than explaining events with the wisdom of hindsight.

Visually, it also works, literalizing King's racial metaphor describing the non-status of every prisoner – that 'every con's a nigger'.[4] The film also by-passes a practical problem – the novella describes how Red picks up information about the myths surrounding Andy but, here, what we see is a tale told in retrospect, juxtaposing subjective first-person views with omniscient camera work, allowing us to trust what could only be Red's partial view in reality. Red, the first person teller of the tale, as the 'man who can get things', even Rita Hayworth, in a manner of speaking, cannot easily work out Andy Dufresne, who remains an enigma to him (and therefore also to the viewer), generating curiosity, sympathy and suspense at the end about whether Andy has committed suicide after the hope that Tommy represented has been cruelly plucked away. Red is another writer: the narrative we see/read is supposedly his retrospective account of Andy's time at Shawshank. The novella explicitly states: 'It's all about me … Andy was the part of me they could never lock up'.[5] In that sense, it is Red who finds redemption through the model of Andy, and the primacy of Red's view is established as we follow Freeman, via a long take, walking across the prison yard, blurred figures walking through the shot. His voiceover begins, striking a typical tone: relaxed, representative, laconic ('There must be a guy like me in every prison in America …').

The long take which rises up from the back of the van bringing Andy to Shawshank, passes right over the compound and picks up the van again at the front entrance. More than an establishing shot to fix the geography of the main setting, this also suggests Andy's key gift that he manages to pass on to those around him – the transcendent power of the imagination (and by extension cinema: film shows feed the fantasy lives of the men inside) to fly over the walls. This POV shot also evokes aerial food-drops in famine or disaster zones, casting Andy as the bringer of some kind of nourishment to the masses below. Darabont credits his production designer, Terence Marsh, with a number of key contributions to the film: the huge interior Escher-like prison set (which most viewers assume is shot on location), the climactic field of alfalfa and this aerial sequence, which does even not appear in the script. The human figures we see scurrying to the front gate show the best of humanity (curious despite themselves about someone new) and the worst (looking for fresh meat to exploit) in an ambivalent mix of supportive applause and baying mob (particularly from Andy's POV through the wire where soon he will be without the protection of class or social status). With the guards above, brandishing their shotguns, the most human welcome comes from the other inmates. Alfonso Freeman, Morgan's son, delivers the taunting 'Fresh fish' dialogue (as well as providing an eerie mug-shot for the younger Morgan).

Authority figures always feature in prison narratives but in Warden Norton, Darabont creates an arch hypocrite: spouting scripture and Christian teachings whilst overseeing a completely corrupt system. In an inverted system of values, his main rule, 'No blasphemy' supersedes all others. The hypocrisy of the sampler, 'His judgement cometh and that right soon' covering the safe, where he keeps the details of the bribes from the prisoner work programme and other varied scams, comes back to haunt him, and the sequence in which Andy carefully puts the papers inside (including a shot from within the safe), is repeated later to show the switch. Andy assumes the fraudulent identity set up for the Warden, shown via flashback like that in *The Usual Suspects*, whereby we re-evaluate written text, repeated actions and the setting up of a phantom identity in the light of new information. Kermode stresses similarity between Norton and Nixon as an example of a hypocritical politician, linked later with Red's description of the term 'Rehabilitation' as 'a politician's word'. However, in terms of body language and appearance, including glasses, actor Bob Gunton actually bears a closer resemblance to a young Henry Kissinger, who, although not accused over the Watergate scandal, nonetheless, as National Security Advisor in Nixon's first term, could be identified as the guiding hand behind his flawed foreign policy over Vietnam, Cambodia and the bombing of Laos.[6]

Kermode ultimately concludes that the attraction of the film remains an 'unresolved mystery' but many viewers identify the scene when Andy barricades himself in the library and plays the Mozart aria '*Sull'aria? Che soave zeffiretto*' over the prison tannoy (a key addition to King's novella), as key to its appeal.[7] As the first bars drift across the institution, everyone, prisoners and guards, those inside and, most dramatically, those outside, all look upwards in roughly the same direction. As Spielberg shows in films like *Close Encounters of the Third Kind* (1977), close-ups on faces looking up at some miraculous entity greater than themselves can create a transcendent effect, especially so when complemented by powerful music. Andy leans back in his chair with a beatific smile on his lips and his only response to the fury of the Warden at the door is to lean forward and turn up the volume (an improvisation from Robbins). Like Kubrick's *Paths of Glory* (1957), we see the effect on an all-male, brutalized group of a young girl singing in a language alien to her audience (Christiane Harlan, the future Mrs Kubrick, singing 'The Faithful Hussar'). Freeman's voiceover makes the significance clear: 'I have no idea to this day what those two Italian ladies were singing about. The truth is I don't wanna know. Some things are best left unsaid ... It was like some beautiful bird flapped into our drab little cage and made those walls dissolve away.' The beauty of the something ineffable and uncrushable (its power enhanced by its forbidden status), gives hope and nourishment to the men's spirits (as McMurphy's use of a fictional TV picture of the World Series in *One Flew Over the Cuckoo's Nest*). Afterwards, Andy asks his fellows, 'Haven't you ever felt that way about music?' and that the importance of the act was so they 'don't forget there are places in the world that aren't made out of stone.'

In terms of the title of King's source story, *Shawshank* is clearly an intertextual work but more specifically, film and art more generally, offer escapism, literally via the Rita Hayworth film poster, but also the opportunity for men to escape in shared screenings (reflected in the transcendent images of Red and Andy looking up). Even Andy's attempted escape from Bogs occurs in the projection room and reels of film offer a weapon against brutalization. In a small link missed by Kermode, Glenn Ford and George Macready's dialogue in *Gilda* (Charles Vidor, 1946) uses the term 'canary', linking back both to Red's comments on the music and the specific word he chooses to describe Andy after his escape, which carries connotations of captivity, tunnelling and a thing of beauty too great to be suppressed. Kermode notes that 'Andy appears to have become some sort of god, the writer/director of his own movie, the creator of a fictional character' – Randall Stephens, the alter ego he creates superficially for Norton but actually for himself, literalizing the cliché of filling another man's shoes.[8] It is the fact that such literalization is not seen (like the 'salvation lies within' concept of the rock hammer in the Bible), which adds piquancy to Andy's audacity – the belief that Norton, a very literal adversary, would miss the clues right in front of his face. Red claims that 'You can't just make a person up' to which Andy replies 'Sure you can' – his triumph is one of the artistic imagination over all those forces which would seek to crush it, reflected in Norton's habit of citing by rote the words of others rather than creating something original. Furthermore, Andy not only crafts a narrative himself, one is created about him after his departure, in which he becomes a 'star' in his own right and a symbol of hope for those left behind.

Many prison movies detail repeated escape attempts against the odds, such as *Papillon*, *The Great Escape* (referenced in Andy's dropping of soil from his trouser pockets during exercise out in the yard) or John Frankenheimer's *The Birdman of Alcatraz*, (1962) alluded to in Hatlen's crow, Jake, but *Shawshank* has something more. It dramatizes how, in a brutalizing system, one individual refuses to be brutalized. Andy refuses to adopt the hate-filled behaviour by which he is surrounded. Andy certainly has a hope, a dream, to which he clings (how hard we only discover by the end) but it is more than just a tale of mere survival. Brooks survives in the prison but at the expense of part of his humanity, which leaves him lost once outside the prison walls. The film examines, in an explicitly practical way, the same philosophical question that, in a different generic area, is explored by Philip K. Dick: what it is to be human. Music (his stunt in the library), Art (his rock carvings), Literature (his library project) – these are the things an appreciation of which make us human. Andy preserves those parts of himself (or discovers them within him) which allow him not just to endure but to transcend adversity without becoming bitter, cynical or despairing. From his first steps into the prison, we do not see him griping about his unjust conviction or weeping on his first night – he personifies his later advice in that from the outset, he 'gets busy living'. This is the pleasure in beating the system – the beers he secures for the work on the roof (in which he does not partake), the library building and books, the literacy teaching of his fellows, are all for others. His first reaction after being told about the fat guy's death is to ask what his name was. Even the maggot he finds in his food he gives to Brooks for his bird. He subverts the expectations of the system by not only looking after himself.

From the outset, Andy, pictured sitting erect in the bus, in the middle of the T-frame, wearing a suit but no cap, is visually set apart from the other passengers. His question to Hadley on the roof, 'Do you trust your wife?' sounds like provocative foolishness but sets up the first deal to use his knowledge for the benefit of his peers. The risk he runs is conveyed by Darabont's camera positioning, using a bird's-eye crane shot, showing the vertiginous drop down the side of the building and then falling back behind Hadley for an over-the-shoulder shot as the danger recedes. We cut back several times to the other workers who are watching – first in fear, then puzzlement, and finally admiration – guiding the viewer's response as the balance of power shifts from brutality to selflessness.

The film also subverts the expectations of viewers: there is relatively little violence, sex or scenes of action. The beatings of Andy and the consequent revenge of the guards on Bogs mostly occur off-camera and are suggested by sound effects rather than direct visuals. The climactic escape is told in flashback, low-key for the most part apart from his transcendent ripping off his prison uniform and raising his arms in triumph to the stormy night. Matters of gender are almost irrelevant: Andy's wife, seen briefly at the beginning, is virtually the only woman shown on screen. The film raises questions of value: Andy appears guilty but is actually innocent; the Warden appears saintly to the outside world but is in truth mired in corruption; and a small rock hammer achieves something momentous. Red wishes he could say that Andy 'fought the good fight and the Sisters let him be … but prison's no fairy tale world.' The camera withdraws round a corner as Andy is beaten into submission. He is repeatedly gang-raped but it is his reaction which is important, resisting physically but also with guile. When cornered by Bogs in the projection room, he appears to give in but grabs a reel to fight with and then, when faced with the prospect of oral sex under duress, he uses mental agility, describing how sudden brain injury causes the human jaw to lock down instinctively. Even from a low-life like Bogs there is genuine sense of admiration in his reaction: 'Where d'you get this shit?' The superhuman patience of his letter-writing campaign (cynically dismissed by the Warden) makes sufficient nuisance of himself until the hard-hearted Senate board relent and donate money, pleading for him to stop (and prompting 'Good for you, Andy' from a guard – the only positive comment from the staff in the whole film).

Kermode's analysis focuses very much on working through all the religious references, particularly the instinctive cursing and swearing in the dialogue, and symbolic actions, such as the number of men on the roof and Andy's abstinence from drinking, (casting him as Christ amongst the apostles). He puts a strong emphasis on the ambiguity over Andy's guilt from the outset, making his redemption and acceptance of some moral responsibility for his wife's death all the more powerful when his innocence is later underlined with Tommy's appearance in the narrative. Mitigating factors in Andy's favour (that his wife seems to be having an affair and that he needs drink to steel himself to act), encourage us to sympathize with him. Kermode does see Andy's 'beatific smile', both in Norton's office and on the roof, as confirmation of his role as 'the spiritual saviour of Shawshank's inmates', although he does not analyse fully the precise nature of this divinity.[9]

Dufresne keeps something of himself inside (he sits apart from the other men on the roof), which a Christian reading might call his soul, but at the table he taps his head and his heart, suggesting these are the sources of his humanity: his intelligence and his emotional being. Kermode talks of 'relative clumsiness' of 'overly explanatory' dialogue where Andy says how he survived solitary because he had 'Mr Mozart to keep him company' and, like the final reunion on the beach, overtly sentimental.[10] However, it serves to emphasize how he does not fear solitary confinement, because the prison cannot take these things away from him unless he lets them. As the Warden fails to realize, short of killing him, Andy is beyond punishment, making him a dangerous enemy. Reading is important for him, not just as a trained accountant but as one who appreciates literature, becoming a pseudo-teacher to fellow inmates to whom he enthuses about particular texts that they might enjoy. Education is also the source of his particular skill, causing first Hadley, next other officers, then the Warden, and finally the whole staff and those from visiting prisons, to queue up at his desk – knowledge is power. It could be said that he abuses this knowledge in covering up the Warden's illegal dealings but, as the film goes on to show, he redeems himself (part of the significance of the title) by an elaborate 'sting', using the only weapons at his disposal (time and his knowledge) to build a water-tight criminal case against the authorities at the prison, which is triggered by his escape.

Although he has some features of a Christ-figure (absence of hate, concern for his fellow man, even talking Brooks out of attacking Heywood), Andy reacts in a very human way to his situation. Red's admiration ('some fellows collect stamps, others build matchstick houses, Andy built a library'), is a tribute to his force of will rather than any saintly resignation. The point at which Andy might be most prone to despair, after he had allowed himself to hope that Tommy might testify only for the Warden to have him killed, sees him threatened by the Warden with having the library burned and protection from the Sisters withdrawn. He sits against a wall, with every reason to be dejected, and the shot stays on him as Red comes and talks to him. The novella talks about 'an invisible coat' that he seems to have on, which we might later see as faith or hope, an image which is transposed into Red's intrigued narration about the month's delay before he approaches Red to ask about the rock hammer.[11] It is precisely this inner serenity which infuriates the warden and which he tries (and fails) to crush.

Although the film focuses on Andy, we should not forget the absolute brutality of the system which holds him. On his first night, one of his fellow new inmates is beaten and left for dead in the infirmary. The revenge beating of Bogs leaves him paralysed. The sudden shooting of Tommy, whom King does not kill off in the novella, is shocking but that is because we have been focused on Andy; the brutal system against which he is opposed is still in place. The guards, who had largely disappeared from the narrative and feature less heavily on-screen in the second half of the film, are still there and the Warden, stubbing out the life of a nineteen-year-old boy as he stubs out his cigarette before stepping over the body (shown in God-like birds-eye view), shows no qualms in murdering to maintain his power.

There is a tight ensemble-cast element to the film. Scenes with Andy's immediate circle at dinner or talking outside (as when they discuss Brooks) are tightly framed to squeeze seven–eight figures into the shot. At the suggestion of cinematographer Roger Deakins, Darabont radically reduced the number of complex set-ups in the ensemble shots, using, for example, slow forward tracking shots up to a close-up on Robbins in the scene where he talks about music. Heywood's description of Dumas as 'dumbass', or digging up petrified lumps of horseshit thinking they are rocks, provide rare moments of light relief in what, on paper, might seem a bleak film. In his later account, at the table, of Andy's escape, we see prison mythology evolving before our eyes in a credible way through the ability of the cast, especially William Sadler as Heywood, to improvise dialogue.

The pay-off of the escape tunnel behind the poster is deliciously simple, outwitting the authorities (and possibly viewers). King's novella is slightly overwritten, with a cellmate repeating that there was always a strange draught in that cell and Andy asking, 'didn't you ever feel that way about a picture?' (which Darabont shifts to comments about music) or feeling 'that you could almost step right through it?' There is a brief moment of the Todorovian fantastic: a moment of hesitation where something apparently impossible and (until the poster is removed) inexplicable and, in that short time, there is the tantalizing prospect of being witness to something impossible that, albeit momentarily, makes us re-assess what we know about the world. Like Red and the Warden, we are kept in ignorance of the tunnel until it is explained to us in extended flashback. The library, the accountancy 'sting' and his own escape are all possible because of his patience and forbearance linked to the one thing he has lots of – time. It is entirely fitting that his particular pet subject is geology, the study of the combined forces of pressure and time. The irony of the scripture (missed by the Warden), symbolized by the Bible that Andy knows well enough to quote, which the Warden even picks up and which secretly contains his rock hammer, reflects the underlying humanist impulse of the film: 'Salvation lies within'. The object that was a Lilliputian joke to Red has now achieved the apparently impossible. The significance of Andy's surname ('Dufresne' is a French derivation of 'mineralogist') could have been a weakness since, as with Dickens, such nomenclature inhibits the notion of character development. However, it is not the only reference to this word field and also fittingly suggests character as defined by a process of revelation rather than actual change. In a sense, over the course of the film (and his sentence), alongside Red, we are invited to chip away at the enigmatic surface of Andy's true self. The irony of Andy's knowledge of Alexandre Dumas' *The Count of Monte Cristo* (1845), a classic text about lengthy incarceration, deception and dramatic escape, and his recommendation to file it under 'Education materials', gains particular resonance in retrospect. The action where Andy begins to carve his name imitates that of many others but he goes beyond just literally writing his name to making a mark, leaving an indelible legacy behind.

Unlike a conventional prison narrative, a minor character takes over the narrative for a time. Brooks Hatlen's role is greatly expanded from the novella where his parole and demise in an old-folks home is described in a paragraph.[12] Like the basis for *The Green Mile* story, Brooks is a trusty given the responsibility for the book-cart. The narrative follows this apparently minor character for a substantial digression and he takes over the voiceover, motivated as a final letter (a suicide note in effect), when we cut back to the jail. This is the best future awaiting the inmates – a life in a dismal half-way house, doing a tedious, low-paid job, unable to find a place in a society that they neither know nor, in some cases, understand. As Red realizes, Brooks is so institutionalized that he does not have the means to cope outside. A slow track up to Red gives emphasis to his philosophy about the walls that 'first you hate them, then you get used to them, then you depend on them'. Shot in extreme long shot, Brooks (James Whitmore) cuts a pathetic, lonely figure in a world that he does not recognize, at first reluctant to leave the gates and then being harassed by cars (Darabont blending features of Red's feelings on parole as described by King) or feeding birds in the park, hoping to meet Jake (definitely buried in a poignant but unfilmed scene).[13] He has bad dreams and states that he is 'tired of being afraid all the time'. The sequence where Brooks commits suicide is both touching and even suspenseful. We see him dress smartly, stand on a table and do something with a knife, the camera focusing on his shoes upon which sawdust falls. Only when the camera slowly tracks back do we have confirmed what we may have feared. When Red is finally released, he treads in Brooks' footsteps but crucially does not take the final step. Under the influence of Andy, he chooses to make his mark but remain in the world and 'get busy living' rather than share Brooks' fate.

Castle Rock, and particularly Executive Producer Liz Glotzer, really wanted to bring the two protagonists together, a feeling reinforced by test screenings, and so King's ending on the bus is translated to Red's final words which begin 'I hope...' and the mythic paradise of Zihuatanejo. Like the men on the roof, who 'feel like free men' and 'the lords of all creation' because they can sit and drink with their friends in the open air, freedom is primarily freedom to express the bonds of friendship. The pair retain their integrity despite, not because of, a deeply flawed prison system in which the granting of Red's parole is as random and absurdly Kafkaesque in its clemency as in its severity. Kermode reads Red's attitude as representing the atonement of a guilty man and it is tempting to believe that Red's more honest, direct answers and his ultimate attitude (symbolized by his 'I don't give a shit') win over the board, but this is really wishful thinking. The comments on rehabilitation appear at the beginning of the novella, reflecting that Red has always known this.[14] The apparently random granting of parole now only underlines its cruelty in being delayed so long and, in hindsight, undermines Andy's years of digging – after all, he too might just have waited and been lucky. That said, the final sequence is still powerful. Red's actions are almost Pavlovian: asking permission for a toilet break at the store and dramatically, even though he is in the middle of open countryside, having chosen a compass rather than a handgun, he instinctively looks around him and peeks over a wall before opening the box (a nice piece of improvization from Freeman).

The basic plot elements, and importantly their structure (the holding back of the details of the escape, the ending, and much of the dialogue), all derive from King's original novella, which should be attributed its due, especially its central uplifting theme, placed as it is in *Different Seasons* under the section 'Hope Springs Eternal'. Darabont's additions, often at the suggestions of others, (the first arrival at the prison, the ensemble mealtimes, the music scene and the final reunion on the beach), his omissions (Red wondering if Andy bribed the guards so they did not search his cell, which would make the escape somehow less miraculous), his alterations (the centrality of the Warden, who has Tommy killed rather than merely transferred), his extensions (the sequence with Brooks' parole and suicide), all effectively complement King's tale, producing the strange sensation in rereading the novella, of finding oneself missing those sections absent in the original.

The script is only one of two currently available for sale of any King adaptation (the other, inexplicably is *Dreamcatcher*), testament to the power of the film but also as a desired piece of literature, complementary to King's novel. It is certainly not flawless – Andy's ability to strike a pipe with a rock in exact time with a lightning strike, is somewhat unlikely. However, there is an almost Biblical weightiness to parts of the script, which Freeman's voiceover conveys with conviction: after Andy's escape, we see Red tending a graveyard and pausing to look up, pondering (almost verbatim from the novella): 'some birds aren't meant to be caged. Their feathers are too bright. And when they fly away, the part of you that knows it was a sin to lock them up, does rejoice but still, the place that you live in is that much more drab and empty that they are gone.'[15] Ultimately, the film is a paean not just to human endurance and strength of purpose (waiting twenty years and then crawling 500 yards through a sewer) but ultimately to a generosity of spirit, which makes Andy always look within himself for the means to help others. His dream on the beach is not for him alone. In inviting Red to join him it is clear that matters of race, nationality, class do not prevent Andy from offering his money, his dream and his heart, to another. Perhaps part of the film's enduring appeal is the relatively-rare filmic means that it employs. The persistence of first-person voiceover from first to last powerfully conveys the survival of the spirit, the interior voice (in a similar way to *Forrest Gump*, despite multiple pressures to the contrary, both within the narratives and in the film industry itself). There is a slight bumper-sticker quality to the gnomic utterances that start to stack up towards the end of the film but Red's three-part conclusion that 'Hope is a good thing. Maybe the best of things. And no good thing ever dies,' (similar to King's 'Nothing is ever lost' in his conclusion to *The Dead Zone*), is at least two-parts convincing.[16] The need to protect and nurture a particular kind of hope has been personified powerfully by Andy, a selfless humanist, sensitive to the transcendent needs of our nature. The third part of an eternal value is a step too far – good things (Tommy, Brooks, the fat guy at the beginning) do die and so can hope. That is precisely what makes its survival here so poignant.

The Green Mile (Frank Darabont, 1999)

Only five years apart, with the same writer and director, both prison dramas with at least one A-list star, *The Green Mile* certainly benefited from a perception and a linkage with *The Shawshank Redemption*, whose reputation had been growing steadily. As noted previously, limited exposure to prison itself and related movies both make intertextual linkages more potent – all the more so when the other text is a recent King adaptation.

Even beyond this, *The Green Mile* adds an intertextual awareness to the prison genre, particularly in relation to John Steinbeck. The film opens with an impression of a lynching party, close to the style of the 1992 version of *Of Mice and Men*, directed by Gary Sinise (who appears here as Burt Hammersmith). Like *Shawshank*, Steinbeck's narrative is also set in the 1930s Depression and also like the victimization of Coffey, features a strong but harmless giant of a man, Lenny Small, who is persecuted by those around him. The story of Mouseville for Delacroix (Michael Jeter) has the same kind of tragic, childish element of wish-fulfilment that George Milton's tale about living off the 'fatta the lan' has for Lennie, calming both receivers of the tales. There is even an explicit allusion to the phrase in King's novel about what Coffey (Michael Clarke Duncan) could do 'to mice and to men.'[17] The warden's final bemused search of Andy's cell in *The Shawshank Redemption* also touches on Steinbeck's description of Crooks' room: an examination of a man's accumulated personal possessions over many years tells us something about him. King's 'trunk novel', *Blaze*, which has been partly-rewritten and released, was originally conceived (according to George Beahm) as 'a literary homage' to Steinbeck's book, featuring a large, semi-retarded character who falls under the influence not of a benign helper but a small-time crook called George.[18] For attentive viewers, Darabont also places a metatextual joke in casting Harry Dean Stanton (who had already appeared in *Christine* many years before) as Toot-Toot in a film which has another character called Dean Stanton.

There is also explicit cinematic intertextuality in allusions to *One Flew Over the Cuckoo's Nest* in its characterization of the Georgia Pines nursing home, such as the mindless music played to subdue residents, the presence of a Native American character called 'the Chief' and Billy's pose of drugged-up stupor before his sudden attack on the guards, echoing McMurphy, back from shock therapy, in Foreman's film. Although there is no Nurse Ratched figure here, King's novel does feature Brad Nolan, a mean orderly who tells sick jokes and bullies Paul Edgecomb, the narrator and main character (shared between Dabbs Greer and Tom Hanks) as he wants to go out on his daily walk. However Darabont softens this in the film to mere wistful curiosity and even makes his character willing to turn a blind eye to his breaking of minor rules (rather than Brad's officious enforcement of them), setting up audience interest in what the old man is doing outside every day, in all weathers. For an opening to a major feature film, the pace is gentle, reflected in the use of dissolves for most cuts here.

The narrative structure is more complex than a standard prison movie. In King's novel, in part because of the way in which it was originally published in Dickensian-style regular parts, there is an 'eddying' structure, with new sections recapping and sometimes repeating verbatim a page or so before taking the story forwards, and these recapping sections usually take us back to the nursing home and Paul telling his story to Elly (Eve Brent), a close friend. This serialized form does require regular cliffhanging elements, which could be said to inject dramatic tension but it can also make the narrative seem a little episodic. In the written form, serialization allows the writer to ration and tantalize the reader, who cannot skip to the end to find how the narrative plays out. Darabont bundles all these elements together in an opening section and also, thereby, juxtaposes one (possibly repressive) institution with another. Paul's thoughts are converted into dialogue, sometimes expressed by others, so the intellectual aridity of the place is conveyed by arguments over the ubiquitous daytime TV. *Top Hat* (Mark Sandrich, 1935) comes on (Darabont shifting King's narrative on three years to allow him to use this film and the keynote song 'Cheek to Cheek'), upsetting Paul and triggering the main narrative. Later, when Paul looks through Coffey's notes, and we cut to a dramatization of the crime, drawing the beginning, middle and end of the film together, we will see a more complete picture of events. In taking Edgcomb's hands, Coffey motivates a cut to a slow-motion sequence, ultimately revealing Wharton as the guest at the Detterick family table, although this supposed dramatic climax is rather clumsily held back for dramatic effect and raises the question why Coffey did not say something straight away.

The parading of a new prisoner is a standard feature of prison movies. Here, it is the nature of the prisoner that is different. The close-up of John Coffey as a black man led in chains by an abusive little white man feels like an emblem of slavery. However, at the same time, there is something comically absurd about Coffey's physical incongruity (the guards are described in the novel as 'like children walking along with a captured bear').[19] He has to duck his head to enter his own cell and a tilt shot inside the cell shows Paul's POV as he looks up at Coffey's face. Indeed, the cropping of Coffey's head by the framing is reminiscent of the running sight gag of the freakily-tall lab technician in *Police Squad* (ABC, 1982). Far from irrelevant, this underlines how he is physically out of his element (a dissonance so pronounced that all the prison officers, despite their professionalism, cannot help but stare, even the film form struggles to accommodate him) and, in such circumstances, one possible reaction is humour. Here, we also see one of the stylistic motifs of the film when all the main characters look up in a mixture of curiosity and almost 'Spielbergian' awe before we see what they are looking at. The same occurs when Coffey blows on the mouse, or 'kisses' Percy (Doug Hutchison) or Mrs Moores (Patricia Clarkson).

The setting is unusually claustrophobic (even for a prison narrative) and Darabont uses low angles to create a sense of perspective and depth on the Mile to enforce Edgecomb's comments about how long it feels for the prisoner's last steps and also to prepare us for the appearance of Mr Jingles, shot almost entirely in alternate high and low angles (except for Delacroix's POV as the mouse shoots past his cell).The appearance of the mouse represents an unexpected moment of humour, variety and connectedness between people in a very serious, routine-based, isolated situation, underlined by the light, quirky xylophone score at this point. Darabont also pulls focus with the mouse in the extreme foreground, looking down the Mile to draw our attention to its fragility. The mouse humanizes those who watch it and helps demonize Percy further by his rabid and illogical hatred of the animal. It represents his attitude to the men supposedly in his care. For Edgecomb, the Mile is like 'an intensive care ward' but for Percy it is 'a bucket of piss to drown rats in'.

The stock character of the abusive guard is represented by Percy Wetmore, whose on-screen presence feels like a stereotypical homosexual in denial as he constantly preens his hair, uses frequent homophobic abuse of prisoners but, beneath his hostility, he is petrified of being in close proximity with 'Wild Bill' Wharton (Sam Rockwell), as seen when he wets himself rather than help his colleagues fight him off and, later, when he is tied up in a straight jacket. His reading of pornographic comics inside academic textbooks reflects a nature that is divided and sexually repressed. His murder of Wharton is an attempt to negate a part of himself which, with tears streaming down his face, he cannot accept. When he is finally placed in a mental institution, he appears to have found his rightful place, hinted at earlier in his fascination with the store-room which doubles as a padded cell. His behaviour throughout the film is unstable and potentially violent (ironically much more so than most of the prisoners). The sadism he shows towards Delacroix, not just pretending to wet the sponge but also disabusing him about Mouseville, is particularly cruel. His backing away from the sight of the prisoner on fire, and the involuntary raising of his hand to his mouth, might suggest that this experience also plays a part in fragmenting his already fragile sanity.

Like Dufresne, Christ-figure associations seem to surround Coffey. The initials device has been used before, but not in a prison narrative, from William Faulkner's morally-ambiguous Joe Christmas in *Light in August* (1932) to John Conner in *Terminator II*. He is given to appreciating the simpler things of life (his final meal request includes some cornbread baked by Edgecomb's wife and he stoops to smell a handful of leaves during the night-time 'excursion' to see Mrs Moores). Powerful yet meek, he is a figure who apparently 'dropped from the sky' (according to Hammersmith) and takes away the pain of others (Paul's bladder infection, Mr Jungle's injuries and Melinda Moores' tumour) at a physical price to himself. His actions are termed 'miracles' by Edgecomb, whose judgement, as the first person narrator, we are encouraged to trust, and there is a slow zoom into a close-up of Coffey's face, back-lit by the projection room, open-mouthed and transfixed, watching Fred Astaire and Ginger Rogers in *Top Hat* (the film that had triggered Edgecomb's memory in the prologue), calling the dancers 'angels'.

Faced with the prospect of carrying out an execution on an innocent man, Edgecomb pleads with Coffey to 'tell me what you want me to do'. However, the Christ-like overtones are also a little ambiguous– he directs his power, perhaps vindictively, to punish Percy, and use him by proxy to punish Wharton and he seems weary of the world (or perhaps just his place in it). However, there is also something of the Uncle Tom stereotype in his obsequious 'Yessah', his moon-like face and his repeated mantra about his name and its spelling. The lip-to-lip kiss Coffey gives Melinda, the wife of the warden, in 1930s America is certainly a challenging image but ultimately no more believable than the *Poltergeist*-style shaking furniture, glowing lights or grandfather clock stopping.

However, it is actually *Edgecomb* who has greater claims as a Christ-figure. The first time we see him, he definitely seems like a new kind of hero whose main problem is trying to urinate, and later at home, crawling outside at night to pee by a woodpile. His trauma is distinctly personal and domestic. He bears wrongs and clear insults with such magnanimity, like Percy's unprovoked attack on Delacroix, that it is hard to see how he got this job in the first place or continued in it for so long. Despite Percy's influential aunt, and not wanting to upset the men on the Mile, the fact that Paul does not really show anger, even in more personal moments, makes his character less human. Making Percy look at Delacroix's burning body before extinguishing the flames still seems more educational than justifiably vindictive. He feels more like a personification of sensitivity than a real human being. Even after the Delacroix debacle, when Percy showed his truly sadistic nature, Edgecomb virtually covers for Percy in front of the warden when he could clearly make his guilt plain. In a sense, Coffey 'punishes' Percy, because Edgecomb does not.

The saintliness of Edgecomb spills over to his crew, who, under his tutelage, become disciples of a similar creed, practising executions when prisoners are absent to make the actual process as painless as possible. Brutus Howell invents the mawkish concept of Mouseville; Harry Terwilliger (Jeffrey DeMunn) wishes Delacroix to 'knock em for a loop' in demonstrating his mouse to visitors; and the slogan first intoned by Edgecomb is later repeated by Howell (whose nickname 'Brutal' is largely ironic):'What happens on The Mile, stays on The Mile'. This applies to Percy, too, whom they do not humiliate although they have ample opportunity (when he wets himself) and motivation to do so.

When Toot-Toot (Harry Dean Stanton) cracks a tasteless gag that makes everyone laugh, Edgecomb is the one who pulls them together, maintaining his composure at all times. When Arlen Bitterbuck (Graham Greene) is awaiting his final hours, we see a very private moment with Edgecomb in which the latter almost acts as a confessor, coaxing comforting thoughts out of him of what heaven might be like. The novel includes Edgecomb's unspoken (and arguably hypocritical) thoughts, which clearly show that while he is saying these soothing words, he clearly thinks that the man is going straight to hell. Also, King has Edgecomb suggest the plan to help Mrs Moores in part as atonement for guilt he feels over Delacroix. Darabont cuts all this, making Edgecomb's motivation seem pure and casts self-doubt as engaging weakness – he asks what he is going to say on Judgement Day and, earlier, confessed to his wife that he feared he might be going to Hell for such an execution. In the novel, Edgecomb is considering moving out of the job even before we see any executions taking place, but Darabont's pushing this to the end makes him seem more affected by his experience with Coffey and closer to his spiritual heir. Edgecomb suffers sleepless nights thinking about Coffey and physically suffers, collapsing to the floor on the Mile itself after Billy's initial rampage. He is a model husband, still finding his wife desirable, and with the help of Coffey, able to show that. The fact that Edgecomb cannot continue the job strongly suggests that, to a sensitive and humane individual, it is a process that cannot and should not be borne.

The climactic execution, another prison movie staple, is pure Hollywood sentiment. In a reversal of earlier roles, Coffey has to assure the guards that it will 'be alright fellas' and, on entering the execution room, Coffey recoils at the hate-filled audience but is reassured by Edgecomb (using a line attributed to Brutal in the novel), encouraging him to 'feel how we feel'. We cut between all the guards, tearfully trying to avoid eye contact, and there is another iconic handshake between Edgecomb and Coffey, paralleling their first meeting, juxtaposing black and white, captor and captive, strong and relatively weak and also contrasting with Percy who shakes Edgecomb's hand but does not keep his word. We hear Coffey's thoughts via voiceover, like a telepathic message to Edgecomb, echoing how Wharton had managed to abduct the girls by swearing to hurt the other if they called out: 'He kill them with they love. That's how it is every day. All over the world.' This might both describe Coffey's attempt to help people or Edgecomb's job on the Mile.[20] Coffey murmurs 'Heaven, I'm in Heaven', the lyrics from 'Cheek to Cheek', as the equipment is attached. We have seen the full horror of the process twice already in the film, so when the second switch is thrown here, we only see a moment of Coffey's pain before cutting to several reaction shots, with bulbs blowing in slow-motion in the background, lending the scene a transcendent quality. After the death, Edgecomb puts the St Christopher back round Coffey's neck, which could be seen as a promise kept or an ironic comment on a pointless death.

The film pays little regard to social realism. Given the saintliness of Edgecomb, Darabont's vision is open to the charge of sentimentalizing what was a brutal system. The first glimpse of the chain-gang, accompanied by energetic singing, almost appears as if the prisoners are working 'happily', and this seems quite a relaxed regime with fairly minimal supervision (one guard on foot and one on horseback). The escape seems ridiculously easy with apparently no sign of external guards around the prison. In the film, apart from Coffey (who is innocent), the crimes of Bitterbuck, Delacroix and even Billy Wharton are not given to us until near the end (unlike the novel), which has the effect of humanizing and lightening their characters. In the film Delacroix appears an amenable eccentric, befriending the mouse, apologizing and showing regret in the electric chair even though, in the novel, his unequivocal conviction for rape and multiple murder make the reader respond to him more coolly.

However, in other ways, Darabont makes King's novel darker. Edgecomb visits Burt Hammersmith, a reporter in King's novel but here made a lawyer, and Coffey's defence lawyer at that. This casts the negro-as-unpredictable-mongrel metaphor as particularly telling. Visitors are barely referred to and no visits are seen from family or indeed legal counsel – Darabont's vision is of a place where all legal means have been exhausted, making The Mile a place of no return, a wait before certain death. The film's position may not be as overt as Alan Parker's *The Life of David Gale* (2003), and Darabont does not include lines from the novel like 'we had once again succeeded in destroying what we could not create', but the clear portrayal of the mechanics of legalized killing (the chair, the sponge, the words said) leave little doubt that its author is not a proponent of the death penalty.[21] Each of the three executions we see shows us further details of the process, including the occasional need for two doses of electricity. Delacroix's execution probably could not be shown in the graphic, eye-popping nature that King describes without gaining an R-certificate in the US, so Darabont focuses on the sound of sizzling flesh, Delacroix's screaming, the stampeding crowd and the appalled reaction of guards held in close-up. For similar reasons, Melinda's swearing is reported rather than heard directly.

We may not expect the clichéd sudden reprieve as parodied at the end of Robert Altman's *The Player* (1992) but for a prison narrative, the film ends on an unusually downbeat note. Even though we also do not see the horrific death of Edgecomb's wife in a bus crash, as in the novel, Darabont has Edgecomb looking back at the book he has written (perhaps a little like King himself), wondering 'if there is some meaning here' that is 'supposed to be uplifting and ennobling.'[22] Clearly, Coffey is not reprieved and Edgecomb's narrative ends with him intoning that 'each of us are walking our own Green Mile', i.e. that life is a death sentence. Far from a blessing, his extended life (like the gifts of Carrie White, Johnny Smith and even John Coffey, who refers to feeling the pain of the world as like having 'pieces of glass' in his head) ultimately seems more of a curse (we dissolve to him laying flowers at Elly's funeral, whom he has outlived), from which death would be a release.

The Running Man (Paul Michael Glaser, 1987)

The Running Man was the first adaptation from work written by King under the Richard Bachman pseudonym to allow him to produce more than the publisher's expectation of one-novel-a-year. It may seem an odd choice for this section but, shorn of its social subtext by cuts to King's narration and by the sheer in-built obsolescence of its visualization, the prison break plot device is more prominent.

Like the previous two films, *The Running Man* is textually allusive but, here, that is more a sign of imaginative poverty than textual depth. In terms of visual style, the film is highly derivative. The opening credits, with Harold Faltemeyer's tinny, synthesized score, evokes less the upbeat style of *Beverly Hill's Cop* (Martin Brest, 1984), more a poor man's *Terminator*, complete with similar on-screen graphics. The prologue, set in a high-tech helicopter using surveillance devices to control and monitor crowds in an urban setting, is a pale echo of *Blue Thunder* but whereas the earlier film generates real tension, here the unconvincing fight in the confined space of the helicopter and the obvious use of a blue screen make the refusal of Ben Richards (Arnold Schwarzenegger) to obey an order, and his hanging out of the helicopter, unwittingly amusing. Badham's film creates an effective sense of narrative drive based around the viewing of a video-tape of surveillance footage, which would expose the manipulation of images for political ends. A similar outline plot here produces zero suspense – Amber (Maria Conchita Alonso) is caught quite easily trying to steal the tape and Arnie shows no interest in exposing the falsity of the TV programme (he is not the one who wants to crash the satellite system), just in exacting personal, righteous and violent revenge on his tormenter. However, despite superficial similarities between the confrontation with Fireball in an apparently-abandoned foundry with the closing sections of *Terminator* or its precursor films like *Westworld* (Michael Crichton, 1973), there is no sense of dread or jeopardy. The urban landscape of L.A. is every inch low-budget *Blade Runner* (Ridley Scott, 1982) – skyscrapers shown at night, search-lights raking the scene and street-level shacks, some with fires. Even the large neon screens (accompanied by a soft, reassuring female voice) promoting the show, evoke Scott's ads for the Off-World colonies.

The film could have blended a prison break motif with social criticism of the reality TV phenomenon, in which both regulars on the show (such as the Stalkers here) and contestants become instant celebrities. However an inherent problem with the game-show-as-a-glimpse-of-the-future motif is that the film is woefully unambitious. The host's insincere patter, the introduction of competitors with an emotively-edited video package, a call-and-response relationship with the audience, given to outbursts of ecstatic whooping and ending the feed-lines of the host, all scarcely seems futuristic. By 1989, shows like *American Gladiators* were already a globally-syndicated reality. The casting of Kurt Fuller as Killion's studio side-kick, Tony, now comes to us viewed through the prism of *Wayne's World* (Penelope Spheeris, 1992), in which, as Russell, he reprised and parodied this exact role, making it hard to take seriously the hand-wringing of the programme-makers here. Similarly, the elision/blurring of the Justice and Entertainment arms of government is part-and-parcel of a US news media that funds news crews to race to scenes of crime. Killion's amoral response to a potential candidate – a schoolteacher who killed his wife and mother-in-law with a steak knife ('I like that quality') – hardly seems surprising. The amphitheatre of *Rollerball* (Norman Jewison, 1975) had already conveyed state suppression of dissent by promoting violence-as-sport on television, over a decade earlier.

In comparison to *Rollerball*, The game itself seems quite tame. Contestants fly down a tunnel in an experience that is a cross between a luge and a roller-coaster ride (both usually seen as pleasurable by those who choose to do them), creating a very low-tech version of the Stargate sequence in *2001*. Having 'landed', there is little sense of geography and each of the subsequent confrontations with Stalkers takes place on dim sound stages or patches of wasteland that could be anywhere. The violence of the game, like the names of the Stalkers and, to a large degree, Schwarzenegger's character, is cartoonish. Although the opening motorbike attack by Buzzsaw seems quite menacing, as Arnie is dragged along behind the bike in a parody of the western punishment of 'keel-hauling', we never really expect the kind of brutal, stylized violence of Ridley Scott's *Black Rain* (1989), where Andy Garcia's character, Charlie, is decapitated in similar circumstances.

However there are some effective satirical touches. In Killion's office, we see posters for 'The Hate Boat' and, later, 'Pain – American Style', juxtaposed with a number of statuettes, suggesting that he knows what his public want. Similarly, the brief ad for 'Climbing For Dollars,' involving a man climbing a rope above a pack of baying Rottweilers, neatly encapsulates the corrupted-heart or simple beauty (depending on your view) of exploitation TV. The twist of having a blast of air knock the man down, just as he is about to escape, and the freeze-frame as he begins to fall, would be the kind of programme of which Max Renn in Cronenberg's *Videodrome* (1982) would approve. Killion's essentially duplicitous nature is established by his two-faced friendliness to a cleaner who accidentally trips him as he crosses the foyer and the subsequent throwaway comment in the lift to have the man sacked. The state's use of media manipulation extends beyond re-editing footage of Ben's dissent to the production of crude propaganda and the wholesale manipulation and fabrication of material when we see Captain Freedom overcoming figures supposed to be Arnie and Amber, although the assault on the TV studio looks as bizarre as the initial prison break-out, with the numbers of men in both cases barely reaching double figures.

Magistrale writes interestingly about the shift from the dystopian, socially-engaged vision of the novel to the individualistic Republican hero of the film and, certainly, the film is shorn of most of the book's more radical, political element. However, what Magistrale misses is the manipulation of Schwarzenegger's image, which overshadows all other generic expectations. At this point in his career, his simply being in a film makes it an 'Arnie movie' but the ways in which audiences derive intertextual meanings from this is more complex than it may appear. The original novella had ended with a creepily-prescient 9/11-style attack on the skyscraper HQ of the enemy (a plot device also used in *Insomnia*) but socially-engaged suicide for a higher moral purpose is not something that meshes neatly with Schwarzenegger's screen persona. Star theory, as developed by academics such as Richard Dyer, posits that the attraction of a star's persona is created by the tension between the delivery of expected items and the possibility of something original. The pleasure lies in the integration of old and new, familiar and unfamiliar. The casting of Schwarzenegger is crucial. Apart from in the apocalyptic *End of Days* (Peter Hyams, 1999), he has not died in any of his film roles (he has been rebuilt as a Terminator), meaning, effectively, that there is little on-screen jeopardy. We know he will be back. How, not whether, he will despatch his opponents is the viewing pleasure on offer. What we have here is not a serious attempt at social satire or even an action film. *The Running Man* represents a pivotal point in the crafting of Schwarzenegger's screen image. He certainly is involved in action sequences with car chases and explosions, he strides purposefully as the Terminator in two further sequels but after this film, the only running we see him do is for political office.

As in previous films, the film's main special effect is his body. However, this literal embodiment of 'the self-made man' remains largely covered from direct view. A skin-tight cat-suit makes the sheer dimensions of the man clear and there are repeated shots of him in the initial prison break-out, standing and firing a rifle one-handed, Rambo-style, at stuntmen falling melodramatically from gantries but, soon after this, one of his first actions is to urge caution and to think rather than rush the perimeter fence before the force-field is down. The original casting of Christopher Reeve would have retained some of these cartoonish elements but Schwarzenegger's on-screen persona encompasses more than this. The first time we see him, he is leisurely carrying an iron girder single-handed whilst puffing on a very phallic cigar, like a mixture of John Wayne and Popeye. In contrast to convicts on the run in a standard prison movie, Schwarzenegger shows no fear, makes no attempt to hide and, still chewing the cigar, he travels to the city dressed in a hybrid of previous iconography – a Gold's Gym vest top, boots and a toolbox, looking like a cross between his body-building days, his Terminator character and even a slight Village People allusion to his gay fanbase.

In *Terminator II*, his character, the T-1000, intones that the more contact he has with humans, the more he learns. In a dialogue echo here, he claims 'I'm a quick learner' and even before the family-centred, 'touchy-feely' Ivan Reitman comedies *Twins* (1988) and *Kindergarten Kop* (1990) there is already evident here a kinder, gentler, Arnie. Compared to earlier films such as *Conan the Barbarian* (John Milius, 1982) or *Commando* (Mark L. Lester, 1985), dialogue- and language-coaching allow him to deliver a greater amount of relatively complex language. Granted, some of this is only in the stiff, unfunny, Bond-like quips delivered upon dispatching his victims – Buzzsaw ('He had to split'), Fireball ('What a hothead') and Sub Zero/Dynamo ('He was a real pain in the neck') – but even the infamous 'I'll be back' is given a sad farewell as Killion replies (ironically referring to the catchphrase), 'only in a re-run'.

Unlike his earlier action roles, he shares significant screen time with a woman, whom he manages to win over by his status as dissident and falsely-accused victim of the state as much as by his animal magnetism and is rewarded in an affirmation of his heterosexual credentials with a kiss at the end. However, it must be said that, from the viewpoint of 1987, it will still be a few years before balanced gender participation occurs in a Schwarzenegger film. Having been caught trying to expose the truth about the Bakersfield massacre, Amber is sent into the game after Ben. Once in the game, she fulfils the conventional role of women around Arnie: showing plenty of fear and needing to be protected at all times. However, attempts to 'sex up' Arnie's screen persona are not wholly successful. On seeing Ben, a colleague of Amber's notes that it was lucky that 'he didn't kill you and then rape you. I mean a guy like that. What would stop him?' eliciting a mumbled 'What would?' from Amber. However, this reflects the ambition of Arnie in Hollywood more than any real shift into obvious sexual deviance.

In former films, Arnie would have been the one playing a Stalker – a one-dimensional, robotic-like figure. As a bridge between the two *Terminator* films, the first where he is a cold-bloodied killer, the second where he is a model father and saviour of the Christ-figure, John Conner, his character here refuses to fire upon unarmed women and children. He is not quite at the stage of dancing the tango or flying a jet fighter, as he does in *True Lies* (James Cameron, 1993), but we see him working out problems by brain as well as brawn, improvising weapons against his better-equipped adversaries and stealing Amber's travel pass through some computer trickery. He still shows occasional feats of strength, such as lifting Alonso's work-out bench out of its fixtures on the floor or, later, pushing against the door of his cell. However it is Alonso's fitness routine, which he interrupts, rather than his own and in both scenes he does so wearing a white vest-and-shorts combination and, like the Hawaiian shirt he sports in travelling on the bus, makes him look oddly child-like and thereby less threatening (a sartorial pattern developed further in his *Twins*). The presence of gags unrelated to despatching one of the enemy, such as that she could throw up on the shirt and no one would notice, is also new.

Effectively, by the end, little has changed. The opening prison sequence appears to be long forgotten but in the totalitarianism that they accept there is a sense of imprisonment by consent. The audience of the TV show might realize they have been cheated but there is no impression that they will hold the government to account or be willing and able to stand up against it. The moronic whooping which greets Ben's dispatching of Killion seems no different from their earlier reaction to the game. Killion's speech about a culture dependent on television still rings true and, as long as Arnie gives them what they want, they will cheer for him. Despite the genre aspirations of an action film, the ideological underpinning of the film is paradoxically bound to political inertia. As the future Governor of California states to his fellow escapees, 'I'm not into politics, I'm into survival.' In Darwinian terms, that means only survival of the fittest. Killion can instantly spot Ben's star quality precisely because it is so rare. In being mesmerized by footage of slow-motion Arnie, Killion is articulating the star quality that Schwarzenegger brings to a project. In describing Richards, Killion says, 'You've got talent, you've got charisma, you've got balls.' It is debatable whether Schwarzenegger shows all three qualities in this film but then, the role does not really demand it of him. In shifting Ben Richards from Everyman to Superman, character changes and casting choices mean that the only way to effectively overthrow, or even bring into question, the actions of a totalitarian state is not by collective, democratic action but by individual acts of heroism – a role for which only former Mr Universes need apply.

Conclusion

The representation in this section of prison as a machine, crushing the life out of its inmates by repetitive, arduous routine, in a sense creates a more fearsome and (because based in reality) more believable 'monster' than many of King's techno-monster movies (discussed in chapter 5). Kafka's 'In the Penal Colony' (1919), like *The Trial* (1925), features inmates charged without any logical evidence being brought forward and subject to a sadistic, dehumanizing system, whose only purpose seems to be to destroy them. King adaptations do not aspire to such random, existential notions of punishment: rituals, however unpleasant, have an internal logic in the context of managing the prison. In *The Green Mile*, we see the inexorable process of preparing prisoners for execution and in *The Running Man*, a TV show creates fundamentally the same scenario but for mass entertainment on television. Rafter suggests that

> the quintessential prison movies are fantasies, films which purport to reveal the brutal realities of incarceration whilst actually offering viewers escape from the miseries of daily life through adventure and heroism. Presenting tales in which justice is miraculously restored after long periods of harsh oppression, prison movies enable us to believe, if only briefly, in a world where long suffering virtue is rewarded.[23]

Both *Shawshank* and *The Green Mile* are set in a mythic past, have endings which might be described as uplifting (if we see Edgecomb's heroism and Coffey's sacrifice as the foci of *The Green Mile*, not the state-sanctioned murder of an innocent black man] and *The Running Man* has the definitive action-adventure hero as its star. However, any sense of justice restored is set firmly at the level of the individual, not the institution, and comes with strong caveats. Justice is only restored in *Shawshank* by an almost unbelievable act of personal endurance (Andy is not pardoned, he only flees the system) as well as financially benefitting from the Warden's fraudulent schemes. In *The Green Mile*, although Edgecomb walks away from the system, that same system remains essentially intact and the ridiculous rebellion in *The Running Man* rings less true than the suicidal plane crash in King's original story. Albeit fortified by drink and 'justified' by his wife's adultery, injustice appears to play little part in *Shawshank*, since we see, or think we do, Andy commit the crime from the outset. The plot only later becomes a more conventional 'clearing-of-one's-name' narrative with the introduction of Tommy and the new plot information about Elmo Blatch. Similarly, Coffey seems clearly guilty from the outset and only towards the end do we have the fuller version of the flashback with the real perpetrator, Billy, fully in view. *The Running Man*'s plot establishes clear injustice from the outset, blending the personal motivation of Ben Richards to clear his name with that of a political rebel, exposing the TV fake show for the instrument of state oppression it is.

Movies like *I am a Fugitive from a Chain Gang* (Mervyn LeRoy, 1932), sometimes feature an element of almost Dickensian social comment, making us aware of aspects of incarceration systems about which we might be encouraged, implicitly or explicitly, to protest. Although Steve Neale also asserts that genre films can help direct and shape ideological concerns as well as reflect them, in the case of *Shawshank* and *The Green Mile*, by setting the narratives back in time, there is the suggestion of a reassuring 'buffer', a comforting prism of nostalgia, that implies that the horror of the death penalty, or prison conditions generally, are no longer quite so brutal.[24] *The Green Mile* features graphic dramatization of the death penalty and *Shawshank* has the brutal power structures of a prison based on physical, financial and even sexual power. Both, however, are mediated by Christ-like protagonists and distanced in time from the present, reducing the explicit political content and making them more historical, backward-looking pieces than 'calls-to-arms' to the contemporary viewer.

Notes
1. John Fiske, *Television Culture* (London: Routledge, 1987), p. 115.
2. Nicole Rafter, *Shots in the Mirror: Crime Films and Society* (Oxford: Oxford University Press, 2000)
3. See Deral Cheatwood, 'Prison Films: 1929–1995,' in Donna Hale and Frankie Bailey, eds., *Popular Culture, Crime and Justice*, (Belmont, CA: Wadsworth, 1998).
4. Stephen King, 'Rita Hayworth and the Shawshank Redemption' in *Different Seasons*, op. cit., p. 42.
5. Ibid., p. 106.
6. Mark Kermode, *The Shawshank Redemption* (London: BFI Modern Classics, 2003), p. 47.

7. Ibid., p. 88.

8. Ibid., p. 61.

9. Ibid., p. 39.

10. Ibid., p. 40.

11. Stephen King, 'Rita Hayworth and the Shawshank Redemption' op. cit., p. 76.

12. See ibid. pp. 48–49.

13. Ibid., p. 108.

14. Ibid., p. 12.

15. Ibid., p. 106.

16. Ibid., p. 112. See also Stephen King, *The Dead Zone*, op. cit, p. 467.

17. Stephen King, *The Green Mile* (London: Orion Books Ltd, 1996), p. 285.

18. George Beahm, *The Stephen King Companion*, op. cit., p. 297.

19. King, op. cit., p. 9.

20. Ibid. Darabont's script blends two clauses from King, *The Green Mile*, op. cit., p. 416 and p. 417.

21. Ibid., p. 97.

22. Ibid., p. 448.

23. Nicole Rafter, *Shots in the Mirror: Crime Films and Society*,op. cit., p. 117.

24. See Steve Neale, *Genre* (London: BFI, 1980), p. 16.

CHAPTER SEVEN

BOOKS OF BLOOD: THE WRITER

'Never believe what you publish. Never publish what you believe.'[1]

Many of King's characters (central and peripheral) are writers, especially since the early 1990s, and many are also male and suffering a recent loss, especially of a spouse, which appears to give them an extra level of creative sensitivity. Writing is an inherently interior act and whilst not impossible, it is certainly a challenge to the filmmaker to make writing a dramatically powerful activity. Graham Greene, whom King has cited as his favourite writer when he talks about writing, suggested 'writing is a form of therapy'.[2] For a number of King's characters, writing down experience becomes a way to understand it, come to terms with it and continue to live a relatively normal life. This becomes especially important when that experience happened in childhood and can only be understood through the filter of adulthood, as in the case of Gordie Lachance and Bill Desborough. That applies not just to professional writers (Paul Sheldon, Jack Torrance, Thad Beaumont, Ben Mears), but also to private individuals like Paul Edgecomb, struggling to make sense of their lives. *Secret Window* clearly touches on plagiarism but also the strangely isolated nature of a writer's life and that, at times of stress, it is an activity that can paradoxically both maintain and threaten an individual's sanity. The appearance of Shooter as a potential stalker evokes *Misery* and King's oft-repeated anecdote of signing an autograph for Mark Chapman – the man who went on to shoot John Lennon.

It might seem as if King is drawing upon a shrinking range of subject matter or that, not surprisingly perhaps, the act and processes of writing are of particular interest and importance to him. Certainly, a man who writes as many words a day as he does should be fairly knowledgeable about it but may find it just hard, logistically, to experience much else of life. The nature of the relationship between artist and character, particularly the use of pseudonyms, which take on a life of their own (*The Dark Half*), the sometimes obsessive relations of fans for authors, refusing to let them change/develop (*Misery*), the risks of plagiarism and solipsism (*Secret*

Window, Secret Garden) and the whole question of writer's block (*The Shining* and *Bag of Bones*) are all issues that have affected King directly. He claims that *Secret Window* is 'the last story about writers and writing' but has been drawn back to this particular muse in *Lisey's Story* (2006), exploring the literary legacy of a writer.[3]

In terms of the actual process itself, that is more problematic. King's *On Writing* was an attempt to answer the perennial question about 'Where do you get your ideas?' only to be met by relatively lukewarm sales. *Misery* dramatizes what writing under duress might look and feel like, *The Dark Half* only shows an act of writing at the close as George Stark tries and fails to emulate his creator, and *Secret Window* dramatizes a denial of writing altogether. Rather than challenge the film form directly, like Peter Greenaway in *The Pillow Book* (1996) or his version of *The Tempest* in *Prospero's Books* (1991), which uses the Paintbox system to create text on screen in a range of fonts, here it is, the life of the writer, which is visualized on screen. What we see in the films in this section, are individuals facing an interruption to their income stream. Reflecting the attractions and tyranny of generic pressures in the film adaptations elsewhere in this book, their work operates successfully within a specific genre but difficulties arise when they try to move beyond that.

Misery (Rob Reiner, 1990)

Annie Wilkes: For a while, I thought I might go crazy.

Having demonstrated his ability to create powerful small-scale, character-driven drama in *Stand by Me*, Rob Reiner's narrative here plays like a theatre piece, concentrated in one place and with a limited cast. King describes *Misery* as articulating 'the powerful hold fiction can achieve over the reader' and *The Dark Half* 'the converse', with *Secret Window* as the attempt 'to tell both stories at the same time'.[4] Where *The Shining* and *Bag of Bones* explore the horror of writer's block, *Misery* explores how artists can be compromised.

Paul Sheldon (James Caan) is a writer trapped by his own success, suggested by the opening tight shot – a close-up of a bulky, openly-anachronistic typewriter and the sound of tapping keys (the writer, by contrast, is initially a blurry figure in the background). Later, we see Paul looking straight at the camera in close-up before cutting to a reverse shot of the typewriter, reflecting the intensity of relationship between a writer and his/her means of production. Scriptwriter William Goldman chooses not to use King's adversarial dialogue between the two, like the talking pig's skull in *Lord of the Flies*.[5]

Paul's crazed outburst of typing is juxtaposed with a humorous reverse shot – a close-up of 'fuckfuckfuck...', like Nicholson's repeated proverb in *The Shining*. King's own practice as a writer is echoed in the rituals on completing a novel and Sheldon's conclusion to his story: 'Breathing might not seem like much but without it, what else was there?' gains ironic resonance following King's own accident in 1999.

The satchel (shown twice in close-up in the car), suggests a self-importance/satisfaction/absorption, and provides a link to a flashback with Paul explaining its importance to his publisher (Lauren Bacall), as a symbol of his hard-won ideals as a struggling writer. The publisher role is fleshed out to give some contrast and relief from the sheer claustrophobic nature of Paul's experience. He is clearly jaded, describing that 'I was a writer then,' regarding himself now as just in 'the Misery business'. His agent describes Misery's symbolic value as financial, countering that he is 'still a writer', and points out that Misery effectively put his children through college, and paid for the luxuries of a wealthy life. His success has been, to him, a poisoned chalice and this is all that his readers, and therefore his venal publishers, want him to produce. Annie Wilkes (Kathy Bates) is the extreme representative of an adoring, insatiable reading public, demanding more of what they like rather than something original. He has created a monster that needs feeding annually. All through this conversation, Misery is described as if she were real. The different levels of identification with fictional entities become the core battleground between Annie and Paul, who is taught a humbling lesson about the responsibilities of the author (as Annie sees it). Unhinged though she is, in a sense she is right – he is not what he appears to be and he comes out of his experience a better writer. A harsh editor is what he actually needs and she is ironically correct when she notes of his current writing that 'it's not worthy of you'.

Central to the film's portrayal of writing is the means of characterizing the relationship between Paul and Annie. Paul wakes to Annie's defining statement, 'I'm your number one fan', imbued with all its juvenile hyperbole and latent impossibility. A wide shot of the room shows a spare wooden floor, the bed, one chair and no other furniture, establishing the geography of what will limit his existence for months. He is initially framed in the doorway, complementing his captive status and inevitably, since he is in bed, he is often shot in high angle, underlining his vulnerability, and with Annie (from a low angle), sometimes with wide angle lenses distorting her features and emphasizing her monstrosity, leering into his face or symbolically filling the doorway, such as when she discovers he wants to kill off Misery. Magistrale struggles with the terms 'high-' and 'low-angle' and claims that 'throughout the film the camera's angle and perspective is almost exclusively Paul's, cementing the audience's identification with his victimization while distancing us from Annie herself.'[6] However, in their most intense scenes, Reiner alternates POV shots to allow us to empathize with both protagonists, such as when he wakes to a low angle close-up of Annie's face and then we cut to her looking down at him. As Paul starts to write, Reiner begins to shoot more closely to one another's eye-line and also often uses a static camera, remaining within the room with Paul as Annie talks, effectively using different sound level perspectives as she hangs her coat up or works in other parts of the house, providing the kind of small naturalistic detail alongside overlapping dialogue, as Annie's lies start to break down, which increases our identification with Paul's situation.

Ian McEwan's *Enduring Love* (1997), filmed by Roger Michell in 2004, dramatizes a case of de Clérambault's Syndrome, which lists amongst its symptoms, an obsessive identification with a beloved person with whom the individual imagines a reciprocal relationship to the point of a cataclysmic suicide pact and the belief that they are acting out some kind of divine destiny. With religious zeal, Annie sees it as 'a kind of miracle' that she found Paul but her unquestioning adoration for the 'world's greatest writer' already suggests an underlying instability to her hero-worship. Her faith is made overt through her prominent crucifix, her stance on profanity and her claim that God answered her prayer, telling her 'I delivered him unto you so that you may show him the way.' She also rationalizes to herself that 'in a way, I was following you', imagining that the strength of her desire brought its object to her. Religious and secular worship combine in the 'shrine' to Paul in the lounge, based around a signed photo. Her hyperbolic praise also ironically touches upon the artistic lie he is living – when she asserts 'What a poet you are', part of the pain in his expression is the knowledge that he is not. She declares that 'I love you', adding quickly 'your mind, your creativity', showing a girlish propensity for adolescent crushes (a breathless 'Oh, Paul' is a standard response) and belief in a 'special, perfect love' (picked up later in her spinning around in adolescent joy that 'Misery's alive' and rushing off to put on a Liberace record). Her emotional development has been arrested and she finds adult relationships difficult, choosing to watch dating shows on TV with her soft toy pig and a bag of potato chips. This even goes as far as being unable to engage in small-talk so that when Paul talks about winters getting shorter, she cuts him off with 'Yeah, well it's a theory.'

Annie adopts a number of roles. Rather than kidnapper and hostage, she casts herself in the role of unappreciated housewife ('I feed you, I clean you, I dress you and what thanks do I get?'). She also adopts the pose of a lover from the kind of romantic fiction Paul writes, turning in the doorway to blow him a kiss and, in a sense, he is the author of his own downfall, having scripted her actions and clichéd dialogue ('I have faith in you, my darling'). In her response to his writing, she is a savage critic and in the guise of a teacher, admonishes him that it is 'all wrong. You'll have to do it again.' Annie excises those elements in the world which do not match her preconceived view of it: the swearing in the manuscript; the burning of the book in which Misery is killed off; Saturday morning serial cinema where heroes miraculously escape; people she does not like (the sick that she nursed or the Sheriff who asks questions). Her vanity, however, does allow her to bypass her solipsistic tendencies, permitting Paul to name a gravedigger after her as the only acceptable feature in his first attempt at *Misery's Return*. When, at the end, Buster calls at the house, Annie reveals a further stage in her perverted identity, telling him that God has called her to be Paul's 'replacement' and to make up new stories as if she were him. Identification has been replaced by absorption. She is also Paul's self-appointed nurse and, early in the film, Annie draws the covers back and Reiner gives us a slow head to foot top-shot, like a CAT-scan, showing Paul's complete injuries for the first time. The shot is reversed, later, revealing Paul's home-made weapon in his sling, like Travis Bickle (Robert de Niro) in *Taxi Driver* (Martin Scorsese, 1976) – a suitable intertextual allusion to another deluded, potentially-violent solipsist.

Paul intuits her condition, starting to praise her, claiming to like Liberace too, allowing her the fantasy that they have a relationship as a means to try and engineer his escape. Annie is also a tragic figure – self-pitying, perhaps, but there is a core of truth in her observation to Paul that 'You'll never know the fear of losing someone like you if you're someone like me.' She also replies to his assertion that he likes it there that 'that's very kind of you but I'll bet it's not altogether true.' Like his dawning awareness of Annie's deluded character, Paul is forced to realize the gap between fiction and reality in his frustrated inability to open the door with a bobby-pin, ('C'mon, I've written about this'). It is only on finally escaping the room that we realize that we, like Paul, do not know the geography of the house, having been denied omniscient views beyond his room, prompting whip pans up and down the hall, as he is unsure which way to go. The phone that he dials and then lifts to reveal an empty shell parallels Annie, who might look normal but has something missing inside her. Returning from a shopping trip, her off-screen gossip becomes more pointed when she sees his physical state and throws an aggressive question at him – 'What have you been doing?' Goldman's script (using King's dialogue almost verbatim here) often repeats her lines back ironically and here Paul deflects the suspicion, 'You know very well what I've been doing', adopting the role of victim, intuitively sensing that this will distract her.

Reiner conveys the essentially undramatic nature of writing with a montage dissolving repeated graphic matches of Paul typing day and night, taking paper out of the typewriter, the Sheriff reading, and side-on and top shots of the typewriter keys. Accompanied by Liberace, the montage suggests the process is easy but that may be because he has only one reader to please, however exacting she may be. In the novel, King makes this explicit: 'Annie Wilkes was the perfect audience, a woman who loved stories without having the slightest interest in the mechanics of making them. She was the embodiment of that Victorian archetype, Constant Reader.'[7] Paul tries to explain the process of writing (such as the kind of paper he uses) to Annie but, at bottom, she does not want to know. Ironically, Goldman reflects the problem by cutting King's sections where Paul works out the narrative problems of *Misery's Return*. It is the fact that he finishes the book that is important, not the actual words he writes. This devotion is the cause of his material wealth, but also of his present incarceration: it leads to delusional fantasies of identification but this also allows him to ultimately trick Annie and escape.

Much has been made of Bates' performance, for which she won an Oscar, but Caan's work is no less impressive, especially since he is on-screen most of the time and physically incapacitated, often reduced to communicating through facial expression alone. The novel's recording of his dependence on painkillers is replaced by Caan's wincing and heavy breathing that accompanies every movement. When she starts to complain about the swearing in his manuscript, her voice gets progressively louder, edging into hysteria, symbolized by her spilling soup and aggressively blaming him ('See what you made me do'). Compressing several scenes in the novel, Reiner zooms in slightly on Paul, whose eyes, skipping across to the window, convey increasing distress verging on panic at the reality of his situation, which is only now dawning on him – he is in the hands of potentially-violent maniac given to unpredictable outbursts of temper at the same time as being in an isolated house, dependant on painkillers and with smashed-up legs.[8] Like Scheherazade, as long as the story lasts they can maintain a precarious equilibrium. The completion of the book provides inevitable closure to the narrative, which Annie herself senses in her drift towards suicide.

Annie's inability to synthesize sexual physicality with her world-view erupts in her speech, which is a bizarre mix of childish terms ('oogy', 'dirty bird', 'cockadoodie' and 'Mr Man'), almost pathological aversion to swearing (profanity has 'no nobility') and eccentric outbursts such as when she makes pig noises. There is also a graphic insensitivity to her attitudes to illness (anticipating her failings as a nurse) – she talks of 'popping' his dislocated shoulder back in and 'hearing the bones moving about' in his leg. Most obviously, we have a shot down the bed, cropping Annie's head but focusing on Paul's panicked expression as she waves his bedpan around, perilously close to his legs, anticipating the same actions later with the lighter fuel and then the block of paper (viewed from above).

In such an apparently-bleak, intense drama, there are tiny comedic elements for contrast – when Annie wheels in the barbecue to burn his book, he says 'when I mentioned a snack, I was thinking more along the lines of cheese and crackers'. When Annie produces a wheelchair, he declares 'Great, I always wanted to visit the other side of the room.' Annie gives Paul a pad and invites him to 'think of me as your inspiration'. He does, but not in the way she imagines. The perkiness between Buster and his frisky wife (played by Frances Sternhagen, reprising a similar role a year later in *Golden Years*) produces some good lines too – after one of her acidic comments about his reading, he replies 'it's just that kind of sarcasm that's given our marriage real spice'. A great shot down the length of the hall, with Buster in the lounge and Annie in the kitchen, neither appearing to be honest with the other, shows both peeking out at the same time (twice in fact) before the Sheriff has the chance to sneak upstairs. Annie appears in the frame behind him but carries nothing more threatening than cocoa.

Elements of explicit gore more associated with the horror genre, such as Annie's sadistic running over a second cop's face with a lawnmower, are (perhaps not surprisingly) cut, although the sudden brutality of shooting Buster, seen in low angle from Paul's POV down in the cellar, is still quite shocking. Annie's calm delivery about the Kimberly diamond mine and the faint sound of Liberace makes the horror of the 'hobbling' scene all the more powerful (an addition scripted by Reiner and Producer Andrew Scheinman that most interested Goldman in the whole project and which he fiercely argued should stay). Less bloody, perhaps, than the amputation of a single foot in the book, it conveys its power from a momentary glimpse of Paul's ankle at an unnatural angle, a sickening crunching sound but perhaps most particularly by the gradual way in which Annie leads up to it, juxtaposed with Paul's utter physical helplessness. We do not need to see the second strike, the first is sickening enough – a conclusion also shared by Goldman when he saw the finished cut.

At the end, writing provides literal escapism for Paul as he burns Annie's script, even stuffing paper in her mouth (like the 'oral-rape' of Ripley in *Alien* and possibly revenge for Annie's repulsive mouth-to-mouth in the opening of the novel).[9] She becomes closer to a personification of the female grotesque who survives a blow from the typewriter, his Molotov cocktail and being impaled on the machine itself before being punched by a Misery-style doorstop and falling on Paul in an orgasmic parody. In the novel, Annie escapes somewhat improbably from a window, like Frankenstein's unkillable monster, and a subsequent nightmare of her trying to kill him is given without markers, so the description of her actual death out in the barn, is quite anticlimactic. By contrast, the coda in the film shows Paul lunching with his publisher to celebrate the critical, if not commercial, success of his new novel. Whilst not displaying the obvious generic markers of horror, the film ends, like *Carrie,* with an unsignalled subjective vision: a recurrent, living nightmare (as he is still approached by a reader claiming to be 'his number one fan') and, like Sue Snell at the end of De Palma's film, there is a muted tone to the final frames as a zoom-in shows his smile fading slightly and the final line, 'I don't know if anyone can ever totally get over something like that', is left hanging.

The Dark Half (George A. Romero, 1993)

'I hope it's not you Thaddeus. I'd hate to think of George Stark taking over your lecture group'. (Beaumont's colleague Reggie Delesseps)

Hodder and Stoughton subtitled King's 1989 novel *The Dark Half* 'his masterpiece'. Director George Romero, who has dedications in the novels of *Christine* and *Cell,* shows slightly less hubris in his treatment of the text. The concept of basing a film not so much on where a writer gets his ideas from as much as where they go, and what happens if a larger-than-life character will not 'die', is certainly interesting. King clearly draws on the Bachman experience ('the novel could not have been written without him', the author's note states) and his desire to kill off an alter ego who writes characters that are more dynamic than his other work. However, the problem, both in the book and the film, is in its realization. Both take a far-from-convincing concept, the psychopomp (from Greek mythology and Jungian psychology), literalize this in flocks of sparrows and then expect readers and viewers to take this as literally true and work backwards to its metaphorical meaning as a messenger between life and death. Romero may be closely associated with the living dead (the gravedigger who crosses himself as Homer merrily clicks away in the foreground is an intertextual joke, reminiscent of the minor figures in Romero's seminal *Night of the Living Dead*) but as extremely physical and visceral entities, not as a vague abstract concept.

Generically, the film is pulling in different directions – crime story, philosophical fantasy, horror and family drama surrounding the life of a writer – and eventually cannot cohere. The film struggles to convey convincingly a sense of duality. The impact on the Beaumont family of working as a writer is clear from the material benefits of a comfortable house to the drinking, the mood swings whilst writing and, particularly in Thad's case, identifying too closely with unpleasant fictional characters. When Thad adopts his jokey, tough-guy talk whilst changing the babies, and when journalist Donaldson reads an extract on the way to the photo-shoot, Liz, his wife, looks away and later leaves the 'Stark study', a dark, windowless room accessed by a Gothic-style sliding bookcase, clearly repulsed by his persona. However, flaws in the basic premise undermine attempts at characterization and audience empathy. Certainly, there are many films which defy logic and do not necessarily need a wholly rational plot, but here we are supposedly dealing with a crime narrative, which is quintessentially involved with cause and effect, including a detective looking for clues. Trying to understand the complex motivation of a projection does not stand up to scrutiny. Although there is some ambiguity in Tim Hutton's performance (threatening blackmailer Clawson or saying to the doctor that George will 'have his balls for breakfast'), there is not enough threat in the part of Beaumont or humanity in the part of Stark to see a convergence of characters as likely (apparently suggested by Thad's growing clumsiness).

The central problem here, as elsewhere in this study, is a crushing tendency towards literalization (seen in the denouement at 'Endsville'). King and Romero are taking a simile and converting it into a straightforward metaphor – a writer's character is treated as if he were alive. This is even reflected in intertextual allusions. The nurse's vision in the hospital (the final scene's extremely high angle over the house with very slight movement, simulating a bird's POV shot) and most obviously in the attack on Stark, are clear references to Hitchcock's *The Birds*. Although Hitchcock plots are not always watertight, they are best known for their ability to convey suspense – a quality singularly lacking here. We see Beaumont at home with an alibi although, to the police, prints at the crime scenes and eye witnesses seeing someone who looked like him start to build a powerful case of circumstantial evidence. At the point when Beaumont takes a phone call from Stark we know that Beaumont cannot be literally be responsible for the murders but Pangborn finds the notion of Stark hard to accept (as indeed we might) because, unlike a belief in ghosts, this is a man who has never existed before. We may share Beaumont's feelings that, as in the novel, 'reason and rationality told him that Stark could not be out there'.[10] Also, unlike the final scenes of narrative exposition in a standard crime/mystery narrative, even used by Hitchcock, here there are several scenes where plot momentum dies and we are invited to consider the actuality of a character created by the projection of another's subconscious. This not only lacks credibility, it is inconsistent. Stark is more decisive and violent, certainly, but he kills people with whom Beaumont has no argument; i.e. he is only acting out his wishes in the style, not the actuality of his actions.

Moments of visceral horror surrounding bodily transgression deliver the pleasures audiences might expect from a Romero film, such as a top shot during surgery into Beaumont's brain, which reveals a moving eye, or the final attack on Stark by the sparrows that peck out his brain and rib-cage. There are tiny glimpses of attempts to break out of a generic straightjacket, such as a surreal sequence, which in retrospect we can read as an unsignalled dream, with Beaumont moving through the house and seeing a vase which shatters, an oven which cracks, revealing a putrid turkey, and a sitting figure, who looks like his wife but on closer examination has no face, only a mask which also cracks to reveal a skull beneath. All of these images are drawn directly from King's novel and are effective because they obey a nightmarish, surreal logic.[11] The images are replayed at the climax, where the vase, oven and sitting figure do not crack in two, casting the earlier scene as a precognitive experience.

The film actually works most effectively where writing is not part of the narrative – in generically 'straightforward' kill scenes when Stark is purely a homicidal maniac. These do use the horror clichés of abrupt movement into the frame (Miriam grabbed into her apartment) or sudden noise (a piece of paper suddenly blowing in the cop's face in the parking lot). However, to gain a family rating and to allow the film to be shown on television (its likely prime exhibition environment), brutal acts of violence take place off-frame (like the kicking of Donaldson's head, conveyed by sound effect alone) or out of plain view (as with Clawson's death). The presence and then withdrawal of a sense of threat is also used effectively to unsettle audiences: Homer stops to pick up a man in the dark but looking back, the road is empty. Reversing, he stops again and we share his POV down the side of the truck before cutting back to his face as, suddenly, hands reach into the frame and drag him bodily out of the window (albeit using a very obvious dummy). A slow track up to the truck shows his leg left dangling there, a variation on 'the hook' urban myth (and an effectively macabre change from the arm used in the novel). Rick, Thad's agent, is seen in his apartment with a pair of legs slowly coming into the frame behind him on a window-cleaning gantry, only to reveal the friendly face of a cleaner. Allowing the viewer to recover, Romero then has Rick going into his bathroom, finding two dead cops and then, suddenly, Stark leaps out, stabs him and exits via the window. Stark's slow descent becomes the last thing Rick sees (this is also a meta-textual editing gag, completing a previous action) and the killer leaves with the Bond-like quip: 'It's a cutthroat business.'

The final sequence, where George tries to write, attempts to reassert the focus of the film on the writer. Like Paul Sheldon, Beaumont uses the tools of his trade to defeat George, first stabbing him in the neck with a pencil and later knocking a gun out of his hand with the typewriter. However, intertextual allusions in the final sequence only serve to underline how the notion of the body at war with itself, in George's case, a kind of Invisible Man in reverse, has several, more effective, cinematic precursors. The sparrows peck their way into the study, sending shafts of light through the room, like the arrival of the cenobites in Clive Barker's *Hellraiser* (1987), and the animatronic birds attacking Stark, ripping his skin off, feel a little like Frank Cotton's generation in reverse. In the words of Ridley Scott's Roy Batty from *Blade Runner*, George wants 'more life, fucker' but, unlike Roy, the character of Stark is never developed enough to provoke any sense of tragic empathy. Stark and Beaumont gradually converge spatially and in appearance, meeting face to face, both wearing a hat and dark glasses and each carrying a baby.

Like David Cronenberg's Mantle brothers in *Dead Ringers* (1988), the attempted convergence of twins at the denouement is reflected in on-screen symmetry but unlike Jeremy Irons' finely-nuanced performance in the earlier film which teases out similarities as well as differences in character, and even with the hints that Beaumont is drawn to parts of Stark's character, we still have the clichéd contrast here of 'normal' with the psychotic. Stark's bodily deterioration (recorded in some detail in the novel) also echoes that of Seth Brundle in Cronenberg's *The Fly* (1986).[12] Stark dispassionately pulls out a tooth and doubts if their voice-prints would match any longer. However, unlike Brundle, there is no coherent existential 'Insect philosophy' underlying this action. In the novel, Stark evasively states, 'The word became flesh, you might say. How it happened doesn't much matter – what matters is that I'm here.'[13] If Beaumont needs to give expression to his dark half ('It's all me', he tells his wife), this does not square with his desire to kill him off as he needs to integrate Stark's dynamism into his writing and his everyday character. Another Cronenberg film, *Scanners* (1980), dramatizes a more convincing and ultimately tragic final battle, also between brothers, in which only one will survive, assimilated by the other.

The generic confusion extends to the Danny Elfman-style opening theme that suggests a fantasy film but, elsewhere, for example when Beaumont drives to work, we have *Miami Vice*-style synthesizer. The novel describes the denouement as 'a scene from some malign fairy tale ... as if a hole had been torn in the fabric of reality'.[14] Unfortunately parts of the 'reality' of the book are never firmly established. The concept of an unabsorbed twin is interesting but the division of human nature into two halves, one light the other dark, is a very crude dichotomy – Timothy Hutton as George Stark is cartoonish, dressed all in black, including gloves and boots, slicked back hair and with a different accent – but as soon as we move from cropped shots and actually see his full physical form, articulating a desire for Beaumont to write, the idea no longer works. Although a doctor notes that Beaumont is displaying classic symptoms of schizophrenia, this is not actually true, and the fact that Romero uses same-sex twins (Sarah and Elizabeth Parker) to play William and Wendy Beaumont suggests a director who is not fully engaged with detail. George Stark, his projected fantasy character, is strong, dynamic and decisive and supposedly inhabits part of Beaumont's brain that was originally a twin but, logically, the undeveloped twin and he should contain both elements.

There is a final generic contradiction here. The film, the book and the horror genre upon which they rest are all intrinsically interested in 'the dark half' of human nature – remove that and what we are left with are anodyne scenes of domestic bliss (after all, we do see quite a lot of baby-related domesticity on-screen). Without transgression there is no story. The plot ends before we see the kinds of more worthy, literary work that Beaumont can now produce, but there is little sense that it will be more interesting (in the novel we are given an epilogue with the moral, 'He was not a man who believed in happy endings. What little serenity he knew came chiefly from that.')[15] The film ameliorates the book's darker ending, which features a clear hint that the Beaumont's marriage does not survive, and also ducking the impact on Thad, who later commits suicide (according to *Bag of Bones*).[16] More than the question expressed by AC/DC in *Maximum Overdrive*, 'Who made who?', it is a matter of who needs who(m) and, implicitly, this is a warning to those who would wish to undermine the primacy of the author. King has never written an overt sequel, although his critics might say that he recycles ideas instead. This is largely what Romero does here.

Secret Window (David Koepp, 2004)

Director and screenwriter David Koepp had already shown ability to create tension in confined spaces in writing credits such as *Panic Room* (David Fincher, 2002) and *Jurassic Park* (Steven Spielberg, 1993). In relation to *Secret Window*, based on the novella 'Secret Window, Secret Garden' collected in *Four Past Midnight* (1990), most readers, and not a few viewers, will have spotted the plot twist quite a while before the 'revelatory' scene, where we see the elision of Shooter and Rainey's identity. This is a result of a fairly predictable plot (including Mort's blindingly-obvious symbolic name) and previous films like *Fight Club* (David Fincher, 1999), which use the same basic premise. However, there is also more artistry at work here than might at first appear and the film does reward repeat viewings.

Intertextuality is present from the fluidity of the opening long take, up to and through the window of Rainey's lakeside house (almost certainly with a 'cheat cut' at some point), evoking Hitchcock's *Psycho*, which might also make a cine-literate viewer wonder if Rainey, like Marion Crane, has stolen something. The 'floating' camera appears to be searching for a subject: passing slowly across a laptop and down and round until we can see a figure lying on a couch. The occupation, relative wealth and current slothfulness of the owner are all contained within this shot. The allusion to Lewis Carroll's *Alice in Wonderland* (1865) in passing through the mirror, with only a slight visual effect to convey this, is likely to be missed on first viewing and its full meaning only available with hindsight. Similarly, in the climactic recognition scene, we see multiple Raineys on-screen, simultaneously, one looking straight at the camera and each manifestation using a slightly different voice (Marlon Brando, Christopher Walken and Roman Polanski) – the intertextual allusion planted as a clue for cultural experts to display their credentials by recognition (an inherent genre pleasure). This extends to allusions to King's own work: when the camera has tracked back through the mirror, Amy sees the house as it was all along, a chaotic mess with 'Shooter' carved into several parts of the house (an elision of Rainey's underlying desire, 'Shoot her'), a less subtle version of the 'Redrum' idea from *The Shining*.

Even though the film does not specifically mention a nervous breakdown, unlike the novella, clues about Rainey's guilt are all there from the outset: the cleaner, Mrs Gavin, assuming the manuscript in the bin is Rainey's; his private investigator asking point-blank if he stole it; and even his wife Amy (Maria Bello) wondering if the situation is 'like before', i.e. a previous plagiarism lawsuit. After a flurry of nervous (and possibly guilty) activity close to the camera as he hunts through his drawers for some cigarettes, he addresses the camera directly, as if talking to his dog, and states that 'I didn't steal that story' several times, giving the impression of protesting rather too much, subsequently knocking over a drink as he reads it, which might suggest a deeper recognition. His following dream features a door, wobbling as if holding back a great force, and his discomfort in the Post Office and in the Sheriff's office suggest a strange unease around women. Over the latter part of the film, his guilt becomes even more obvious, focused on the iconic hat, which he brings in, carries around and finally and puts on, clearly identifying him as 'Shooter' (whose accent he also adopts).

The film is an odd generic hybrid. Despite the appearance of a mystery story, Depp's portrayal of Morton Rainey extracts every potential morsel of comedy from Koepp's script. The flashback sequence, in which Rainey emerges from the house, is typical. He jokingly protests that Amy has left $100 when his sexual favours are free and tells her she has something round her mouth, even though he is the one covered in shaving foam and wearing a dressing gown. This almost feels like a compilation of many of Depp's previous eccentric outsiders – from *Benny and Joon* (Jeremiah S. Chechik, 1993) to *Pirates of the Caribbean* (Gore Verbinski, 2003) and its sequels. Much of the interest of the film centres on close-ups of his face – from the opening glazed stare through a windscreen, prior to confronting his adulterous wife, to the final snapshot of him taking a bite from his corn, grown over her dead body. We see him caught smoking by his cleaning lady, like Chandler smoking in his cubicle in *Friends* (Series 3, episode 18, 1997); gesturing aggressively at the phone when his wife starts to tell him about one of 'her feelings'; going 'Ra' like a small dog; or developing a nervous jaw tic as his identity implodes (all features added to the film). In the novella, the line 'I killed a mirror' is part of a screaming, unhinged fit but Depp's calmer delivery makes his antics more absurd than unstable. Kelsch asks Rainey if he has 'done anything to piss Ted off', at which point we have a quick shot of Rainey screaming in his face after surprising him in the motel room with Amy. We then cut straight back to a close-up on Depp, who admits in an off-hand manner, 'I might have'. We are denied views of his attacks on Kelsch and Greenleaf and even his final murders of Ted and Amy are partly obscured. His tomfoolery with the dog, singing Mexican songs to it while wobbling his Adam's apple, sitting with a bag of Doritos staring at a phone which he himself has unplugged, make him an engaging, empathetic figure. The comedic elements even extend to Ted, whose attempts to fight Rainey at the gas station culminate with him punching the car window by mistake and injuring his own hand.

Juxtaposed with this, are some more measured, darker moments. The crack that spreads up the wall and across the ceiling, as a metaphor of his divided and fragmented self, (even with a POV shot from the ceiling) is too obvious but the superimposition of memories of Amy over shots of the window (used in a similar way in Nic Roeg's *Bad Timing* from 1980) and, later, of the burned house are quite touching. His true feelings for Amy are reflected in the almost subliminal flashback of them making love as they meet by the burned-down house and his look at her momentarily-bared shoulders during the insurance assessment interview (apparently unseen by the others).

The disruption of framing conventions aligns sections of the film more closely with a mystery narrative, albeit in a slightly unusual style. In the truck scene, Koepp uses Depp's head to conceal part of the frame until we track back through the driver's window and see the screwdriver sticking out of the head of Tom Greenleaf, the sole witness, on the other side. Although, logically, Rainey cannot see that clearly from where he is, he reacts viscerally, throwing up (suggesting he is being forced to recognize his own actions). Rapid cutaways of the weapon, Rainey framed through a blood-stained window and Kelsch, the investigator, dead on the back seat, convey the shock and reality crashing in on Rainey's (and possibly our) consciousness. King's novella also mentions, early on, that Rainey needs new glasses, underlying his flawed vision, and Koepp conveys this by using close-ups of Depp peering, for example at a lone squirrel. Koepp also frames only half of Depp's face here, in extreme close-up – all clues that we are looking at a severely-divided personality. Koepp does at least try to extend some generic conventions, and his camera positioning raises questions about what the 'true' subject of a shot actually is. In several places, Koepp directs the camera at an apparently 'empty' space a few moments before the main subject enters the frame, such as the shot of the motel door through the windscreen at the opening; the couch, onto which Rainey happily collapses almost as if he is a part of it; and Rainey approaching the burned remains of his former home. When Rainey goes for a walk by the lake, Koepp places the camera very close to the back of Depp's head so that, when he slaps a mosquito, it is almost as if he senses he is being watched.

Intertextual allusions in the dialogue often add a bitter-sweet resonance. In rejecting Shooter as ignorant, Rainey spells out (literally) his marital status by referring to Tammy Wynette's song *D-I-V-O-R-C-E*. Later, on viewing Amy and Ted together, he says the Talking Heads lyric to himself: 'This is not my beautiful house. This is not my beautiful wife.' He is very much a 'talking head' for much of the film and displays some of the same eccentric qualities associated with singer/writer David Byrne. The exchange with the woman in the Post Office works like the dialogue in Brett Easton Ellis' *American Psycho* (adapted by Mary Harron in 2000), whereby it is not one hundred percent clear what a character has actually said. The woman says 'They'd shoot me if you did' (her superiors would be angry if they knew she gave Rainey a parcel) but he first hears, presumably distorted by his guilty conscience, 'I know what you did'. However, the *Rebel Without a Cause*-style running of the truck into the lake does seem a rather desperate attempt to import some action into the plot.

The title 'Secret Window' reflects an essentially Romantic view of writing and King dramatizes some of his own rituals, such as going for walks, but the only actual writing we see occurs at the very beginning and ending of the film as a largely interior act. Rainey's life is really very empty. The meal that he promised the cleaner he will make consists of some unappetising sandwiches and we see him lying in his dressing gown, listening to a dripping tap and talking to his dog. His isolation is not only a matter of the physical location of the house (stressed in the opening approach across an expanse of water) but also seen in the fact that the killing of the dog deprives him of his closest companion. As a careful reader, Shooter knows about the minutiae of his life, including his 'stupid little naps' because he read it on a book-jacket. Rainey-as-author is a product, manufactured by the joint collusion of the needs of marketing departments and audiences.

The narrative focuses on ownership of ideas, and the impact that has on authors and those around them. Notably, this film is not called 'Stephen King's Secret Window' but Koepp claims, on the DVD, that King approved the script, viewed a rough cut and 'made some suggestions', although what these were exactly, remains unclear. King's plot is essentially a triangular love story seen through Rainey's distorting subjective prism. Much of King's text is composed of Rainey's thoughts and Koepp adopts a number of means to suggest this, most obviously voice-over, but he also has Rainey speak his thoughts aloud – credible given his isolated position – his career as a writer and the ubiquitous mirrors, which seem to invite direct address. Koepp also gives him a dog for company, the ageing blind Chico (originally 'Bump' the cat in King's novella), to act as a sounding-board.

The horror clichés of a woman pursued by a male killer and a car that will not start are made more interesting by a top-shot showing Amy being dragged out of the car, a rescuer almost-comically walking onto Rainey's shovel and being despatched out of sight, and a restrained cutting away from Amy's demise. Instead we have a double-coda with a newly-invigorated, clean-cut Rainey some months later. Now he flirts with the woman from the Post Office and ignores attempts by the Sheriff to warn him off, replying, before putting his headphones back on and returning to writing, 'The only thing that matters is the ending' and 'This one's perfect.' As if to prove the point, Koepp tracks past him, through the secret window and down to the crop of corn under which, it is implied, the bodies lie. A deleted scene actually showed this but Koepp wisely felt the voiceover reading the last lines of the story ('in time every bit of her will be gone and her death will be a mystery, even to me') would be more effective. The *deus ex machina* ending of the novella, where insurance investigator Fred Evans appears just in time to shoot Rainey before he can harm Amy, is rejected. In the film, a deluded killer survives, unpunished, and in a better state than he was at the beginning; turning his experience into a new literary work. Indeed, the fact that Rainey wrote his story so long ago might suggest that the homicidal impulses, and their final realization that we see at the end of the film, have been many years gestating.

The film does use standard horror techniques and what has become the all-too-predictable device of an unreliable narrator. However, there are redeeming features that raise the film beyond generic expectations – particularly a memorable performance by Johnny Depp – and Koepp's camera placement and movement try hard to conceal a lack of cinematic drama in the plot. In the novella, witness Tom Greenleaf sees a transparent ghost-like figure with Rainey; there is a back-story about a tale stolen from a student, John Kintner, in the past; and the narrative ends with a mysterious note, which may be from an entity calling itself Shooter. To convey a fractured psyche, Koepp chooses a fragmented narrative form but, like Stark in *The Dark Half*, Shooter cannot be taken seriously as both a projection and a real individual. King's ambivalence in the earlier text finds its way into Romero's film but Koepp takes the braver decision to choose one alternative and stick to it, add a far bleaker ending (a rarity in King adaptations) and, as King claims to do with the fiction, 'take familiar elements and put them together in an entirely new way'.[17]

Ultimately, subtext is heavily signposted and there is no equivalent of the 'pulling of the rug' from beneath the reader/viewer, as at the end of Bryan Singer's *Jacob's Ladder* (1991), Richard Kelly's *Donnie Darko* (2001) or M. Night Shyamalan's *The Sixth Sense* (1999). The line from the TV ad used in both books, *The Dark Half* and 'Secret Window, Secret Garden': 'Is it real or is it Memorex?' does not really resonate in the film versions – both aim for a domestic, psychological drama rather than a braver, P.K. Dick-style full disorientation narrative and, with slightly modest ambitions, their success is proportionately reduced.

Conclusion

Misery is explicitly about authorship and more precisely, about consumer rights. Annie Wilkes, as Sheldon's 'Number 1 fan' is asserting her right, as the prime shareholder in his work, to influence the writing process. She shows no real interest in the mechanics of writing, becoming angry when Paul tries to explain the creation of characters and mapping relationships, although, having played a part in his commercial success by buying his books, she expects to be consulted. Paul's abduction and imprisonment is an embodiment of the notion that an author is 'created' by an audience and therefore owes them loyalty by producing more texts that they like. More particularly, *Misery* dramatizes the pleasure of genre consumption taken to an extreme and the tyranny of its consequences for an author. The film, therefore, not only reflects King's dilemma as an author but also that of directors of any King adaptations – desiring to produce a distinct work but also likely to face the wrath of Wilkes-like fans if it is perceived that an adaptation stretches generic expectations too far. This ready-made audience allows projects to be green-lit in the first place but ironically, at the same time, creates a creative environment which is disproportionately averse to risk-taking.

There is very little actual writing in these films, which do not attempt to challenge the conundrum of how to show an interior, cerebral act of creation, but instead they dramatize the writer as public property and commodity: a figure destined to have meanings projected upon him, whether he wishes it or not. In a sense, what we have in the on-screen readers are uncritical auteurists, convinced of their own elision of authors with their work. Thus we see writers as celebrities (*Misery*), as the creators of popular fictional personae which, rightly or wrongly, are often taken to reflect part of their own character (*The Dark Half*) and as the object of law suits and personal attacks (*Secret Window*). It is ironic that at the same time as King is encouraging this myth of authorship, with signed copies, personal appearances and possessory credits, his fiction, and the films based upon them, portray this as delusionary. Writers are portrayed almost as shamanic figures, creating alternative imaginative dimensions for the real world – beyond works of fiction. The most ambitious of the three, *Secret Window*, uses a relative rarity in mainstream cinema – an unreliable narrator – as we track through the mirror into Rainey's supposed solipsistic universe, and although the film may be considered as only partially successful and messily plotted, it is a rare example of a film text that at least tries to yield a different meaning on repeat viewings.

Notes

1. Stephen King, 'The Night Flier', in *Nightmares and Dreamscapes* (London: New English Library, 1993), p. 138.
2. Cited in Don Herron (ed.), *Reign of Fear: The Fiction and the Films of Stephen King*, op. cit., p. x.
3. Stephen King, *Four Past Midnight* (London: New English Library, 1990), p. 305.
4. Ibid., p. 306.
5. Golding, *Lord of the Flies* , op. cit., p. 70.
6. Magistrale, *The Hollywood Stephen King*, op. cit., p. 65 and p. 66.
7. Stephen King, *Misery* (London: New English Library, 1987), p. 69.
8. See ibid., pp. 10, 13 and 15.
9. Ibid., p. 5.
10. Ibid., *Stephen King The Dark Half*, (New York: Viking, 1989). p. 165.
11. Ibid., pp. 36–38.
12. See ibid., pp. 291–2.
13. Ibid., p. 415.
14. Ibid., p. 461.
15. Ibid., p. 463.
16. Ibid., p. 468.
17. King, *Four Past Midnight,* op cit.,p. 306.

CHAPTER EIGHT

THE TERROR OF EVERYDAY LIFE AND FINAL GIRLS

'Doors were mouths, stairways throats. Empty rooms became traps'.[1]

(Cujo)

The title of Jonathan Lake Crane's *Terror and Everyday Life* suggests a new movement towards the domestic and the mundane as sources of fear,[2] perhaps reflecting wider cultural shifts such as bookstores routinely carrying a section for 'Survivor Literature' (e.g. David Pelzer's 1995 *A Child Called It*), towards which even King's own *Misery* could be said to contribute, or even the cultural phenomenon of 'Panic Rooms', underlining how citizens no longer feel safe even within their own homes. However, this can be traced back at least as far as Hitchcock's *Psycho,* and the reference above, which might describe John Carpenter's closing frames in *Halloween* (1978), reflects an enduring interest in King's work with small-scale, domestic fears. Magistrale describes *Shawshank*, *Apt Pupil* and *Dolores Claiborne* as being 'devoid of the requisite supernatural monsters and concerned instead with the monsters of everyday reality'.[3] The first two are generically placed elsewhere in this study but there is an element of these fears in King's techno-horror narratives, and the underlying fear of death, an everyday reality for us all, is mentioned in the 'Body under the sheet' section.

The Shining is as much about family breakdown as it is a horror narrative and *Dolores Claiborne,* focusing on the reaction of an abused wife and the gradual uncovering of abuse of a daughter, is couched in terms of a present-day all-female relationship: the consequences of the terror. In the film of *Cujo*, although Tad's fear of the monster in his closet (echoing 'The General' segment of *Cat's Eye*) is placed near the film's opening, the novel (but not the film) includes consideration of Vic's fear of failure, at work and as a husband. In the novella, the lines above actually apply to Donna and the nightmare of her empty, loveless marriage, which is the real underlying subject of both the book and film.

Cujo (Lewis Teague, 1983)

'There's no such thing as monsters. Only in stories.' (Vic Trenton)

'Why do grown-ups say there are no monsters?' (Newt in *Aliens*,1986)

'Nope. Nothing wrong here.' (the Sharp Cereal Professor)

Generically, *Cujo*, as book and film, is routinely promoted as a horror story with images of a demonic, slavering dog dominating covers and posters. However, problematically, it fails to deliver generic expectations, either because of poor directing decisions from Teague or, more importantly, because its underlying structure is not that of a horror film but family drama. This is particularly apparent in the character progression of Donna Trenton (Dee Wallace-Stone), the realization of the rabid Cujo and the climactic ending in which both Donna and her son, Tad (Danny Pintauro), are trapped in their car by the dog.

There are several problems with *Cujo* as a horror narrative. Firstly, and most obviously, there is a clear case of miscasting. Rather than a breed known for its aggressive qualities, the film (and book) choose a St Bernard, known for its size certainly but just as prominently for its intelligence and caring qualities. As a symbol for mountain rescue, this works, but as a way of conveying the horror of a rabid dog, it does not. Rather than a hellish Baskerville hound, here, a giant St Bernard with unconvincing shaving foam round its mouth looks like it might lick you to death in a fit of over-zealous friendliness. With different music, the opening sequence, with its intercutting of POVs from a hunter/hunted perspective, might seem just playful. From the perspective of a rabbit in low angle, it might look threatening but even the dog getting its huge head stuck in a rabbit hole and then bitten on the nose are the ingredients of a children's story. The attack sequences using close shots, rapid cutting and even a stuntman in a dog costume, look more like rough play, with growling sound effects clearly added in post-production. There is some attempt to show a degeneration in Cujo's condition, with more drool, unpleasant-looking discharge and an increased intolerance of noise, but it is ridiculous that nobody notices a prominent red wound on the nose of a large dog.

However, generically, *Cujo* is really a family drama with a horrific final section. The pacing of the first half compared to the scene at Camber's farm is relatively slow but the marital infidelity that occupies two-thirds of the film is actually more than the 'subplot', as Collings describes it.[4] Like Newt's unanswerable question about monsters in *Aliens*, Cujo is also about 'family'. Reflecting Sharp's cereal, which appears dangerous but only emits a harmless, red dye and Vic's professional reputation as an advertising agent, all is not as stable as it seems. There is a sense of disjunction between the Trentons' social aspirations (and possibly pretensions) and the reality of their seemingly-comfortable life. They live in a large house

THE TERROR OF EVERYDAY LIFE AND FINAL GIRLS | 189

overlooking the sea, the husband drives a red sports car and they socialize at a tennis club. However, the husband's job is precarious and threatened by a scandal not of his making, the car looks good but needs repair-work and, at the club, Vic (Daniel Hugh-Kelly) plays against Steve (Christopher Stone), who is part of the adulterous force destroying the family. Vic seems as powerless to limit the damage to his professional reputation as he is to repair his car or his marriage, which are all close to breakdown. He knows that something is amiss, lying awake and replying to Donna's compliment of how good he is with Tad with 'And how am I with you?'

Vic's assurance about monsters proves to be wrong, although in a sense his written 'spell' to keep the monster at bay works in Tad's bedroom and maybe, ultimately, in the car with the dog. However his remedy for a lack of conversation at breakfast is to suggest another baby when domestic drudgery is what Donna yearns to escape. Her own low self-esteem, inability to resist temptation (shown in avoiding eye contact with her own reflection) and the social pretensions come together when the Trentons first go to the Camber's garage. She takes a step towards Mrs Camber, who is peeling some vegetables, but freezes awkwardly, inappropriately over-dressed for a visit to a rural garage in a puffy-shouldered dress and high heels. Steve's attempt to continue the affair leads to a fight in which food is spilt and it is as Donna is mopping up the mess that Vic returns home with Tad. One look at her confirms his worst fears and, despite the feeling that the first half is slow and over-written, he asks succinctly 'Yes or no?', to which she replies, simply, 'Yes'. Right at the close, Vic, having obeyed an inexplicable *Jane Eyre*-like dream, and Tad's voice calling him to come home, runs to give Donna some specific domestic support (lacking up to this point), taking the child she is carrying, and the film closes on a freeze-frame, an icon of a family fractured but enduring.

Carol Clover's analysis of slasher films produced the archetypal Final Girl, who is no passive screaming female, survives by her own wits, and goes on to escape or kill the killer. Clover defines the role of the Final Girl thus:

> She is introduced at the beginning and is the only character to be developed in any psychological detail. We understand immediately from the attention paid it that hers is the main story line. She is intelligent, watchful, and level-headed; the first character to sense something amiss and the only one to deduce from the accumulating evidence the pattern and extent of the threat ...[5]

In a conventional slasher, women are frequently portrayed by critics as passive victims of a crazed, usually lone, male killer, suppressing an element of his sexual identity, which is projected onto those he kills. Clover problematizes such assumptions, especially concerning male and female identification, and raises the possibility of masochistic pleasure and identification with victim as well as killer. As she states:

[t]he Final Girl, on reflection, is a congenial double for the adolescent male. She is feminine enough to act out in a gratifying way, a way unapproved for adult males, the terrors and masochistic pleasures of the underlying fantasy, but not so feminine as to disturb the structures of female competence and sexuality.[6]

However, the kinds of narratives she bases her theories upon are largely absent from this book and none are overt slasher films.

As Linda Badley notes:

[m]ost horror stories offer a message as conservative as their morality: conform. The boogeyman of Halloween and Friday the 13th are the hitmen of homogeneity. Don't do it, they tell us, or you will pay an awful price. Don't talk to strangers, don't dare to be different.[7]

The notion of punishment for sexual activity, although sometimes attributed to *Halloween*, goes back at least to Marion Crane and her extra-marital affair in *Psycho* (1960). King seems very aware of this and the victims of Cujo are punished for their sins.[8] Brett Camber (Ed Lauter) plans to spend his wife's lottery win on a weekend of alcohol and sex. His friend, and accomplice, Gary, pays the price for his mistreatment of the dog and general slovenliness – Cujo attacks him as he is randomly tipping rubbish out in the backyard. Wallace-Stone, subsequently married to Christopher Stone, her on-screen lover here, and seen more recently in Rob Zombie's *Halloween* (2007), draws upon her 'scream queen' experience in *The Hills Have Eyes* (Wes Craven, 1977), *The Howling* (1981), and powerfully conveys the anger, panic and desperation of a mother forced to defend her child in a primal, womb-like setting. The performance that Teague gets from her and the young boy, who has never seen his mother out of control like this, shown in a close-up reaction shot, is impressive, given the speed of shooting and the practical difficulties of working with animals. Her resilience, resourcefulness and a sense of aggressive combativeness mark her as a potential Final Girl. However, there is a sense, too, of punishment and expatiation for the adultery: the 'stupid mistake', from which she thinks she has extricated herself. Even the 'Fuck you, dog', which she snarls at Cujo, proves premature and the engine subsequently dying seems like a punishment for a moment of hubris. Critics who wonder why she does not make a run for the house, try to push the car a little nearer to it or, indeed, why she takes a child to an isolated place in a car she knows is unreliable, overlook the sense of panic that such a situation would induce or that all of these aspects of the plot derive from King's novel.

There are some effective sequences in evoking fear of the everyday. Tad's fear of monsters in his cupboard (a trope also used in *Cat's Eye*) is dramatized in a powerful slow-motion run from light switch to bed, in a single shot from a birds-eye view. The subsequent pan next morning from Tad's bed to his barricade of objects blocking the cupboard door, his description of the monster he fears and the cut to Scooby-Doo, all foreshadow the attempt to keep the dog out of the car. This final extended sequence uses some standard generic horror devices, linking a sense of physical entrapment with the claustrophobic constriction that pervades Donna's family life. As Donna reaches across to help free Tad's belt, the window is half-way down and there is no music for a few seconds before Cujo bounds into shot, barking loudly. Rapid cutting splices low angles from within the car, a close-up of her hand holding the door closed and the dog scrabbling frantically at the window. Like Steven Spielberg's *Jaws* (1975), Teague allows the animal-monster to drift away as quickly as it appeared, only to suddenly bring it back into the frame (as Cujo jumps onto the bonnet or, later, as Donna looks out of the window) and, like Spielberg's shark, Cujo rams the car head first in apparent rage. There is some sympathy created for the 'monster' here as he appears maddened by the sound of the phone and injures himself, appearing bloody and concussed. Using the wing mirror, she spies the means of salvation: a baseball bat, lying on the ground, and we cut in on the axis for a close-up to emphasize its importance for her. An extremely low angle shot through the steering wheel pulls focus slightly to shift attention from them to the keys as the transmission holds the key to life or death. A slow zoom out from the car, now seen standing right in the middle of the yard, emphasizes its isolation and cranes down to Cujo, lying on a step, apparently watching and waiting. The same shot slowly moves round to give us a close-up of Cujo's face, covered in a strange yellow discharge, apparently emitting a slight growl. Later, a low-level shot frames the siege situation with the sunset in the distance, the car in the mid-ground and Cujo settling himself sphinx-like in the foreground.

Pressure outside the car begins to be reflected by pressure inside it, with the boy going through phases of panic and then physical deterioration. Eventually, Donna tries the door and takes a few steps away from the car, still unable to see Cujo. She checks under the car (where we saw him lying in wait when Tad had to pee, earlier) but it is only when she straightens up that Cujo comes into shot, right behind her. As Donna scrabbles back into the car there is an intense series of quick cuts as the dog gets some way into the car and she fights for her life (showing off the developing talents of a young Jan de Bont as cinematographer, shooting using several cut-open cars). After beating the dog away, a slow pan passes from her to the boy but then continues to complete a 360 degree movement, which is repeated faster and faster (reflecting Donna's loss of blood and consciousness) until it creates the effect of a whip pan and we cut to Vic on his business trip, possibly dreaming something is wrong. Cujo comes and lies on the bonnet, looking directly through the windscreen at her, and it is at this point she prays twice: 'Please God, get me out of here.' It seems as if her prayers are answered as a police car arrives but, as in a conventional slasher, recourse to prayer in a godless universe does not yield redemption and Cujo kills the cop (possibly harshly punished for a lack of caution; exploring before radioing in).

With the boy growing delirious, Donna faces Cujo in a final confrontation. Alternate points of view create empathy for both woman and dog and all looks lost for Donna as the bat breaks but luckily (or by divine help) the dog is impaled as it makes a final leap. The nightmare is not yet over as, initially, she cannot get back into the battered car but eventually uses a gun to smash the back windscreen. The drama in the car is cross-cut with Vic outstripping the police to reach the farm and save his wife. However, she is resourceful enough to save herself. Carrying the boy inside, she lays him out on the table, splashes water on his face and eventually, after mouth-to-mouth resuscitation, he finally takes a breath. However, in an addition to the novel, Cujo suddenly smashes through the window (as with the windscreen smash, in slow motion). Repeat edits of the dog's jaws as it springs are juxtaposed with a close-up of Donna firing the cop's gun into the camera (like Tom Mix in Edwin S. Porter's 1903 *Great Train Robbery*). She shows resourcefulness, physical toughness and a stronger will than her antagonist to survive and kill her opponent – all qualities of Clover's Final Girl.

The novel ends with the death of the child, whose slight frame and name suggesting something small adding poignancy to his death. According to King, whilst writing, he had intended the boy to live but found that the story that he had written demanded a more realistic outcome.[9] Therefore, in a sense, when King was persuaded by the film's producers to ameliorate this so that both mother and child survive (although she has been badly bitten and the boy licked by a rabid dog and so, theoretically, they will also develop the disease), there could be said to be a restoration of an underlying structure. King's own script was rejected in favour of additions by Lauren Currier (pen-name for Barbara Turner), Don Carlos Dunaway and director Teague to give the film a more uplifting ending. King felt strongly enough that there was precious little difference with his work to go to arbitration, but failed to secure a writing credit. In 1983, the commercial genre expectations and studio pressures win out over the potential bleak vision of the writer. By 2004, King's position was such that he could insist on a bleaker ending for *Secret Window*, reflecting the growth in his status as a global brand.

Dolores Claiborne (Taylor Hackford, 1995)

Dolores: Now, you listen to me, Mr Grand High Poohbar of Upper Buttcrack, I'm just about half-past give a shit with all your fun and games.

The genre of family drama here is elevated above the norm by director Taylor Hackford's unconventional editing choices and the performances he draws from his two leads, the eponymous heroine, Dolores Claiborne (Kathy Bates) and daughter Selena St George (Jennifer Jason Leigh), who spend much of the film sparring. Through the course of the film these two elements combine to reveal truths, both disavowed and purposely buried.

Evoking the transition after the first reel in *The Wizard of Oz* (Victor Fleming, 1939), we periodically shift from a present devoid of colour to a bright realm of the imagination. Hackford achieves this, however, not only through cuts but also elaborate sequences placing past and present not just in the same scene but sometimes within the same shot, reminiscent of Cronenberg's *Dead Zone*, twelve years earlier. It is an intrinsically theatrical device, using a different part of the set to represent a different time – clearly in the theatre, the option of cutting to a different viewpoint is not available so directing an audience's attention has to happen through use of space and lighting, in particular. It is fitting here as the extremely limited cast gives the film a claustrophobic feel – much of the film takes place within Dolores' run-down house, where mother and daughter square-off against one another.

The narrative structure of the film is also more complex than it first appears and is concerned with juxtaposing chronological links and refocusing generic markers towards the family. In some of the sharp dialogue exchanges and the symmetry of the script's structure we might detect the influence of William Goldman, an uncredited 'film consultant' on the project. The planting of a cassette tape in Selena's car is in keeping with Dolores' wily nature and the knowledge of her daughter (she finds it whilst rooting around for cigarettes) as well as extending the means of storytelling beyond 'talking heads'. As before, flashbacks visualize for us what Selena is being told by Dolores – here the whole eclipse sequence. This constitutes a confession, which runs on as voiceover as we see Selena on the ferry, although she must have heard this whilst still in the car (so events are effectively shifted backwards and forwards in time). In adapting King's novel, Hackford, alongside scriptwriter Tony Gilroy, removes the 'dust bunnies', creatures that live under Vera's bed that only she can see, recasting the prime monstrosity in human, rather than supernatural terms. This is refocused from the novel's battle between Vera and Dolores, particularly over bodily functions, to the domestic battle of husband and wife. The book's extended first-person narrative is used selectively, especially in Dolores' flashback, and we come to understand her less through her own words than through the antagonistic relationship with her daughter. The revelation of abuse comes about a third of the way through the novel but Gilroy holds it back as a final twist.

It is one of the few novels to carry illustrations, possibly suggesting that King was thinking of visualizing his work (although none feature in the film explicitly) and possibly to 'beef up' what is a relatively short King novel. The pictures are actually very literal and add little that is not already in the descriptions, other than adopting a low, childlike eye-line, possibly suggesting that the book is written for Selena to understand what her mother did. Also, since the novel is written in flashback, the illustrations reflect key remembered images. The same points apply to *Gerald's Game* (1992), so far unfilmed, in the small illustrations at chapter openings, which offer literal, key images, often from a low-angle (although, there, reflecting the position of the narrator, hand-cuffed to a bed).

The initial sequence showing the fight between Dolores and her elderly employer, Vera, via shadows at the top of the stairs; Vera's subsequent fall and Dolores' action, on the verge of bludgeoning the woman with a rolling pin, is interrupted by the mailman, who poses the central question of the film: 'What have you done?' The film is not so much a 'whodunnit' as a 'why-she-dunnit' as we see the background to this apparent murder and the suspected attack on her drunken and abusive husband, many years earlier, come together through the obsessive investigations of Detective John Mackey (Christopher Plummer), a figure developed from a sceptical medical examiner in the novel, Dr John McCauliffe. The insult cited in the reference that opened this section is delivered to Mackey but blends Dolores' description of Joe, sitting in state while his wife did all the housework, with a colloquialism from her opening remarks during her confession.[10] Clearly, the film raises moral questions about whether it is ever justifiable to kill, about guilt and the need for absolution, but the film's moral compass is focused very distinctly on the mother-daughter relationship. When the revelation about Vera's will is made, it is Selena's opinion that matters to Dolores, no one else's. She needs Selena to believe in her, which is what happens by the close, after the revelation on the ferry, so that the daughter can come back and defend the mother and the two be reconciled. We later see the initial sequence as attempted suicide rather than murder, underlining that the meaning of a series of images and dialogue is not always what it might seem. Vera's words 'help me' are revealed as a plea to die, not to be saved. Context is everything.

When Selena first comes back to the island, there is a spectacular helicopter shot coming down over the ferry and right up to Selena, standing alone at the front of the boat like a figurehead, clad in widow-like black and with shades, which in retrospect we might see as protective strategies to ward off memories she has only partially suppressed of what happened on that ferry with her father in the past. In contrast with the slightly desperate attempt to inject scale with the ferry shot, the emotional range of the protagonists is decidedly small-scale, perhaps reflecting that the real terror of the everyday is how you can grow apart from your family. Leigh's performance as Selena exudes bored hostility. She never smiles, rarely sustains eye contact for long, frequently rolls her eyes, seeking escape in cigarettes and alcohol and she huffs and puffs her way through the first half of the film like a moody teenager, stomping out of the house ostensibly to get groceries but actually to escape the presence of her mother, which somehow acts as a genetic irritant to her. Like Dolores' phone, which has been out of order for years, the communication between the two has broken down. In the car together (also in the house, particularly at the table, they are often forced into close physical proximity, conveyed by tight framing, showing how they cannot easily escape one another) the tension between them is clear. Dolores prattles on about renting a car by the day or the week and Selena, back in shades and smoking her ubiquitous cigarettes, visibly wishes she were somewhere else. Selena has been forced to return and face events and people she has tried to forget. On first meeting Mackey and his deputy Frank, they both recount childhood memories of her, which she cannot deny except by brusquely cutting through their attempts at small talk.

King describes *Dolores Claiborne* as 'a beautiful film to watch, if simply as an exercise in cinematography and the technical possibilities of using a camera and colours as active vehicles in the presentation of a story'[11] but he underestimates how Hackford's choreography of relationships between shots as well as the acting within them is key to adding depth to this family drama. On entering the battered house, Dolores looks across to the water. The scene in front of her dissolves into a more colourful summer scene, from which we cut back to the pale face of Dolores in the present, but the sound of people shouting 'bleeds' into the present. A younger Dolores in a red checked shirt appears in shot as a younger Selena (the uncannily well-cast Ellen Muth) runs into the shot and when the present-day Dolores calls to her to get inside the house, the present-day Selena answers from behind her that she is, already. The past-Dolores turns and, as she does so, her clothing fades so that momentarily she stands pivotally between past and present – a vision of her past out front and her present behind her. It is very quickly done and Dolores stops to look out once more, as if she cannot quite believe what just happened, but it has returned to its featureless, colourless present.

Inside the house, Dolores unpacks Selena's luggage, although it is ambiguous whether the gesture is helpful and maternal or intrusive and distrustful. Finding the pills, she begins to realize that she does not know her changed daughter and she looks up to the stairwell, at which point we have another flashback. Childish laughter comes up on the soundtrack and bright, warm orange light suffuses the scene before Selena's teenage self appears, followed by a younger Dolores, in a game of hide-and-seek and, again, we cut back to the present-day Dolores watching the scene, bemused. They are now playing an adult version of this game: each possessing secrets which the other needs to know for a new connection to be made between the two. The blend of past and present gets closer as Dolores turns to Selena, sitting at the table, and behind her, in the left side of the frame, a man comes in the door, spilling daylight and colour into the room. Clearly, this must be a flashback as the current scene is set at night and Dolores looks back at Selena, who is still talking, in apparent disbelief that she cannot also see this. Now past and present occur within the same frame, albeit in different depth perspectives. The camera passes behind Dolores, using her head as a vertical wipe, replacing the drab present with a past in sharp colour, and introducing the most fully-dramatized flashback yet.

Everyday items are used as symbols of Dolores' plan so that even the fabric of her home seems to be to prompting her to commit her deed during the lunar eclipse, like Joe's 'mooning' at her with his split trousers, the plate she washes up in slow-motion in the past and the glass she turns upside down in the present. When she first trips over the well cover, we share her point of view looking down at this hole and her hand enters the frame rather strangely to snap off some rotten wood and we cut to a close-up of her looking, apparently amazed, at her own evil thoughts. The sequence featuring the eclipse itself looks as if it is shot on a set with an obvious blue screen, creating a heightened sense of unreality. The climactic scene juxtaposes Joe's perspective, looking up at Dolores, the eclipse framed next to her head, a reverse over-the-shoulder shot with the hole in the background and several wider shots of shifting light, juxtaposing Dolores against a blood-orange sky and the unreality of celebrations and fireworks out in the harbour. There is also a shot from within the dark well up into an otherworldly, orange light and, from the rim of the well, we have a graphic match to the eclipse itself. In the novel, Joe survives the fall, climbs up several times, calls out and his hand even whips out, *Carrie*-like, to grab Dolores' ankle. Such actions would push the narrative closer to a standard horror narrative and make Dolores more culpable (she delivers a killer blow with a rock in the book) and less sympathetic to the viewer.

Some horror devices are used, such as sudden movement into the frame, but alongside theatrical proxemics to emphasize key dynamics in the family relationships. Joe's sudden baseball-style strike on Dolores' back with a piece of wood is shocking, placed in the middle of an apparently flirtatious, domestic scene (only revealed through dialogue with Selena in the novel), underlining that fear is the guiding emotion in this family and that, at any given moment, Joe, fuelled by alcohol, might lash out again unpredictably (Danny Elfman's whimsical score suddenly turning discordant here). It marks Bates' role as victim, the polar opposite of her monstrous Annie Wilkes in *Misery* (with a small visual reference, later, in Vera's porcelain pig collection). She bears the pain over several minutes, hiding this from her daughter, but exacts swift revenge. A close shot of Joe, sitting king-like on his chair in front of the TV, pontificating, is surprisingly interrupted when Dolores' arm breaks into the frame, smashing his head with a milk jug, paralleling his earlier blow. Calmly shielding the axe from her daughter's view, Dolores spells out clearly that if he hits her again he will have to kill her, challenging him to do so, tossing the axe in his lap. He backs down. At this point we cut back to the present and Selena crying, suggesting that what we have just seen is the visual counterpart to some unheard dialogue.

The film dramatizes the enduring power, particularly, of a mother's love, which drives Dolores to work selflessly for years to save money for her daughter's future, symbolized in what she has done to her hands. After years of following Vera's exacting standards, the close-up of her putting up the desired six pegs shows ageing as her hand enters the frame for the second time. Further editing choices suggest connections between mother and daughter which go only partially recognized. The only item she wants from Vera's house is the scrapbook (unlike Annie Wilkes' account of murderous exploits, this book records Selena's articles, and symbolizes Dolores' enduring connection with her daughter, despite lengthy separation). Selena starts to share in the flashback style, although the power of this device to disorientate the viewer is weakened through over-use. Dolores looks anxiously towards the phone, which is picked up by a younger Selena in the past and having to deal with a malicious call, provoking her to a suicide attempt.

Eventually, Dolores grabs Selena and sits her down at the table, sliding her drink across Western-style, trying to make her face some uncomfortable truths. The glass is picked up by a clearly male hand and we shift again to a scene in the past, underlining Joe's alcoholism. Joe and Dolores are arguing over their daughter's poor school report. Selena is sitting in the T-frame, the focus of tensions between them (all of Dolores' hopes for a better future and his secrets of financial and sexual abuse). It is not surprising, then, that with so much pressure, she suffers a breakdown and carries neurotic behaviour into adulthood with its social corollary – smoking, drinking and drug use. Trying to force some recognition of what happened, the adult Selena stomps upstairs and, as Dolores looks at the base of the stairs, younger-Selena comes down in her burgundy work uniform and, as she opens the door, we can see for a split second what is white or grey on the inside is red on the outside. Another effective transition cuts to a bright, sunny day outside.

The final transition into the past on the ferry contains the vital memory of abuse, which Selena has denied up until now. Selena's flight from her mother and the truth about her own abuse is credible but persistent deferral of explanations does seem contrived. We see her father buying a drink, standing right next to her, in the same lighting/colour wash as she is, i.e. past and present collide. Like a ghost in her own past, he shows no sign that he can see her. Selena follows him outside, where the colour levels come up, and, effectively, she stalks her own memory, with Hackford using the detective/thriller trope of forward and reverse tracking POV shots. The eye-lines of the younger- and present-day-Selena meet, at which point her name is called and we cut back to a present, with the colour drained out, and the man from the café giving her the change she had forgotten.

At the final inquest, Dolores is on the point of confessing before Selena comes back and, somewhat melodramatically, turns hotshot lawyer as the scene tips into courtroom drama and she defends her mother, winning the battle of wits with Mackey. What ultimately turns proceedings in her favour is the challenge to Mackey that what he really wants is justice for the previous 'crime' of responsibility for Joe's death. Ironically, if he had not connected the two, he might have succeeded. King is not a fan of the reconciliation between mother and daughter, which he feels is 'tacked on' to the narrative, but actually Hackford achieves it with a sense of restraint (much more so than the saccharine ending of King's script for The Shining (1997), it must be said).[12] At the end, Selena symbolically offers her mother her hand, a gesture which is accepted, and then, later, as the two bid each other farewell, there is an embrace, genuine on both sides and an acceptance of one another. Dolores lets her go without bitterness and Selena shows the neck scar, a sign of the inescapability of the past. Still dressed in black but looking small and even frail, Selena salutes her mother as she travels back to the mainland, reconciled to a life and a mother from which she had previously fled.

Hackford's picture composition, especially using mirror imagery, also elevates the film beyond standard genre expectations. The remains of a broken window, which Dolores smashes, 'holds' her reflection as it breaks like a breaking jigsaw puzzle, in a moment of stylized, slow-motion. More than 'a symbol of the present', as Magistrale describes it, this effect is an image of impossibility, drawing our attention to the filmmaking process and how Dolores is constructing events (for herself and us).[13] She is also seeking to refashion her image, not so much for the community, whose opinion she does really care about, but particularly in the eyes of her daughter. Later, on the ferry, there is a parallel mirror scene where Selena splashes water on her face, shocked by the sudden memory of abuse. The collision of past and present, real and disavowed memory is suggested in the 'false' reflection in the mirror showing the impossible image of the back of her head (an effect used in *Secret Window*, also linked to a subjective projection to obscure an objective truth). Like Dolores' first flashback on the steps of the house, Selena also gives the mirror 'vision' one final look and, as with her mother, everything looks normal. A sign behind Selina reads 'Report all injuries', reflecting the need for a 'talking cure', to verbalize suffering in order to purge it and move on.

Hackford's transition sequences, picture composition and direction of his two female leads elevate the film above narrow genre expectations. The editing is often extremely fluid, dissolves being the predominant means of signalling the transition between sequences and, increasingly in the second half of the film, to cutaways of mottled skylines, partly to show the passage of time but also the strange, otherworldly beauty of the landscape and the light. Unjustly eclipsed (no pun intended) by Bates' performance in *Misery*, the darker, domestic themes and small-scale, theatrical intensity of *Dolores Claiborne* mitigate against high TV ratings but it repays repeat viewings and its critical stock should rise over time.

The Shining (Stanley Kubrick, 1980)

'... there may be some truth in that idea that houses absorb the emotions that are spent in them, that they hold a kind of ... dry charge. Perhaps the right personality, that of an imaginative boy, for instance, could act as a catalyst on that dry charge, and cause it to produce an active manifestation of ... of something. I'm not talking about ghosts, precisely. I'm talking about a kind of psychic television in three dimensions. Perhaps even something alive. A monster if you like'.

(Ben to Susan in *Salem's Lot*)[14]

'... at the centre of the maze there's an encounter with one's self'.

(Carol Shields, *Larry's Party*)[15]

King has talked about literary archetypes of the haunted house horror sub-genre, such as the so-called Bad Place, usually in the lowest or highest point, i.e. cellars or attics.[16] In King's *The Shining*, the boiler is a clear symbolic trigger which will explode at some point and in *Graveyard Shift* and *The Mangler* it is below the lowest level of the main setting, the mill and the laundry respectively, where the true evil resides. *1408*'s setting right in the middle of the building seems a conscious decision to move away from such archetypes and designate psychic space by what has gone on in a room. *The Shining* uses several classic haunted house elements – a large structure, isolated by distance and the elements (in severity and duration) from the nearest human contact. Stanley Kubrick's *The Shining* (1980) and Mick Garris' 1997 remake, in partnership with King himself, provide interesting mirror-images of one another. Garris' version dramatizes a haunted house; Kubrick's a haunted man. For Garris, the house projects its evil onto the man; for Kubrick, it is the other way round. Kubrick departs from King's novel and submitted script; Garris' reinstates excised elements. King's TV work develops these ideas with the Marsten House in *Salem's Lot*, a more objective pursuit of psychic phenomenon in *Rose Red* and a whole surreal, David Lynch-like apparatus around the *Kingdom Hospital* series.

Far from showing an ignorance of horror, as King asserts, the film shows Kubrick's depth of knowledge of film form and its possibilities. It may show a disinterest on Kubrick's part about audience expectations, something King is far more adept at meeting (in literary terms at least), although it could also be said that individuals like Kubrick, and to a lesser extent, De Palma and Cronenberg, are not seeking to meet audience expectations quite as keenly as other directors. Genre theory places a strong emphasis on the audience and the ways in which they read or 'consume' the film but a small number of influential directors, especially by the time they have established themselves in their careers, may care less about meeting those expectations and are willing to accept that a film may find critical acceptance, and a more appreciative audience, over time. In this sense, *Carrie*, *The Dead Zone* and *The Shining*, may be critically received as the next instalment in the sub-genre of De Palma, Cronenberg and Kubrick auteurist statements, i.e. as chapters in an oeuvre.

The film firmly denies us those pleasures that we might expect from a horror film – the pace, like the camera movement, is leisurely, not frenetic; the level of gore is paradoxically restrained and repetitive (in Danny's vision of the girls in the corridor); dialogue is slow and apparently inconsequential at times; and shots are held longer than we are used to, encouraging (possibly even demanding) that we scan the whole frame for meaning, slowly. We are not given a gothic mansion with dark corners, typical of the 'evil house on the hill' subgenre. Kubrick chooses neither an imposing gothic façade for his film or to shoot scenes in shadowy corridors and dimly-lit rooms. The building is clearly an inhabited space (during the non-winter months) and commercially viable as a hotel, not a museum. Even when Halloran returns at night, the rooms are sufficiently well-lit to be able to make out everything clearly. There is some element of a closure in the ending as the mother and child escape but exactly what they have escaped from and how they have managed this, are far from clear. The difficulty even of summarizing the plot suggests that the real horror is achieved by presenting us with a phenomenon which we might describe as impossible and then making no attempt to explain it.

Kubrick is still credited in the Guinness Book of Records with the greatest number of retakes in a scene – 125 for when Wendy climbs the stairs for the final time at the end of the film. Such practices suggest an attempt to capture something not seen before rather than fit the expectations of a genre. Furthermore, is it really likely that a man like Kubrick, known for the time he takes between film projects and who is known for meticulous approach to shooting, would somehow make a mistake with the paper in the type-writer? If a new piece of paper appears in the machine shortly after Jack tore it out, we must assume the director meant it to be there. It is extremely demeaning to Kubrick to assume that such actions are in some way the sign of amateurishness or carelessness. Michel Ciment asserts that *The Shining* is 'most subservient to the laws of genre' but actually Kubrick systematically undermines horror tropes in *The Shining* to show the failure of cinematic forms of representation in conveying evil.[17] When we see Wendy in the bathroom and Jack strikes the door with an axe, Kubrick shows us the events on the other side of the door because he wants us to see them. Rather than this being a sign of a horror amateur who does not know how to generate cheap frights in his audience, Kubrick is repeatedly giving us the generic elements of a horror film but denying us the cathartic pleasure of a genre picture.

Geoffrey Cocks places Kubrick's films at a particular moment in history, seeing holocaust imagery as the means to best explain several aspects of *The Shining*, so that the sequence of the vision of blood pouring from an elevator is taken to represent 'the blood of centuries, the blood of millions, and, in particular, the blood of war and genocide in Kubrick's own century.'[18] It is perhaps Kubrick's reluctance to trivialize evil and suspicion at clichéd representations of cinematic evil that leads to a contradictory impulse to undercut horror film tropes as soon as he starts to use them. Cocks links fairy tale references, such as the wolf at the door, with the rise of fascism, but equally as powerful, especially to an audience in 1980, is the ubiquitous nature of Disney cartoons, including 'Three Little Pigs'(Burt Gillet, 1933), and catch-phrases from prime-time entertainment shows, which dominates Jack's speech in the closing third of the film. Jack Nicholson's seminal 'Here's Johnny!' only really makes sense as a parody of Johnny Carson's familiar call to his nightly audience as presenter of *The Tonight Show* (1962–1992).

Kubrick, a notoriously reclusive figure, gave virtually no interviews during his career, made relatively few films and said very little about them, content to let others argue over their meaning. As a result, critical viewpoints tend to divide quite sharply between those who see the work as immensely profound or as just plain pretentious. Different critical positions read the film as a cautionary tale about the evils of patriarchy (Patricia Ferreira), the breakdown of the family, the failings of US capitalism (Frederic Jameson), a study in madness (Thomas Allen Nelson) or even an anti-colonial statement (Bill Blakemore).[19] It was the first of King's movies to be remade and, on its release in 1980, *The Shining* provoked one of the strongest negative reactions from King himself, whose own script had been rejected during the process. He seems to have mellowed slightly in his views over the years – possibly his own experience at directing in *Maximum Overdrive* in 1986 was a humbling experience. Kubrick's film may have drawn critical attention because the film includes devices that draw attention to themselves, such as languorous camera movement, slow motion, painterly picture composition and deliberate breaks with conventional continuity style of editing.

The grandeur of the opening sequence, especially the helicopter shots following a car as it travels along a winding country road, is a trope palely echoed in *Dreamcatcher*, but shares little of Kubrick's majestic power. Here, the camera appears to close in on the car 'like a bird of prey', as Nelson calls it, and at the point of catching up with it, we cut away, creating a sense of brooding threat and of something waiting to attack the family in a confined space – here a car, later the hotel and finally the maze.[20] On several different occasions and in slightly different forms, King has retold an anecdote of Kubrick calling him in the middle of the night to ask bluntly whether King believed in God, which would thereby suggest an optimistic belief in some continued existence after death. Kubrick seems to have found notions of an afterlife troubling and his film emphasizes the development of human, rather than supernatural, evil. King asserts 'because he could not believe, he could not make the film believable to others,' claiming also Kubrick did not really understand the horror genre and, therefore, the film was doomed to fail.[21] However, that assumes that a horror film was what Kubrick was trying to make. It is not a trivial observation that Joey from *Friends* keeps his copy of the novel in the freezer because it is so scary, not the video. King is dismissive of 'playing games … playing the artiste' but seems to imply it is a simple matter of 'getting the reader or viewer by the throat and never letting go'.[22] However, a similarly-phrased ambition lay behind his script for *Creepshow* and his directorial debut with *Maximum Overdrive*, and not even the kindest critic would suggest that such an effect is achieved there.

As King's novel can be seen as a novel about writing, so Kubrick's film is, in many ways, a film about filmmaking. Many of Kubrick's films are about the inadequacy of language, and how the language of film can suggest what the spoken and written word alone cannot. Halloran and Danny's imaginary friend, Tony, both tell him not to be afraid of visions that he might see as they are 'just like pictures in a book'. The film that we are seeing is composed of 'moving pictures', which we, too, know are representing a manufactured view of 'reality' but which may feel real in the context of a cinema. Kubrick made this film prior to the widespread use of video and so the film is designed to be watched without access to freeze-frame or reverse functions, i.e., the exhibition context for which the film was produced is the visceral effect of it being seen once at normal speed in a cinema setting. This concern with visual story-telling might even extend to the intriguing possibility that, prior to the blocks of repeated text that Wendy sees, Jack Torrance is actually writing the unfolding narrative that we see in *The Shining* – a very Nabokovian device that would be in keeping with Danny's retracing of footsteps in the snow at the end: in a sense playfully 'cancelling' the character being pursued and, with it, the chase sequence and the life of the protagonist. In a film about communication in its widest sense, body language is important too. Whilst Wendy and Danny are lost in the maze, Jack is also feeling strangely constricted. He unleashes a final aimless throw in the hall and does not wait for a rebound. He starts to develop the visual tics of a bored teenager, venting his pent-up frustrations in shaking out his arms (an action he repeats before entering the ballroom later) – an almost ape-like gesture (an echo of *2001*) that gains in prominence as the film progresses.

Like Mike Enslin in *1408*, Jack Torrance tries to explain to those around him what it is like being a writer, but he cannot. Far from being blocked, Jack's problem is that Wendy does not understand the process of creation at all. When he sarcastically agrees with her that 'it's just a matter of getting back into the habit of writing every day. Yep, that's all it is', this is partly King the prolific writer replying to critics who would equate volume of output with literary weakness. Later, Nicholson adds a manic smile and a gesture, as if typing were an easy childish game. The act of creation, writing or filmmaking might seem easy enough but Kubrick suggests it is not. The first cut to the typewriter in the very centre of the shot, from which we zoom out, is only part of the apparatus of the persona of a best-selling writer. We see a cigar and paper laid ready – the material preparations are all meticulously observed but the act of original creation is much harder to define (and harder to create on film). In part, Jack's throwing a ball against a wall is as much a literalization of his inability to generate ideas as a sign of his failing sanity. The novel that Jack writes is not nonsensical, merely a different kind of writing (it is carefully laid out in paragraphs with indents), and the film that Kubrick produces questions its own form.

This is reflected in Danny's visions where the blood pouring out of lift doors (also coloured red), running down the hallway, cannot be real since blood would coagulate and not flow like water. Indeed, it moves in slow motion, like a special effect on *Thunderbirds*, and also ultimately overflows its channel, washing up over the camera lens – highlighting the existence of a 'fourth wall'. What is particularly unsettling here, apart from the flash-cuts of uncanny identical twin girls, is the direction of gaze (directly at the camera) and the framing, which, via the combination of low-angle and wide-angle lens, makes the girls seem like giants, as high as the window behind them and overtly referencing Diane Arbus' photograph 'Identical Twins, Roselle, New York, 1967', with which Kubrick was familiar.[23] Cocks sees Halloran's effective rescue of Wendy and Danny, by distracting Jack and with his subsequent murder, as evocative of Nazi racial persecution but Kael's complaints about the somewhat perfunctory dispatching of Halloran, after a lengthy build-up in terms of screen-time and space, plenty of cross-cutting – all suggestive of dramatic import only to end with the thud of an axe in his chest, is more pertinent here. Kubrick is apparently offering but ultimately denying us the pleasure of suture and of generic expectations fulfilled. Kubrick holds shots slightly beyond the 'content curve', that is, as Louis Giannetti explains, 'the point in a shot at which the audience has been able to assimilate most of its information.'[24] This creates a sense of time being extended, like in a dream or, as with Danny, a vision. Kael is right to observe that 'the horrors involved in the hotel's bloody past usually appear in inserts that flash on like the pictures in a slide show' but rather than a weakness of the film, this is what repays, and even demands, repeat viewings.[25]

Once at the hotel, precise time ceases to have any real meaning. It is wintertime, but day or night seems irrelevant because of electric lighting and, by the 'Wednesday' intertitle, the sense of time has largely been lost. This effectively creates a sense of disorientation but weakens the attempt to increase the tension towards the end by using specific time references, like a clock running down, after Jack is locked in the cupboard. Possibly due to its exhibition context on TV, with commercial breaks, Garris' version re-orientates the viewer a little with a greater number of subtitles, more precision in the dates and a greater use of 'weather shots', purely to signal the passing of time.

Periodically, to disorientate the viewer and draw our attention to the film-making process, Kubrick breaks the conventions of continuity editing. At the bar, Jack looks directly into the camera lens to order a drink. He is already using Lloyd's name and, in combination with Nicholson's great performance as a manic drunk (looking both ways in an empty room), his crazed laugh makes it clear that he is already possessed. In this context, when Wendy staggers in and claims that someone has tried to strangle Danny, Jack's perfectly measured response, 'Are you out of your fucking mind?' is both deeply ironic, given the condition of the speaker, and very funny, drawing on Nicholson's sense of comic timing, also seen in *Easy Rider* (Dennis Hopper, 1969). When Wendy mentions the possibility of leaving the hotel, Jack reacts angrily and storms out of the room, giving a tiny glance directly at the camera. Nic Roeg's *Bad Timing*, released the same year as *The Shining*, also features an A-list actor, Harvey Keitel, performing a similar little in-joke. Later, the transition from Jack to the reflection in the mirror, showing a decomposing old woman, is conveyed via a whip-pan, stressing his shock and horror at being confronted by his own mortality (and possibly shame at his own weakness), the shock of Wendy, in seeing 'Murder' reflected in a mirror, is conveyed by a crash zoom, and Kubrick saves the technique for which he gained notoriety with *2001* (1968), the jump cut, for Jack in the maze, linking his collapsed state to his petrified one in the morning.

Sudden bursts of deep synthesizer score blend György Ligeti, Krzysztof Penderecki and Béla Bartok – the last especially apt as he is named in the novel as one of Wendy's favoured composers.[26] This might seem clumsy and inappropriate but such intrusive editing evokes Jean-Luc Goddard's use of sound as an alienating device, cutting in over the domestic chatter between Wendy and Danny early on and also, later, in the dried goods-cupboard scene. This suggests that something is not right and, perhaps more precisely, expresses an otherworldly 'language' of the hotel trying to contact Danny. Along with the heartbeat, which comes up on the soundtrack when Jack is under stress (such as when he goes to the radio room after the scene in the bathroom with Grady), such sound effects complement the literalized idiom when Grady informs Jack that free drinks are part of 'orders from the house' (the dialogue blending King's original chapter title 'Drinks on the house' with Grady's dialogue 'Orders from the manager'.[27] The synthesizer that cuts in as we see Wendy and Danny playing in the snow outside feels a little like radio interference, a signal which only Jack picks up, reflected in the zoom up to a close-up of him watching them, head down, brow-furrowed, struggling to synthesize the noises that he (and we) hear. Another favourite of Goddard's, the use of intertitles without music, particularly the first one here, 'The Interview', is a little reminiscent of silent film format. For a modern audience, this may seem a little heavy handed, telling rather than showing, but the foregrounding of the film form, such as the fake-looking blue screen shot in the car, underlines the superficial and fragile nature of family harmony as just a veneer. Underlighting is used to make Jack seem slightly less stable, such as when he does the typing mime for Wendy and more obviously at the brightly-lit bar with Floyd, a device that Garris picks up but uses in a more blatant, expressionist and arguably unsubtle fashion.

The interview itself with Ullman, the Manager, forms a strong parallel with a similar scene in Milos Forman's *One Flew Over the Cuckoo's Nest*, his last major role. There, Jack Nicholson, as the mentally unstable but charismatic R.P. McMurphy, undergoes a psychological evaluation with the purpose of trying to determine whether he is faking insanity or not. The rhythm of the question and answer exchange where Nicholson's character is asked for his opinion across a desk and where he gives a spirited, humorous reply to a formal question that is laced with ambiguity as to whether he means the exact opposite of what he says, is strikingly similar. In both examples, the veneer of formality in Nicholson's delivery, speaking as if to a friend in confidence, suggests a suppression of the character's true nature. The same room is used to house the radio, providing a useful reminder, later, when Jack enters the room again and we can see how far his character has changed. As Jack Kroll notes, 'You suspect that Kubrick cast Nicholson in the part chiefly because of Nicholson's unique face – the sharp nose, wide, mobile mouth and angled eyebrows that can redeploy themselves in an instant from sunny friendliness to Mephisthophelean menace.'[28] It is Nicholson's face that carries key scenes of *One Flew Over the Cuckoo's Nest* – think of the World Series, animated by his quick-fire commentary and facial vitality reflected in the blank TV monitor or the penultimate return to the ward and his unbroken resistance, conveyed by his clowning imbecility. The same is true here. Although in his later career, in playing characters like The Joker in *Batman* (Tim Burton, 1989), all he had to do was pull faces, in *The Shining* it is the depth and range of emotion that Kubrick manages to coax from him, and which he captures in close-up, that give the film its power and true metaphysical horror, not cheap scare tactics.

Scatman Crothers also appears in both films. In Forman's work, he is the night watchman, apparently impotent, susceptible to drink and open to bribery as the inmates briefly take control of the facility. In both films, Crothers' character presides over a largely empty space, here a kitchen, touching upon his sexual weakness, he is manipulated by others and ultimately betrayed by them. In King's version, the posters that adorn his bedroom seem like an excessive, strident pose of sexual bravado, masking something less confident. The fact that shots of him, wide-eyed with horror, are followed by the sequence in Room 237 might even suggest that this is his vision or that he shares it with Jack and, therefore, the naked woman becomes his sexual fantasy more than Jack's. That is not to say Kubrick makes Halloran particularly prominent – fans of the book might complain that he cuts too much but that intertextual allusions add depth to even a fairly minor part. King's version, although restoring more lines of dialogue and screen time, does not actually add any further complexity to his character.

In the car on the way to the hotel, Wendy starts to talk about the Donner party and cannibalism. Jack reacts angrily that they should not be discussing this in front of Danny, to which she assures him that he has already seen a documentary about it. Jack's reply ('You see, it's OK. He saw it on the television') and his unsubstantiated claims, during the interview, that his wife loves ghost stories and horror films, suggest Jack, and possibly Kubrick too, share a McLuhanesque cynical scepticism about the visual mass media.

Wendy (Shelley Duvall), in the version seen by most cinemagoers, is reduced to a shrieking mess. Her physical movement is as ineffectual as her character so that her flailing the baseball bat at Jack from the top of the stairs, her racing out into the snow, her arms flapping stupidly or, at the end, her running to Danny make her look like one of Jim Henson's muppets. Her dialogue is shorn of all depth, leaving her with statements which are so banal and repetitive (her empty comments on the radio about the weather are cut short by the police officer) that in context they seem funny rather than pathetic, especially with an annoying verbal tic at the end. Several beats into Halloran's tour of the facilities, she comments 'This is the kitchen, huh?' or the unfunny joke she makes when Ullman tells them that soon everyone will be gone: 'just like a ghost-ship, huh?' In her dialogue, metaphors are literalized (the kitchen is 'such an enormous maze') and fairy-tale elements are made blatantly obvious ('I'll have to leave a trail of breadcrumbs'). Momentarily, Wendy shares Danny's vision of the corridor of blood but this is ambiguous as there is little previous indication that she, too, has any psychic gift, indeed rather the opposite. In terms of appearance, Kubrick has her wear red tights, a shapeless blue dress and a hideous yellow jacket so that she comes across as an unattractive, bug-eyed whiner. However, in the initially-released, US version, 25 minutes of additional footage make her character more balanced, with scenes where she takes Danny to see a doctor, contemplates escape and comes across a room full of celebrating skeletons – all of which, in some fashion, Garris restores.

King claims that he rejected the idea of a maze as it had already been used in *The Maze* (William Cameron Menzies and Richard Carlson, 1953), although such high principles did not prevent him from basing the basic possession plotline of *Carrie* from another 50s B-movie, *The Brain from Planet Arous* (Nathan Juran, 1958).[29] However, Kubrick's maze imagery not only provides a suspenseful climax but pervades the film. The paradoxical pleasures of mazes, blending controlled constriction with apparent freedom, reflects Kubrick's aesthetic of an intellectual game with sporadic moments of panic. Wendy's decision to take Danny into the maze without a map touches upon this as well as showing her naivety (exactly how they get out again is glossed over).

Carol Shields talks about how 'a maze...is a kind of machine with people as its moving parts' and there is a sense of this here as Kubrick's fascination with technology meshes with his portrayal of a fragmenting psyche.[30] The blending of Jack's slow gaze down onto the model of the maze with a bird's-eye view of the actual maze with Wendy and Danny (a shot Magistrale strangely thinks has been overlooked critically), gives Jack the status of a God-like entity, or suggests that perhaps much of what we see in the latter part of the film only occurs in his head. Danny is seen, later, playing with cars on a carpet with a maze-like pattern, making the toys themselves into a similar structure at which point a tennis ball rolls, unmotivated, into the maze. As a symbol or an actual manifestation of the hotel trying to reach him, it is an interesting effect (one which Garris translates to a croquet ball) but it is a little ambiguous as it might also suggest the means of his ultimate salvation, i.e., it remains unclear whether Jack or Danny (or both) are really the object of the hotel's evil.

We cut between Wendy hearing voices in the boiler-room to Jack asleep at his desk, mumbling to himself in sleep, almost as if he were producing the voices. He wakes and confesses his dream, seeming like a 'normal', loving father for a moment but this only lasts until she spots the marks on Danny's neck, instantly accusing him of being responsible. The veneer of trust between the couple is broken. As Jack walks from the empty corridor, with hazy lighting, to the packed ballroom, full of noise, the transition of colour, music and scale provokes no reaction from Jack, suggesting that he is in equilibrium with the hotel. Later, in the bathroom with Grady, Jack is sporting a maroon jacket, bringing him closer to the dominant colour of the décor of the hotel. The jumping of the 180 degree line conveys Jack's disorientation, and the reality that he is Grady's alter ego is underlined by the proxemics, placing them as mirror images of one another, reminiscent of the exchange in *2001* (1968) between Bowman and Poole, shown without dialogue. The gradual realization that he has 'always been the caretaker' is explicit in the close-up showing Jack's fading smile (highly reminiscent of the tragic moment of dawning awareness in *One Flew Over the Cuckoo's Nest* when he realizes that most inmates are voluntary).

Cynthia Freeland's description of the film, terming Kubrick's vision as 'dark and bleak' (although actually not as bleak as King's novel, in either early drafts or finished form), is compromised by assuming from the outset that moral judgements can be made about horror film's presentation of evil.[31] Often, such concepts either lie totally outside the moral scope of horror or are clearly redefined by it, i.e., it is highly debatable how far rigid categories of what constitutes 'evil' can, without major caveats, be applied to a genre which often challenges, or even ignores, what might be seen as cultural norms. It is true that the generic expectations of visceral pleasures of horror or a sense of tension-and-release are not much in evidence in *The Shining*. Stylistically, the film is full of leisurely tracking shots, especially behind pillars, as in The Gold Room, or through walls, (Freeland strangely says 'as if' this movement were happening but it is, literally so) like in the storeroom or the Torrances' sleeping area.[32] This is sometimes taken to be a weakness of the film, giving it a cold, glacial feel so that we do not empathize closely with characters in a more conventional way. However, this may be precisely Kubrick's intention. Like the long, fluid tracking shots in Peter Greenaway's work, such as *The Cook, The Thief, His Wife and Her Lover* (1990), it draws our attention to the process of composition and the set as a set. Rapid cutting, especially around Danny's visions, the juxtaposition of images without a comforting voiceover, subtitles or even a character within the fiction (a typical King feature), helping us articulate or understand what we are saying, force us to think about the meaning of what we are witnessing when we see Danny's second vision of the twins, who just look at each other and then walk away, or Wendy's glimpse of two men at the end of a long corridor, engaged in some kind of sex act, one dressed as a bear (foreshadowing Kubrick's *Eyes Wide Shut*, 1999).

The extensive use of slow-moving Steadicam, rather than cutting in on the action, creates some of the sense of floating otherness used in *Alien* and, especially, the opening of *Halloween*, which also conveys unease in a domestic space. Jack's entrance into Room 237 is a good example where this helps to establish a sense of claustrophobic subjectivity but also limits our available viewpoints. We cut between Jack's POV and reverse tracking shots to record his reaction as we explore the room through his eyes, his hand coming into the frame to push the door open. The shots following Danny on the Big Wheels trike, especially when he swings round corners, effectively conveys the childish pleasure in pure, visceral speed (although there is no explanation of how Danny moves between floors with what looks like a heavy trike), complemented by the use of different sound perspectives, such as the rolling wheels of Danny's trike across bare flooring and then over carpet, muffling the sound. Freeland claims that 'our perspective is not quite identified with his in these scenes' but that is not actually so.[33] We occupy his eye-line directly in looking back at Room 237 and, later, looking up at the visions of the twins. The precise positioning of the camera, i.e., right behind Danny's head, is less-often noted, making it the internal counterpoint to the opening helicopter shots. Later, when Danny pedals furiously away from Room 237, it is the break in expectation, the fact that the camera suddenly stops and follows his progress into the distance and round the corner from a static position, which in theory lessens the tension but in effect maintains it. The camera no longer has to literally 'chase' the little boy to convey the sense of him being pursued – the demons are in his head.

As the visions intensify in detail, so the methods of introducing them change. On the third occasion of seeing the girls, Kubrick tracks Danny with Steadicam, lets him move away from the camera and then, as he disappears around the corner in the distance, adds a sudden, dramatic violin note. We cut to his vision of the girls, accompanied by a cymbal crash. The hotel and its apparitions are becoming more powerful, reflected in the fact that the girls address him directly by name and invite him to play. Kubrick rapidly cuts between them lying dead in the corridor, with an axe lying on the floor and blood up the walls, a close-up of the girls as they are now and Danny's horrified reaction, moving to closer shots of this same sequence. The final chase brings the stylistic motifs together. Low angle forward and reverse tracking shots (now at the boy's standing head height) convey the hunter/hunted battle through the maze, whilst a motivated light source (Danny's torch) and a wide angle lens create a ghostly otherworldly quality to the setting. In simple plot terms, we have been prepared for the fact that the boy knows the way round the maze, whereas his father does not. Jack's POV, looking down at the prints, suddenly stops as the prints disappear and the camera tilts up to show his bemusement. In theory, having escaped his pursuer, Danny might be safe but in sprinting away, and in shifting to his POV, we (and he) no longer know exactly where the pursuer is, making this sequence more frightening. Shots of Jack slowly limping forward, however, dissipate this effect and, like this physical movement, the tension now runs down as Danny escapes and Jack collapses. The final Steadicam shot draws up to the picture hallway outside The Gold Room and, via a series of dissolves, we see Jack as the caretaker back in 1921, suggesting a destiny he was bound to play out.

Jack is framed, with the typewriter in the background, in The Colorado Lounge, whose scale and grand furnishings dwarf the human figure, increasing the pressure bearing down upon him. Swirling, discordant music makes clear that something is not right here, underlined as it abruptly stops when Wendy wanders up, oblivious to this subtext, and Jack takes the paper out before she can read it. The sound feels almost like the 'voice' of the hotel, which is exerting an increasing influence over Jack and warns him of her impending approach. Although Wendy asserts 'OK, I understand', it is clearly a language from which she is excluded. Reading the sound in this way recasts the opening as a call to Jack from afar, and to which he is unwittingly drawn, even from the outset. It would be an overstatement to cast the film as possessing the depth of a Shakespearean tragedy (although interestingly, King did originally conceive the novel in the form of a five-act tragedy) but there are echoes of *Macbeth*, here, in the character trajectories of a couple who cease to talk to one another and the husband drawn increasingly to murderous thoughts under supernatural influences. One of the interesting aspects of such a parallel is the possibility that Jack had such dark thoughts from the beginning and that he was selected as someone who could be manipulated. In Jack's interaction with Danny, there is something of the Macbeth-Banquo relationship – an apparently loving, close relationship underpinned by plans to murder (when Danny sits on Jack's lap, there is no eye contact between father and son until the hotel is mentioned). Magistrale notes the tendency to frame Jack in mirrors, in his bedroom, the hallway, the bathroom with Grady and in Room 237, suggesting either that Jack has a darker schizophrenic side or that, more existentially, he is already a ghost.[34] Like Macbeth, Jack is tortured by nightmares, including murderous thoughts, and Grady's offer to clean up the drinks spilled down Jack echoes Lady Macbeth's 'a little water clears us of this deed'. There is the sense of him being offered expatiation but for future, rather than past, sins. Interestingly, in cutting from a forward tracking shot that ends in a close-up of Danny, eyes wide in terror, to a further corridor vision of the girls, Kubrick is referencing a famous cinematic manifestation of Shakespeare, echoing the filmic means used to introduce Lawrence Olivier's 'To be or not to be' soliloquy in *Hamlet* (Olivier, 1948).

Wendy's discovery of Jack's writing is conveyed in a powerful, extremely low-angle shot as her face emerges, looking over the machine. The real horror is not only that he is clearly mad but that to produce such a volume of 'work', he has been mad for some time. It makes her (and us) wonder exactly how far back this mania stretches, making us rethink the apparent normality of earlier scenes. The discordant strings that accompany the scene grow progressively louder and we cut to a POV from behind a pillar while she is still looking. As Danny experiences a further vision of the hotel corridors running with blood (with furniture being carried away, like in DH Lawrence's *The Virgin and the Gypsy* (Christopher Miles, 1970), Jack confronts her, playing out more fully the roles of hunter and hunted as we repeatedly cut between alternating forward and reverse tracking shots. Kubrick gives us fourteen shot-reverse-shot patterns, including closer over-the-shoulder shots, as Jack slowly stalks Wendy across the hall and up the stairs, growing more and more like the Big Bad Wolf character, building to his fake clawing actions on the stairs and his overt speech at the bathroom door later ('Little pig ...'). Wendy, here, is little more than a grizzling mess, cruelly mimicked by Jack (possibly deliberately created by a merciless Kubrick, who insisted on at least 45 takes for the scene). Although, in some senses, she is in a dominant physical position, above him on the stairs, emphasized by the low angle, and she has a weapon, she seems powerless, reflected in the way she backs off and the symbolic, ineffectual swipe she gives halfway up the stairs. His appeal to her ('Wendy, darling, light of my life') alludes to the famous opening lines of *Lolita* (1962), a previous Kubrick project (also featuring a child abuser), and there is a similar knowing playfulness, mixing absurdity with comedy, in Jack's repeated command to 'Give me the bat', to the extent that he sounds like an actor trying out different ways to deliver the line, including a jokey, ridiculous, deep-voiced parody. The scene constitutes a domesticated version of a standard feature of swashbuckling movies, a fight on the stairs, but Jack expresses surprise and shock in the pain caused by a blow first to his hand and then to his head, which sends him tumbling to the foot of the stairs, releasing the tension that had been building as he slowly ascended towards her.

Although Conner describes *The Shining* as 'an 'anti-horror' film' and Collings asserts that Kubrick 'did not use conventional treatments to create terror or horror,' the film does draw on some standard tropes of the horror film, as when the decomposing woman walks forward, arms outstretched, like a mummy from *Scooby-Doo*, but it is true that, generally, clichés are avoided.[35] As Wendy pulls Jack through the doorway to the dry-store cupboard, Kubrick avoids the temptation to have him grab either the doorframe or her. Kubrick uses creative, unusual camera placement, such as at the bathroom door, when we see Nicholson with his head leaning against a door, shot by Kubrick lying on his back below, looking up. This makes the door seem like a constrictive ceiling and suggests an immense pressure bearing down on the central character who, with hair falling past his ears, and with the light on the door, has the look of a caged and deranged animal. Garris' argument that he did not want to show Grady opening the door, as it would be distracting, really makes no sense. Here, we hear his voice and the bolts slide back. As the door can only be opened from the outside, we need to have some clue as to who or what frees Jack to maintain the coherence of the film.

Nicholson's performance can be criticized as histrionic but he has produced moments of lasting iconic power, particularly the 'Here's Johnny' at the bathroom door. King's criticism of the casting is, in retrospect, quite naïve. He may decry Hollywood's preference for a star who is 'bankable' but that is exactly what he himself has become and one of his suggestions, Michael Moriarty, went on to give a fairly awful, wooden performance in *Return to Salem's Lot* (1987).[36] Besides, Nicholson's performance contains many examples of great subtlety too, all too often missed, like his little shimmy in the ballroom, made much more theatrical by Stephen Weber in the Garris remake. Collings' assumption, echoed by Magistrale, that the film fails because 'it has ceased to be King's' is just too simplistic in assuming one can only be 'faithful' to a novel if the script is written by the same author.[37] *The Shining* (1997) is a good example of how greater 'faithfulness' to a source text does not, in itself, yield a more memorable film. Film is not in the business of producing fully-rounded, psychological entities. The remake may include more depth to Jack's alcoholism, fractured marriage and psychic breakdown but, in filmic terms, that does not in itself produce a better product. In the closing fifteen minutes, Magistrale dismisses Nicholson as just 'a monster' and it is certainly true that he becomes a blend of howling Big Bad Wolf, and a loping, limping Hunchback of Notre Dame figure (fusing both in the maze), appearing absurd.[38] However, King does describe his character as

'It' just prior to the boiler explosion in the novel and, even so, there are also several examples of an engaging and tragic wounded childishness, such as when he is hurt with the bat or the knife, or the few seconds of calculation in phrasing an appeal to Wendy, when he is locked in the cupboard, alternating between crying, begging and throwing an outright tantrum. In the food locker, when Jack comes round, it is only when he tries to stand that he winces in pain at an injury to his ankle, which is logical as he has been dragged to that particular spot.

King himself felt the film was emotionally cold and, unlike his book, foregrounded Jack's mental instability, thereby making a descent into madness impossible. Lack of 'faithfulness' to the novel was reason enough to damn the film in some fans' eyes (and implicitly exonerating King, who as Beahm claims, 'had nothing to do with it').[39] However, ultimately, it is unfair to see *The Shining* as failing in this sense or as a horror film when that is not what it is trying to be. King's assertion that Kubrick does not understand horror film may or may not be true, but if the film of *The Shining* is about horror, it is a different kind: the horror of mortality, the horror of being trapped in a confined space (even with those you love) and, perhaps, King's greatest fear, the horror of having to write when inspiration eludes you. For some, it will always be a cautionary tale that too much Steadicam is bad for your health but it also shows Kubrick's ready embrace of developing technology. Kubrick claims that 'I wanted very much to make a film in which the story is told in ways different from those to which the sound film has accustomed us…I believe that without doubt there is a more cinematic manner of communicating, closer to silent film.'[40] In the multi-layered soundtrack, the allusions to *Cuckoo's Nest*, and the deflating of audience identification with horror conventions, Kubrick is reflecting an aesthetic that is inherently intertextual and thereby requires viewing strategies from the audience that are equally sensitive to marker of genre and textual allusion. Compared to the Garris version, it is a film about the potential of film-making rather than demonstrating its limits.

The Shining (Mick Garris, 1997)

Jack Torrance: Women – can't live with them; can't kill em.

Delbert Grady: Can't you, sir?

Superficially, Garris' version offers a more powerful expression of terror of the everyday with hedges, wasps providing supposed sources of threat. Mick Garris' two-part TV version of *The Shining* reads like a list of features that Kubrick chose to omit. Chief amongst these, the hedge creatures were much anticipated by fans of the novel. However, there is a fundamental problem in how the written word and moving images evoke fear in their respective audiences. It is debatable whether, in a film context, a monstrous entity can actually be frightening, beyond a moment or two, if it cannot move. In the case of the hedge creatures, under the guiding hand of Visual Effects Supervisor Boyd Shermis and Steve Johnson's XFX Inc, initially they only move, Grandmother's Footsteps-style, when they are unobserved – looked at directly, they stay still. The 'movement' is supposedly created by whip pans, rapid tracking up to static figures in close-up oblique angles, crane shots that rotate as they descend and one single frame where there appears to be a moving foot (via puppetry). Adding sound effects of growling or snow supposedly falling as the figures move are attempts to paper over this fundamental flaw. Secondly, in the sequence when the creatures do move, approaching Danny at play in the snow, the computer effects are so bland (identical in movement and Day-Glo colour similar to that used by the BBC for the pre-school show *Teletubbies*, Ragdoll Productions, 1997–2001) that there is no sense of depth of shot and therefore no threat, since the creatures are supposedly approaching from some distance. The point here is that this section of the cinematic colour palette is reserved almost exclusively for very young children. A descending, rotating crane shot feels like a contrived way to suggest Danny is under threat whilst innocently playing but, like the other camera movement around the hedge creatures, it is just trying too hard. In the book, the creatures do actually attack Halloran and Danny, cutting his leg, but there is a loss of nerve here (or an underlining of technical limitations) as the game of Grandmother's Footsteps is suddenly halted when the grown-ups appear.

The wasp sequence is equally devoid of threat. Fear of a phenomenon in the real world should be easier to create than suspending disbelief in a fictional entity but, even here, the wasps seem no more bothersome than flies. An instructive comparison is with Jonathan Swift's *Gulliver's Travels* (1726), where, in the second book, the hero is accosted by giant wasps and must fight them off with his sword. The 1996 Channel Four adaptation of this text, directed by Charles Sturridge, dramatizes an exciting battle between Ted Danson as the eponymous hero and wasps produced by a blend of computer-generated effects, Jim Henson puppetry and animatronics, which really do look as if they could kill.

The small effect of the hotel hose is underplayed nicely. It appears in Tony's first 'vision', uncoiling and leaping into the camera, revealing *Langolier*-looking teeth. In the hotel, it is seen through Danny's POV first of all. Later as he investigates Room 217, the hose swings out as if ready to spring and is shot from a high angle, like a security camera, as he walks warily past into the frame. After ignoring Tony's warnings, the hose flies out, blood oozes from the nozzle and it gives one more twitch, but the outcome of these effects is strangely sequential, not cumulative; one follows another without any palpable increase in tension. The things which he senses almost immediately – Almond's picture, the voices in the Presidential suite and the blood on the walls – are not unsettling because, unlike the visions in *It* that only children can see, these can be easily wished away.

Despite repeated protestations on the DVD by Garris that he is 'doing the book', he is clearly aware of the weight of Kubrick's film. Tracking shots are used for the hotel corridors but here at adult eye-level rather than at the height of Danny's go-cart and mostly POV – not over-the-shoulder-shots as in the earlier film. Later (in a mini Kubrick homage perhaps) we float, via Steadicam, through the living space of the Torrances but here, rather than Kubrick's sense of isolation, we are exploring their domestic happiness, with Jack typing and Wendy and Danny reading together. The Steadicam only really starts to swoop down the corridors in Part III, when Jack is losing his grip on reality. The only low-level tracking shots we have are specifically-motivated, like when we follow Jack's unconscious body as he is dragged through the kitchen to the freezer.

The casting of Melvin Van Peebles in the role of Halloran adds credibility to his link with Danny and, certainly, the sartorial decision of a dark red suit and placing him in an open-top red car gives him a 'Pimp my Halloran' feel. King had reservations about this Huggy Bear-with-a-makeover look but it effectively makes his character more active, in tune with the boy and draws on the considerable talents of Peebles: charismatic star, writer and director of the groundbreaking *Sweet Sweetback's Baadasssss Song*, (1971). Rather than Scatman Crothers' more stereotypical 'Yessah' servant, Peebles, in a white suit, listening to Wilson Pickett on the jukebox out in Miami, exudes an impression of 'cool'.

This film does not have the enigmatic quality of Kubrick's version but, at times, we are also not given visual access to what is going on within, i.e., not always given an omniscient view, as when Danny locks himself in the bathroom. This can be said to create purposely slight viewer frustration, build suspense and reduce the sense of a god-like authorial presence but it does not feel part of a coherent aesthetic, as in Kubrick's film. The extra time of a two-part TV series allows for apparently extraneous shots to create atmosphere, such as the lingering shot of the kitchen door, which slowly shuts on its own, or the extended scene where Wendy tries to seduce Jack. The opening sequence, introducing the hotel, self-consciously seeks to break with Kubrick's glacial vision as we see colour, warmth and happy families – a normality to be disrupted. The double-sized 'Denver croquet' suggests a playing, *Alice in Wonderland*-style, with proportions but this does play out in the rest of the film (as in the fairly prosaic wasps).

The iconic scene of Jack breaking down the bathroom door is given an interesting twist by Wendy opening a window, to be met by a wall of snow, and Weber's great improvised, underplayed 'Boo' instead of Nicholson's 'Here's Johnny !' However, the distracting of Jack at this point by Delbert reminding him to focus on Danny (and then again, soon after attacking Halloran), does seem like a dramatic 'stringing out' of a final conflict for which we have been waiting for nearly four hours. Nicholson's tennis ball finds its counterpart here in the croquet ball, which rolls spookily into Wendy's path, enticing her into the office where she is trapped, leaving Danny vulnerable outside and also, ultimately, provides her with a weapon to save herself and Danny. Unlike Kubrick's film, there is a very unconvincing 'winning back' scene between

Jack and Danny, when the father is quickly shaken out of his madness, only to lapse back into it and lope off down the corridor, like the Hunchback of Notre Dame, en route to sacrificing himself by the boiler.

Danny's experience in Room 217 works quite well, including a POV from inside the room looking out, via a wide-angle lens, at Danny on a chair, giving the 'ghostly presence' more substance. As Danny slowly approaches the bath with a shower screen, we have alternating POV shots, not just his but also from within the bath. The putrid woman, revealed when he pulls back the curtain, opens her eyes and addresses him, causing him to flee in panic to the door, setting up the cross-cutting axis between his static, increasingly-panicked attempt to open the door and the slow, inexorable approach of the woman. We see an ankle-level shot of her feet as she steps out and walks towards him, her POV as she turns the corner and, then, the two finally in the same shot – the past is almost colliding with the present. The door eventually opens, Danny escapes but inexplicably stands inches from the door. Therefore, the hands that shoot out and grab him back into the room do shock the viewer but the stupidity of standing waiting for this, undermines that shock. Like the events in the locked bathroom, we do not see what transpires next – Danny appearing later, marked with lipstick. Whilst in theory, this might create a sense of unease that we are not always placed in a position of omniscience, the omission of these scenes, the last one especially, represent a real lost opportunity. Jack's exploration of the room turns up nothing at first, until he walks out of the bathroom and hears the shower curtain swish back, causing him to run. It is such smaller, more subtle touches that are more unsettling than full-screen effects, like the 'visual bleed' between the cut from the ballroom to the scene out with the snow-mobile, where, for a second, a few pieces of confetti fall snow-like inside the shed (in the novel, streamers in the elevator are an early suggestion of the other presences in the hotel), and the liquid-like shadows that appear under the door are more effective than the 'wasp woman', viewable amongst the DVD deleted material.

The DVD mentions a 'visual manifesto' that Garris explained at the start of the project, including the use of natural and reflected light, low angles and a moving camera. Jack's gradual breakdown is signalled fairly early with his slightly excessive shaking of Danny after the apparent fit he has in the bathroom. Alone, looking at his face in the mirror, Jack starts speaking to himself and there is a slight under-lighting shift on his face, something which is more obvious in later scenes, like the red tint as he speaks to his 'father' over the radio or the spotlight used on him when he is locked in. This is a theatrical way of suggesting Jack's duality, an expressionist approach used elsewhere in the film by Garris (an avowed fan of psychological horror such as Polanski's *Repulsion* (1965), such as when individual lights are used underneath each bottle at the bar or Horace Derwent appears sporting luminous face-paint. Ciment notes how Kubrick 'makes very sparing use of expressionistic lighting and plays on the ambiguous relation between imagination and reality almost to the end of the film.'[41] Contrast this with Garris' approach – fluorescent make-up, coloured disco-style lighting in the bar and little sense of Jack (as played by Weber) as anything other than a man undergoing a psychic breakdown. As Danny wanders down the corridors in Part II, strong top-lighting creates pools of light and shadow for him to pass through. Despite the seventeen-year gap since Kubrick's film, Garris seems to want to keep most of the effects (barring the hedge creatures and final explosion) within the shot and on-set, such as the stop-motion of 'Redrum' appearing on the wall, which is probably fair, when the post-production effects are examined. Wisely, he cuts elaborate effects of putrefaction of King as band leader Creed in close-up, which are more overtly horror-orientated (and more evocative of a 1960s Roger Corman Poe-exploitation vehicle) than the rest of the film. The final explosion of an obvious model house at the end looks no more convincing than *Carrie*, twenty years before.

The casting of children in major roles is always difficult. In retrospect, Kubrick's script wisely shifts the focus from Danny's POV in King's novel to Jack's descent into madness. The problem, here, is that Courtland Mead as Danny has an expression of almost permanent surprise and very slow, adenoidal speech, which makes a shift of emotional gears difficult (especially when he keeps repeating 'like pictures in a book'). Danny Lloyd in Kubrick's version had weaknesses too but could convey terror effectively. Garris' limitations are in part due to pressures of network television in the US, where scenarios with children in jeopardy are an instant cause for censorship. At the very heart of this narrative we are supposed to believe an evil house wishes harm to come to a child with a special gift. A subtle little touch is to put Danny in pyjamas with the same cowboy design as the wallpaper of his room, as if he is part of the fabric of the hotel (or a reflection of its 'desire' for him).

King's script has plenty of parts that resonate, especially in retrospect. Jack's promise that, in reference to his family, 'I'll take care of them' is protective in context but threatening, later. However, it must be said that, unlike Nicholson's manic pursuit with the axe, there is much less sense here that Jack will do real harm to either Wendy or Danny. The choice of 'weapons' is significant. The croquet mallet (from King's novel) and the baseball bat have the potential to hurt but their literal and dramatic impact is blunted compared to that of an axe, making the 'pursuit' down the corridors quite a half-hearted affair. On the other hand, this does allow the showing of the full blow to Halloran's head (from which he might also credibly survive) and the strike to Wendy's chest (also from King's novel). Expository dialogue is served up directly and frankly with little artistry through conversations between Jack and Watson and then Almond, providing an explicit history of the hotel. The final twist of making Tony Danny's older self (in the novel) is logical, as his gift is partly precognitive and very King-like in subsuming a 'twin' within the self, à la *The Dark Half*. Unfortunately, the effectiveness of this is undone by the awful sentimentality of the blown kiss and lingering, routine exchange with his father, painfully reminiscent of the ridiculous farewell between 'Dead Meat' and his wife in *Hot Shots* (Jim Abrahams, 1991). With a lower US rating than Kubrick's version (fifteen rather than R), a domestic exhibition format on terrestrial television (thereby juxtaposed with commercials) and a running time more than four times the original, such intertextual comparisons are much more likely. If we are supposed to accept that Jack poses a serious threat, then Kubrick's refusal to resolve the father-son conflict seems much more believable. Here, even in Part III, an argument by the lift ends in a group hug, not an axe-attack. King's description of the script that Kubrick originally rejected contains several elements that resurface here – domestic tragedy, Jack's alcoholism, previous events at the Overlook and the cutting of the interview scene. Even his description of the opening, a black screen and the dialogue between mafia hit-men, reappears seventeen years later, perhaps suggesting more might have been done to hone and improve rather than shoe-in an existing script.

As with many of King's mini-series, pacing is a problem. The family standing on the hotel steps as the camera cranes up, dwarfing them, with Danny slightly separated from his parents, looks like (what it is) a posed shot for a trailer or linking section back from a commercial break – it does not fit in the drama of the film. Part I ends without any real climax – ghostly happenings are starting (fires self-lighting and chairs dropping off the tables) but if the narrative charge is supposedly lit, it is a very long fuse. There are some witty lines – in addressing his father over the radio, Jack asks: 'Pardon me for asking… but aren't you dead?' By 1997, King can use the Arnie catch-phrase ironically, so, when Jack goes to explore Room 217, he promises 'I'll be back.' There is an allusion to *Psycho* (the seminal madman-in-a-h/motel-scenario) in the echo of Norman Bates' line, 'I'm not myself when I drink'. Typical of King scripts, one character (here Wendy) has rather unlikely leaps of perception about supernatural phenomena and 'explains' to Jack that the hotel wants Danny. Later, after the ballroom scene, she suddenly starts carrying a large knife without any clear threat being apparent. The closing shots signal the rebuilding of the hotel – opening the way for a further film. Evil endures as we have a shimmering glimpse of the old building and snatches of dialogue from a croquet game.

The relationship of the Torrances is a clear departure for Garris. The casting of Rebecca de Mornay and the running time (three times longer than Kubrick's) gives him plenty of opportunity to make Wendy a strong, intelligent, slightly-overprotective but resourceful woman (who slashes her husband with a razor) and not the one-dimensional shrieking face of Shelley Duvall (for which Kubrick must also take responsibility). Small gestures, like not just sniffing but tasting the bottle of tea in Jack's office, capture the uneasy state of trust between the couple and between any recovering alcoholic and those around them. King's own alcoholism (now acknowledged) can play much more of an overt part of Jack's character, so we see an AA meeting (along with Garris' obligatory cameo). At King's suggestion, Wendy was cast as blond, beautiful and potentially a high-school cheerleader, foreshadowing Maria Bello in Cronenberg's *A History of Violence* (2005).

King has claimed, on many occasions, that Kubrick did not understand what the novel was about, that he could not believe that a house could be innately evil. However, the remake does not fare any better at conveying a possessed house. To be effective, the haunted house genre needs credible effects, drawing on a credible script. The effect of Tony floating seems out of place here and better suited to a more traditional vampire/ghost narrative, as Danny Glick in *Salem's Lot*. We do not really see that much of Danny's gift. Certainly Halloran senses his potential in sending telepathic messages, making his car lights blow, but apart from knowing that Jack got the job and that, later, he is not writing but researching the hotel and drinking, it is not easy to see exactly why the house would want him (but this is a quibble with the source novel too). Some of the frights are less creative, like the horror cliché of sudden movement into the frame when Derwent pops up in a wolf mask. Garris' repeated use of low oblique angles, albeit of The Stanley Hotel in Colorado, the very place where King thought up the premise of the novel, accompanied by 'angry' synthesizers, does not make a building, an inanimate object, scary. On the contrary, this version focuses all the more on the psychological pressures on Torrance, fleshing out his alcoholism, failed teaching career and strict upbringing, his supernatural encounters with the topiary and the CB radio, all underlined, from the outset, by the heavy-handed symbol of the boiler, which, predictably, blows up at the end, triggering the Usher-like collapse of the building.

The ballroom scene is a slight echo of *Carrie* and initially conceals the identity of King himself as leader of the band, Gage Creed (the boy who returns from death in *Pet Semetary*). What is only suggested by Kubrick, that much of what we see in the hotel is often the subjective world of Jack, is made explicit here when Garris cuts from Jack in a crowded ballroom, apparently bumping into Preston Sturges (played by the legendary director's own son) to him dancing alone in an empty room in the present. To 'corroborate' the subjectivity, Garris also places Wendy, later, in the Halloran attack scene, cutting between Jack seeing Horace at the bar and Wendy staring in bemusement at thin air (like the appearance of Banquo's ghost in *Macbeth*).

More broadly, King has claimed that Kubrick does not understand the horror genre but it is debatable whether, in filmic terms, he does either. Garris' remake, which failed to repeat the ratings success of *The Stand*, makes much of being 'faithful' to King's book and including elements missing from the first version. However, the reinstatement of Jack writing a play rather than a novel or the officiousness of Ullman (Elliot Gould) add little and do not produce a better film. Anything needing clarifying, such as the history of the hotel via the scrapbook, is clearly shown to us. Problematic elements, like the glimpse of the man in the dog-mask, are smoothed over. Nevertheless, for all its qualities, it is not the performance of Stephen Weber but that of Jack Nicholson (perhaps able to draw on all his extra-filmic baggage as an, alleged, womanizing hellraiser) that sticks in the mind and it is the direction of Kubrick that has spawned a whole critical industry, not Mick Garris (who has yet to have a single book written about him). This may be unfair but it shows a clear distinction between a cinematic and a televisual aesthetic, between the relative stature of the actors and directors concerned and that slavishly including all available material from a book over six hours, and with a bigger budget, will not produce a better film. Here, King has his usual mini-series deal – Executive Producer role, directorial oversight, his script, a cameo role, a reasonable budget – but can only produce character-based drama with some interesting features but with substantially less art than Kubrick. Garris is, ironically, correct on the DVD commentary, intoning that 'less is more'.

1408 (Mikael Hafström, 2007)

'The autobiography of a nightmare.' (Mike Enslin)

'It's an evil fucking room.' (Olin)

The oddness of hotel rooms, particularly of the sense that they contain some kind of residual element of the lives that have passed through them, is not a wholly original idea, (think of Ali Smith's 2005 *Hotel World*). However, *1408* is one of the most allusive films in this book, demanding an approach that is sensitive to its intertextual references and attempts to extend generic conventions. This is particularly so, given its genesis as a drafting exercise in King's *On Writing*, used as part of a competition and eventually made into a script, initially by Matt Greenberg and then by Scott Alexander and Larry Karaszewski. *Cavalier* magazine had done something similar with 'Cat From Hell' in 1977, used as the basis for a segment of *Tales from the Darkside*, and only anthologized many years later in *Just After Sunset* (2008). Superficially, *1408* has similarities with *The Shining* (ghosts in a hotel, getting lost in anonymous corridors) but it is actually closer to *Battleground* (albeit with dialogue and the shared addition of elaborate special effects), blending Aristotlean unities of a specific timeframe in one particular location (once inside, the protagonist never leaves the room) with filmic influences from Roman Polanski's claustrophobic and expressive works like *Repulsion* (1965) and *The Tenant* (1976). Like *Misery*, the protagonist, Mike Enslin (John Cusack), is a man trapped by a writing career and a product in which he no longer believes, a man used to describing feelings rather than actually experiencing them, reflected in the formulaic and derivative names of his titles – *Ten Haunted Hotels*, *Graveyards*, *Lighthouses*. Hotel manager Gerald Olin (Samuel L. Jackson) perceptively describes him as 'a talented and intelligent man who doesn't believe in anything or anyone except himself', the emptiness underlying his success, reflected in the poorly-attended reading.

Greenberg's script originally had a murder in the opening section, but its relevance in the finished film is as a foreshadowing. Enslin walks round a supposedly-haunted room, unimpressed. Loss of proportion is emphasized by his drinking miniatures and sitting on a tiny Alice-style chair. Rather than a mindless teen protagonist, Enslin's intellectual scepticism gives credence and dramatic weight to his initial reaction, looking round 1408, where his glib description is interrupted by the radio coming on with The Carpenters' 'We've Only Just Begun'. Music frequently provides an ironic intertextual subtext in King adaptations, most obviously in *Christine* and *Sleepwalkers* but even in *Graveyard Shift,* where the rats cling to logs to the accompaniment of The Beach Boys' 'Surfing USA'. When the clock comes on for a second time, it also shows time counting down, marking the last hour of the film in real time and underlining that is how long guests usually survive (Enslin rationalizes this as a trick, albeit 'very effective'). There is a period of Todorovian hesitation and slow-burn increase in unease as he cannot explain the chocolates on the pillow and feverishly searches the apartment, convinced someone else is there. Later, several wide-angle lens panning shots of the room from Enslin's POV, as he scans the room, suggest a slipping into insanity and he clutches at the temporarily-satisfying explanation of Olin's drink as the source of the hallucination.

In a rare scene outside 1408 itself, Hafström uses a high top-shot above London's Reform Club (standing for New York's Dolphin Hotel). To make the most of the opulent décor and to foreshadow the tussle to secure the room key and the dizzying loss of proportion that will soon envelop Enslin, Hafström follows this with a rotating camera (an intertextual allusion to a favourite De Palma device) around Olin and Enslin. The casting of Samuel L. Jackson (originally short, chubby and white in King's story), allows Olin to embody a stronger counterpoint to Enslin (like the casting of Morgan Freeman in *The Shawshank Redemption*), enhances the sense of threat of the room and allows the film's one swear word to be delivered with greater conviction, also evoking his role as loquacious killer, Jules, in Quentin Tarantino's *Pulp Fiction* (1995).

A variety of effective sound perspectives are used, such as the grinding synthesizer that accompanies Enslin's first look round the room, the later effect of toys running down and a muffled heartbeat audible just before the window slams on his fingers. The effect is reminiscent of Kubrick's sound of a boy's trike over the opening credits of *The Shining* and the ambient, industrial noise of *Seven* (David Fincher, 1995). The sudden cutting of sound (as when he first enters the room) can be as unsettling as sudden unexpected noise. The shot of the picture, which he tries to straighten, is accompanied by a creaking sound of ropes and boards (later the mewing of seagulls when he throws a chair against the wall), anticipating the flood erupting outwards at the climax. Some of this is prompted by King's description – '[i]t made him think first of scary movies where the director tried to indicate mental distress in one of the characters by tipping the camera on the point-of-view shots,'[42] and a crooked door 'had a little of that old *Cabinet of Dr Caligari* charm'.[43]

There are standard horror devices, like the use of sudden movements, as when the bell-boy bobs up into shot and then disappears just as quickly, or sudden sounds, such as the radio coming on unexpectedly. However there are also more creative decisions on show. Unusual camera angles, such as the high angle shot from the corner of the room, evoke security camera footage (increasing the sense that he is being watched). The extreme close-up from inside the lock mechanism adds to the distortion of perspectives, especially when Enslin breaks his key off and he bangs uncontrollably on the door as if the fabric of the hotel is conspiring against him. Sporadic use of wide angle lenses, particularly focusing on Enslin's glass in the corner of the frame, creates a distorted, almost drug-induced, effect and camera movements like the slow rising shot over the back of the TV is reminiscent of Kubrick's shot of Shelley Duvall looking over her husband's typewriter for the first time in *The Shining*, creating a sense of an agency in the room beyond Enslin's control.

However one of the most uncanny effects is derived from intertextual references rather than generic devices. Enslin starts to signal to a figure in a building opposite only for the man to mimic his actions until they are completely in synch. What starts out as comic (reminiscent of the Marx Bros.' 1933 mirror routine in *Duck Soup*) becomes threatening, in a nightmarish twist, as the figure reveals his face as Enslin's own, about to be attacked by a man with a claw hammer. However, the speed with which his own attacker disappears from 1408, at the moment of delivering the final strike, cheapens the shock effect a little and retrospective knowledge that the casting of the actor here, Cusack's own personal trainer (Benny Urquidez), is a metatextual joke almost casts the scene in the light of Inspector Clouseau's tussles with his man servant Cato (Burt Kwouk) in Blake Edwards' *The Pink Panther* series.

Generically, a ghost story needs some evidence of the supernatural. The first clear appearance of a ghost occurs when a man in grainy black and white, and then a woman in 1940s-style dress walk, through the room, take a baleful glance at him and then jump from the window. These are very human ghosts, clearly from different eras, and signal a bond with Enslin, suggesting that he is, or soon will be, a ghost himself. Knocked out by a wave whilst surfing, we see 'Psycho I' on Enslin's wetsuit, marking (perhaps only in retrospect) the subjective nature of the body of the film. The apartment becomes progressively more expressive and rooms 'host' scenes from other places – the Director's Cut features Enslin's father, alone in a nursing home bathroom, delivering the gnomic utterance to his son: 'As you are, I was. As I am, you will be.' Like the crack across the ceiling in *Secret Window*, the walls here start to crack, oozing blood, and Enslin tries to escape the room by climbing out onto the ledge, only to discover (which we see by a crash zoom-out) that there are no further windows – he really is in a room of the mind, reflected in the altered fire drill information. Hafström however adds little touches to keep a dream-like logic (and the echoes of the second part of *Cat's Eye*), so that Enslin is startled by the ghost-woman, destined to repeat her suicidal jump *ad infinitum*. A room is transformed into a hospital scene, so that we have more back-story about the death of his daughter (Katy), an addition to King's plot, and the room appears to communicate more and more directly with him – from his daughter's dress, sent via the fax machine, to the final exchange with the receptionist over the phone, advising him to use 'the rapid check-out system', before the camera pulls back through a noose that has miraculously appeared, neatly framing Enslin's head within it.

The effects, including freezing and fire scenes, are primarily on-set rather than created in post-production, which adds to the sense of authenticity and claustrophobia in the room but these become gradually more excessive. By the time of the flooding sequence, we have tipped into disaster movie territory, à la *The Poseidon Adventure* (Ronald Neame, 1972). For all the technical complexity of tilting the set 45 degrees (featured heavily in the DVD extras), ultimately, Hafström cuts this latter sequence as just excessive. That said, the storm sequence, with flash cuts of the pictures changing to feature more grotesque, sexualized figures, possibly including his mystery attacker from earlier, is still impressive, but the overall impact of such effects is to underline them as effects. If we are marvelling at the logistics of the hydraulics, we may not feel genuine jeopardy for the characters.

The subjective frame-story alludes to other similar rhetorical devices, particularly so as it is a relatively-rare generic feature. His coming round on the beach and staring up at a plane carrying a banner with the number '1408' on it feels like an unconscious version of the 'Keyser Söze' ending of Bryan Singer's *The Usual Suspects* (1995). However, we are in a false dawn as the plot slips into a slower pace, apparently heading towards resolution, and closer to a love story as Lilly and Mike reconcile and talk about their daughter's death and separation. Like Nic Roeg's *Don't Look Now* (1973), the death of a daughter is the tragic subtext to the hero's weakening sanity and premonitions of his own death, particularly poignant in his meeting Katy, only for her to die again in his arms. However, the bubble of the love story ('I can't believe I'm sitting here with you') is burst in the restaurant scene. In a metatextual reference to *Misery* (where a writer is also encouraged to exploit a personal experience), Enslin sees the ghost from 1408 but when we cut back to her, she is just a normal waitress. The past bleeds into the present, madness into sanity, death into life, anticipating the Post Office scene (where a shot from inside his mail-box references the close of *The Shawshank Redemption* but here there is no possible redemption) where he gradually recognizes figures from the hotel, such as the bell-boy, who knock down the fabric of the set in a Nabokovian 'cancelling' of the scene, revealing that he never left the room at all.

There is a slightly episodic feel to parts of the film, such as the vent sequence and the later appearance of a black monolith-like door in the room (both references to Kubrick's *2001*). In the vent, Enslin bumps into a mummified figure (apparently O'Malley, the room's first victim but this is rather unclear), looks down at an argument between himself and his father (who declares he is 'a bullshit writer' and looks knowingly and directly up at him). There is a sense of the Ghost of Enslin's Christmas Past giving him snapshots from his life (as if the room is already treating him as a ghost) and his tumble back into the room (and later opening of the black door) is reminiscent of part of Cusack's own past in Spike Jonze's *Being John Malkovich* (1999), which also features moments of surreal crossing of borders between the everyday and an existence just beyond it. Back in the room, Enslin opens the fridge only to see a vision of Olin in a long hallway. Referencing the fridge effect in *It* with Kubrick's underlying philosophical question in *The Shining*, Olin asks 'Why d'you think people believe in ghosts?' answering himself: 'the prospect of something after death.' The reverse shot with Enslin screaming at the fridge door evokes the sequence, ultimately cut from David Cronenberg's *Videodrome* (1982), where we see a reflection of the protagonist, Max Renn, still wearing a VR helmet, problematizing the status of the preceding scenes as subjective hallucination.

The Director's Cut DVD features a different ending, which, by implication, was too bleak for a theatrical release and contributes to the marketing of the DVD as distinctive. Here, apart from a cheap flash cut of a scarred Enslin, suddenly appearing in Olin's rear-view mirror, there is little gained by the extra scene. Olin tries to return Enslin's possessions and convey a sense of gratitude that, by his sacrifice, the room has somehow been exorcised. The final shot, up the building to the room, evokes the *Kingdom Hospital* credit sequence and the close of *Red Rose*, with Enslin as a ghost looking down over the city (smoking a final, satisfying cigarette, reminiscent of *Misery*'s Paul Sheldon) before being called away by his daughter. Forward narrative momentum is compromised by the increasing piling up of intertextual references, including King adaptations, so that spotting them becomes a game for the knowledgeable viewer, validating their generic credentials.

There is some technical updating from King's story, adding the ability to communicate visually via a laptop, although why this machine alone works in 1408, is a little unclear. The written story uses a *Blair Witch*-style reconstruction from recovered tape recordings and evolves into a fragmented blend of snatches of fairy-tales, surreal dream-like sensual impressions and interior thoughts. Hafström linearizes these elements and, to broaden the visual drama from the source text, uses a Dictaphone to verbalize Enslin's thoughts, and King's original 'voice of the room' is transposed into telephone messages; the recorder talking back with King's dialogue resurfaces in Cusack's adlibbed non-sequiturs. Enslin calls 1408 part of 'this Kafkaesque hotel' and where this leads to a questioning of boundaries, like the mysterious alter-ego in the building opposite, the post office scene or the ledge sequence, the film works well. Images slightly out of key with on-screen events, such as flies on food left outside in a corridor, a woman pushing an over-sized pram into a nearby room (with echoes of Polanski's 1968 *Rosemary's Baby*) and persistent crying heard through walls, suggest something untoward just beyond our sight. As Enslin describes his new novel, the film works best when expressionist elements reflect subtext, 'Truman Capote meets HR Giger', rather than slipping into pure spectacle.

1408 is sensitive to other film works, playing with the viewer's sense of reality and, through the performance of Cusack, there are some nice satirical touches about hotel life: Enslin gets lost initially in the anonymous corridors; the toilet paper is neatly-folded into a point, the epitome of pretentiousness; and the robotic voice reciting irrelevant, impersonal information rather than listening to an individual. When the clock later reaches zero and Enslin receives the call from room service, there is the sense that he is not caught in the comedy of *Groundhog Day* (Harold Ramis, 1993) but the nightmare of *Storm of the Century* in which 'Hell is repetition'.

Conclusion

Tanya in *Sleepwalkers* survives but spends that film within the confines of stereotype as a screaming, wide-eyed, passive victim. She does nothing to save herself and only survives because of the sacrifice of several cops, parents and many cats – in short, everyone except her. By contrast, in this chapter, Clover's Final Girl theory works, in part. Donna, Wendy and Dolores are observant, aware of danger and do survive. However, they are not the only characters to be given any psychological depth and certainly not the only ones 'whose perspective approaches our own privileged understanding of the situation.'[44] There is no shift from literal point-of-view and audience identification with the killer to the teller of the tale, none have androgynous names (Wendy, Donna, Dolores) and not one is a member of a peer group against whom they can be measured. On the other hand, there is an element of 'phallic appropriation', in Wendy's use of a knife and Donna's use of a baseball bat, but none of the names are masculinized and we see the heroines as abused rather than the killer as a male in a crisis of sexuality (unless the abusive behaviour is read as an expression of sexual conflict). All three are 'masculinized' in the sense of actively directing the narrative (if narrative influence is seen in gender terms) – Dolores sets a trap, Donna sets out to the garage (a stereotypical male environment) and Wendy seeks escape in the world outside the hotel. Most notably, there is less emphasis on a virginal abstinence from sexual activity than on an accommodation within a family setting. All three examples here are wives, casting the genre closer to family drama than teen kill-pic. In fact, teenagers are almost wholly absent from these films.

Moreover, as we noted in chapter two on portmanteau films, in the words of Jonathan Lake Crane, 'older forms of horrific imagery and storytelling have vanished. Horror films that rely on the hallowed legends of the past, spiced with just a hint of spurious violence, are gone.'[45] This includes the haunted house tale, intrinsically linked to a literary form from a previous century and a cinematic genre from a bygone era. Crane adds how

> [s]pooky tales stressing the importance of group solidarity in the face of evil have also been driven from the multiplex. And films that assayed the meaning of dread ... while eschewing vulgar and bloody spectacle, have faded from view as well.[46]

Ultimately, the difference between the two versions of *The Shining* is that King's own scripted version tries to reanimate a dead sub-genre, the haunted house movie, in thrall to his muse Shirley Jackson, whereas Kubrick, perhaps wisely, does not. The difficulty of persuading an audience that an inanimate object can be either inherently evil or threatening failed to convince Kubrick, who rejected King's script outright, and also the audience, who may find Kubrick's version puzzling and pretentious but at least memorable in its stylized camerawork and the power of Nicholson's performance.

Fundamentally, objects which cannot move can only be threatening in an extremely closeted environment. In theory, a snowed-in hotel, cut off from the outside world for months, should provide such an environment but Kubrick never tries to generate a sense of threat from the building itself and Garris tries, but fails. As with the zombie movie, as soon as some distance is placed between oneself and the source of evil, such as Danny playing outside in the snow, the threat is negligible. Kubrick raises questions about cinematic representation whereas Garris opts for atmospheric dread, largely undercut by the extended running time and the lack of monstrous manifestation as a pay-off, beyond some highly unconvincing hedge creatures.

It could be said that a remake is perhaps the definitive intertextual text. Garris' version might then be described as a 'clinamen', Harold Bloom's term for a conscious turning away from an influence – a reaction which, arguably, is still an influence and, more precisely, a predictable one.[47] In this sense, the second film becomes an anti-Kubrick film. Where the first film used compression, Garris uses expansion and even sloth: harsh reality of filming in freezing conditions is replaced by cinematic effects, and one show-stealing central performance is diffused into a stronger, wider cast.

Christine Gledhill observes that genres can function as a way to prevent texts from shifting into 'individualism and incomprehensibility'.[48] However, in the case of *The Shining*, these very elements form part of the Kubrick brand so that the film is marketed as a piece of auteurist art, partly defined as such by the presence of enigmatic elements, which may be difficult to synthesize into conventional generic categories. At the same time, although it appears a defiantly anti-auteur text, Garris' version actually still remains one at its core – it just replaces the work of a famous cinematic auteur with that of a literary one. All of the influences of a visual specialist are systematically stripped out and replaced with literal, visual parallels from King's text. What might be seen as an extended moment of the Todorovian fantastic actually stretches for much of the length of Kubrick's movie as we are not entirely sure who opened the pantry door, whether Jack is talking to himself or 'real' ghostly apparitions and whether he is actually in the picture in the final shot. This ambiguity and openness is replaced by specific and codifiable motivation, especially alcoholism, and thereby universality reduced in favour of biographical linkage to King himself. In short, intelligent, challenging ambiguity is foresworn for crushing literalism. Nabokov used to open lectures at Cornell with the line: 'Literature does not tell the truth – it makes it up!' Kubrick understands the burden and the potential of creativity, producing (with the help of Production Designer Roy Wood) an incredibly elaborate set, with giant rooms, corridors and kitchens. Garris opts for the actual hotel where King was staying when he thought of the story. Fidelity to a source replaces creativity. Just as fidelity criticism in Adaptation Studies produces writing that is often sterile and repetitive, an unwavering commitment to 'fidelity' as a director produces similar results.

Notes

1. Stephen King, *Cujo* (New York: Viking, 1981), p. 53.
2. Jonathan Lake Crane, *Terror and Everyday Life: Singular Moments in the History of the Horror Film* (London and New Delhi: Sage Publications, 1994).
3. Tony Magistrale, *Hollywood's Stephen King*, op. cit., p. xiv.
4. Richard Collings, *The Films of Stephen King*, op. cit., p. 83.
5. Carol J. Clover, *Men, Women and Chainsaws: Gender in the Modern Horror Film* (London: BFI, 1992), p. 44.
6. Ibid., p. 51.
7. Linda Badley, *Film, Horror, and the Body Fantastic* (London: Greenwood Press, 1995), p. 102.
8. Stephen King, *Cujo*, op. cit., p. 187.
9. See George Beahm, *The Stephen King Companion*, op. cit., p. 92.
10. Stephen King, *Dolores Claiborne* (London: New English Library, 1993), p. 2 and p. 107.
11. Stephen King, cited in Magistrale, *Hollywood's Stephen King*, op. cit., p. 18.
12. Ibid., p. 19.
13. Ibid., p. 74.
14. Stephen King, *Salem's Lot* (London: New English Library, 1976), p. 43.
15. Carol Shields, *Larry's Party* (London: Fourth Estate Ltd, 1998), p. 313.
16. See King, *Danse Macabre* op. cit., pp. 296–330.
17. Michel Ciment, 'Kubrick & The Fantastic' in *Kubrick* (trans. Gilbert Adair, New York: Holt, Rinehart & Winston, 1983), p. 126.
18. Geoffrey Cocks, *The Wolf at the Door: Stanley Kubrick, History, and the Holocaust* (New York: Peter Lang, 2004), p. 2.
19. See Patricia Ferreira, 'Jack's Nightmare at the Overlook: the American Dream Inverted' in *The Shining Reader*, Anthony Magistrale (ed), (Washington: Starmont House), pp. 23–32; Frederic Jameson, 'Historicism in The Shining' in *Social Text* 4 (1981), pp. 114–125; Thomas Allen Nelson, *Kubrick: Inside a Film Artist's Maze* (Bloomington: Indiana University Press, 1982); and Bill Blakemore, 'The Family of Man', *San Francisco Chronicle*, 29 July (1987), available at www.visual-memory.co.uk/amk/doc/0052html.
20. Nelson, op. cit., p. 203.
21. Stephen King, interview with Eric Norden, *Playboy* (June 1983) in Tim Underwood and Chuck Miller (eds.), *Bare Bones: Conversations on Terror with Stephen King* (New York: McGraw-Hill, 1988), p. 29.
22. Stephen King, cited in Tim Underwood and Chuck Miller, *Feast* 85, p. 100.
23. See Vincent LoBrutto, *Stanley Kubrick: A Biography* (New York: Penguin Books, 1997), p. 411.
24. Louis Giannetti, *Understanding Movies*, (Englewood Cliffs, NJ: Prentice-Hall, 1987), p. 159.
25. Pauline Kael, 'Devolution', *The New Yorker*, June 9, 1980, p. 130.
26. Stephen King, *The Shining* (London: New English Library, 1977), p. 209.
27. Ibid., pp. 319 and 321.
28. Jack Kroll, 'Stanley Kubrick's Horror Show', *Newsweek Magazine*, June 2, 1980, p. 52.
29. See Conner, *Stephen King Goes to Hollywood*, op. cit., p. 5 and p. 22.

30. Carol Shields, op. cit., p. 218.
31. Cynthia A. Freeland, *The Naked and the Undead: Evil and the Appeal of Horror* (Boulder, Colorado: Westview Press, 2000), p. 223.
32. Ibid., p. 219.
33. Ibid., p. 218.
34. See Magistrale, *The Shining Reader*, op. cit., pp. 94–95.
35. See Conner, op. cit., p. 28 and Collings, op. cit., p. 59.
36. Stephen King, 'Shine of the times', an interview with Marty Ketchum, Pat Cadigan and Lewis Shiner cited in Underwood and Miller (eds.), op. cit., p. 122.
37. Collings, op. cit., p. 62.
38. Magistrale, op. cit., p. 100.
39. George Beahm, *The Stephen King Story*, (London: Warner Books, 1994), p. 118.
40. See Ciment, op. cit., p. 187.
41. Ibid., p. 8.
42. Stephen King, '1408' in *Everything's Eventual*, (London: Hodder and Stoughton, 2002), pp. 448–449.
43. Ibid., p. 452.
44. Clover, op. cit., p. 44.
45. Crane, op. cit., p. 2.
46. Ibid.
47. Harold Bloom, *The Anxiety of Influence*, (Oxford: Oxford University Press), p. 14.
48. Christine Gledhill, in 'Genre' in Pam Cook (ed.), *The Cinema Book* (London: British Film Institute 1985), p. 63.

CONCLUSION

'It wasn't horror – not quite'. (*Gerald's Game*)[1]

Van Gennep's anthropological theories about rites-of-passage rituals have a useful parallel in terms of film viewing. If a film is 'consumed' within a cinema environment, we enter a dark place amongst strangers, experience something akin to a limbo state, the exact like of which we have not seen before, possibly learn something about ourselves and emerge some two hours later to re-engage with the world. If the film is a pure genre film, meeting all of our expectations, we may return to the world much as we left it but, if our generic expectations have been challenged, we are somehow changed and we may feel that we are not exactly the same person who went into the cinema. This may also operate at the level of expanding our awareness of the possibilities of film or it may represent a change in attitudes to broader issues in the world around us. Watching a film becomes a rite-of-passage experience. The greater our generic boundaries have been stretched, within our own personal levels of tolerance, the greater level of disorientation we may feel.

In approaching almost any film, viewers bring with them a set of generic expectations, against which a new film is compared. The result is a kind of palimpsest, leading to pleasure where the match is either exact or close enough to be recognizable. Where the match appears to be too poor, the difference between expectations and experience too radical, viewers may react with confusion, disappointment and possibly even anger. A key problem with many of the King adaptations in this book is that either they fail to challenge the generic expectations with which they are most logically associated or, in a few cases, notably *Cujo* and *The Shining*, they are misrepresented at the marketing stage as belonging to a genre – horror – not borne out by the majority of the text.

In Oscar terms, King's adaptations are most warmly received when they feature redeeming sentiment (*Shawshank*, *The Green Mile*) or outlandish eccentricity (Piper

Laurie in *Carrie* and Kathy Bates in *Misery*). There is recognition, too, of the difficulty of conveying repressed emotion, especially women being bullied or abused (Sissy Spacek and Kathy Bates in *Carrie* and *Dolores Claiborne*), although it is tempting again to see a moralistic redemptive element in both examples of the latter. Male suffering (James Caan in *Misery*), direction generally (Frank Darabont – nominated for Best Adapted screenplay but not direction; Golden Globe but not Oscar winner, Rob Reiner, for *Stand by Me*), and art design where it seems to be transparent (Terence Marsh's giant prison set for *Shawshank*, which many assumed was shot on location), are less publicly recognized. The effective elements from the best films are due to the contributions of ambitious direction (De Palma with *Carrie*), intelligent scripting (Cronenberg with *The Dead Zone*) and powerful performances, which should also be partially attributed to the direction (Kathy Bates and James Caan in *Misery*, Ian McKellen in *Apt Pupil*, Anthony Hopkins in *Hearts in Atlantis*, Christopher Walken in *The Dead Zone* or the four protagonists in *Stand by Me*). As Herron points out, 'a "Stephen King movie", as we now know, looks just like *Maximum Overdrive*'.[2]

Conner talks about the possibility of dividing films into two categories: those with and those without the writer's involvement.[3] However, things are not that simple. King's involvement as a writer ranges from none at all (Kubrick's *The Shining*), to virtually none (*The Lawnmower Man*) to contested/uncredited (*Cujo*), to partial (*The Dead Zone*), to collaborative (*Creepshow*) to complete (*Pet Sematary*). That said, whatever his level of overt involvement, his standard deal, including script approval, means he bears a substantial responsibility for the films made if they carry his name above the title. Critics persistently assume (often wrongly) than an author is the person best placed to comment on his own written work, or on adaptations derived from it, without arguing why this should be so. As critic Bill Warren notes, 'Stephen King is not the best person to adapt Stephen King to the screen'.[4] It is always debatable how well an author knows his or her own work, a point that King himself has admitted.[5] In the case of *The Dead Zone*, scriptwriter Jeffrey Boam went as far as to say that King 'missed the point of his own book' – the impossibility of emotional and social denial.[6]

It is also debatable how well King actually understands film. Herron puts this rather more bluntly – 'every time King makes a statement about the art of film he sounds like a moronic twelve-year-old'.[7] Whilst certainly no masterpiece, King describes *Cujo* as 'this big dumb slugger of a movie … [i]t has no finesse,' skipping over the marital subtext and the orchestration of the climactic battle.[8] At the same time, he calls much of *Carrie*, the film which helped him become a global brand, 'light and frothy' and as a 'surprisingly folly'.[9] He claims that 'as a kid in Connecticut I watched the *Million Dollar Movie* over and over again. You begin to see things as you write – in a frame like a movie screen', and yet still had little idea of film form when he tried to direct *Maximum Overdrive*. He claims to 'know my right from my left in any scene', which, along with the positioning of furniture, might be considered more basic imaginative geography than purely filmic.[10]

His dismissive comments of directors like Scorsese or Kubrick, whom he implies make a very different kind of movie than he is interested in ('[s]ophisticated movies demand sophisticated reactions from their audiences... [h]horror movies are not sophisticated'), ironically perpetuate the high/low artistic divide that he rails against in a literary context.[11] Furthermore, he seems to have a fairly low opinion of the medium generally ('I can't think of half a dozen movies that would compare with the books that spawned them') and those who make them ('[m]ost movie people are pinheads').[12] He assumes a Hollywood business model, based around committee-orientated, low-risk mediocrity, which he contrasts with auteur-driven, integrity-rich projects, a view also uncritically accepted by Magistrale. King's attitude to the horror is highly judgemental, dismissing the work of Wes Craven at a swipe and asserting that critics often 'don't know what they are seeing' but at the same time, arguing that 'the gross-out is art'.[13]

Describing the difference between literature and film, he claims:

> because I am one person and I do everything myself, the creative instrument I use is like a scalpel, it cuts deftly and deep. With films, every time you add another layer of production, the surface gets blunted more and widens.[14]

He does have a knowledge of film history, particularly relating to the horror/sci-fi genres, and it is certainly true that his fiction is replete with references to moments in specific films. However, there is a gap, again reflected in critical works upon his films, between having seen films and being able to analyse how they work – symbolized in the forced admission during the filming of *Overdrive*, that he did not know about 'crossing the continuity line', a basic building block of conventional film grammar.[15] In this light, his comments about the director of *The Shining*, a film which can be read explicitly about film-making, as having 'a basic ignorance of the field' and 'not very good at casting', producing 'a maddening, perverse, and disappointing film', can seem fairly arrogant.[16] On the one hand we have a director credited as the driving creative force behind some of the most innovative and influential works in cinematic history, such as *Lolita*, *Dr Strangelove* (1964), *2001*, *A Clockwork Orange* (1971), *Barry Lyndon* (1975) and *Full Metal Jacket* (1987), amongst others, compared, on the other hand, to King's sole directorial experience – the highly-unambitious and deeply-flawed *Maximum Overdrive*.

In general, in comments by King, one often finds a conflation of 'visual' with 'cinematic'. King buys into the notion of himself as a cinematic writer. When signing copies of *Night Shift*, 'what I usually sign is, "I hope you've enjoyed these one-reel movies", which is essentially what they are.'[17] Such a phrase might be true in terms of the time that it takes to read one, i.e. about twenty minutes, and it might suggest some link to King's own childhood in the 1950s when movies certainly played an important part in his life. However, it does not follow that the two art forms work in the same way. There is also an important underlying point to his choice of phrase.

Short stories need fleshing out if they are to make successful films. The key question is how. It might seem easier to expand short stories than reduce massive novels to a 90-page screenplay but both processes need a blend of ruthlessness and creativity. It is worth noting that of the adaptations most commonly seen as critical (and commercial) successes (*Carrie*, *The Shawshank Redemption*, *Stand by Me*, *Misery*, *Apt Pupil*, *The Green Mile*), not one script was written by King. Even *The Dead Zone* and *The Shining*, where he had some contested involvement, bear the mark of their directors more than the original source. By contrast, the greater his writing/directing involvement in a project becomes, the poorer the eventual result, with an extreme example in *Maximum Overdrive*. Not all reviewers are impressed by King's ability as a scriptwriter – in reference to *Sleepwalkers*, Susan Wloszczyna sniped that 'ol' Cujo Breath can come up with his own lousy script.'[18] Cronenberg described King's rejected script for *The Dead Zone* as 'a really ugly, unpleasant slasher script', which opened with Stillson torturing a child and gave little context of Johnny's past.[19]

Increasingly, what occurs in King adaptations is a tendency to meta-textual referencing so that the ubiquitous brand names used in his fiction are replaced by references to his own work: *King-as-product-placement*. This occurs literally in his cameo appearances, which he either writes for himself or chooses. He may not appear as frequently as Hitchcock but King's choices remain interesting. His roles tend to fall into specific categories: 'fetchers-and-carriers' (Cemetery Worker in *Sleepwalkers*); commentators on main action (Truck Driver in *Creepshow 2*); satirical figures of authority (Minister in *Pet Sematary* and Gage Creed, bandleader in Stephen King's *The Shining*); hick figures of fun (the uncredited 'ATM man' in *Maximum Overdrive* and Jordy Verrill in the 'Lonesome Death of Jordy Verrill' in *Creepshow*, possibly name-checking his long-serving editor Chuck Verrill); and as parodies of himself (Insane Clown Poppy in *The Simpsons*, 1999, voice of Brian in *Frasier*, 'Merry Christmas' episode 2000, and an obsessive Red Sox baseball fan, i.e. himself, in *Fever Pitch*, the Farrelly Bros., 2005). He has no illusions about his qualities as an actor. His appearances provide a game for die-hard King fans to spot him, constituting a more populist version of what David Bordwell describes as a feature of European art films – the *cognoscenti* are challenged to spot a stylistic feature and by doing so they are marked as one of a select few.[20]

This visual referencing extends to King's own preferences in cult films seen or heard on-screen – in *Tales From the Darkside*, TVs playing in the background of scenes provide references for fans of Romero, who may hear snippets of *Dawn of the Dead* (1978) in 'Lot 249' and *Martin* (1977) in 'Cat From Hell'. Through the late 1980s and 1990s, this intertextual referencing occurs less often, but include King's momentary tongue-in-cheek appearance as a romantic hunk on the cover of 'Misery's Return' in *Misery*, paralleled by Kathy Bates dusting Vera's collection of porcelain pigs in *Dolores Claiborne*. *Cat's Eye* probably represents an overload situation – beyond this, a 90-minute film cannot support the number of King films which might be mentioned without becoming a kind of episodic *Scary Movie*, where forward narrative momentum is hamstrung by setting up the next visual gag. In portmanteau films, with their inherent episodic quality, this is less important, perhaps, but in a feature film it becomes just a distraction. The sheer number of films also means that whilst there are probably few people on the planet with access to a television who have never seen a film based on a King text, albeit unwittingly, the number who have seen them all is relatively small.

What this mixture of King as brand name and blatant product placement produces is a very obvious example of author intrusion, one of the key things that King rails against in his fiction. Granted, many of his films have little direct involvement from him, but many do. His script, Producer and Director approval package, his standard cameo, his increasingly frequent role as Executive Producer and his visible publicity around the time of a film's release mean he cannot easily distance himself from the films – their weaknesses as well as their strengths. This culture of appropriation also appears to the point in *Cat's Eye*, where it almost becomes the subject of the film. As Herron notes, '[i]f only in-jokes could make a movie... but it doesn't work that way.'[21]

Fourteen reasons why King texts resist adaptation

It is not completely facetious to note the rather ridiculously portentous tag-line used on King's books for a while by Hodder & Stoughton: 'Words are his power'. Perhaps this is literally so. Clearly, films involve words too, most obviously via the script, but they are primarily a visual medium. Books-on-tape of a number of his works have also proved popular. Might it be that King's works work best in a purely verbal medium? The slogan was later replaced by the more factually-accurate 'The Number One Bestseller' or the more modest 'His New Bestseller'. That said, there are more specific reasons why King adaptations often disappoint:

1. In-built obsolescence

Clearly not a fan, reviewer Joe Queenan described King's fiction as '[big], dumb, plodding and obvious, Mr King's books are the equivalent of heavy metal'.[22] However, the weakest film adaptations from his work also display similar features. The music comparison is instructive and reflects what King likes to have playing while writing and uses when given the opportunity to direct. Those films frequently deemed critical successes draw upon music that complement the aesthetic of the film with a degree of subtlety, such as *Secret Window* (Philip Glass), *Stand by Me* (B.B. King), *The Shining* (an eclectic mix of Wendy Carlos, Rachel Elking, György Ligeti, Krzysztof Penderecki and Béla Bartok) and of course *Shawshank* (Mozart). By contrast we have AC/DC in *Maximum Overdrive* and The Ramones in *Pet Sematary* (in which Louis even uses 'Dee Dee Ramone' as an assumed name). In print, King often draws music from American rock and roll of the 1950s and 1960s, possibly linked to his own childhood. In period pieces like *Stand by Me* this works fine but in a mainstream movies this may not mesh with the 16–35 demographic of contemporary audiences. If all narratives featuring childhood are set in the 1950s or 1960s, that is inherently limiting and open to accusations of nostalgia. Carpenter's powerful, self-composed keyboard refrains that add suspense to *Assault on Precinct 13* and *Halloween* are replaced in the film of *Christine* by the much more obvious, melody-based, snatches from existing 1950s songs, chosen purely to provide a one-dimensional gag.[23]

2. Characterization

Despite priding himself on characterization ('I don't care how the gadgets work; I care how the people work'), elsewhere King admits that 'if I can have a situation, if I can have an opening scene, if I can see a progression to an end, then I can write the book. The characters don't matter.'[24] Basic motivation is often severely lacking, only underlined by clumsy expositional scenes, often placed near the end the end of narratives, forcing characters to expound ridiculous theories on subjects they could not possibly know, like Marty on werewolves in *Silver Bullet* or *Maximum Overdrive*'s comet explanation, which suffers by comparison with John Wyndham's integrated ambiguity in *Day of the Triffids*. There are also potential differences between how King views characterization and how film directors see this issue. The speed of Arnie Cunningham's transformation in the film of *Christine* or Jack Torrance's breakdown in *The Shining* (1980) may unsettle some viewers but it is possible that Carpenter and Kubrick, respectively, view characterization as a process of revelation rather than actual change: the more we see of characters, the more we see of their deeper nature, which was always there but dormant. It is a little like Wittgenstein's notion of 'aspect dawning', that it is impossible to see a visual image in two contrasting ways absolutely simultaneously but there comes a moment when we shift from one to the other and for some viewers it can be too big a shift to easily accept.

3. Politics out

Typically, political elements are excised as too difficult, diffuse and possibly dated. Thus the film *Hearts in Atlantis* strips out the core from the book about Vietnam; *The Dead Zone* moves the Stillson plot into the final third rather than opening and centring the narrative; The Shop in *Firestarter* is cut down to a shadowy, somewhat ridiculous, clichéd body, whose function in the film narrative remains unclear; and the portrayal of government agencies at war with one another, running roughshod over civil liberties in times of national crises are marginalized in *Dreamcatcher* amidst all the special effects. There is also politics with a small 'p' in the sense of lengthy narratives, often filled with a panoply of minor characters who resist being reduced in the adaptation process, resulting in strange hybrids that were initially conceived as movies but only really work as a two or three-part TV mini-series (like *Needful Things*, *It*, *Salem's Lot* and *The Stand*). This local 'colour' is something which diehard King fans certainly miss. One reason *The Dead Zone* does work is because Cronenberg, despite the fact that politics and melodrama are like kryptonite for him ('I try to completely clear my head of all the intellectual and cerebral considerations of the times I live in'), elects to blend the politics with the more generic, Norman Rockwell-style portrayal of small-town America, rather than link it to a specific issue (Vietnam in the book).[25]

4. Film audiences are more intelligent than Studios (and King) appear to think

King's glowing description of *Maximum Overdrive* as 'a wonderful moron picture' underestimates viewers' capacity for visual sophistication.[26] For example, there is a tendency in King adaptations to literalize their central metaphor: *The Dark Half's* more violent literary alter ego becomes an actual murderer and the 'memory warehouse' in *Dreamcatcher* becomes an actual warehouse. Even the shot that Magistrale strangely feels critically neglected in *The Shining*, when Jack looks down at the model of the maze, is fairly obviously a parallel for his mind (hence the brain-like layout), the labyrinthine nature of the hotel corridors, and the means of Danny's final escape by intuiting how his father's mind works. Even fans of Kubrick might admit that it is just too blatant and intrusive as a device. However, King's novel does feature Danny showing his mother a wasp's nest he has found and 'for one comic-horrible moment Wendy thought it was a brain'.[27] It is still more subtle than the King-scripted remake which uses a boiler as the means to convey increasing pressure on Jack and which predictably explodes at the end. This crushing literalism finds its apotheosis in this film when, rather than using a set and sound stage to create something new as Kubrick does, King favours the actual location where he conceived the novel. For all the interviews that King did around the time of the release of *Dreamcatcher*, claiming that he was breaking the cancer-related taboo about what goes on behind the toilet door, essentially audiences were faced with a turd-like CGI monster that wants to kill people.

5. Double standards between attitudes to film and to print

Courtney Mead, the actor who played Danny Torrance in *The Shining* (1997), could legally purchase a copy of King's novel in a bookstore but could not rent a copy of the film, even though he actually starred in it. In a digital age, one might argue about the effectiveness of the concept of age as a 'gatekeeper' but with a censorious apparatus surrounding the visual media, possibly with the added factor that King movies are also regularly shown on network TV, adaptations frequently have scenes of graphic violence excised (such as the death of the cop being run over by a lawnmower in the novel of *Misery*), or the film is given an R-rating for cinematic release in the US, signalling a commercial death knell (as experienced by *Maximum Overdrive* and *Silver Bullet*), especially since these films also seem fatally mis-pitched, thereby satisfying neither family audiences nor gore-hounds. From *Carrie* onwards, one of the legacies of King is to bring horror fiction into the mainstream. At the same time, features of horror films that used to be only seen in specialist fare, and gain an obligatory R-rating, are now appearing in 'family' films. Gore Verbinski's *Pirates of the Caribbean* (2003) and its sequels feature murderous undead pirates, whose limbs can be lopped off and yet still function à la Robert Wiene's 1924 *The Hands of Orlac*, which spawned a whole subgenre of horror films featuring unkillable hands. Along with the revival of the teen slasher, as in *Scream I*, *II* and *III* (Wes Craven, 1996, 1997, 2000), and their later egos in overt parodies such as *Scary Movie*, there is an increasingly fragmented horror market in which devotees are finding more extreme, often sadistic, franchises, rarely shown on network TV. With the evolution of the sadism of *Saw* (James Wan, 2004), *Saw II* and *III* (Darren Lynn Bousman, 2005, 2006); *Hostel I* and *II* (Eli Roth, 2005, 2007) and the game-playing motifs of *Cube* (Vincenzo Natali, 1997), *Cube 2: Hypercube* (Andrzej Sekula, 2002) and *Cube Zero* (Ernie Barbarash, 2004), it is hard to see a place for a King-related horror movie, except in the mainstream. Such audiences are unlikely to find their dose of 'gross-out' in a King adaptation, made directly for, or ultimately finding its natural resting place amongst, TV schedules of fairly conservative, censorious broadcasters. In the last decade or so, King adaptations have shifted closer to mainstream entertainment with isolated horrific scenes, and all of the critically-acclaimed films have occurred outside the horror genre.

6. Generic differences between film and literature, specific to King's style
Even as early as *Rage*, King, in his writing, uses italics to show the interior thoughts of characters, especially the protagonist, for example in *Cujo, Dolores Claiborne, Misery, The Shining, Pet Sematary* and *Apt Pupil*. How to show interior states of mind has always been a problem for film. It is possible to use voiceover or more subtle techniques like expressionist symbolism, as in *The Cabinet of Dr Caligari* (Robert Wiene, 1920), which Romero does in the lighting and framing of *Creepshow,* but the technique is so prominent in King's work that readers may not engage so strongly with character motivation in the films as they did with the book. The film of *Cujo* cannot give us the dog's thoughts like the novel without evoking an aesthetic like Disney or films like *Babe* (Chris Noonan, 1995). Extended voiceover is possible but this is a clumsy cinematic tool from which most directors shy away – *The Shawshank Redemption*, as discussed, is an extremely rare example of where this works. Garris uses it in his remake of *The Shining* to convey telepathic thought between Halloran and Danny, which is effective enough at the level of basic comprehension, but Kubrick does not, creating a more enigmatic effect. A further technique that King uses exacerbates this difficulty as he often creates not just one interior voice but two in a very contrived dialogue between sides of a character's consciousness, as in *Rose Madder*. *Apt Pupil* presents a particular problem here as the italicized interior thoughts of Todd Bowden strongly foreshadow Patrick Bateman's misogynistic, murderous ranting in Brett Easton Ellis' *American Psycho* (1991), so that we are not always sure whether such feelings have actually been spoken aloud. It is more than a passing similarity, since in the novella, like Bateman, Bowden channels his sadistic sexual fantasies into acts of violence on the detritus of society, killing a tramp for no good reason – a 'rough edge' to the narrative that is smoothed over in the adaptation. King's *Apt Pupil* and *Dolores Claiborne* also use a character, Dussander and Dolores respectively, to speak thoughts aloud to themselves. The adaptations retain a little of this but film is more squeamish of such an overtly theatrical device, which audiences may more commonly associate with mental illness.

A favourite technique of King is a deliberately-misleading flash-forwards to generate tension, particularly around a character death. In *Cujo*, we are told that Brett Camber 'never saw his father alive again'; in *Dreamcatcher*, we are told Duddits 'would die a child, and long before he turned forty'; and in *Pet Sematary*, we are told that Gage 'now had less than two months to live'.[28] The actual death of Gage in King's novel is reminiscent of John Irving's *The World According to Garp* (1978), where the death of a young child, Walt, is skipped over and we have to piece together the chain of events from fragments of information given by traumatized adults, in retrospect. In film, the flash-forward is a rarely-used device as it tends to destroy suspense and signal the possession of some supernatural ability, like Donald Sutherland's character in Nic Roeg's *Don't Look Now,* or foreground the presence of the director deliberately, as used by directors of *la nouvelle vague*. It can also signal a comedic moment, as in Steven Spielberg's *Jaws* (1977), when the sarcastic question from Matt Hooper (Richard Dreyfuss) 'Have you got a better idea?' is answered by a jump cut, effectively a jump forward in time, to a close-up of a shark cage. A further stylistic tic, particularly in King's later work, is for a character to use a term for an idea or an image, which is almost instantly picked up by other characters without question (like 'deathbag' in *Insomnia* or 'phoners' in *Cell*).

7. King's attachment to subgenres that are played out

He seems to retain an interest in horror icons that are largely redundant in filmic terms, like the mummy in *Creepshow II* and the werewolf in *Silver Bullet*. This is closely linked with the 1950s in a simplistic fear of domestic technology or the landing of hostile aliens (continued in *Dreamcatcher*), which have little contemporary cinematic credibility and closer to parody. Machines running out of control are more likely to yield a **batteries not included*-style film, most probably aimed at children. Allied to this, there is the sense that plotlines are recycled. Any prolific artist is likely to have recurrent concerns but King seems particularly dependent on *The Monkey's Paw* for dramatic impetus: the idea that you should be careful what you wish for, resurfacing in *Apt Pupil*, *Pet Sematary* and even *1408*, where Enslin claims that '[n]othing would make me happier than to experience a paranormal event' just before being overwhelmed by several of them.

8. The visualization of evil

Apt Pupil works, in part, because it is played out in recognizable, small-scale human terms. By contrast, the unmasking of an otherworldly monster is often the point at which a film is greatly weakened. A reader may have many different images in his or her head but a filmmaker can only choose one to put on screen. The relatively vague description in the novel of *Dreamcatcher* of the 'shit weasels' has to be realized by a specific effect. This also extends to those films focusing on characters with a psychic gift, which requires a special effect to show what they can do. As King recognizes, 'the writer is much more fortunate than the filmmaker, who is almost always doomed to show too much...including, in nine cases out of ten, the zipper running up the monster's back.'[29]

As King notes, 'the artistic work of horror is almost always a disappointment' because ultimately '[y]ou have to open the door and show the audience what's behind it'.[30] Once the object of fear, usually a form of monstrosity, is revealed, in the words of theorist W.H. Rockett, it 'becomes finite' and therefore manageable.[31] This is certainly true in films like *Pet Sematary*, which set up an interesting first half only to be followed by a predictable 'gruefest'. Rockett's solution is to follow Lovecraft in violating norms of the genre by allowing chaotic events to occur and remain unexplained, in effect to spin out the period of Todorovian hesitation without end. Thus, to create real terror, a filmmaker would give us generic conventions as a 'crutch' by which we might codify and normalize our reaction to unexpected events only, then, to pull them away and leave us disorientated. However, this is some way away from King's own definition of effective horror films, which he declares 'were always supposed to be fun'.[32]

A further problem relates to the genres with which King is most closely associated. Both horror and science fiction require a leap of the imagination to imagine something that has no objective correlative in the real world. It becomes more difficult for readers, and therefore viewers of film versions, to necessarily share a common visualization of the purely fictitious. This difficulty partly explains a tendency in adaptation to diminish fantastical or supernatural elements, like the cutting of the 'dust bunnies' from *Dolores Claiborne* or Shooter-as-ghost seen in *Secret Window*. This problem is exacerbated when inanimate objects are supposedly imbued with evil – the difficulty with King's *The Shining*, which Kubrick displaces onto his cast. Possessed objects, whether it be a car (*Christine*) a truck (*Maximum Overdrive*) or a dog (*Cujo*), are hard to convey convincingly if they look exactly like something from the known world. King may describe Cujo as 'some creature from hell', and explicitly tells us that Donna 'knew that the dog was something more than just a dog', but that may not be the impression we get when faced by a large St Bernard covered with shaving foam.[33] In *Pet Sematary*, the addition of glowing eyes and snarling sound effects for Churchill do not suddenly make a cuddly cat scary (even the bringing of killed vermin to a master is natural behaviour).

9. Lack of generic ambition

Thematically, King's novels break little new ground. He lists typical themes: 'how difficult it is…to close Pandora's technobox once it's open'; 'the thin line between reality and fantasy'; 'the terrible attraction violence has for fundamentally good people'; 'the fundamental differences between children and adults'; and 'the healing power of the human imagination'.[34] Those films that have been grouped in 'The Rise of the Machines', (chapter 5, this volume) are typically unambitious. In King's novels they might have a social or even political subtext but, in the films, the only resonance they carry is the 'machines-running-out-of-control' motif, overtly from 1950s sci-fi (but not original even then, dating back to German Expressionism of the 1920s). Problematically, film audiences are not only surrounded by machines and labour-saving devices, many of these are sentient and to which we, for the most part, are completely accustomed. King's assertions, such as 'we have been betrayed by our machines and processes of mass production' simply do not tally with people's daily experience.[35] That is not to say that the dangers posed by technology are no longer present (they have arguably increased) but automation has been normalized and integrated into everyday life. The small-scale examples of frustrations at machine malfunctions, like the electric knife in *Maximum Overdrive*, sound a recognizable note of plausibility. However, when machines become malevolent for no apparent reason and gain the power of moving beyond their physical restrictions, they become mere figurative antagonists that offer no believable threat. *Christine* is a slight exception to this as the car acts as a surrogate for Arnie Cunningham's libido, destroying his high school tormentors. However, typically for films in this section, the machines only possess an exaggeration of their expected operating functions. The only otherworldly power the car seems to have, apart from the Herbie-like ability to drive on its own, is the ability to renovate itself, and neither of these is, in itself, frightening. For those who do not share King's personal suspicion of technology, scenes like the ATM machine in *Maximum Overdrive* running out of control are more likely to evoke slapstick comedy than horror.

As King himself recognizes, horror is historically a conservative genre with monsters killed, villains punished and convincing narrative resolution the norm. Films only tend to be memorable milestones in the development of the genre if they are prepared to step outside this genre convention, like *Night of the Living Dead*. However, this level of ambition is rarely visible. Most genre pieces operate safely within recognizable conventions. On the other hand, few of the adaptations could really be said to be trying to transcend their genre – it is profitable for Studios to give audiences more of what they appear to want rather than challenge and extend what they might accept. The indeterminacy with which *Silver Bullet* closes (where, despite reverting to human form, Lowe's final 'surprise', i.e., sitting bolt upright and giving one last snarl after being shot) is almost a generic feature by 1985 (and a clear *Carrie* rip-off), and the slight extension of werewolf lore that Lowe can elect to transform himself at times other than the full moon is more to speed up the narrative than challenge genre conventions. King's novels are often limited by place (frequently around the quasi-fictional Derry). Films like *Stand by Me* and *Pet Sematary* (which King insisted should be shot in Maine to boost the local economy) have established this small-town American setting in the minds of a global audience as 'King country', helping to define the 'King brand', but this may also create a certain similarity in the minds of audiences, blurring some of the films mentioned in this book.

In the novel of *Cujo*, King describes the climactic attack of the rabid dog at Donna's car window 'like a horror-movie monster that has decided to give the audience the ultimate thrill by coming right out of the screen.'[36] Lewis Teague gives us a close-up of the window and a sudden object looming into the frame, along with a loud sound effect. It might make us jump but the kind of effect King is describing, one he comes back to in 'The Sun Dog', is only used as a simile. Filmmakers have to translate the written word into something visual, describe something as if it were something else, i.e., use a visual metaphor. Clive Barker's short story 'Son of Celluloid' (1984) also describes the apparently permeable membrane of a cinema screen but provides an alternative glimpse of a more challenging realization, making the outbreak literal as the emotions of audiences are projected onto monsters that break through the screen. Barker's text might not make a better film but it is cinematic in a way that King's is not. Ironically, King mentions how he overcame his kids' preference for sitting right at the front in movie theatres by telling them that people in the background shots had been sitting too close and fallen into a hole in the screen.[37] Without the recourse to 3-D technology, the genuinely frightening effect that King alludes to becomes a flat 2-D cheap shock in Lewis Teague's slow-motion sequence in the denouement where Cujo jumps through a window of the house (which is not in King's novel).

10. Generic confusion

Work by theorists like Steve Neale concludes that genre expectations and pleasures are drawn from a tension between the known and the unknown. Overall, the films in this book often disappoint in terms of either not stretching generic boundaries or being wrongly-marketed. Studios sometimes appear unaware of what they have purchased. Dazzled by the King brand, they promote films assuming them to be horror when actually they are not. Generically, horror is not as dominant in the King oeuvre as might at first appear. Despite posters and refashioned novel covers, *Carrie* is a high school rite of passage, *The Running Man* and *Dreamcatcher* are overt science fiction, *Firestarter* and *The Dead Zone* (both originally overtly political novels) are also close to science fiction, with the latter also a tragic love story. *Shawshank* and *The Green Mile* are prison dramas, *Misery* is a psychological thriller and *Dolores Claiborne* is a family drama. *Secret Window*, *The Dark Half* and even *The Shining* might be seen as studies in mental breakdown. *Cujo*, *Maximum Overdrive* (despite its R-rating) and *Cat's Eye* only offer horror muted and domesticated for a mainstream audience, where real shocks are few and often couched in in-jokes. Besides, both *Cujo* and *Cat's Eye* are actually two-thirds domestic/marital comedy, with a final section closer to horror, and *Maximum Overdrive* is a siege narrative: a mechanical version of John Wayne's *The Alamo* (1960). The surface narratives of the films (and the texts upon which they are based), at times, conceal a different but related narrative. *Silver Bullet* shows less interest in the basics of lycanthropy (lunar phases, transformation scenes and tragically spliced identities) than disruption to the life of a small American town; less *Jekyll and Hyde* than *To Kill a Mocking Bird* (an impression increased by the choice of the protagonist's older sister as main narrator). In general, as Tessier describes it, these are 'hybrid entertainments' likely to yield a mixture of pleasures and reactions, confusion and disappointment amongst them.[38]

With the exception of Dolores Claiborne, Wendy Torrance and especially Donna Trenton, there are very few characters in the adaptations discussed in this book that could be considered Final Girls. In the case of Donna and Wendy, they both undergo lengthy and traumatic threats to their lives but their prime motivation is not self-survival but the protection of their sons – their nurturing role is their prime motivation. The key characteristic they share is that they all survive and in the circumstances in which they find themselves, that constitutes heroism. Perhaps more, they all show a readiness to inflict physical pain in order to survive (Dolores' plot with the well, Donna wielding a baseball bat and even Wendy stabbing blindly with a knife). However, there are differences too. Even if we define femininity along the very narrow grounds of physical attraction, although Donna has enough physical appeal to draw the attentions of a jealous lover and regain the attention of her husband by the end, Wendy is granted none of this. She is closer to the stereotypical, passive female victim, whose screaming face, held in close-up, dominates film posters and promotional material. She escapes largely by luck rather than cunning. It is Danny who has to both save himself and fool the 'monster' in the maze. In an age of family breakdown, perhaps the real Final Girls are those women who are strong enough to break away from an abusive partner and raise their children independently.

11. Compromised endings

King admits that he is 'a sentimentalist at heart' and certainly a number of his narratives have been ameliorated, particularly the endings.[39] Apart from De Palma's bravura sudden shock ending of *Carrie* (something which he repeated in *Dressed to Kill*), the films in this study hardly distinguish themselves with strong finishes. King's script for *The Shining* (1997), rather than his initial conception in which Danny and his mother have their brains smashed out or the Kubrick version with father frozen out in the maze, has a ghost father blowing Danny a kiss at his graduation. If his criticism of Kubrick is that he is a 'man who thinks too much and feels too little', then, in relation to film, his own weakness may be that he thinks too little and feels too much.[40] The script for *Cujo*, to which he contributed and of which he approved, has the boy, Tad, recover (although since he was licked by a rabid dog, a grisly fate may await him beyond the end of the film). Even the critical success of *Stand by Me* distracts audience's attention from the fate of the boys in the book – beaten up by Ace Merrill's gang and all but Gordie dying young in violent accidents, rather than sadly fading away in a cursory voiceover explanation. King's *The Dark Half*, in which Thad Beaumont defeats his own demons, but at the price of his marriage and his sanity, only retains the first half of the equation in Romero's film. Even stories which, in print, remain balanced or open, almost always end with a comforting sense of narrative closure on film. In King's 'The Ledge', Norris waits for Cressner, preparing to shoot him if he does not already fall, but in the film we see (and hear) his life transferred to an absurd little horn. In King's *Apt Pupil*, the cat gets graphically cooked rather than scampering away, and the written narrative ends with Todd Bowden heading off to become a freeway sniper before being shot himself, rather than the film version which, even though portraying Todd as manipulative, shows him with 'his life opening up before him', as his guidance counsellor, Mr French, describes it. As scriptwriter George Goldsmith expresses it, 'it's okay sometimes if the protagonist dies at the end but it's not often that the film succeeds commercially'.[41] For Kermode, the ending of *Shawshank* is a disaster:

this finale reduces the fantastical possibilities of the narrative, in which escapist myth and cinematic magic are splendidly conjoined, to the level of an oddly down-to-earth climax in which a beach and a boat are the greatest rewards imaginable.[42]

However, this is a good example of how genre expectations will not be denied. Darabont's (and King's) original ending, with a bus heading off into the distance, was rejected by test audiences who demanded more demonstrable closure in bringing the two together in a vision of an earthly paradise.

In the rare cases where the counter-movement holds true – King's endings made bleaker on film – this is often symptomatic of an aesthetic approach which is more ambitious, even if not always successful: in King's 'The Raft', Randy waits for death, but in the film he thinks he survives, only to be swallowed by the slick. In *1408*, Enslin is rescued in King's text as a famous burns victim but dies in the film (only to be resurrected as a ghost in the director's cut), and in King's *Secret Garden*, Rainey is killed and his wife saved in a last minute rescue but in the film, Rainey kills his wife and lover, remains at large and gains a new burst of creativity in his writing. Perhaps it is too early to see a trend in this but both these last two films also feature unreliable narrators who attempt to twist their narrative perspective in a radical way. Both films do literalize a projection but at least they are potentially motivated by proceeding from a writer's overactive imagination. This may be seen as a gimmick, and one which some viewers might feel they could have predicted early on, but at least it shows some ambition to do something different with the narrative. Both tales, especially *1408*, resist empirical explanation, which might signal a shift to what might be termed the Kafkaesque fantastic (Enslin calls 1408 part of 'this Kafkaesque hotel'), in which characters do not question the source or reality of extraordinary events – a tendency also found in some of King's early short stories, like 'The Raft'. The two versions of *The Shining* reflect this difference. King and Garris heavily signal the hotel as the cause of Jack's breakdown; Kubrick resists such straightforward (in purely fictional terms) explanations, cutting, for example, references to drink or drugs, which could be seen as motivating Jack's behaviour, or any mention of medical experts who might explain Danny's 'shining' ability with cod psychology.

12. A lack of editing

Beahm repeats the equation of numbers of words and on-screen running time: 'A short story is a snapshot in time. A novella is a short movie. And a novel, a long movie. All are slices in time.'[43] It is certainly true, at a basic level, that a longer novel inherently requires cutting. However, it does not follow that, correspondingly, a short story is easier to make into a high quality film. By that logic, poetry, plays and short stories should be easier to write than novels, which is patently not the case. One criticism of King's written narratives which persist into the films is that of over-writing. Despite citing Quiller-Couch's 'Murder your darlings' and his second foreword in *On Writing* repeating the gnomic advice 'Omit needless words', it is advice he finds easier to give than to follow.[44] In relation to his short stories, he recognized himself that '[t]hey keep wanting to bloat ... I have a real problem with bloat'.[45]

Magistrale bewails the lack of extended extracts from 'Misery's Return' in the film, the narrative that Paul Sheldon is forced to write in captivity, and which are included in King's novel, but to do this would crush momentum from a potentially-static narrative. King is both aware of his status within the publishing and media industries and, at the same time, partly seduced by it: '[a]t this point nobody can make me change anything ... [w]here does a 10,000 pound gorilla sit? The answer is, any place he wants'.[46] He claims that he always tries 'to give good weight', overtly reducing his art to a commodity, evaluated by number of pages.[47] As far as Harlan Ellison is concerned, apart from *It* or the *Dark Tower* series, 'I can't think of any King novels ... that could not have been told just as well as a novella' and that he is not getting 'the kind of editing he needs'.[48] The commercial phenomenon that King has become, in both his written works and in related films, has in many ways immunized the works (in both media) from criticism and done a disservice to both.

13. Weight of expectation
Other novelists like Tom Clancy or Michael Crichton have had several of their works adapted, too, but in terms of worldwide sales, no one competes with King's current global dominance, which creates an unparalleled level of expectation for each King-related release. As King himself describes it: 'I started out as a storyteller; along the way I became an economic force,'[49] The weight of expectation increases massively when there is also a director or star with their own army of admirers – such is certainly the case when Kubrick directed *The Shining*. This affects critical responses, producing a futile, fidelity-obsessed search for the holy grail of a 'faithful' adaptation, without any real understanding of what that might actually look like. Strangely, King's own objection to adapting *The Dark Tower* series also manifests this tendency. His is a standard complaint that a particular film's realization of a literary character would not be what viewers/readers expect. How could it be? A given text can often be read in a wide variety of ways. Magistrale stumbles across this realization, en passant, drawing attention to differences between the book and film of *Dolores Claiborne*: 'the novel and film emerge as uniquely separate entities, two widely varying renditions of the same story', ironically missing the point that this is true of all cinematic adaptations.[50] Similarly, he states that 'individual scenes in Kubrick's cinema must be 'read' carefully, in a process that is akin to experiencing a poem or viewing a complex oil painting', but only accords this to particular films, earmarked as high art worthy of analysis, contradicting his early stridency in making no distinction between high and low art.[51]

14. Dependency on inert plots
King's admission, that several stories, both in print and on screen, began life as a single image, is also relevant. A giant prisoner waits for the old trusty who pushes a cart with a squeaky wheel (*The Green Mile*) or a car whose odometer runs

backwards (*Christine*) – in themselves these situations are static, not dramatic. King's insistence in restating in his 1997 film version many elements from the novel *The Shining*, including the initial image that sparked his interest (an animated hotel fire hose), only underlines this further. King recognizes this limitation in the genesis of his plots – '[m]ost of my fictions are simply situations that are allowed to develop themselves'.[52] Even when expressed as contingency plots, 'what ifs?', this may not necessarily lead to engaging and dramatic incident. What if a pseudonym would not accept being written out? (*The Dark Half*); What if a mother and son were trapped in a car by a rabid dog? (*Cujo*); What if a dead pet cat could be brought back to life? (*Pet Sematary*). However, as Bill Warren points out, 'horror movies, to simply be scary, often require plots and clues'.[53] Ironically, Beahm, talking of the countless King wannabes, believes that their 'most erroneous assumption … is that in fiction the idea is the story; that, they think, is all it takes' – an error of which their idol is also guilty.[54]

The Last Word
Ultimately, having a novel optioned by a film company is like putting up a child for adoption. In most cases, once they sign up, the donor has few visitation rights (certainly writers are not always welcome on set); although King's standard deal over his assembly-line style productions give him more access than most parents. Some identifiable features, which can be traced back to the original parent, may persist in the child but the most noticeable effects occur once the offspring leaves the parental arena. For some parents, the continuation of the name is important and, here, the offspring still has the ability to inflict damage upon, or enhance the prestige of, the family name. It can be a painful process and the desire for a parent to cling to their offspring is strong, fearing that it will be misunderstood. Having experienced the process many times, and having had a few *Lawnmower Man*-experiences, once a few clear ground rules have been set out, King can now afford to be more phlegmatic about the whole affair. Harlan Ellison invokes the concept of xenogenesis, the fact that some children do not look like their parents, to consider King's adaptations but it is not enough to decry the adaptations as dumbed-down, special effects exercizes, shorn of characterization and any vestige of subtlety.[55]

It is worth considering what it is about *The Shawshank Redemption* and *The Green Mile* that sets them apart from the mass of films in this study. Sensitivity to King's own work is paramount. The author himself certainly feels this as far back as Darabont's 1983 student version of 'The Woman in the Room', a short film that captures the unsettling nature of death in the family without resorting to horror clichés. One central factor, however, is the surprising fact that these films are the only ones in this book (with the exception of *Maximum Overdrive* and Kubrick's co-writing with Diane Johnson on *The Shining*) which are written and directed by the same person, allowing an investment of time and creative energy often missing elsewhere. Darabont's skill as a writer should not be overlooked. The time and care that he takes with his scripts, perhaps reflecting his earlier career as a set dresser, where attention to detail and the visual impact of such precision are both paramount, sets his work apart from many of the journeyman efforts of an average adaptation.

Both *Maximum Overdrive* and *Shawshank* feature a scene of crawling through a drainage pipe. In the film directed by King, unsympathetic characters make tasteless gags about rats and swallowing sewage; in Darabont's film, Tim Robbins struggles out and, in a rising high angle, adopts a crucifix pose against the wind, rain and darkness (used on the cover of Kermode's book). It may not be quite as iconic as Shakespeare's Lear on the blasted heath but, as the culmination of a twenty-year fight, the sheer doggedness of which has been held back, from the viewer as well as the guards in the narrative, the contrast with King's film, where the only quality being celebrated is crass stupidity, could not be starker. For all the charges of sentimentality that might be levelled at Darabont's film, at least it aspires to a larger vision of the self: a rising above the prosaic rather than an apparent revelling in it. In contrast to King's overwriting about the cell (see chapter 6), it is not just the escape itself but Dufresne's unembittered imagination that is celebrated.

Consider, too, the scene where Red finds the hidden letter. The alfalfa field by which he slowly walks was not just found, it was allowed to grow over several months and a hand-built stone wall added, to produce the powerful shot of Morgan Freeman carefully making his way in fading afternoon light as grasshoppers spectacularly fly up (albeit after some noisy encouragement from Darabont himself off-camera). Darabont is co-credited on *The Blob* (Chuck Russell, 1988) and *The Fly II* (Chris Walas, 1989) and arguably, like King, has produced his best work away from the horror genre, yet with a residual understanding of it. *Shawshank* has no supernatural horror but plenty of visceral suggestion of the horror of Andy Dufresne's fate at the hands of gang rapists. Darabont also chose to cut a sequence, near the end of the film, of a guard retracing Andy's escape and, most tellingly, of Morgan Freeman, in close-up, laughing with tears pouring down his cheeks: both decisions reflecting a willingness to allow a space for audience response rather than manipulate it unnecessarily. Indeed, part of the uplifting quality of this film is that it got made at all. Lengthy voiceovers; extended running time; the restrained portrayal of sex and violence (Norton's suicide is suggested by sound effects and a blown-out window); only one female character of any note – all are factors that should have made Studios nervous. It is the acceptance of difference in its form as well as its content which mark it as a truly remarkable film.

A further factor about the success of *Shawshank* and *The Green Mile* is generic. Since they are both prison movies, a relatively under-represented genre, it could be said, from a slightly cynical point of view, that they have fewer films against which to be judged and so can exercise a disproportionate influence on audiences. The fact that the most critically acclaimed of King's adaptations have occurred outside the horror genre may also suggest that this represents an enduring value judgement on horror (a genre rarely associated with Oscars) but, contrary to popular opinion, this is also where King's best writing lies. Despite a clear emotional attachment to the films of his youth, attempts to recreate techno-monster movies repeatedly fail whereas relatively slow-paced, human-centred, rites-of-passage narratives, set within prisons or on the cusp of adulthood, provide the most satisfying balance of meeting and exceeding generic expectations.

In studying film noir, James Naremore suggests that 'the Name of the Genre… functions in much the same way as the Name of the Author,' and, in a sense, King perpetuates auteurism by the perception that films based on his work constitute their own genre in a convergence of aesthetic and commercial needs: 'the Stephen King adaptation'.[56] In bookstores, King's works routinely occupy their own section and perhaps the time has come to do the same with the films. For Altman, 'genre films make heavy use of intertextual references,'[57] and this is reflected not just literally in the number of sequels in this book (*Creepshow*, *Carrie*, and *Pet Sematary*) and remakes (*The Shining*, and arguably *Carrie* too) but also by the possibility of spotting overt references by which fans can prove their knowledge and loyalty. Through the 1980s, King adaptations had quite low cultural capital but, over time, the sheer volume of business generated for publishers and film companies has steamrollered most criticism into, sometimes begrudging, acceptance. Somewhat out of step with contemporary trends in horror, which focus on making the infliction of pain visible, the films have shifted away from its roots in horror to the point where the brand has evolved to be more closely associated with fantastical tales which, at their best, can deliver and exceed generic expectations. Due to the sheer number of adaptations already produced, the situation has evolved so that there is the temptation to think of a King adaptation as a safe choice. From what might have been seen as radical, transgressive texts in the 1970s, the volume of films, through the 1980s in particular, has cast them as the norm: in a sense the new conservatism.

Harlan Ellison attributes King's success in large part to his ability to refashion existing ideas 'from a position of cultural currency' which, speaking in 1989, he (along with Don Herron) clearly does not expect to continue for long.[58] However, twenty years on, King has confounded such expectations and renewed currency has been injected into the adaptations by his ability to keep meeting the needs of the marketplace, advances in technology and cultural phenomenon such as TV remakes of earlier film work, like *The Shining* and *Carrie*. The dynasty continues via King's son. Joe Hill's horror tale *Heart-Shaped Box* (2007) has already been optioned and the two have collaborated on 'Throttle' in *He was Legend* (2009), a tribute to Richard Matheson, alluding to his short story 'Duel' (Steven Spielberg's 1971 breakthrough movie). Forthcoming attractions include adaptations of *From a Buick 8* (directed by Tobe Hooper), *Cell* (although some of its plot 'thunder' has been stolen by Night M. Shyamalan's 2008 *The Happening*), a threatened remake of *Children of the Corn* with Producer Donald P. Borcher's original script), the ever-expanding *Dark Tower series*, and, of course, despite having spoken of retirement more than once, King himself is still writing. He has said on different occasions that his interest in childhood, writing and monsters is fading, only to produce a further variation of these elements.[59] Despite producing *Danse Macabre* and *On Writing*, both attempts, in part, to answer oft-posed questions about the nature of writing and the horror genre in particular, the same questions keep coming. If the films were really so terrible, as some critics believe, one might expect that readers would be deterred from buying King's books, which is clearly not happening. Unfazed by poor reviews, he keeps writing and films keep being made and audiences keep coming back, effectively cutting critics out of the commercial loop. While cynics might say that this suggests something about the illiterate nature of film audiences and their short concentration spans, it may also say something about a key feature of the horror genre in particular: deferral. In a genre dominated by sequelization and metaphoric as well as literal cannibalization, there is a sense that any comment upon it can only represent the next word, rather than the final one. In the words of a piece of King juvenilia, already used for three TV-movie incarnations: 'Sometimes They Come Back'.

Notes

1. Stephen King, *Gerald's Game* (New York; London: Signet, 1993), p. 18.
2. Don Herron, *Reign of Terror*, op. cit., p. 233.
3. Jeff Conner, *Stephen King goes to Hollywood*, op. cit., p. xiv.
4. Bill Warren, cited in Magistrale, *Hollywood's Stephen King*, op. cit., p. xvi.
5. Stephen King in Underwood and Miller (eds.), *Bare Bones: Conversations on Terror with Stephen King*, op. cit., p. 69.
6. Jeffrey Boam cited in Collings, *The Films of Stephen King*, op. cit., p. 100.
7. Don Herron, op. cit., p. 225.
8. Jesse Horsting, cited in Herron, ibid. pp. 131–2.
9. Stephen King cited in Conner, p. 6 and in King, *Danse Macabre*, op. cit., p. 199.
10. Stephen King in Underwood and Miller (eds.), op. cit., p. 128.
11. Stephen King, *Danse Macabre*, op. cit., p. 228.
12. Stephen King in George Beahm, *The Stephen King Companion*, op. cit., p. 108.
13. Stephen King, *Danse Macabre*, op. cit., p. 247 and p. 219.
14. Stephen King in Magistrale, *Hollywood's Stephen King*, op. cit., p. 19.
15. See Conner, op. cit., p. viii.
16. Stephen King in Underwood and Miller (eds.), op. cit., p. 143 and p. 159; *Danse Macabre*, op. cit., p. 245.
17. Stephen King in George Beahm, *The Stephen King Story* (London: Warner Books, 1994), p. 110.
18. Susan Wloszczyna in George Beahm, *The Stephen King Story*, op. cit., p. 246.
19. David Cronenberg, in Chris Rodley, *Cronenberg on Cronenberg* (London: Faber & Faber, 1992), p. 113.
20. David Bordwell, *Narration in the Fiction Film* (New York; London, Routledge, 1985), p. 211.
21. Don Herron, op. cit., p. 228.
22. Joe Queenan in George Beahm, *The Stephen King Companion*, op. cit., p. 232.
23. See David Bernand and Miguel Mera, 'Fast and Cheap? The Film Music of John Carpenter' in Ian Conrich and David Woods, (eds.), *The Cinema of John Carpenter: The Technique of Terror* (London: Wallflower Press, 2004), pp. 49–65.

24. Stephen King in ibid., p. 426 and Underwood and Miller, op. cit., p. 115.
25. David Cronenberg, in Rodley, *Cronenberg on Cronenberg*, op. cit., p. 118.
26. Stephen King in Conner, op. cit., p. viii.
27. Stephen King, *The Shining*, op. cit., p. 115.
28. Stephen King, in *Cujo*, op. cit., p. 126; in *Dreamcatcher*, (London: New English Library, 2001), p. 202; and in *Pet Sematary*, op. cit., p. 223.
29. Stephen King, *On Writing*, op. cit., p. 203.
30. Stephen King, *Danse Macabre*, op. cit., p. 133.
31. W. H. Rockett, cited in Collings, op. cit., p. 20.
32. Stephen King, cited in Collings, p. 26.
33. Stephen King, in *Cujo*, op. cit., p. 256 and p. 237.
34. Stephen King, *On Writing*, op. cit., pp. 246–7.
35. Stephen King, *Danse Macabre*, op. cit., p. 156.
36. Stephen King, in *Cujo*, op. cit., p. 172.
37. Stephen King,in Underwood and Miller, op. cit., p. 57.
38. See Tessier in Herron, op. cit., p. 75.
39. Stephen King, cited in Magistrale, p. 13.
40. Stephen King, in George Beahm, *The Stephen King Companion*, op. cit., p. 34.
41. George Goldsmith in Stephen Jones, *Creepshow: The Illustrated Stephen King Movie Guide* (New York: Billboard Books, 2002), p. 36.
42. Mark Kermode, *The Shawshank Redemption*, op. cit., p. 86.
43. George Beahm, *The Stephen King Story*, op. cit., p. 263.
44. Stephen King, *On Writing*, op. cit., p. 233.
45. Stephen King, *Skeleton Crew*, 'Introduction' (London; Sydney: Futura, 1985), p. 6.
46. Stephen King, in George Beahm, op. cit., p. 187.
47. Stephen King, in Herron, op. cit., p. 221.
48. Harlan Ellison, in George Beahm, op. cit., p. 216 and p. 220. See also Charles Willeford expressing a similar point in Herron, op. cit., pp. 54–55.
49. Stephen King, in George Beahm, op. cit., p. 25.
50. Tony Magistrale, *Hollywood's Stephen King*, op. cit., p. 73.
51. Ibid., pp. 86–87.
52. Stephen King, in Underwood and Miller (eds.), op. cit., p. 144.
53. Bill Warren, in Herron, op. cit., p. 124.
54. Beahm, op. cit., p. 258.
55. Harlan Ellison in George Beahm, op. cit., p. 333.
56. James Naremore, 'American Film Noir: The History of an Idea', *Film Quarterly*, 49. 2 (1995–96), p. 14.
57. Rick Altman, *The American Film Musical*, op. cit., p. 25.
58. Harlan Ellison, in Beahm, op. cit., p. 217.
59. See Don Herron, op. cit., p. xiv; and King, *Four Past Midnight*, op. cit., pp. 305–7.

REFERENCES

Altman, Rick, *The American Film Musical* (Indiana: Indiana University Press, 1989).

Badley, Linda, *Film, Horror, and the Body Fantastic* (London: Greenwood Press, 1995).

Beahm, George, (ed.), *Stephen King Companion* (London; Sydney: Futura Publications, 1991).

Beahm, George, *The Stephen King Story* (London: Warner Books, 1994).

Beahm, George, *Stephen King: America's Best-loved Bogeyman* (Kansas City, Andrews McMeel Publishing, 1998).

Beahm, George, *Stephen King from A–Z: An Encyclopaedia of his Life and Work* (Kansas City, Andrews McMeel Publishing, 1998).

Beard, William, *The Artist as Monster* (Toronto: University of Toronto Press, 2001).

Benshoff, Harry M., *Monsters in the Closet: Homosexuality and the Horror Film* (Manchester: Manchester University Press, 1997).

Biskind, Peter, *Seeing is Believing: How Hollywood Taught Us to Stop Worrying and Love the Fifties* (New York: Pantheon Books, 1983).

Blakemore, Bill, 'The Family of Man', *San Francisco Chronicle* , 29 July (1987), available at Accessed 5 March 2009

Bloom, Harold, *The Anxiety of Influence*, (Oxford: Oxford University Press).

Bordwell, David, *Narration in the Fiction Film* (New York; London, Routledge, 1985).

Bordwell, David, *Making Meaning: Inference and Rhetoric in the Interpretation of Cinema* (Cambridge, MA: Harvard University Press 1989).

Bourdieu, Pierre, *Distinction: A Social Critique of the Judgement of Taste*, (trans. Richard Nice, Harvard: Harvard University Press, 1997).

Brophy, Philip, 'Horrality: The Textuality of Contemporary Horror Films', *Screen*, 27:1, (January–February 1986),

Browning, Mark, *David Cronenberg: Author or Filmmaker?* (Bristol: Intellect Books, 2007).

Buckingham, David, *Children Talking Television: The Making of Television Literacy* (London: Falmer Press, 1993).

Burke, Seán (ed.). *Authorship: From Plato to the Postmodern* (Edinburgh: University of Edinburgh Press, 1995).

Cartmell, Deborah and Whelehan, Imelda (eds.), *Adaptations: From Text to Screen; Screen to Text* (New York; London: Routledge, 1999).

Caughie, John, *Theories of Authorship* (London: Routledge, 1981)

Cheatwood, Deral, 'Prison Films: 1929–1995,' in Donna Hale and Frankie Bailey, eds., *Popular Culture, Crime and Justice*, (Belmont, CA: Wadsworth, 1998).

Ciment, Michel, *Kubrick* (trans. Gilbert Adair, New York: Holt, Rinehart & Winston, 1983).

Clover, Carol J., *Men, Women and Chainsaws: Gender in the Modern Horror Film* (London: BFI, 1992).

Cocks,Geoffrey, *The Wolf at the Door: Stanley Kubrick, History, and the Holocaust* (New York: Peter Lang, 2004).

Cohan, Steven and Hark, Ina Rae (eds.), *Screening the Male: Exploring Masculinities in Hollywood Cinema*, (London; New York: Routledge, 1993).

Collins, Jim, 'Genericity in the Nineties: Eclectic Irony and the New Sincerity' in Jim Collins, Hilary Radner and Ava Preacher Collins (eds.), *Film Studies Goes to the Movies* (New York: Routledge, AFI Film Readers, 1993), pp. 242–263.

Collings, Michael, *The Films of Stephen King* (Washington: Starmont House, 1986).

Conner, Jeff, *Stephen King Goes to Hollywood* (New York: New American Library, 1987).

Conrich, Ian and Woods, David, (eds.), *The Cinema of John Carpenter: The Technique of Terror* (London: Wallflower Press, 2004).

Cook, Pam (ed.), *The Cinema Book* (London: British Film Institute 1985).

Crane, Jonathan Lake, *Terror and Everyday Life: Singular Moments in the History of the Horror Film* (London and New Delhi: Sage Publications, 1994).

Darabont, Frank, *The Shawshank Redemption: The Shooting Script* (New York: Newmarket Press, 1996).

De Palma, Brian, interviewed by Mike Childs and Alan Jones, *Cinefantastique* 6:1 (Summer 1977).

Derrida, Jacques, 'The law of genre' in W J T Mitchell (ed.), *On Narrative* (Chicago: University of Chicago Press, 1981).

Dika, Vera, Games of Terror: Halloween, Friday the 13th, and the Films of the Stalker Cycle (Rutherford, N.J.: Fairleigh Dickinson Press; Cranbury, N.J.; London: Associated University Presses, 1990).

Faulks, Sebastian, *Engleby*, (London: Vintage Books, 2008).

Ferreira, Patricia, 'Jack's Nightmare at the Overlook: the American Dream Inverted' in *The Shining Reader*, Anthony Magistrale (ed), (Washington: Starmont House), pp. 23–32.

Feuer, Jane, 'Genre study and television' in Robert C. Allen (ed.), *Channels of Discourse, Reassembled: Television and Contemporary Criticism* (London: Routledge, 1992), pp. 138–59.

Fiske, John, *Television Culture* (London: Routledge, 1987).

Floyd, Nigel, *Sleepwalkers* – a review, *Sight and Sound* 2:4 (August, 1992).

Freeland, Cynthia A., *The Naked and the Undead: Evil and the Appeal of Horror* (Boulder, Colorado: Westview Press, 2000).

Fuss, Diana (ed.), Inside/out: Lesbian Theories, Gay Theories (New York; London: Routledge, 1991), p. 23.

Gagne, Paul, 'Creepshow', Cinefantastique (September/October, 1982), pp. 17–35

Gennep, Arnold Van, *Rites-of-Passage* (New York: Routledge, 2004, first published 1909).

Gerstner, David A. (ed.), *Authorship and Film* (London: Routledge, AFI Film Readers, 2002)

Giannetti, Louis, *Understanding Movies,* (Englewood Cliffs, NJ: Prentice-Hall, 1987).

Gledhill, Christine, 'Genre' in Pam Cook (ed.), *The Cinema Book* (London: British Film Institute 1985)

Golding, William, *Lord of the Flies* (London: Faber and Faber, 1954).

Grant, Barry, (ed.), *Film Genre Reader* (Austin: University of Texas Press, 1986).

Grant, Barry (ed.), *Auteurs and Authorship: A Film Reader* (Hoboken, NJ: Wiley-Blackwell, 2008).

Greenblatt, Stephen, *Learning to Curse: Essays in Early Modern Culture,* (London: Routledge, 2007).

Gunden, Kenneth von and Stock, Stuart H., *Twenty All-Time Great Science Fiction Films* (New York: Arlington, 1982).

Hawkins, Joan, *Cutting Edge: Art-Horror and the Horrific Avant-garde* (Minnesota: University of Minnesota Press, 2000).

Herron, Don (ed.), *Reign of Fear: The Fiction and the Films of Stephen King* (Novato, California: Underwood-Miller, 1988).

Horsting, Jessie, *Stephen King at the Movies* (New York: New American Library, 1986).

Hills, Matt, *Fan Cultures* (London: Routledge, 2002) and The Pleasures of Horror (London: Continuum, 2004).

Jameson, Frederic, 'Historicism in The Shining' in *Social Text* 4 (1981), pp. 114–125

Jancovich, Mark, *Horror,* (London: B.T Batsford Ltd., 1994).

Jancovich, Mark (ed.), *The Horror Reader,* (New York: Routledge, 2002).

Jones, Stephen, *Creepshow: The Illustrated Stephen King Movie Guide* (New York: Billboard Books, 2002).

Kael, Pauline, 'Devolution', *The New Yorker,* June 9, 1980, p. 130.

Kermode, Mark, *The Shawshank Redemption* (London: BFI, 2003).

King, Stephen, *Carrie,* (London: New English Library, 1974).

King, Stephen, *Salem's Lot* (London: New English Library, 1976).

King, Stephen, *The Shining* (London: New English Library, 1977).

King, Stephen, *The Dead Zone* (London; Sydney: Futura Publications, 1979).

King, Stephen, 'The Ledge' in *Night Shift* (London: New English Library, 1979),

King, Stephen, *Danse Macabre* (New York: Berkeley Publishing, 1981).

King, Stephen, *Pet Sematary* (London: New English Library, 1984).

King, Stephen, *Four Past Midnight* (London: New English Library, 1990).

King, Stephen, 'The Body' in *Different Seasons* (London: Warner Books, 1992; originally published 1982).

King, Stephen, 'The Night Flier', in *Nightmares and Dreamscapes* (London: New English Library, 1993).

King, Stephen, *Dolores Claiborne* (London: New English Library, 1993).

King, Stephen, *Gerald's Game* (New York; London: Signet, 1993).

King, Stephen, *The Green Mile* (London: Orion Books Ltd, 1996).

King, Stephen, 'Rita Hayworth and the Darabont Redemption'– Introduction to Frank Darabont, *The Shawshank Redemption: The Shooting Script* (New York: Newmarket Press, 1996).

King, Stephen, *On Writing* (London: New English Library, 2000).

King, Stephen, *Dreamcatcher*, (London: New English Library, 2001).

King, Stephen, '1408' in *Everything's Eventual*, (London: Hodder and Stoughton, 2002).

Kroll, Jack, 'Stanley Kubrick's Horror Show', *Newsweek Magazine*, June 2, 1980, p. 52.

Langford, Barry, *Film Genre: Hollywood and Beyond* (Edinburgh: Edinburgh University Press, 2005).

Leitch, Thomas, *Film Adaptation and Its Discontents* (John Hopkins University Press, Bloomington and London, 2007).

Livingstone, Sonia M., 'The rise and fall of audience research: an old story with a new ending', in Mark R. Levy & Michael Gurevitch (eds.), *Defining Media Studies: Reflections on the Future of the Field* (New York: Oxford University Press, 1994), pp. 247–54.

LoBrutto, Vincent, *Stanley Kubrick: A Biography* (New York: Penguin Books, 1997).

Lloyd, Ann, *The Films of Stephen King* (New York: St. Martin's Press, 1994).

McFarlane, Brian, *Novel to Film: An Introduction to the Theory of Adaptation* (Oxford: Oxford University Press, 1996).

McCloud, Scott, *Understanding Comics: The Invisible Art* (New York: Harper Collins, 1993).

Magistrale, Tony (ed.), *The Shining Reader*, (Washington: Starmont House, 1991).

Magistrale, Tony, *The Hollywood Stephen King* (New York: Palgrave Macmillan, 2003).

Magistrale, Tony and Spignesi, Stephen, *The Essential Stephen King* (Career Books, 2003).

Matthews Jnr., Melvin E., *Hostile Aliens, Hollywood and Today's News: 1950s Science Fiction Films and 9/11* (New York: Algora Publishing, 2007).

Naremore, James, 'American Film Noir: The History of an Idea', *Film Quarterly*, 49. 2 (1995–96).

Naremore, James, *Film Adaptation* (London: Athlone, 2000).

Neale, Steve, *Genre* (London: BFI, 1980).

Nelson, Thomas Allen, *Kubrick: Inside a Film Artist's Maze* (Bloomington: Indiana University Press, 1982).

Paul, William, *Laughing Screaming: Modern Hollywood Horror and Comedy* (New York; Chichester: Columbia University Press, 1994).

Phillips, Kendall R., *Projected Fears: Horror Films and American Culture* (Westport: Praeger Publishers, 2005).

Rafter, Nicole, *Shots in the Mirror: Crime Films and Society* (Oxford: Oxford University Press, 2000).

Rodley, Chris, *Cronenberg on Cronenberg* (London: Faber & Faber, 1992).

Ryan, Michael and Kellner, Douglas, *Camera Politica: The Politics and Ideology of Contemporary Hollywood Film* (Bloomington: Indiana University Press, 1988).

Schatz, Thomas, 'Film Genre and Genre Film' in L. Braudy and M. Cohen (eds.), *Film Theory and Criticism* (New York: Oxford University Press, 2004), pp. 691–702.

Schatz, Thomas *Hollywood Genres: Formulas, Filmmaking and the Hollywood Studios*, (Random House, New York, 1981).

Sconce, Jeffrey, 'Trashing the Academy: Taste, Excess and the Emerging Politics of Cinematic Style' in *Screen*, vol. 36:4 (Winter,1995), pp.371–393.

Sconce, Jeffrey, *Sleaze Artists: Cinema at the Margins of Taste, Style and Politics* (Durham, NC: Duke University Press, 2007).

Shields, Carol, *Larry's Party* (London: Fourth Estate Ltd, 1998)

Sinyard, Neil, *Filming Literature: The Art of Screen Adaptation* (Beckenham, Kent: Croom Helm, 1986).

Skal, David *The Monster Show: A Cultural History of Horror* (London: Faber & Faber, 2001).

Sobchack, Thomas and Sobchack, Vivian, *An Introduction to Film* (Boston, MA: Little, Brown & Co, 1980).

Stam, Robert, *Film Theory: An Introduction*, (Malden, MA: Blackwell, 2000).

Steinbrunner, Chris and Goldblatt, Burt, *Cinema of the Fantastic* (New York: Galahad Books, 1972).

Stevenson, Robert Louis, *Strange Case of Dr Jekyll and Mr Hyde* (London: Longmans, Green & Co., 1886).

Todorov, Tzvetan, *The Fantastic: A Structural Approach to a Literary Genre*, trans. Richard Howard (Ithaca, New York: Cornell University Press, 1975).

Tudor, Andrew, *Monsters and Mad Scientists: A Cultural History of the Horror Film* (Cambridge Massachusetts: Basil Blackwell Inc., 1989).

Turner, Victor, *The Ritual Process: Structure and Anti-Structure* (Aldine Transaction, 1995; first published 1969).

Underwood, Tim and Miller, Chuck, *Bare Bones: Conversations on Terror with Stephen King* (New York: McGraw-Hill, 1988).

Wellek, René & Warren, Austin, 'Literary Genres' in *Theory of Literature* (Harmondsworth: Penguin, 1963).

Wexman, Virginia Wright (ed.), *Film and Authorship* (Piscataway, NJ: Rutgers University Press, Depth of Film Series, 2002).

Wiater, Stan, Christopher Golden and Hank Wagner, *The Stephen King Universe* (Los Angeles: Renaissance Books, 2001).

Wilson, David, and O' Sullivan, Sean, *Images of Incarceration* (Bristol: Waterside Press, 2004).

Wolfman, Marv, 'King of the Comics' in Don Herron (ed.), *Reign of Fear: The Fiction and the Films of Stephen King* (Novato, California: Underwood-Miller, 1988).

Wood, Robin, 'An Introduction to the American Horror Film', in Andrew Britton, Richard Lippe, Tony Williams and Robin Wood (eds.), *The American Nightmare: Essays on the Horror Film* (Toronto: Festival of Festivals, 1979), pp. 7–28.

Wright, William, *Sixguns and Society*, (University of California Press, Berkeley, 1975).

Žižek, Slavoj, *The Fright of Real Tears* (London: BFI Publishing, 2001).